# Positive Psychology

# Positive Psychology
## An International Perspective

Edited by

Aleksandra Kostić
Derek Chadee

**WILEY** Blackwell

*Registered Office(s)*
John Wiley & Sons, Inc., 111 River Street, Hoboken, NJ 07030, USA
John Wiley & Sons Ltd, The Atrium, Southern Gate, Chichester, West Sussex, PO19 8SQ, UK

*Editorial Office*
111 River Street, Hoboken, NJ 07030, USA

For details of our global editorial offices, customer services, and more information about Wiley products visit us at www.wiley.com.

Wiley also publishes its books in a variety of electronic formats and by print-on-demand. Some content that appears in standard print versions of this book may not be available in other formats.

*Library of Congress Cataloging-in-Publication Data*

Names: Kostić, Aleksandra, editor. | Chadee, Derek, editor.
Title: Positive psychology : an international perspective / edited by
    Aleksandra Kostić, Derek Chadee.
Description: First edition. | Hoboken : Wiley, 2021. | Includes
    bibliographical references and index.
Identifiers: LCCN 2020048416 (print) | LCCN 2020048417 (ebook) | ISBN
    9781119666448 (paperback) | ISBN 9781119666431 (adobe pdf) | ISBN
    9781119666363 (epub)
Subjects: LCSH: Positive psychology.
Classification: LCC BF204.6 .P65857 2021  (print) | LCC BF204.6  (ebook) |
    DDC 150.19/88–dc23
LC record available at https://lccn.loc.gov/2020048416
LC ebook record available at https://lccn.loc.gov/2020048417

Cover Design: Wiley
Cover Image: "Happy Windows" by Aleksandra Kostić

Set in 10/13pt Minion Pro by SPi Global, Pondicherry, India

Printed and bound by CPI Group (UK) Ltd, Croydon, CR0 4YY

10  9  8  7  6  5  4  3  2

We dedicate this book to two outstanding persons in their own right, a successful Caribbean entrepreneur and founder of the ANSA McAL Group of Companies, and an academic and founding member of positive psychology, both of whom have uniquely and positively contributed to the development of the field of psychology.

To Dr. Anthony N. Sabga for his philanthropic contribution towards the establishment of the ANSA McAL Psychological Research Centre at The University of the West Indies, St. Augustine Campus and by extension to the development of psychology within the Caribbean – DC

To Professor Mihaly Csikszentmihalyi for his early and lasting contributions to the development of positive psychology – AK

# Contents

# List of Contributors

**Aleksandra Kostić** is a Professor of Social Psychology at the Faculty of Philosophy, Department of Psychology at the University of Niš, Serbia. She teaches courses on Introduction to Social Psychology, Social Perception, Nonverbal Behavior, and Psychology of Interpersonal Behavior. Her research interests include nonverbal communication, emotional experience, time perspective, ethnic identity, and similarities and differences between cultures in perception of category, intensity and antecedents of emotion. She has published four books in Serbian including *Facetalk: Signs and Meanings and Studies of Time Perspective in Serbia, Talk Without Words*, and coedited four international books in the area of social psychology – *Social Psychological Dynamics* (2011); *Time Perspective: Theory and Practice* (2017); *The Social Psychology of Nonverbal Communication* (2014); and *Social Intelligence and Nonverbal Communication* (2020).

**Derek Chadee** is a Professor of Social Psychology and Director of ANSA McAL Psychological Research Centre at The University of the West Indies, St. Augustine Campus. His current research interests include the social psychology of fear of crime and general fear, antecedents of emotions, copycat behavior, and media influence on perception. He has published with the *British Journal of Criminology, International Review of Victimology, Crime Media and Culture, Journal of Applied Social Psychology, Journal of Cross-Cultural Psychology*, and *Psychology of Popular Media Culture*. He has a strong interest in social psychological theories and his second edition of Theories in Social Psychology ,Wiley, is forthcoming in 2021.

**Massimo Agnoletti** graduated in general and experimental psychology at the University of Padua (Italy) and received his PhD at the University of Verona (Italy) where he is a research assistant. His experience is internationally based (Massachusetts Institute of Technology, University of California, Berkeley, Massachusetts General Hospital, Osaka University, University College of London, etc.) and his main scientific focus is on flow experiences, time perspective, psychological aspects in telomeres, and vagus nerve activation.

**C. Daniel Batson** is an experimental social psychologist. He is currently a Professor Emeritus of Psychology at the University of Kansas. His extensive research on the empathy-altruism hypothesis is reviewed in *Altruism in Humans* (2011) and *A Scientific Search for Altruism* (2019). He is also the author of *What's Wrong with Morality? A Social-Psychological Perspective* (2016).

**Celina Benavides**, is an Assistant Professor in the Child & Family Studies Department at California State University, Los Angeles. She earned a PhD in developmental psychology at Claremont Graduate University, an MA in human development and psychology at Harvard, and an MA in education and mathematics credential at Whittier College. She conducts research in two related topic areas: the educational experiences and outcomes of students of color, and the role of schools and communities in supporting the positive development of adolescents and young adults, namely through civic engagement initiatives and fostering purpose.

**Ilona Boniwell** is one of the European leaders in positive psychology, having founded and headed the first master's degree in applied positive psychology (MAPP) in Europe at the University of East London. She heads the International MSc in Applied Positive Psychology (I-MAPP) at Anglia Ruskin University, teaches positive management at l'Ecole Centrale Paris and HEC, and consults around the world as a director of Positran. She founded and was the first chair of the European Network of Positive Psychology (ENPP), organized the first European Congress of Positive Psychology in June 2002 (Winchester), and was the first vice-chair of the International Positive Psychology Association (IPPA). She is now the vice-president for the Francophone Association of Positive Psychology, serves on the board of directors of the International Positive Education Network (IPEN) and is a coeditor of the *Applied Positive Psychology Journal*. She is well-published and author of *Positive Psychology in a Nutshell* (2006, 2016); coauthor of *The Happiness Equation* (2008), *Positive Psychology: Theory, Research and Applications* (2011, 2019), *Well-Being Lessons for Secondary Schools* (2012); coeditor of *The Oxford Handbook of Happiness* (2013); and coauthor of *Motivated Adolescents* (2015) and *PEPS: Positive Education for Parents and Schools* (2018).

**Jolanta Burke** is a chartered psychologist (British Psychological Society) and an assistant professor at Maynooth University, Ireland, where she teaches well-being. Prior to that, she was a master's program leader in applied positive psychology at the University of East London, and lectured at Trinity Business School, where she developed a series of highly popular lectures about positive cyber psychology. Her latest books are *The Ultimate Guide to Implementing Wellbeing Programmes for School* and *Positive Psychology and School Leadership: The New Science of Positive Educational Leadership*. For her work on well-being, she was acknowledged by the *Irish Times* as one of 30 people in Ireland who make it a better place.

**Gian Vittorio Caprara** is Professor Emeritus at Sapienza University of Rome where he served as chair of the Department of Psychology and dean of the Psychology Faculty. He has been president of the European Association of Personality and is a member of the Academia Europaea. He is author and coauthor of over 500 scientific publications, including several volumes, among which: *Personality: Determinants, Dynamics and Potentials* (with D. Cervone, 2000); *Personalizing Politics and Realizing Democracy* (with M. Vecchione, 2017). His research has addressed several topics across personality psychology, social psychology and political psychology.

**Mihaly Csikszentmihalyi** received his PhD in psychology from the University of Chicago, where he taught for 30 years and served as chair of the Department of Psychology. He is Professor Emeritus of Psychology at Claremont Graduate University, where he founded and codirected the Quality of Life Research Center (QLRC). He is the author of *Beyond Boredom and Anxiety: Experiencing Flow in Work and Play* (1975), *Flow: The Psychology of Optimal Experience* (1990), and *Creativity: Flow and the Psychology of Discovery and Invention* (1996). A wide range of his work was reprinted in the 2014 three-volume set, *The Collected Works of Mihaly Csikszentmihalyi.*

**Ed Diener** is a Professor at the University of Utah and the University of Virginia, a distinguished emeritus professor at the University of Illinois, and senior scientist for the Gallup Organization. He is one of the most eminent research psychologists in the world. With over 400 publications and a citation count over 230,000, he is one of the most highly cited scientists in the world. He has been the president of three scientific societies and the editor of three scientific journals, including being a cofounder of the *Journal of Happiness Studies*. He was the founding president of the International Positive Psychology Association. He has received major awards in psychology including the Distinguished Scientific Achievement Awards from the American Psychological Association.

**Scott I. Donaldson** is a postdoctoral scholar in evaluation, statistics, and measurement at the University of California, San Diego School of Medicine, Moores Cancer Center. Scott received his PhD in psychology with a concentration in evaluation and applied research methods and a co-concentration in positive organizational psychology from Claremont Graduate University. He received his BA in psychology from the University of California, Los Angeles, and his MS in organizational psychology from the University of Southern California. His research focuses on the design and evaluation of behavioral health interventions at work.

**Stewart I. Donaldson** is Dstinguished University Professor and executive director of the Claremont Evaluation Center at Claremont Graduate University. He is a cofounder of the first PhD and research-focused master's programs in positive psychology at Claremont Graduate University. He currently teaches, mentors, and employs numerous students specializing in positive organizational psychology, positive health and sports psychology, and evaluation science. He serves on the Council of Advisors for the International Positive Psychology Association (IPPA) and was chair of IPPA's World Congress of Positive Psychology in Los Angeles (2013). He has published numerous articles, chapters, and books on the science of positive psychology, including his latest book *Positive Psychological Science: Improving Everyday Life, Well-Being, Work, Education, and Societies Across the Globe (2020)*.

**Sandro Formica** teaches Managing Self, Others and Positive Organizations in Hospitality at Florida International University and The Economics of Happiness in selected European universities. His book, "*Personal Empowerment: Empower the Leader within You*," is highly experiential and contains over 200 self-awareness practices and exercises. He is the academic director of the Chief Happiness Officer in the Hospitality and Services Industries certificate program, granted by WOHASU (World Happiness Summit) and Florida International University. As an academic, he published in international peer-reviewed journals on human motivational factors and behavioral decision-making, executive education needs, United States versus Europe training systems, and predictability of human preferences in future global business.

**Burkhard Gniewosz** received his diploma in psychology from the University of Jena, Germany, in 2002. He is currently Professor of Quantitative Research Methods in educational science at the Paris-Lodron-University in Salzburg, Austria. His major field of research concerns socialization processes during adolescence. He mostly focuses on contextual (family and school) influences on adolescents' political and academic development. In recent years, his research interest centered on students' motivation within a developmental context.

**Saeideh Heshmati** is an Assistant Professor of psychology at Claremont Graduate University. She is a positive developmental psychologist interested in how optimal development unfolds over time in diverse samples, especially in at-risk adults. Using her expertise in positive relationships and love, human development, and state-of-the-art analytical methods, she examines authentic or embedded assessments of large datasets related to individual and group characteristics that influence everyday well-being and positive development. Her work has brought together a suite of measurement tools such as experience sampling methods, observational analysis, cognitive psychometric modeling, and wearable physiology monitors in the service of understanding how individuals' sense of well-being – and love as one component of well-being – unfolds moment-to-moment in their everyday lives.

**Jessica Kansky** is a sixth-year graduate student in clinical psychology at the University of Virginia and graduated summa cum laude with a BA in psychology from the University of Pennsylvania. She will be completing her doctoral internship at the Charleston Consortium this year. Her research focuses on psychosocial predictors and outcomes of romantic experiences from adolescence through adulthood. Her interest is in the role of romantic relationships in optimal interpersonal and individual development and well-being and she has recently published several reviews of romantic development across the lifespan. She has received numerous accolades for her teaching, receiving the University's only Distinguished Teaching Award for Social Sciences in 2019 and the Society for a Science of Clinical Psychology Outstanding Student Teacher Award in 2020.

**Shari Young Kuchenbecker** is Associate Director and cofounder of the Western Positive Psychology Association (WPPA), Claremont, California. Her BA is from Stanford and PhD is from UCLA. She chose to tenure-retire at the age of 32 to raise three kind efficacious children – one DVM and two PhDs. She continues to write, teach/do research at SoCal universities, presenting at conferences with colleagues and students, many now PhDs, EdDs, MAs, and parents. Her Stanford role model and lifelong mentor was Dorothea Ross. Albert Bandura, her academic grandfather, and she began regular "Salons" across the last two decades. Collaborating with Phil Zimbardo, Al's and Phil's positive educational role models, theories, research legacies, and their social activism inspired the chapter included here.

**Marija Pejičić** is a PhD student and teaching assistant in the Department of Psychology, Faculty of Philosophy, at the University of Niš. Her teaching and research areas focus mainly in the area of interpersonal relations, specifically, communication and emotional experience.

**Vesna Petrović** is a Professor of Psychology at the Union University of Belgrade, where she has served as head of the master's program in psychotherapy. She is an integrative psychotherapist, founder and director of the Serbian Association for Integrative Psychotherapy, and national representative of Serbia in the European Association for Psychotherapy. Her research has addressed issues in mental health, positive psychology, trauma psychology, integrative psychotherapy, and systemic family psychotherapy.

**Wendy-Ann Smith** is a registered psychologist in her native country Australia and her current home France. She is the co-editor of *Positive Psychology Coaching in the Workplace* (in press) and author in the domains of positive and coaching psychology, specifically in the domains of positive leadership, strengths and emotions coaching, and coaching for high quality relationships. She is a reviewer for the *European Journal of Applied Positive Psychology* and co-leads the French chapter for the International Society for Coaching Psychology. She is an executive coach at high ranking international and French business schools and teaches in the domains of positive and coaching psychology at both French and UK academic institutions. She founded her first coaching psychology practice in Australia, Inspirations Coaching and Development and has translated that to France with her positive psychology business Eclorev Coaching.

**Robert J. Sternberg** is a Professor of Human Development at Cornell University and honorary professor of psychology at the University of Heidelberg, Germany. His BA is from Yale, his PhD from Stanford, and he holds 13 honorary doctorates. He is a past winner of the Grawemeyer Award in Psychology and the William James and James McKeen Cattell Awards from the Association for Psychological Science. He is past-president of the American Psychological Association and the Federation of Associations in Behavioral and Brain Sciences. He has been cited over 184,000 times in the professional literature, with an h index of 207. He is the author of *Adaptive Intelligence* (in press).

**Sara Wilf** is a doctoral student in the Department of Social Welfare at the University of California, Los Angeles. She researches the development and practice of youth civic engagement with a focus on youth activism on social media. She received her BA from Brown University and her MPA from Columbia University.

**Everett L. Worthington Jr.** is Commonwealth Professor Emeritus at Virginia Commonwealth University. He continues an active research, writing, and speaking career studying forgiveness, humility, hope, gratitude, patience, and other positive psychology topics. He originated the REACH Forgiveness intervention, which has been investigated in over 30 randomized control trials and continues to be studied and used around the globe. He also continues to do research in the hope-focused approach to couple enrichment and therapy.

**Laura Wray-Lake** is an Associate Professor of social welfare in the Luskin School of Public Affairs at University of California, Los Angeles. She received her PhD in human development and family studies from Penn State University. Her research focuses on how and why young people become civically engaged. She has published over 60 research articles and book chapters, including a 2020 SRCD Monograph on pathways to civic engagement among urban youth of color. Her work uses multiple methodologies and takes developmental, cultural, and contextual perspectives in studying youth civic engagement.

**Dragan Žuljević**, PhD, is an Assistant Professor at the Faculty of Law and Business Studies, Dr Lazar Vrkatić, Novi Sad, Serbia. He received his PhD in psychology with a concentration in psychotherapy treatment evaluation. He authored over 100 research reports and publications focused on psychological treatment evaluation, resilience, mental health, and positive psychology. His current research is focused on practice and evaluation of acceptance and commitment therapy and contextual behavioral science.

# Acknowledgment

This book would not have been possible if not for the contributions and dedicated commitment from a number of persons. We express our deepest and sincerest thanks to the following individuals for their invaluable contributions toward the successful completion of this volume. First, we say thanks to all of our diligent contributors: Mihaly Csikszentmihalyi, Daniel Batson, Robert J. Sternberg, Massimo Agnoletti, Celina Benavides, Ilona Boniwell, Jolanta Burke, Gian Vittorio Caprara, Ed Diener, Stewart I. Donaldson, Scott I. Donaldson, Sandro Formica, Burkhard Gniewosz, Saeideh Heshmati, Jessica Kansky, Shari Young Kuchenbecker, Marija Pejičić, Vesna Petrović, Wendy-Ann Smith, Sara Wilf, Everett L Worthington Jr., Laura Wray-Lake, and Dragan Žuljević. A special thanks to Steve Dwarika, Mala Ramesar, and Shenelle Matadeen for their administrative assistance.

This book is an output of the ANSA McAL Psychological Research Centre of the University of the West Indies. Our sincerest thanks to The University of the West Indies and the ANSA McAL Psychological Research Centre and the Faculty of Philosophy, Department of Psychology, at the University of Niš (Serbia) for their support. Our earnest gratefulness to the staff at Wiley Publishers. To all those who provided technical and other kinds of support resulting in this publication, we would like to indicate our deepest appreciation. And to those we may have inadvertently overlooked in this acknowledgment, we say thank you for all the encouragement and assistance that you have rendered.

# 1

# Embracing Psychology Positively

## Derek Chadee and Aleksandra Kostić

Positive psychology conjures the notion of a soft approach to addressing hard psychological issues. Though this is far from the truth, academia quite often focuses on removing of the negative and thinking critically of issues that adversely impact on our lives. Focusing on the other side, the positive, somehow implicitly summons the notion of not assessing the core of a problem. Martin Seligman in 1998, recognizing the usefulness of critically assessing the cause and impact of the negative, also saw the need to focus theorization, research, policy, and a paradigm toward the other side of the coin – the positive. In fact, positive psychologists go even further to emphasize that by encouraging the development of positive attributes many of the negative issues may be systemically addressed.

Martin Seligman the father of positive psychology defined this area of psychology as "a scientific and professional movement with a new goal to build the enabling conditions of a life worth living" (2011) and studied not only the frailties and problems but the strengths and virtues of the human being (Seligman, 2002, p. 630). Later, Duckworth, Steen, and Seligman (2005) clarified positive psychology from clinical psychology noting that as a "scientific study of positive experiences and positive individual traits and the institutions that facilitate their development, a field concerned with well-being and optimal functioning, positive psychology at first glance seem peripheral to mainstream clinical psychology. We believe otherwise." In fact, they noted that positive psychology expands the emphasis of clinical psychology from distress and interventions for improvement and moving the discourse to continuance of well-being. Taking this principle of positive psychology, its contributions toward well-being expands beyond that of the clinical branch of

*Positive Psychology: An International Perspective*, First Edition.
Edited by Aleksandra Kostić and Derek Chadee.
© 2021 John Wiley & Sons Ltd. Published 2021 by John Wiley & Sons Ltd.

the discipline of psychology. Gable and Haidt (2005) argued that the prominence of the negative in psychology may be a result of prioritizing of compassion, the history and pragmatism of focusing on distress and disease, the nature and theorization of psychology. But they also posited that a positive psychology in no way implies a negative psychology, nor prior or future theorization, and research outside of this emerging branch are not in any way inferior.

Core to the discipline is the fact that positive psychology has the characteristics of a scientific intellectual movement and has over a short period develop a paradigm of a mature science (Simmons, 2013). Seligman, Gillham, Reivich, Linkins, and Ernst (2009) acknowledged the growth of positive psychology as a scientific paradigm to study positive emotions, engagement, and meaning and the importance of these characteristics in the development of life satisfaction. But one may ask why the ease in which this discipline has so quickly navigated toward respectability. The answer obviously lies in the content of positive psychology and the simplicity of the assumptions and premises on which, over a hundred years prior, the discipline of psychology studied with interventions. However, psychology fell short of ensuring the continuance of the well-being of the inner being (Duckworth et al., 2005). Simmons (2013) referred to an interesting quotation from Abraham Maslow's classic book, *Motivation and Personality*, in a chapter titled "Toward a Positive Psychology":

> The science of psychology has been far more successful on the negative than on the positive side. It has revealed to us much about man's shortcomings, his illness, his sins, but little about his potentialities, his virtues, his achievable aspirations, or his full psychological height. It is as if psychology has voluntarily restricted itself to only half its rightful jurisdiction, and that, the darker, meaner half. (Maslow, 1954, p. 354)

The genesis of positive psychology has been attributed to the works of humanistic psychologists such as Carl Rogers, Rollo May, Abraham Maslow, Gordon Allport, and Marie Jahoda, who in 1958 wrote on the continuance of well-being in patients (Duckworth et al., 2005). One can possibly say that the spirit of humanistic psychology manifested in positive psychology, one discipline in its evolution. However, Peterson and Seligman (2004, see also Simons, 2013) noted the reluctance of the humanistic school to emphasize scientific rigor.

Happiness and well-being are partly influenced by positive emotions, engagement, and purpose (Seligman, 2008). Concerns about the past, present, and future influence our levels of contentment, serenity, somatic and complex pleasures, optimism, and hope (Duckworth et al., 2005; Seligman, Rashid, & Parks, 2006). Our engagement is reciprocally conditional to strengths which are constructed on core virtues such as wisdom, integrity, and honesty. Purpose and life meaning are derived from interaction within the institutional core to our self. These three domains are not mutually exclusive but the ideal is a harmonious balance. The interplay of the three domains provide hedonic, emphasis on happiness and pleasure, and eudaimonic emphasis on life's meaning, purpose, and satisfactions. Both hedonic and eudaimonic models were synergized by Seligman and Adler (2018; see also Altmaier, 2019) to understand a blended engagement in the derivation of happiness and life satisfaction. Seligman articulated this blend in the PERMA model which is an acronym for positive emotion, engagement, relationships, meaning, and accomplishment.

Positive psychology has distinguished between the absence of the negative and the presence of the positive. Consider, cold is the absence of heat or poverty the absence of wealth, though debatable, these analogies have their insights but also their limits. Similarly, consider the issue of delinquency. The resolution of this issue by addressing the core causes of the problem means that the issue has been addressed with temporal and spatial specificity. But has the well-being of persons involved with or affected by delinquency been addressed or sustained? Has the social environment and parties feel engaged, or have a greater sense of well-being, or have more positive emotions? The positive psychology emphasis of beyond time and space limitations is a core distinguishing factor. Duckworth et al. (2005) observing that the positive is not simply the absence of the negative, noted with an example that the removal of incivility, revenge, and anger, does not necessarily lead to the presence of civility, cooperation, and loyalty. Both the former, removal of the negative, and the latter, creation and sustenance of the the positive, require different interventions.

Within this context and sharing the assumptions and theorization of positive psychology, the contributors to this book are from a wide range of cultures and have diligently articulated significant issues of interest on positive psychology to an international audience. Their contributions include the areas of altruism, positive creativity, science of well-being, forgiveness, coaching for leadership, cyberpsychology, intelligence, responding to catastrophes like COVID-19, time perspective, physiological and epigenetic, youth civic engagement, ups and downs of love, flow and good life, global perspectives on positive psychology, self and collective efficacy, positive psychology interventions, and positive orientation.

Do we humans ever, in any degree, care for others for their sakes and not simply for our own? Daniel Batson, renowned for his research on empathy and altruism, in his chapter utilizes the empathy-altruism hypothesis to address this question. The egoism–altruism debate is briefly discussed, touching on the egoism trend that prevails in Western societies. The empathy-altruism hypothesis, which states that altruistic motivation is produced by empathetic concern is discussed distinguishing empathetic concern (the perceived welfare of a person in need elicits and is congruent with other-oriented emotion) and altruistic motivation (increasing another's welfare in the main goal). Other aspects of empathy-altruism are articulated such as self-benefits falling within the realm of the goal of egoism as opposed to the consequence of altruism. The author notes that empathy-induced altruistic motivation is within the human repertoire and the biological roots of such motivation may lie in generalized parental nurturance. Practical implications of the empathy-altruism hypothesis are then discussed in relation to its benefits and liabilities. Some benefits include the inhibition of aggression, the increase of collaboration in conflicts, and improved attitudes toward stigmatized groups. Some liabilities include the potential risk of harm (e.g., through time, money, and physical injury) by performing some altruistic acts and some needs may not necessarily arouse empathetic concern.

Distinguished psychologist, Robert J. Sternberg, differentiates between positive and negative creativity, highlighting that while fundamentally being the same, the distinguishing factor is the function they serve. The author contends that creators need to think beyond the short-term requirements of creative solutions since solutions which have outlived their purpose may become negative in the wrong hands, for example, nuclear weapons and carbon-based fuels. Acknowledging the prevalence and impact of negative creativity globally, the article outlines some of the fundamental reasons for negative creativity. These include enhancing reputation, responding in anger, responding to fear, and revenge.

Creators need to also pay attention to whether creativity is adding value both in the short and long term, that is whether it is positive, negative, or neutral. Citing social media and a form of creativity once intended to be positive, it has evolved into a medium which has been used to distort elections and spread hateful propaganda. One of the many conclusions from this chapter is a discussion on how creativity can be uncomfortable and potentially dangerous, but, despite this, there is a need for more positive creativity, decency in discourse, reflection, and civility.

In their chapter Jessica Kansky and Ed Diener extend the concept of subjective well-being (SWB) beyond happiness. The primary causes of well-being (e.g., income, social relationships, genetics, strengths and positive behaviors, and health) were discussed as well as its critical outcomes. SWB consists of three independently related facets: positive, negative, and life satisfaction. The dynamic nature of SWB has seen a growing interest in the field which has been matched by evolving methods of measurement which range from self-report methods to physiological and neuroimaging methods. These methods, however, are constrained by their inability to provide causal conclusions. To address this limitation, experimental methods and long-term follow-up assessments were viewed as a way forward allowing researchers to understand the causal relationship between moods and affect. The influence of programs such as ENHANCE strongly suggest the malleability of happiness. As the authors pointed, "an individual may have multiple happiness set points, rather than one global point and that different aspects of well-being can move in different directions independently". Inclosing an emphasis is given to the strong need for further research on the conceptual and theoretical foundations of SWB and its globalization.

How can positive psychology be applied to leadership styles not only for the direct benefit of organizations but for overall human development? Ilona Boniwell and Wendy-Ann Smith discuss the merit of positive leadership for organizations challenged by global competition. Employees who belong to teams which are guided by greater opportunities for recognition, whose leaders are seen as more ethical, authentic, and charismatic, tend to demonstrate greater engagement at the individual level, and those organizations are better able to achieve their corporate goals. Positive leadership is an umbrella term encompassing several leadership styles which places the human at the center of the value creation process. The authors distinguish among positive organizational scholarship, positive organizational behavior, and positive leadership as critical tools of positive psychology within the workplace. Guided by the competing values framework, which posits that leadership has the capacity to hold and integrate contrasting tensions, the chapter discusses the major theoretical underpinnings of leadership.

Some of the major tools in coaching of employees are articulated and include perceiving emotions, understanding emotions, using emotions to facilitate thinking, and managing emotions. Perceiving emotions extends beyond just that of the individual leader but also of members of the team since this directly impacts leadership thought and behaviors. Understanding emotional reactions provides a greater awareness of the causes of certain emotions and some predictability to the consequences of such emotional responses. Using emotions, both positive and negative, to facilitate thinking can have beneficial outcomes. Positive emotions make one more receptive and creative while negative emotions, guided by support have the potential for creative problem solving. Finally, the authors insightfully discuss that the managing of emotions as a coaching tool is critical since emotions can be contagious and can impact the mood and morale of work teams. Leadership is an integration between positive opposites, which can become negative when viewed in isolation, and that effective coaching supports and challenges employees to go beyond the either/or choices presented by these positive opposites.

Jolanta Burke integrates positive psychology and cyberpsychology into the new and novel field of positive technology. Merging cyberpsychology and positive psychology draws attention to the use of technology in addressing human needs and the development of well-being programs which are delivered using technology. Positive cyberpsychology aims to study three broad areas: the positive impact of technology in directly improving individual and group level well-being, the positive subjective experience of technology, and the positive subjective impact of online content at the individual and group level.

With respect to the positive impact of technology in directly improving individual and group level well-being, there are currently available interventions used in the medical field which serve as a stepping stone since they primarily focus on health rather than well-being. The author contends that cyberpsychology can inform positive psychology in this regard by focusing researchers on the effectiveness of and optimal use of cyberpsychology. To understand the impact of technology on well-being requires further research attention to ensure end-users' positive experiences with technology. Specifically, there is a paucity of research on the positive impact of technology with much greater attention being given to the negative physical and mental outcome of technology. Initial studies have demonstrated how technology can improve lives and this should serve as a guide to developing positive cyberpsychology interventions.

Robert J. Sternberg, in another contribution, is empathetic and expresses his concern as an academic and a world citizen on how pandemics and issues such as COVID-19 are addressed. Guided by relevant research he notes the failure of human beings to truly adapt to catastrophes highlighting several ways in which human beings have failed to adapt to changes. Citing the mismanagement of the Spanish flu pandemic as the perfect example of what world leaders should avoid, he posits that twenty-first-century world leaders instead choose to either ignore those events or implement decisions which arguably have made the current COVID-19 pandemic worse. The chapter challenges the traditional notions of intelligence, drawing a comparison between competence, which refers to our capabilities, and performance which refers to what we do. Applying academic definitions of intelligence may be flawed in real-world settings since pandemics, catastrophes, and climate change oftentimes require practical solutions for which there is no predefined right or wrong answer.

Sternberg argues for the need to incorporate social psychology in the study of intelligence since real-world problem solving and decision making occur within a sociocultural context. Cognitive dissonance theory was used to succinctly explain changes in behaviors and decisions and to demonstrate the utility of incorporating social psychology in the study of intelligence. The role of rational thinking and personality traits are important consideration for realization of the fruits of social intelligence. The chapter outlines the use of positive psychology in helping individuals make important decisions which have health and well-being implications.

What is the relationship between time perspective and feeling good? Aleksandra Kostić, Derek Chadee, and Marija Pejičić's chapter addresses this issue. Psychological research on time indicates that the attitude toward time has a strong and even powerful influence on how we live. The way we relate to different time intervals and the way in which we separate and connect them, and then separate again, influence our perception of the world and sense of well-being. The authors' interest is directed toward the analysis of the connection between the subjective experience of time and an individual's positive affective experience, which implies finding answers to some unresolved questions. Therefore, an important question to ask is whether a certain preferred temporal orientation implies a higher number of positive effects, and another one implies a higher number of negative effects. Core to this chapter is understanding how our motivation, activities, achievements, and transformations are influenced by our time perspective and in turn influence our well-being.

Massimo Agnoletti and Sandro Formica's chapter on physiological and epigenetics builds on research which explored emotions and physiology to demonstrate the deeper impact that emotions, both positive and negative, can have on physical health and well-being. The authors acknowledge the gap between medically researched interventions, which focus on physical and chemical processes of acute illness and trauma, and the psychological impact of illnesses and progressive treatments on humans. Progressive treatment of patients has sought to narrow the mind–body gap since there is new and compelling empirical support for the integration of both methods of treatment. This integration of biomedical and psychological knowledge brings a new and valuable understanding of the physiological and cellular dynamics of positive emotions.

To demonstrate adequately the benefits of physiological and epigenetic effects of positive emotions, the authors use three elements: the dopaminergic neural pathway, the cholinergic anti-inflammatory pathway (CAP), and the interoceptive information. The dopaminergic pathway provides an understanding of the motivational influences governing repeating of behaviors which have positive emotional experiences and promotes better health. The CAP mediates the relation between life experiences and cellular information of the immune system which means that both the quality and quantity of life experiences can trigger epigenetic changes which can affect the quality of life and perception of personal identity. Finally, the interoception information is a continuous bidirectional communication between emotions and external sensory exchanges. The quality of life will be improved when human beings become aware of their thoughts, deeds, and lifestyle and advocate for the further narrowing of the mind–body gap and a move toward developing a platform for a holistic approach to the well-being of individuals and society.

Youth civic engagement is multidimensional with a synergy among individuals, institutions, cultures, and subcultures with a social and economic, among others, context. Laura Wray-Lake, Burkhard Gniewosz, Celina Benavides, and Sara Wilf adopting a developmental and cultural perspective, provide a micro–macro understanding of factors contributing to youth civic engagement and how these levels and their interaction influence engagement. The authors distinguish civic engagement from citizenship noting that the latter is a formal and legal status of being a member of a society while the former is the subjective representation of citizenship with psychological or tangible interactions with others where individuals express rights and acts on responsibilities without the requirement of citizenship. For engagement to take place there must be interaction between the individual and community. An emphasis of this chapter is the importance of socialization in civic development in both childhood and adolescence allowing for a sense of purpose in connection to their social world. The authors embolden discourses to build a consensus across cultures and disciplines on the understanding of youth civic engagement.

In his third contribution, Robert J. Sternberg focuses on the several elements of love and the contribution of these elements to the satisfaction and maintenance of a relationship including elements of trust, compassion, and communication. These core elements are utilized in a holistic analysis and identification of malfunctions within the relationship, and perception of the degree to which the relationship helps the individual to self-actualize. Crucial to an understanding of love are intimacy, passion, and commitment. These form the author's triangular theory of love, the understanding of which is posited to be essential for a success-ful relationship. The theory of love as a story is discussed, along with the formula-tion and functions of the stories of love. The roles of jealousy and envy within current and future relationships are also considered, with situational and personal jealousy and envy being the focus. These constructs were noted as being either harmful or beneficial to a relationship. The chapter provides an angle into the meaningfulness, the eudaimonic, of love and positive relational development.

The celebrated and one of the major contributors to the genesis of positive psy-chology, Mihaly Csikszentmihalyi writes on the flow concept, a major contribu-tion he has made to positive psychology. He notes that this concept arose out of research on low to nonextrinsic rewarding activities. Csikszentmihalyi provides an understanding of the development of the flow concept. He describes the state of flow as an intense concentration in which we tend to lose self-consciousness, though being in control of actions and sensations, but the experience being its own reward. The concept of flow remains an important concept in positive psy-chology. The eudaimonic relationship between flow and realization of intrinsic motivation is core to the distinction of positive psychology from main stream psychology. And this point is clearly articulated in Csikszentmihalyi's chapter.

In the rebalancing of the field of psychology, a call for an increase in positive psychological science was made. Positive psychological science's aim is to increase the understanding of how to build the factors for the prevention of pathologies that result from purposelessness. Stewart I. Donaldson, Saida Heshmati, and Scott I. Donaldson's chapter starts with a brief history of the impact and development within positive psychology. Positive psychology has seen a tremendous increase in peer-reviewed positive psychological scientific studies and research and many of the critiques of positive psychology as nonscientific result from reviewing of some literature that has not passed the examination of scientific peer review. Fundamental to the global development of a scientific psychology is the establishment of reliable and valid measures. The several meta-analyses strongly reaffirm the empirical validity of positive psychological interventions. The chapter deliberates on poten-tial new directions and includes areas of cultural context and relationships and their related issues. The purpose of positive psychology as a new science is to develop and utilize knowledge to address pathologies that arise when life is barren and meaningless. The authors conclude by asserting that "the global perspective on positive psychological science will inspire much more sound peer-reviewed research, and facilitate the design and evaluation of many more evidence-based positive psychology interventions across the world."

Shari Young Kuchenbecker expands on Albert Bandura's social cognitive theory (SCT) utilizing self-efficacy at the center of human agency. Her chapter provides a brief history of Albert Bandura's concept contextualizing them within a positive psychological perspective. The widespread usefulness of his theories and experi-ments are emphasized, this includes the concept of self-efficacy. Of import is the ability to connect with others and the role of self-efficacy in interpersonal and intrapersonal relationships. The essentiality of the interaction between an infant and the caregiver to the social development of the child is emphasized. The link between the care of a child and the healthy development of self-efficacy and other social competencies such as emotional regulation, communication skills, and the ability to form positive functioning social relationships are contextualized in the development of a psychologically healthy person. Self-efficacy and collective efficacy are core to our holistic development and the chapter differentiates these concepts. The relationship between self-efficacy and well-being is considered with an emphasis on the concept of moral disengagement, first introduced by Bandura. Moral disengagement is designed to justify an individual's actions. If moral disengagement exists then so too does moral engagement, which, the author postulates, is the key to the success of the collective efficacy. The chapter acknowledges the contribution of Albert Bandura in creating a map to understand the relationship between community and positive psychology.

As the name suggests, REACH Forgiveness is an intervention with the purpose of assisting persons in the forgiveness of others and becoming more forgiving generally. Everett L. Worthington Jr. begins his chapters by giving a brief history of the development of the intervention as well as some research conducted in efforts to inspire the audience with potential ideas for possible future positive psychological interventions. Taking the REACH Forgiveness intervention as a case study, the author describes the use of scientific principles to create quality psychological interventions, to conduct research on their efficacy, effectiveness, and dissemination. Some origins of ideas for new interventions are discussed, identifying some sources including  clients, teachers, and real-life experiences. Interestingly, the author also focuses on how to create an intervention from an idea. Populations in need of assistance that can potentially be provided through intervention are proposed as a key sample for ethically testing of ideas. Intervention go through multiple testing before the results are published and the intervention is used. An example of the development of an intervention is provided through a case study of the REACH Forgiveness intervention. Methods of disseminating an intervention are outlined, these include dissemination through speeches, scientific publications, and presentations and books. An important take home is that interventions must have relevance and utility.

Vesna Petrović, Dragan Žuljević, and Gian Vittorio Caprara present a series of studies in their chapter that demonstrate the relationships among positive evaluations about oneself, life, and future and these relationships can be traced to a common latent dimension of "positive orientation" and positivity. Their review of findings validates the relationship between positivity and being well adjusted. Positive orientation is a stable evaluative disposition that assists in coping with adversities and has been identified as a latent factor in self-esteem, life satisfaction, and dispositional optimism with evidence of positivity having a genetic influence. The first two studies demonstrated the universality of the positivity scale by testing variance levels across age, gender, and different languages. Positivity should be considered a superordinate variable to self-esteem, life satisfaction, and dispositional optimism. The fourth study highlighted the moderate relation between positivity and the Big Five personality traits which has direct implications for techniques used to improve positivity and general well-being. The fifth study investigated the potential mediating role of positivity in the relation between unresolved family traumatization and variables of subjective well-being. Unresolved family traumatization significantly affects well-being as it predicted higher scores of general distress and negative affect, as well as lower scores of satisfaction with life and positive affect. The same can also be said for positivity, but in the opposite direction.

Based on the arguments made within this article, several areas of future research were noted which include the impact of positivity on different spheres of life and domains of functioning, such as physical health, family, job, coping, and other domains. The authors advocate for research which provides an understanding of the biological correlates of positivity and the ways positivity may moderate stress, illness, and pain to promote overall health and well-being. Research of this nature is essential for designing interventions based on practices that promote and sustain individuals' positivity.

Lopez and Snyder (2009; also quoted in Almaier, 2019, p. 21), succinctly expressed the essence and emphasis of positive psychology as:

> Positive psychology is the "scientific study" of what makes life most worth living. It is a call for psychological science and practice to be as concerned with strength as with weakness; as interested in building the best things in life as in repairing the worst; and as concerned with making the lives of normal people fulfilling as with healing pathology. (Lopez & Snyder, 2009, p. xxiii)

The engagements in this volume provide multidimensional perspectives consistent with the emphasis of positive psychology.

## References

Altmaier, E. M. (2019). Promoting positive processes after trauma. London: Academic Press.

Duckworth, A. L., Steen, T. A., & Seligman, M. E. P. (2005). Positive psychology in clinical practice. *Annual Review of Clinical Psychology*, 1, 629–651.

Gable, S. L., & Haidt, J. (2005). What (and why) is positive psychology? *Review of General Psychology*, 9, 103–110.

Lopez, S. J., & Snyder, C. R. (Eds.). (2009). Oxford handbook of positive psychology (2nd ed.). New York: Oxford University Press.

Maslow, A. (1954). Motivation and Personality. New York: Harper.

Peterson, C., and Seligman, M. E. P. (2004). Character strengths and virtues: A handbook and classification. Oxford: Oxford University Press.

Seligman, M. E. P. (2002). Authentic happiness: Using the new positive psychology to realize your potential for lasting fulfillment. New York: Free Press.

Seligman, M. E. P. (2008). Positive health. *Applied Psychology: An International Review, 57,* 3–18.

Seligman, M. E. P. (2011). Flourish: A new understanding of life's greatest goals and what it takes to reach them. New York: Free Press.

Seligman, M. E. P., & Adler, A. (2018). Positive education. In J. Helliwell, R. Layard, & J. Sachs (Eds.), Global Happiness Policy Report 2018 (pp. 53–74). Dubai: Global Happiness Council.

Seligman, M. E. P., Gillham, J., Reivich, K., Linkins, M., & Ernst, R. (2009). Positive education. *Oxford Review of Education, 35*(3), 293–311.

Seligman, M. E. P., Rashid, T., & Parks, A. C. (2006). Positive psychotherapy. *American Psychologist, 61,* 774–788.

Simmons, J. (2013). Positive psychology as a scientific movement. *International Journal of Science in Society, 4*(12), 43–52.

# 2

# The Empathy-Altruism Hypothesis

## C. Daniel Batson

Think of all the time and energy we spend helping others. In addition to daily courtesies and kindnesses, we send money to aid disaster victims halfway around the world – and to save whales. We stay up all night with a friend who just suffered a broken relationship. We stop to comfort a lost and frightened child until his or her parent appears. Sometimes, the help is truly spectacular – as when Wesley Autrey jumped onto a subway track with the train bearing down in order to save a young man who fell while having a seizure. Or when rescuers in Nazi Europe risked their own lives and the lives of family members to shelter Jews.

Why do we do these things? What motivates such behavior? Is it true that "the most disinterested love is, after all, but a kind of bargain, in which the dear love of our own selves always proposes to be the gainer some way or other" (La Rochefoucauld, 1691, Maxim 82)? Or are we also capable of caring for others for their sakes, not just ours? That is, is altruism within the human motivational repertoire?

The significance of the latter possibility depends on what you think altruism is. If, like most behavioral and social scientists, you think of it as personally costly helping – or as helping to gain self-administered rewards (e.g., a warm glow or avoidance of guilt) rather than to gain material and social rewards – the existence of altruism can't be doubted. But to say we're capable of such altruism tells us nothing we didn't already know. These conceptions trivialize the centuries old egoism–altruism debate. In that debate, altruism refers to a motivational state with the ultimate goal of increasing another's welfare; egoism refers to a motivational state with the ultimate goal of increasing our own welfare. The dominant view in Western thought has long been that our motivation is always exclusively egoistic – as La Rochefoucauld said.

*Positive Psychology: An International Perspective*, First Edition.
Edited by Aleksandra Kostić and Derek Chadee.
© 2021 John Wiley & Sons Ltd. Published 2021 by John Wiley & Sons Ltd.

## Empathy-Altruism Hypothesis

The empathy-altruism hypothesis takes the motivational conceptions of altruism and egoism seriously. And, importantly, it challenges the dominant exclusive egoism view by proposing that empathic concern produces altruistic motivation. To understand this deceptively simple hypothesis, we need to be clear about what is meant both by empathic concern and by altruistic motivation.

### Empathic concern

In the empathy-altruism hypothesis, empathic concern refers to *other-oriented emotion elicited by and congruent with the perceived welfare of a person in need*. This other-oriented emotion has been called by several names other than empathic concern, including compassion, tenderness, sympathy, and pity. The label applied isn't crucial. What's crucial is that the emotion involves feeling *for* the other, not feeling *as* the other feels. (*Feeling as* is a currently popular conception of empathy employed by, for example, Paul Bloom [2016]; Nancy Eisenberg [Eisenberg & Strayer, 1987], and Tania Singer [De Vignemont & Singer, 2006].) Empathic concern also is not a combination of other-oriented emotion and motivation. Although many people use the terms compassion and sympathy to refer to the emotional state I am calling empathic concern, there are some scholars who use one or both of these terms to refer to other-oriented motivation as well as to emotion, making the terms more equivalent to the whole empathy-altruism hypothesis (see, for example, Goetz, Keltner, & Simon-Thomas, 2010; Wispé, 1986). For me, empathic concern *produces* motivation but is not itself a motivational state. I think the question of the nature of the motivation produced by empathic concern – egoistic or altruistic – should be left open for empirical investigation, not finessed by definitional decree.

To further clarify what is meant by empathic concern, let me add four quick points:

1. To say that the other-oriented emotion is "congruent with the perceived welfare of a person in need," refers to a congruence of valence. The emotion's valence is negative because the perceived welfare of a person in need is negative. But this congruence doesn't mean that the empathizer and the person in need are feeling the same negative emotion. It would be congruent, for example, to feel sad or sorry for someone who's upset and afraid. Or to feel compassion for the unconscious victim of a mugging (as did the Good Samaritan: Luke 10:33), even though an unconscious victim is feeling nothing at all.
2. Although the term *empathy* is broad enough to include situations in which there is no perceived need – such as when we feel empathic joy at a friend's good fortune (Smith, Keating, & Stotland, 1989; Stotland, 1969) – not all

empathic emotion is hypothesized to produce altruistic motivation. The empathy-altruism hypothesis refers specifically to empathic concern felt when another is perceived to be in need, because without a perceived need, there's no reason to increase the other's welfare.

3.  Empathic concern isn't a single, discrete emotion but includes a whole constellation of emotions. It includes feelings that people report as sympathy, compassion, softheartedness, tenderness, sorrow, sadness, upset, distress, concern, grief, and more.

4.  Although feelings of sympathy and compassion are inherently other-oriented, we can feel sorrow, distress, and concern that is self-oriented – as when something bad happens directly to us. Both other-oriented and self-oriented versions of these emotions may be described as feeling sorry or sad, upset or distressed, concerned or grieved. This breadth of usage invites confusion. The relevant psychological distinction doesn't lie in the emotional label used – sad, distressed, concerned – but in whose welfare is the focus of the emotion. Are we feeling sad, distressed, concerned for the other? Or are we feeling this way as a result of what has befallen us (including, perhaps, the experience of seeing the other suffer)?

In recent years, the term empathy has been applied to a range of psychological phenomena in addition to the other-oriented emotion just described (see Batson, 2009, for a partial review). Here's a quick list:

- Knowing another's thoughts and feelings.
- Adopting the posture or matching the neural response of another.
- Coming to feel as another feels.
- Feeling personal distress at witnessing another's suffering.
- Imagining how you would think and feel in another's place.
- Imagining how another thinks and feels.
- A general disposition (trait) to feel for others.

Each of these phenomena is distinct from empathic concern. The empathy-altruism hypothesis makes no claim that any of them produces altruistic motivation except if and when it evokes empathic concern. Further, the hypothesis makes no claim that any of them is either necessary or sufficient to produce empathic concern.

## Altruistic motivation

As said earlier, altruism in the egoism–altruism debate refers to a motivational state with the ultimate goal of increasing another's welfare. It's juxtaposed to egoism, defined as a motivational state with the ultimate goal of increasing our own welfare. As these definitions highlight, altruism and egoism have much in common.

Each refers to a motivational state; each is concerned with the ultimate goal of that motivational state; and, for each, the ultimate goal is to increase someone's welfare. These common features provide the context for focusing on the crucial difference: Whose welfare is the ultimate goal – another person's or our own?

(Note that "ultimate goal" in the two definitions refers to means–end relations in the psychological present, not to a metaphysical first or final cause, and not to biological function. An ultimate goal is an end in itself. In contrast, an *instrumental* goal is a stepping stone on the way to some other goal. Both instrumental and ultimate goals should be distinguished from unintended consequences – results of an action that aren't a goal.)

Each of a person's ultimate goals defines a distinct goal-directed motive. Hence, altruism and egoism, which have different ultimate goals, are distinct motives even though they can co-occur. Moreover, they are motivational *states*, not personal dispositions or *traits*. The disagreement in the egoism–altruism debate is over the nature of our motives – egoism versus altruism – not over the kind of people we are – egoists versus altruists.

## Self-benefits as ultimate goals (egoism) or unintended consequences (altruism)

Many forms of self-benefit can be derived from helping. Some are obvious, as when we get material rewards or thanks, or when we avoid censure. But even when we benefit others in the absence of external rewards, we can still benefit. Seeing a person or animal in need may cause us to feel distress, and we may relieve the other's distress in order to remove our own. Or we can benefit by feeling good about ourselves for being kind. Or by escaping guilt and shame for failing to do what we think we should. The empathy-altruism hypothesis doesn't deny that altruistically motivated helping brings self-benefits like these. But it claims that, insofar as our motivation for helping stems from empathic concern, any self-benefits that result are unintended consequences rather than the ultimate goal.

## Two non-claims of empathy-altruism hypothesis

Let me also mention two things that the empathy-altruism hypothesis does not claim. First, it doesn't claim that a person feeling empathic concern must experience only – or even primarily – altruistic motivation. Such a person can also experience motives, including motives to help, that are produced by thoughts and feelings other than empathic concern. Second, the hypothesis doesn't claim that empathic concern is the only source of altruistic motivation. There may be other sources, such as certain personality characteristics or personal values. To date, however, no other source has been carefully tested.

## Why worry about our motivation for benefiting others?

As long as a person in need receives help, why worry about whether the underlying motivation is altruistic or egoistic? The answer to this question depends on your interest. If you're only interested in getting help in this situation for this person (you perhaps?), the nature of the motivation may not matter. But if you're interested in knowing more generally when and where help can be expected – and how effective it is likely to be (perhaps with an eye to creating a more caring society) – then to understand the underlying motivation is essential. If, for example, I am motivated to help in order to impress you, then if you won't know whether I help or not, this motivation and my help will disappear.

As argued by Kurt Lewin (1951), explanatory stability for human action is found in the link of a given motive to its ultimate goal, not found in behavior or in behavioral consequences. Behavior is highly variable. Occurrence of a given behavior, including helping, depends on the strength of the motive or motives that might evoke this behavior, as well as on (a) the strength of competing motives in the situation, (b) how the behavior relates to each of these motives, and (c) other behavioral options available at the time. It also depends on whether the behavior promotes an instrumental or an ultimate goal. The more directly a certain behavior promotes an ultimate goal, and the more uniquely it does so among the behavioral options available, the more likely the behavior is to occur. Behavior that promotes an instrumental goal can change if either (a) the causal association between the instrumental and ultimate goal changes or (b) better behavioral pathways to the ultimate goal appear that bypass the instrumental goal.

Yet, complicating matters, we infer motivation from behavior, although not from a single instance of behavior. Instead, we infer motivation from the *pattern of behavior* across situations that vary in the best way to reach different possible ultimate goals. Inference from such a pattern has allowed us to identify the ultimate goal of empathy-induced motivation to help.

## Current status of the empathy-altruism hypothesis

Across the past four decades, more than 35 experiments have been conducted to test the empathy-altruism hypothesis against a range of egoistic alternative hypotheses – hypotheses claiming that the motivation produced by empathic concern is directed toward the ultimate goal of obtaining one or another self-benefit. As just suggested, the research strategy has been to experimentally vary situations so that we can use the pattern of behavior to make a meaningful inference about the ultimate goal of empathy-induced motivation. (See Batson, 2011 and 2018, for a comprehensive review of the experiments.)

With remarkable consistency, results of these experiments have supported the empathy-altruism hypothesis. The few results that initially seemed to contradict the hypothesis haven't stood up to further examination. To the best of my knowledge, we now have no plausible egoistic explanation for the cumulative results. This experimental evidence has led me to conclude – tentatively – that the empathy-altruism hypothesis is true: Other-oriented feeling for a person in need (empathic concern) produces motivation with the ultimate goal of removing the empathy-inducing need (altruistic motivation). The evidence has also led me to conclude that this motivation can be surprisingly powerful. And it has led me to wonder how this empathy-induced altruistic motivation is possible. What evolutionary function could it serve?

## Evolutionary function of empathy-induced altruism

Rather than inclusive fitness (Hamilton, 1964) or reciprocal altruism (Trivers, 1971), the most plausible answer seems to be that empathy-induced altruistic motivation evolved as part of the parental instinct among higher mammals, especially humans (Batson, 2010, 2011, 2018; Bell, 2001; De Waal, 1996; Hoffman, 1981; McDougall, 1908; Zahn-Waxler & Radke-Yarrow, 1990). If mammalian parents were not intensely interested in the welfare of their very vulnerable progeny, these species would quickly die out.

We humans have no doubt inherited key aspects of our parental instinct from ancestors we share with other mammalian species (Preston, 2013). But in humans this instinct seems less automatic and more flexible. Human parental nurturance goes well beyond nursing, providing other kinds of food, protecting, and keeping the young close – activities that characterize parental care in most mammalian species. It includes inferences about and anticipation of the desires and feelings of the child ("Is that a hungry cry or a wet cry?" "She won't like the fireworks; they'll be too loud."). It also includes goal-directed motives and appraisal-based emotions (Scherer, 1984). Crucially, it seems to include (a) other-oriented feelings of empathic concern for the child and (b) empathy-induced altruistic motivation to protect and increase the child's welfare.

Parental care based on empathic concern didn't supplant the more primitive cue-based responses of our ancient ancestors. Instead, it supplemented these responses by increasing the flexibility with which they are employed (see Bell, 2001; Damasio, 2002; MacLean, 1990; Sober, 1991; Sober & Wilson, 1998; S. E. Taylor, 2002; Zahn-Waxler & Radke-Yarrow, 1990). This flexibility permits anticipation and prevention of needs – even evolutionarily quite novel ones such as the need to avoid sticking a pin in an electrical outlet.

Importantly, the empathy-altruism research shows that we humans don't experience empathy-induced altruistic motivation only in response to the needs of our own children. As long as there's no preexisting antipathy, we can feel empathy for a wide range of others in need, including nonhumans (Batson, Lishner, Cook, & Sawyer, 2005; Shelton & Rogers, 1981). Speculating, let me suggest that this breadth of human empathy-induced altruism may reflect cognitive generalization whereby we "adopt" cared-for others as progeny, producing empathic concern and altruistic motivation when they are in need (Batson, 2011; Hoffman, 1981).

To the extent that the human nurturant impulse relies on appraisal-based other-oriented emotions such as empathic concern, it should be relatively easy to generalize. And two specific factors may have facilitated the emergence of such generalization: (a) human cognitive capacity, including the capacity for symbolic thought and analogic reasoning; and (b) lack of evolutionary advantage for limiting empathic concern and parental nurturance to offspring in early human hunter-gatherer bands. In these bands, not only were those in need often one's children or close kin, but survival of one's genes was tightly tied to the welfare even of those who weren't close kin (Hrdy, 2009; Kelly, 1995; Sober & Wilson, 1998). In contemporary society, the prospect of generalization of parental nurturance appears more plausible when you think of the emotional sensitivity and tender care that can be provided by nannies, workers in day-care centers, adoptive parents, and pet owners.

If the roots of human altruism lie in generalized parental nurturance, then altruism is woven tightly into our nature and into the fabric of everyday life. Empathy-induced altruism isn't exceptional or unnatural, but a central feature of the human condition. Rather than looking for such altruism only in acts of extreme self-sacrifice, it should be manifest in our everyday experience. The empathy-altruism research provides evidence that it is.

## Practical Implications

Now that we have the "what" of the empathy-altruism hypothesis before us, we can turn to why it's important – the implications. Research shows that empathy-induced altruism isn't an unalloyed good. It offers important benefits but also has important liabilities, and we need to be aware of both. Let me highlight some of the key benefits and liabilities. (For more extensive discussion and review of relevant research, see Batson, 2011, 2018.)

### Benefits of empathy-induced altruism

*More, more sensitive, and less fickle help.* Perhaps the least surprising benefit is that feeling empathic concern leads us to help the target(s) of empathy more. Even before the empathy-altruism hypothesis was tested, there was evidence that empathic concern can increase the likelihood of helping (e.g., Coke, Batson, & McDavis, 1978; Krebs, 1975). Now, knowing that empathic concern produces altruistic motivation, we have reason to believe it can improve the quality of help as well – producing help that is more sensitive to the needs of the person for whom empathy is felt.

Egoistic goals such as gaining rewards and avoiding punishments can often be reached even if our help doesn't alleviate the needy individual's suffering. For these goals, it's the thought that counts. But for empathy-induced altruism, the other's welfare counts; our focus is on the other's need and its relief. Experimental evidence supports this reasoning. Unlike those feeling little empathy, individuals induced to feel empathic concern tend to feel good after helping only if the other's need is relieved (Batson et al., 1988; Batson & Weeks, 1996). And our concern for the other's welfare includes sensitivity to future needs. Sibicky, Schroeder, and Dovidio (1995) provided experimental evidence that empathic concern *reduced* helping when the help, although meeting an immediate need, would be detrimental in the long term (e.g., think of parents who refuse to give their beloved child unhealthy treats).

In addition to producing more sensitive help, empathy-induced altruistic motivation is also likely to be less fickle than egoistic motives for helping. Research indicates that individuals experiencing relatively low empathy – and so a predominance of egoistic over altruistic motivation – are far less likely to help when either (a) they can easily escape exposure to the other's need without helping or (b) they can easily justify to themselves and others a failure to help (Batson, Duncan, Ackerman, Buckley, & Birch, 1981; Batson et al., 1988; Toi & Batson, 1982). The practical implications of these findings are disturbing because easy escape and ready justification for not helping are common characteristics of many helping situations. Amid the blooming, buzzing confusion of everyday life, we can almost always find a way to direct attention elsewhere or to convince ourselves that inaction is justified. Given this, the practical potential of empathy-induced altruistic motivation looks promising indeed. In the research just cited, individuals experiencing relatively high empathy showed no noticeable decrease in readiness to help under conditions of easy escape, high justification, or both.

*Less aggression.* A second benefit is inhibition of aggression. To the degree that feeling empathic concern for a person in need produces altruistic motivation to maintain or increase their welfare, it should inhibit any inclination to aggress against or harm that person. This inhibitory effect was impressively demonstrated by Harmon-Jones, Vaughn-Scott, Mohr, Sigelman, and Harmon-Jones (2004). They assessed the effect of empathy on anger-related left-frontal cortical electroencephalographic (EEG) activity following an insult. As predicted based on the empathy-altruism hypothesis, relative left-frontal cortical EEG activity, which is typically increased by insult and which promotes aggression – and which increased in a low-empathy condition – was inhibited in their high-empathy condition.

Note that empathic feelings shouldn't inhibit all aggressive impulses, only those directed toward the target of empathy. Indeed, it's easy to imagine empathy-induced anger and aggression, in which empathy for person A leads to increased anger and aggression toward person B if B is perceived to be a threat to A's welfare (see Buffone & Poulin, 2014; Hoffman, 2000; Vitaglione & Barnett, 2003).

More broadly, empathy may counteract a particularly subtle and insidious form of aggression – blaming the victims of injustice. In his classic work on the just-world hypothesis, Melvin Lerner (1980) found that research participants were likely to derogate a person whom they perceived to be the innocent victim of suffering.

This derogation presumably served to maintain participants' belief that people get what they deserve and deserve what they get. Protecting our belief in a just world in this way can lead to what William Ryan (1971) called *blaming the victim*. Ryan suggested that we're likely to react to the victims of unjust discrimination and oppression in our society – racial minorities, the poor, immigrants – by unconsciously blaming them. If they have less, they must be less deserving.

Derogation and blaming the victim are all-too-common alternatives to caring about the suffering of others. These processes can lead to smug acceptance of the plight of the disadvantaged as just and right. But empathy-induced altruism may counteract this tendency. In an important follow-up to Lerner's classic experiments, Aderman, Brehm, and Katz (1974) found that perspective-taking instructions designed to evoke empathy eliminated derogation of an innocent victim.

*Increased cooperation and care in conflict situations.* There is also evidence that empathy-induced altruistic motivation can increase cooperation and care in conflict situations. Paradigmatic of such situations is a one-trial prisoner's dilemma. In this two-person dilemma, it's always in each person's material best interest to defect (i.e., compete) regardless of what the other person does. Theories that assume we humans are always and exclusively self-interested – such as game theory (Von Neumann & Morgenstern, 1944) and the theory of rational choice (Downs, 1957; Sen, 1977; M. Taylor, 1976) – predict no cooperation in a one-trial prisoner's dilemma. In contrast, the empathy-altruism hypothesis predicts that if one person in such a dilemma is induced to feel empathy for the other, this person will experience two motives – self-interest and empathy-induced altruism. Although self-interest is best satisfied by defecting, altruism is best satisfied by cooperating. So, the empathy-altruism hypothesis predicts that empathy should lead to increased cooperation in a one-trial prisoner's dilemma. Batson and Moran (1999) reported an experiment in which they found precisely these results (also see Batson & Ahmad, 2001; Rumble, Van Lange, & Parks, 2010).

What about real-world conflicts? Might the introduction of empathy-induced altruism be worth pursuing there too? Stephan and Finlay (1999) pointed out that the induction of empathy is often an explicit component of techniques used in conflict-resolution workshops designed to address long-standing political conflicts, such as between Arabs and Israelis. Workshop participants are encouraged to express their feelings, their hopes and fears, and to actively adopt the perspective of those on the other side of the conflict (Burton, 1987; R. Fisher, 1994; Kelman, 1997; Kelman & Cohen, 1986; Rouhana & Kelman, 1994). These efforts should facilitate both perception of the other as in need and sensitivity to the other's welfare – consequences that should, in turn, increase empathic concern.

*Improved attitudes and action toward members of stigmatized groups.* Is it possible that empathy-induced altruism might be used to improve attitudes toward and action on behalf of stigmatized groups? There is reason to think so. Batson et al. (1997) found that inducing empathy for a member of a stigmatized group improved attitudes toward the group as a whole. This attitude-improvement effect has now been found for many stigmatized groups, including people with physical disabilities, homosexuals, people with AIDS, the homeless – even for convicted murderers and drug dealers (Batson, Chang, Orr, & Rowland, 2002; Batson et al., 1997; Clore & Jeffrey, 1972; Dovidio et al., 2010; Finlay & Stephan, 2000; Vescio, Sechrist, & Paolucci, 2003). There is also evidence that the improved attitudes can, in turn, increase action to help the group (Batson et al., 2002).

Underscoring the broad applicability of empathy-induced attitude change, Shelton and Rogers (1981) found that inducing empathy for whales led to more positive attitudes that were reflected in increased intention to help save whales. Both Schultz (2000) and Berenguer (2007) found that empathy induced for animals being harmed by pollution improved attitudes toward protecting the natural environment.

There are practical reasons to employ empathy to improve attitudes toward and action on behalf of the disadvantaged and stigmatized of society – at least initially. The induction of empathy is likely to be easier than trying to improve attitudes through methods such as direct intergroup contact (Pettigrew, 1998). Novels, movies, and documentaries show that it is relatively easy to induce empathy for a member of a stigmatized group. Moreover, this empathy can be induced in low-cost, low-risk situations. Rather than the elaborate arrangements required to create positive personal contact with members of an outgroup, we can be led to feel empathy for a member of a stigmatized group as we sit comfortably in our own home. Further, empathy-inducing experiences can be controlled to ensure that they are positive far more readily than can live, face-to-face contact. (For real-world examples of the induction of empathic concern to improve attitudes toward stigmatized groups, see Stowe, 1852/2005, and Paluck, 2009. For a review of the range of programs that have used empathy to improve such attitudes in educational settings, see Batson & Ahmad, 2009.)

*Self-benefits.* Shifting focus from benefits for those in need, empathy-induced altruism may also benefit the person who is altruistically motivated. Studies of volunteers and providers of social support have noted improved psychological and physical well-being among these help-givers (Brown, Nesse, Vinokur, & Smith, 2003; Luks, 1991). And there is evidence that volunteers who provide personal care live longer than non-volunteers – even after adjusting for the effect of other predictors of longevity such as physical health and activity level (Oman, 2007). Importantly, the effect on longevity seems to be limited to those who volunteer for other-oriented rather than self-oriented reasons (Konrath, Fuhrel-Forbis, Lou, & Brown, 2012).

However, it is not yet clear that these health benefits are due to empathy-induced altruism. They might instead be due either to the esteem-enhancement that doing a good deed provides or to the feelings of accomplishment and competence. And even if the benefits are due to empathy-induced altruism, a caution is in order: Intentional pursuit of these health benefits may be doomed to failure. To use empathy-induced altruism as a way to reach the self-serving ends of gaining more meaning and better health involves a logical and psychological contradiction. As soon as benefit to the other becomes an instrumental means to gain self-benefits, the motivation is no longer altruistic.

## Liabilities of empathy-induced altruism

Not all practical implications of the empathy-altruism hypothesis are positive. Along with the benefits described, empathy-induced altruism has some serious liabilities.

*It can cause harm.* Altruistic motivation is potentially dangerous. As evolutionary biologists have long pointed out (e.g., Dawkins, 1976), altruism may lead us to incur costs in time and money, even loss of life. When 28-year old Lenny Skutnik was asked why he dove into the ice-strewn Potomac River to rescue a drowning plane-crash victim, he said, "I just did what I had to do." When first responders at the World Trade Center on 9/11 pushed forward to help trapped civilians despite flames, toxic gasses, and other obvious dangers, many died. I can't say to what extent these heroic acts were motivated by empathy-induced altruism, but I can say that whatever motivated them put the actors squarely in harm's way.

Not only can empathy-induced altruism be harmful to the altruistically motivated person, it can also hurt the target. Balzac, one of our most astute observers of the human condition, graphically portrayed this irony in his classic novel, *Pere Goriot* (Balzac 1834/1962). Goriot's selfless love spoiled his daughters, drove them from him, and ultimately destroyed both them and him. Balzac's message: Altruism may be part of human nature but, like aggression, our altruism must be held carefully in check, lest it prove destructive. Graham Hancock made a similar point in his scathing indictment of international aid programs in *Lords of Poverty* (1989).

Even when helping is clearly appropriate, empathy-induced altruism can at times make matters worse. This is especially true when effective help requires a delicate touch. Think of surgeons. It is no accident, argued neurophysiologist Paul MacLean (1967), that surgeons are prohibited from operating on close kin. When operating on one's sister rather than a stranger, deep feelings of concern and a desperate desire to relieve her suffering may cause a normally steady hand to shake.

Testimony to an especially tragic circumstance in which a warm heart made it more difficult to do what was needed comes from survivors of the death camps in Nazi Europe. In the camps, members of the underground worked to save lives but couldn't save everyone. At times, they had to decide who would live and who would not. Survivors reported that empathic concern felt for those who had to die made it difficult if not impossible to do what would save more lives. In the words of Terrence Des Pres:

> Compassion was seldom possible, self-pity never. Emotion not only blurred judgment and undermined decisiveness, it jeopardized the life of everyone in the underground . . . Hard choices had to be made and not everyone was equal to the task, no one less than the kind of person whose goodness was most evident, most admired, but least available for action. (Des Pres, 1976, p. 131)

*It can lead to paternalism.* As said earlier, the most plausible account of the evolutionary roots of empathy-induced altruistic motivation seems to be cognitive generalization of human parental nurturance. If true, this account reveals a potentially serious liability. It suggests that a person for whom empathic concern is felt is metaphorically seen as childlike – as dependent, vulnerable, and needing care – at least with regard to the need in question. Consistent with this possibility, research has found that we feel greater empathic concern for more baby-faced and more vulnerable adults (Dijker, 2001; Lishner, Batson, & Huss, 2011; Lishner, Oceja, Stocks, & Zaspel, 2008).

Sometimes, to be perceived as dependent, vulnerable, and needing care poses no problem. Most of us happily defer to the expertise of physicians, police, and plumbers when we need their help. At other times, the consequences can be tragic. Teachers and tutors can, out of genuine concern, fail to enable students to develop the ability and confidence to solve problems themselves, thereby fostering unnecessary dependence, low self-esteem, and a reduced sense of efficacy (Nadler, Fisher, & DePaulo, 1983). Physical therapists, physicians, nurses, friends, and family members can do the same for patients with physical or mental disabilities. So can social workers trying to care for the poor and disadvantaged. To see the person in need as dependent and vulnerable may lead to a response that perpetuates if not exacerbates the problem. It may produce paternalism.

Effective parenting requires sensitivity about when to intervene and when to stand back, as well as sensitivity about how to structure the child's environment to foster coping, confidence, and independence. Effective help requires much the same (J. D. Fisher, Nadler, & DePaulo, 1983). Recall the adage about teaching the hungry to fish rather than giving them fish.

*Not all needs evoke empathy-induced altruism.* Many of the pressing social problems we face today don't involve personal needs of the sort likely to evoke empathic concern. Such concern is felt for individuals, but many of our pressing problems are global. Think of environmental protection, nuclear disarmament, and population control. These problems aren't encountered as personal needs; they're broader and more abstract. It's difficult if not impossible to feel empathy for an abstract concept like the environment, world population, or the planet – although personalizing metaphors like "Mother Earth" may move us in that direction.

Not only is it difficult to evoke empathy for these pressing global needs. Such needs can't be adequately addressed with a personal helping response. They must be addressed in political arenas and through institutional and bureaucratic structures. The process is long and slow, not the kind of process for which emotion-based motives, including empathy-induced altruism, are apt to be very effective (Hardin, 1977). Like other emotions, empathic concern diminishes over time.

Empathy's limited endurance may also undercut its ability to motivate the sustained helping efforts often required of community-action volunteers (see Omoto

& Snyder, 1995). Empathy-induced altruism can be effective in initiating volunteer action, but other motives may need to take over if a volunteer is to continue for the long haul.

*It can lead to empathy avoidance.* What if you don't want to be altruistically motivated? After all, altruistic motivation can cost you, leading you to spend time, money, and energy on behalf of another. Awareness of this cost may arouse an egoistic motive to avoid feeling empathic concern and the resulting altruistic motive. Shaw, Batson, and Todd (1994) provided evidence that this *empathy-avoidance motive* is likely to arise when you are aware – before exposure to a person in need – that (a) you will be asked to help this person and (b) helping will be costly (also see Cameron & Payne, 2011). Empathy avoidance might be aroused, for example, when you see a homeless person on the street, or hear about the plight of refugees, or see news footage of the ravages of famine. It may lead you to cross the street, close your eyes, change channels.

Empathy avoidance may also be a factor in the experience of *burnout* among those who work in the helping professions (Maslach, 1982). But the conditions for empathy avoidance among helping professional don't seem to be the ones specified by Shaw et al. (1994). Among professionals, empathy avoidance is more likely to result from the perceived impossibility of providing effective help than from the perceived cost of helping. Aware of the impossibility imposed by limited resources (e.g., insufficient time) or the intractability of the need (e.g., terminal illness), some physicians, chronic-care nurses, therapists, counselors, and welfare case workers may avoid feeling empathy in order to avoid the frustration of thwarted altruistic motivation (López-Pérez, Ambrona, Gregory, Stocks, & Oceja, 2013; Stotland, Mathews, Sherman, Hansson, & Richardson, 1978). These professional helpers may view their patients or clients as objects rather than people – and treat them accordingly. Other professionals may, over time, find that their ability to feel empathic concern is exhausted, leading to what has been called *compassion fatigue* (Figley, 2002). There are limits to how often one can draw from the emotional well. (For some possible antidotes, see Halpern, 2001.)

Empathy avoidance may also occur in response to the suffering of members of the opposition in intergroup conflicts. Whether your opponents are a rival sports team or a national, tribal, or ethnic outgroup, their suffering may be more apt to produce *schadenfreude* – malicious glee – than empathic concern (Cikara, Bruneau, & Saxe, 2011; Hein, Silani, Preuschoff, Batson, & Singer, 2010).

Empathy avoidance may even have played an important, chilling role in the Holocaust. Rudolf Hoess, the commandant of Auschwitz, reported that he "stifled all softer emotions" in order to carry out his assignment: the systematic extermination of 2.9 million people (Hoess, 1959).

*It can produce immoral action.* Perhaps the most surprising implication of the empathy-altruism hypothesis is that empathy-induced altruism can lead to immoral action. This implication is surprising because many people equate altruism with morality. The empathy-altruism hypothesis does not.

Often, altruism produces action judged moral – as when it leads us to help the needy or comfort the sick. But not always. Batson, Klein, Highberger, and Shaw (1995) found that empathy-induced altruistic motivation can also lead people to give preferential treatment to a person for whom they feel empathy even though doing so violates their moral standards of fairness (also see Blader & Rothman, 2014). Egoism, altruism, and moral motivation are, it seems, three distinct forms of motivation, each of which can conflict with another (see Batson, 2011, 2018, for discussions of the distinctions).

More broadly, there is evidence that empathy-induced altruism can lead to partiality in our decisions as a society about whom among the many in need will get our assistance. Several decades ago, *Time* magazine essayist Walter Isaacson (1992) commented on the photogenics of disaster. He raised the possibility that the decision to intervene in Somalia but not the Sudan occurred because those suffering in Somalia proved more photogenic – their faces evoked empathic concern and altruistic motivation in a way that those in the Sudan did not. Isaacson reflected: "Random bursts of compassion provoked by compelling pictures may be a suitable basis for Christmas charity drives, but are they the proper foundation for a foreign policy?" (Isaacson, 1992; similarly, see Bloom, 2016; Prinz, 2011).

*It can undermine the common good.* Not only does the empathy-altruism hypothesis predict that empathy-induced altruism can lead to immoral action but also that it can lead us to act against the common good in social dilemmas. A *social dilemma* arises when three conditions co-occur: (a) Persons have a choice about how to allocate their scarce resources (time, money, energy, etc.). (b) Regardless what others do, to allocate the resources to the group is best for the group as a whole, but to allocate to a single individual (oneself or another group member) is best for that individual. (c) If all allocations are to separate individuals, each individual is worse off than if all allocations are to the group. In modern society, social dilemmas abound. They include recycling, carpooling, pollution reduction, voting, paying taxes, contributing to public TV – to name but a few.

Guided by the assumption of universal egoism that underlies game theory, it has been taken for granted that in a social dilemma the only individual to whom we will allocate scarce resources is ourselves. But the empathy-altruism hypothesis predicts that if you feel empathic concern for another member of the group, you will be altruistically motivated to benefit that person. So, if you can allocate resources to them, then rather than the two motives traditionally assumed to conflict in a social dilemma – self-interest and the common good – three motives are in play. And if, along with egoism (self-interest), the altruistic motive is stronger than the desire to promote the common good, the latter will suffer.

How often does empathy-induced altruistic motivation arise in real-world social dilemmas? It's hard to think of a case where it doesn't. It arises every time we try to decide whether to spend our time or money to benefit ourselves, the community, or another individual about whom we especially care. I may decline to participate in a neighborhood clean-up project on Saturday not because I want to play golf but because my son wants me to take him to a movie. Whalers may kill to extinction – and loggers clear-cut – not out of personal greed but to provide for their families.

Consistent with this empathy-altruism prediction, Batson, Batson, et al. (1995) found that research participants placed in a social dilemma allocated some of their resources to a person for whom they felt empathy, reducing the overall collective good. And Oceja et al. (2014) found that if there is reason to believe that one or more other individuals in the group have needs similar to the need that induced empathy, resources may be preferentially allocated to them as well.

Highlighting a situation in which empathy-induced altruism poses an even greater threat to the common good than does self-interested egoism, Batson et al. (1999) found that when allocation decisions were to be made public, empathy-induced altruism reduced the common good whereas self-interest did not. Why would this be? There are clear social norms and sanctions against pursuit of self-interest at the expense of what's best for all: "Selfish" and "greedy" are stinging epithets (Kerr, 1995). Norms and sanctions against showing concern for another person's interests – even if doing so diminishes the common good – are far less clear. How do whalers and loggers stand up to the public outcry about over-depletion of natural resources? It's easy. They aren't using these resources for themselves but to care for their families.

If altruism poses such a threat to the common good, why don't we have societal sanctions against altruism like those against egoism? Perhaps it's because society makes one or both of two assumptions: (a) altruism is always good and (b) altruism is weak (if it exists at all). We now have good reason to think that each of these assumptions is wrong.

## Conclusion

Research over the past four decades designed to test the empathy-altruism hypothesis and its implications suggests not only that this hypothesis is true but also that empathy-induced altruism can be a powerful positive force in human affairs. It offers benefits in the form of more and more sensitive help for those in need, less aggression, increased cooperation in competitive situations, reduction of intergroup conflict, and improved attitudes toward and action on behalf of stigmatized groups. It may also provide health benefits to the altruistic helper.

Yet empathy-induced altruism is not always a force for good. To use its power wisely, we need to be aware not only of its potential benefits but also its liabilities. It can, at times, bring harm to the altruistically motivated individual and to those in need. It can produce paternalism. It is more suited to addressing personal than global needs. It can arouse motivation to avoid feeling empathic concern when people know that to act on the resulting altruistic motivation will be either costly or ineffective. It can produce immoral action by leading us to show partiality toward those for whom we care, despite our moral standards dictating impartiality. And it can lead us to act against the common good in social dilemmas. Indeed, when our action is public, empathy-induced altruism can pose a more serious threat to the common good than does self-interested egoism.

These liabilities need to be taken into account in any attempt to promote human welfare by building on the empathy-altruism research. Although we now have clear evidence that empathy-induced altruistic motivation exists and can be pervasive and powerful, we also have clear evidence that unless handled with sensitivity to its limitations as well as its promise, it can harm not help.

If this conclusion is correct, how does the research on empathy-induced altruism relate to positive psychology? Abraham Maslow, who is credited with first advocating positive psychology (in his *Motivation and Personality*, 1954), felt the discipline of psychology had made far more progress understanding our human shortcomings – our pathologies and weaknesses – than our strengths and potentialities. Without denying the importance of understanding and addressing pathology and weakness, Maslow sought to expand the scope of psychological theory and research to include the positive aspects of our nature. The empathy-altruism hypothesis and related research also calls for an expansion of psychology. It calls for expansion of our understanding of human motivation to include more than self-interested egoism. So, the empathy-altruism research may seem a paradigm example of positive psychology – especially given that many people consider altruism a quintessentially positive attribute.

Personally, I think the relationship of empathy-induced altruism to positive psychology is not as an exemplar but as a challenge: The empathy-altruism research poses two questions for positive psychology. First, despite extending our view of human nature beyond deficiencies, has positive psychology extended it far enough? Not only for Maslow but also for the field of positive psychology when established 40 years later in the 1990s by Martin Seligman and others, the positives at issue are almost always positives for the individual – the individual's happiness, creativity, subjective well-being, social skills, self-efficacy, flourishing, and so on. But if I actively seek one or more of these positives as an ultimate goal, my motivation is directed toward self-benefit. And no matter how noble the sought self-benefit, my motivation is egoistic. Even if, for example, I dedicate my life to caring for others as the way to live a full, meaningful life, this is still a form of egoism because my care for others is an instrumental goal on the way to the ultimate goal of living a full, meaningful life.

In contrast, the ultimate goal of empathy-induced altruistic motivation isn't self-benefit, not even the noble self-benefits extolled by positive psychology. Its ultimate goal is to benefit the person for whom empathy is felt. Thus, to find that the empathy-altruism hypothesis is true extends our view of human nature beyond self-interest – even in its most positive forms. If we can care for others for their sakes, our potential exceeds what positive psychology has envisioned.

Second, should not the "positive" and the "psychology" in positive psychology be kept distinct? Positive psychology focuses on what's good about people. In contrast, the research reported in this chapter suggests that empathy-induced altruistic motivation isn't inherently good. Sometimes it leads us to act in ways that we or others judge good, and sometimes, in ways judged bad. Like any other natural phenomenon, empathy-induced altruism isn't inherently positive or negative; it just is. What we do with it is what is positive or negative.

Science, including psychology, can help us understand what is, but to decide whether and when some personal attribute is positive, negative, and neutral is a value judgment that takes us beyond science, including psychology. Should not the distinction between what is and whether and when what is good be applied not only to empathy-induced altruism but also to the personal attributes that are the focus of positive psychology? Doing so would encourage exploration of possible negatives associated with these attributes, not only positives.

## References

Aderman, D., Brehm, S. S., & Katz, L. B. (1974). Empathic observation of an innocent victim: The just world revisited. *Journal of Personality and Social Psychology, 29*, 342–347.

Balzac, H. de. (1962). *Père Goriot* (H. Reed, Trans.). New York, NY: New American Library. (Original work published 1834).

Batson, C. D. (2009). These things called empathy: Eight related but distinct phenomena. In J. Decety & W. Ickes (Eds.), *The social neuroscience of empathy* (pp. 3–15). Cambridge, MA: MIT Press.

Batson, C. D. (2010). The naked emperor: Seeking a more plausible genetic basis for psychological altruism. *Economics and Philosophy, 26*, 149–164.

Batson, C. D. (2011). *Altruism in humans.* New York, NY: Oxford University Press.

Batson, C. D. (2018). *A scientific search for altruism: Do we care only about ourselves?* New York, NY: Oxford University Press.

Batson, C. D., & Ahmad, N. (2001). Empathy-induced altruism in a prisoner's dilemma II: What if the target of empathy has defected? *European Journal of Social Psychology, 31*, 25–36.

Batson, C. D., & Ahmad, N. (2009). Using empathy to improve intergroup attitudes and relations. *Social Issues and Policy Review, 3*, 141–177.

Batson, C. D., Ahmad, N., Yin, J., Bedell, S. J., Johnson, J. W., Templin, C. M., & Whiteside, A. (1999). Two threats to the common good: Self-interested egoism and empathy-induced altruism. *Personality and Social Psychology Bulletin, 25*, 3–16.

Batson, C. D., Batson, J. G., Todd, R. M., Brummett, B. H., Shaw, L. L., & Aldeguer, C. M. R. (1995). Empathy and the collective good: Caring for one of the others in a social dilemma. *Journal of Personality and Social Psychology, 68*, 619–631.

Batson, C. D., Chang, J., Orr, R., & Rowland, J. (2002). Empathy, attitudes, and action: Can feeling for a member of a stigmatized group motivate one to help the group? *Personality and Social Psychology Bulletin, 28*, 1656–1666.

Batson, C. D., Duncan, B., Ackerman, P., Buckley, T., & Birch, K. (1981). Is empathic emotion a source of altruistic motivation? *Journal of Personality and Social Psychology, 40*, 290–302.

Batson, C. D., Dyck, J. L., Brandt, J. R., Batson, J. G., Powell, A. L., McMaster, M. R., & Griffitt, C. (1988). Five studies testing two new egoistic alternatives to the empathy-altruism hypothesis. *Journal of Personality and Social Psychology, 55*, 52–77.

Batson, C. D., Klein, T. R., Highberger, L., & Shaw, L. L. (1995). Immorality from empathy-induced altruism: When compassion and justice conflict. *Journal of Personality and Social Psychology, 68,* 1042–1054.

Batson, C. D., Lishner, D. A., Cook, J., & Sawyer, S. (2005). Similarity and nurturance: Two possible sources of empathy for strangers. *Basic and Applied Social Psychology, 27,* 15–25.

Batson, C. D., & Moran, T. (1999). Empathy-induced altruism in a prisoner's dilemma. *European Journal of Social Psychology, 29,* 909–924.

Batson, C. D., Polycarpou, M. P., Harmon-Jones, E., Imhoff, H. J., Mitchener, E. C., Bednar, L. L., . . . Highberger, L. (1997). Empathy and attitudes: Can feeling for a member of a stigmatized group improve feelings toward the group? *Journal of Personality and Social Psychology, 72,* 105–118.

Batson, C. D., & Weeks, J. L. (1996). Mood effects of unsuccessful helping: Another test of the empathy-altruism hypothesis. *Personality and Social Psychology Bulletin, 22,* 148–157.

Bell, D. C. (2001). Evolution of parental caregiving. *Personality and Social Psychology Review, 5,* 216–229.

Berenguer, J. (2007). The effect of empathy in proenvironmental attitudes and behaviors. *Environment and Behavior, 39,* 269–283.

Blader, S. L., & Rothman, N. B. (2014). Paving the road to preferential treatment with good intentions: Empathy, accountability, and fairness. *Journal of Experimental Social Psychology, 50,* 65–81.

Bloom, P. (2016). *Against empathy: The case for rational compassion.* London, UK: Bodley Head.

Brown, S. L., Nesse, R., Vinokur, A. D., & Smith, D. M. (2003). Providing social support may be more beneficial than receiving it: Results from a prospective study of mortality. *Psychological Science, 14,* 320–327.

Buffone, A. E. K., & Poulin, M. J. (2014). Empathy, target distress, and neurohormone genes interact to predict aggression for others – even without provocation. *Personality and Social Psychology Bulletin, 40,* 1406–1422.

Burton, J. W. (1987). *Resolving deep-rooted conflict.* Lanham, MD: University Press of America.

Cameron, C. D., & Payne, B. K. (2011). Escaping affect: How motivated emotion regulation creates insensitivity to mass suffering. *Journal of Personality and Social Psychology, 100,* 1–15.

Cikara, M., Bruneau, E., & Saxe, R. R. (2011). Us and them: Intergroup failures of empathy. *Current Directions in Psychological Science, 20,* 149–153.

Clore, G. L., & Jeffrey, K. M. (1972). Emotional role playing, attitude change, and attraction toward a disabled person. *Journal of Personality and Social Psychology, 23,* 105–111.

Coke, J. S., Batson, C. D., & McDavis, K. (1978). Empathic mediation of helping: A two-stage model. *Journal of Personality and Social Psychology, 36,* 752–766.

Damasio, A. R. (2002). A note on the neurobiology of emotions. In S. G. Post, L. G. Underwood, J. P. Schloss, & W. B. Hurlbut (Eds.), *Altruism and altruistic love: Science, philosophy, and religion in dialogue* (pp. 264–271). New York, NY: Oxford University Press.

Dawkins, R. (1976). *The selfish gene.* New York, NY: Oxford University Press.

Des Pres, T. (1976). *The survivor: An anatomy of life in the death camps.* New York, NY: Oxford University Press.

De Vignemont, F., & Singer, T. (2006). The empathic brain: How, when, and why? *Trends in Cognitive Sciences, 10,* 435–441.

De Waal, F. B. M. (1996). *Good natured: The origins of right and wrong in humans and other animals.* Cambridge, MA: Harvard University Press.

Dijker, A. J. (2001). The influence of perceived suffering and vulnerability on the experience of pity. *European Journal of Social Psychology, 31,* 659–676.

Dovidio, J. F., Johnson, J. D., Gaertner, S. L., Pearson, A. R., Saguy, T., & Ashburn-Nardo, L. (2010). Empathy and intergroup relations. In M. Mikulincer & P. R. Shaver (Eds.), *Prosocial motives, emotions, and behavior: The better angels of our nature* (pp. 393–408). Washington, DC: American Psychological Association.

Downs, A. (1957). *An economic theory of democracy.* New York, NY: Harper & Row.

Eisenberg, N., & Strayer, J. (1987). Critical issues in the study of empathy. In N. Eisenberg & J. Strayer

(Eds.), *Empathy and its development* (pp. 3–13). New York, NY: Cambridge University Press.

Figley, C. R. (2002). Compassion fatigue: Psychotherapists' chronic lack of self-care. *Journal of Clinical Psychology, 58,* 1433–1441 (Special issue on chronic illness).

Finlay, K. A., & Stephan, W. G. (2000). Reducing prejudice: The effects of empathy on intergroup attitudes. *Journal of Applied Social Psychology, 30,* 1720–1737.

Fisher, J. D., Nadler, A., & DePaulo, B. M. (Eds.). (1983). *New directions in helping. Vol. 1: Recipient reactions to aid.* New York, NY: Academic Press.

Fisher, R. (1994). Generic principles for resolving intergroup conflict. *Journal of Social Issues, 50,* 47–66.

Goetz, J. L., Keltner, D., & Simon-Thomas, E. (2010). Compassion: An evolutionary analysis and empirical review. *Psychological Bulletin, 136,* 351–374.

Halpern, J. (2001). *From detached concern to empathy: Humanizing medical practice.* New York, NY: Oxford University Press.

Hamilton, W. D. (1964). The genetical evolution of social behavior (I, II). *Journal of Theoretical Biology, 7,* 1–52.

Hancock, G. (1989). *Lords of poverty: The power, prestige, and corruption of the international aid business.* New York, NY: Atlantic Monthly Press.

Hardin, G. (1977). *The limits of altruism: An ecologist's view of survival.* Bloomington: Indiana University Press.

Harmon-Jones, E., Vaughn-Scott, K., Mohr, S., Sigelman, J., & Harmon-Jones, C. (2004). The effect of manipulated sympathy and anger on left and right frontal cortical activity. *Emotion, 4,* 95–101.

Hein, G., Silani, G., Preuschoff, K., Batson, C. D., & Singer, T. (2010). Neural responses to ingroup and outgroup members' suffering predict individual differences in costly helping. *Neuron, 68,* 149–160.

Hoess, R. (1959). *Commandant at Auschwitz: Autobiography.* London, UK: Weidenfeld and Nicholson.

Hoffman, M. L. (1981). Is altruism part of human nature? *Journal of Personality and Social Psychology, 40,* 121–137.

Hoffman, M. L. (2000). *Empathy and moral development: Implications for caring and justice.* New York, NY: Cambridge University Press.

Hrdy, S. B. (2009). *Mothers and others: The evolutionary origins of mutual understanding.* Cambridge, MA: Harvard University Press.

Isaacson, W. (1992, December 21). Sometimes, right makes might. *Time,* p. 82.

Kelly, R. L. (1995). *The foraging spectrum: Diversity in hunter-gatherer lifeways.* Washington, DC: Smithsonian Institution Press.

Kelman, H. C. (1997). Group processes in the resolution of international conflicts: Experiences from the Israeli–Palestinian case. *American Psychologist, 52,* 212–220.

Kelman, H. C., & Cohen, S. P. (1986). Resolution of international conflict: An interactional approach. In S. Worchel & W. G. Austin (Eds.), *Psychology of intergroup relations* (pp. 323–432). Chicago, IL: Nelson Hall.

Kerr, N. L. (1995). Norms in social dilemmas. In D. A. Schroeder (Ed.), *Social dilemmas: Perspectives on individuals and groups* (pp. 31–47). Westport, CT: Praeger.

Konrath, S., Fuhrel-Forbis, A., Lou, A., & Brown, S. (2012). Motives for volunteering are associated with mortality risk in older adults. *Health Psychology, 31,* 87–96.

Krebs, D. L. (1975). Empathy and altruism. *Journal of Personality and Social Psychology, 32,* 1134–1146.

La Rochefoucauld, F., Duke de (1691). *Moral maxims and reflections, in four parts.* London, UK: Gillyflower, Sare, & Everingham.

Lerner, M. J. (1980). *The belief in a just world: A fundamental delusion.* New York, NY: Plenum Press.

Lewin, K. (1951). *Field theory in social science* (D. Cartwright, Ed.). New York, NY: Harper.

Lishner, D. A., Batson, C. D., & Huss, E. (2011). Tenderness and sympathy: Distinct empathic emotions elicited by different forms of need. *Personality and Social Psychology Bulletin, 37,* 614–625.

Lishner, D. A., Oceja, L. V., Stocks, E. L., & Zaspel, K. (2008). The effect of infant-like characteristics on empathic concern for adults in need. *Motivation and Emotion, 32,* 270–277.

López-Pérez, B., Ambrona, T., Gregory, J., Stocks, E., & Oceja, L. (2013). Feeling at hospitals: Perspective-taking, empathy, and personal distress among professional nurses and nursing students. *Nurse Education Today, 33*, 334–338.

Luks, A. (with Payne, P.). (1991). *The healing power of doing good: The health and spiritual benefits of helping others.* New York, NY: Fawcett Columbine.

MacLean, P. D. (1967). The brain in relation to empathy and medical education. *Journal of Nervous and Mental Disease, 144*, 374–382.

MacLean, P. D. (1990). *The triune brain in evolution: Role in paleocerebral functions.* New York, NY: Plenum Press.

Maslach, C. (1982). *Burnout: The cost of caring.* Englewood Cliffs, NJ: Prentice-Hall.

Maslow, A. H. (1954). *Motivation and Personality.* New York, NY: Harper.

McDougall, W. (1908). *An introduction to social psychology.* London, UK: Methuen.

Nadler, A., Fisher, J. D., & DePaulo, B. M. (Eds.). (1983). *New directions in helping: Vol. 3. Applied perspectives on help-seeking and -receiving.* New York, NY: Academic Press.

Oceja, L. V., Heerdink, M. W., Stocks, E. L., Ambrona, T., López-Pérez, B., & Salgado, S. (2014). Empathy, awareness of others, and action: How feeling empathy for one-among-others motivates helping the others. *Basic and Applied Social Psychology, 36*, 111–124.

Oman, D. (2007). Does volunteering foster physical health and longevity? In S. G. Post (Ed.), *Altruism and health: Perspectives from empirical research* (pp. 15–32). New York, NY: Oxford University Press.

Omoto, A. M., & Snyder, M. (1995). Sustained helping without obligation: Motivation, longevity of service, and perceived attitude change among AIDS volunteers. *Journal of Personality and Social Psychology, 68*, 671–686.

Paluck, E. L. (2009). Reducing intergroup prejudice and conflict using the media: A field experiment in Rwanda. *Journal of Personality and Social Psychology, 96*, 574–587.

Pettigrew, T. F. (1998). Intergroup contact theory. *Annual Review of Psychology, 49*, 65–85.

Preston, S. D. (2013). The origins of altruism in offspring care. *Psychological Bulletin, 139*, 1305–1341.

Prinz, J. (2011). Against empathy. *The Southern Journal of Philosophy, 49*, 214–233.

Rouhana, N. N., & Kelman, H. C. (1994). Promoting joint thinking in international conflicts: An Israeli–Palestinian continuing workshop. *Journal of Social Issues, 50*, 157–178.

Rumble, A. C., Van Lange, P. A. M., & Parks, C. D. (2010). The benefits of empathy: When empathy may sustain cooperation in social dilemmas. *European Journal of Social Psychology, 40*, 856–866.

Ryan, W. (1971). *Blaming the victim.* New York, NY: Random House.

Scherer, K. R. (1984). On the nature and function of emotion: A component process approach. In K. R. Scherer & P. Ekman (Eds.), *Approaches to emotion* (pp. 293–317). Hillsdale, NJ: Lawrence Erlbaum.

Schultz, P. W. (2000). Empathizing with nature: The effects of perspective taking on concern for environmental issues. *Journal of Social Issues, 56*, 391–406.

Sen, A. K. (1977). Rational fools. *Philosophy & Public Affairs, 6*, 317–344.

Shaw, L. L., Batson, C. D., & Todd, R. M. (1994). Empathy avoidance: Forestalling feeling for another in order to escape the motivational consequences. *Journal of Personality and Social Psychology, 67*, 879–887.

Shelton, M. L., & Rogers, R. W. (1981). Fear-arousing and empathy-arousing appeals to help: The pathos of persuasion. *Journal of Applied Social Psychology, 11*, 366–378.

Sibicky, M. E., Schroeder, D. A., & Dovidio, J. F. (1995). Empathy and helping: Considering the consequences of intervention. *Basic and Applied Social Psychology, 16*, 435–453.

Smith, K. D., Keating, J. P., & Stotland, E. (1989). Altruism reconsidered: The effect of denying feedback on a victim's status to empathic witnesses. *Journal of Personality and Social Psychology, 57*, 641–650.

Sober, E. (1991). The logic of the empathy-altruism hypothesis. *Psychological Inquiry, 2*, 144–147.

Sober, E., & Wilson, D. S. (1998). *Unto others: The evolution and psychology of unselfish behavior.* Cambridge, MA: Harvard University Press.

Stephan, W. G., & Finlay, K. (1999). The role of empathy in improving intergroup relations. *Journal of Social Issues, 55,* 729–743.

Stotland, E. (1969). Exploratory investigations of empathy. In L. Berkowitz (Ed.), *Advances in experimental social psychology* (Vol. 4, pp. 271–313). New York, NY: Academic Press.

Stotland, E., Mathews, K. E., Sherman, S. E., Hansson, R. O., & Richardson, B. Z. (1978). *Empathy, fantasy, and helping.* Beverly Hills, CA: Sage.

Stowe, H. B. (2005). *Uncle Tom's cabin.* Mineola, NY: Dover. (Original work published 1852)

Taylor, M. (1976). *Anarchy and cooperation.* London, UK: Wiley.

Taylor, S. E. (2002). *The tending instinct: How nurturing is essential to who we are and how we live.* New York, NY: Time Books.

Toi, M., & Batson, C. D. (1982). More evidence that empathy is a source of altruistic motivation. *Journal of Personality and Social Psychology, 43,* 281–292.

Trivers, R. L. (1971). The evolution of reciprocal altruism. *The Quarterly Review of Biology, 46,* 35–57.

Vescio, T. K., Sechrist, G. B., & Paolucci, M. P. (2003). Perspective taking and prejudice reduction: The mediational role of empathy arousal and situational attributions. *European Journal of Social Psychology, 33,* 455–472.

Vitaglione, G. D., & Barnett, M. A. (2003). Assessing a new dimension of empathy: Empathic anger as a predictor of helping and punishing desires. *Motivation and Emotion, 27,* 301–325.

Von Neumann, J., & Morgenstern, O. (1944). *Theory of games and economic behavior.* Princeton, NJ: Princeton University Press.

Wispé, L. (1986). The distinction between sympathy and empathy: To call forth a concept, a word is needed. *Journal of Personality and Social Psychology, 50,* 314–321.

Zahn-Waxler, C., & Radke-Yarrow, M. (1990). The origins of empathic concern. *Motivation and Emotion, 14,* 107–130.

# 3

# Positive Creativity

## Robert J. Sternberg

*Creativity* is usually defined in terms of the production of an idea or product that has two properties. First, it is novel; second, it is effective or useful for some purpose (Csikszentmihalyi, 1988, 2013; Kaufman & Sternberg, 2010). Positive creativity is the production of ideas that are not only novel and useful but also beneficial to humanity (see also Clark & James, 1999; James, Clark, & Cropanzano, 1999; James & Taylor, 2010; Sternberg, in press, for further discussion of positive creativity as well as negative creativity). Positive creativity is a natural object of study for positive psychology, which is conceived of studying human strengths and modes of flourishing (Lopez, Pedrotti, & Snyder, 2018).

Creativity, whether positive or otherwise, probably is not just a single entity, any more than intelligence is (Sternberg, 1985b, 1986; Sternberg & Smith, 1985). A variety of scholars have argued that creativity, although it often is viewed as a single thing, actually is composed of multiple kinds of things.

For example, some scholars have distinguished between Big-C (world-class) Creativity and little-c (everyday) creativity, among other types (see, e.g., Kaufman & Beghetto, 2009). In contrast, Sternberg (2018) has distinguished among types of creativity that depend on different combinations of defying the crowd, defying oneself, and defying the zeitgeist. For example, consummate creativity would involve defying the crowd, oneself, and the zeitgeist. Sternberg and his colleagues (Sternberg, 1999; Sternberg, Kaufman, & Pretz, 2002) also have distinguished among different kinds of creative "propulsions," such as *forward incrementation*, which involves advancing a field through a small step, versus *redirection*, where one steers a field in an entirely different direction. Similarly, Kuhn (1970) has distinguished between the creativity of normal versus revolutionary science (see also

*Positive Psychology: An International Perspective*, First Edition.
Edited by Aleksandra Kostić and Derek Chadee.
© 2021 John Wiley & Sons Ltd. Published 2021 by John Wiley & Sons Ltd.

Simonton, 1994, 2004, for a discussion of greatness in science). The division of creativity can be seen in terms of (a) whether it changes a field or society, and (b) if it does make a change, how much it changes. But neither Kuhn nor Sternberg has classified creativity with regard to the extent to which it serves good (or bad) ends for that society.

Another way in which to divide up creativity would be in terms of its influence on a field, such as science, or even on society as a whole. For that purpose, I will distinguish among positive, negative, and neutral creativity.

## Positive Creativity and Negative Creativity

I will define *positive creativity* as the generation of an idea or product that is both novel and useful or effective in some way, but that also serves a positive, constructive function for the domain or field in which it is useful or effective and also for society. Similarly, I will define *negative creativity* as the generation of an idea or product that is both novel and useful or effective in some way, but that also serves a negative, destructive function for the domain or field in which it is useful or effective as well as for society (see also Clark & James, 1999; Cropley, Cropley, Kaufman, & Runco, 2010; Cropley, Kaufman, & Cropley, 2008; Cropley, Kaufman, White, & Chiera, 2014; James, Clark, & Cropanzano, 1999; James & Taylor, 2010; Runco, 2017; Sternberg, 2010, for discussions of positive and negative creativity and of the "dark side" of creativity). Negative creativity is sometimes distinguished from malevolent creativity, where not only the outcome, but also the intention is negative (Cropley et al., 2008). I will not pursue this distinction in this chapter, because sometimes "the road to hell is paved with good intentions." That is, seriously negative outcomes can occur even when scientists or others are well intentioned. *Neutral creativity* is the generation of an idea or product that is both novel and useful or effective in some way and that serves neither a positive nor negative function for the domain or field in which it is useful or effective.

An idea or product can be positively creative at one time or in one place and yet negatively creative at another time or in another place. For example, in the context of World War II, the development of nuclear weapons may have seemed like a positive contribution to the world – a way of ending a prolonged and extremely costly war. But in creating, creators need to think not only about the short run but also about the long run. In the long run, the positivity of the creation of nuclear weapons is, to say the least, highly questionable. As was almost inevitable, they have spread and it is reasonable to fear that they will be acquired by terrorists, if they have not already been so acquired. At that point, the weapons that seemed at one time like they might save the world now potentially could destroy it.

As another example, carbon-based fuels have had many positive effects on the world. Chances are that you or whoever is in charge of heating your living unit relies on carbon-based fuels. Automobiles, buses, trains, planes – all have served a vital role in industrial and other forms of development. But now the world is paying the price for the proliferation of cheap carbon-based fuels. And the collateral damage of such fuels, like that of nuclear weapons, may be immensely destructive. Indeed, one easily could argue that it already has been highly damaging and that the damage in terms of global climate change is likely to continue for some time to come.

## Causes of Negative Creativity

In *Anna Karenina*, Tolstoy said that "Happy families are all alike; every unhappy family is unhappy in its own way." Similarly, I suggest that positive creativity is instigated to help make things better for one or more persons or entities – one's life, the life of one's family, the life of a nation, science, art, or whatever. But negative creativity, like unhappy families, seems to have many different causes. What are some of these causes? And why is negative creativity so prevalent as well as malevolent in the world? What are the reasons?

1. *To enhance one's reputation by diminishing the reputation of one or more others.* In this case, negative creativity serves a somewhat parasitic function. One latches onto someone else in order to draw fame, renown, or resources from that person toward oneself. Usually, some flimsy justification is offered of how one is doing a public good.
2. *To cause harm or destruction as a result of anger.* One is angry at another, at the world, at oneself, or at whomever or whatever. One creatively plans destruction to appease one's anger. In the extreme, negative creativity results from hate (Sternberg, 2020a, 2020b).
3. *To cause harm or destruction as a result of fear.* One is afraid that something bad will happen and proactively seeks to neutralize a potential enemy before one is oneself neutralized.
4. *To gain resources for oneself.* One may be paid, whether monetarily or otherwise, for negative creative ideas or products.
5. *To gain revenge on someone.* One may seek to avenge oneself for a perceived slight or harm. How many wars have been started as a way of seeking revenge for a real or imagined slight?
6. *To gain renown as an "evil genius."* Some people want to be recognized not for the good things they do, but for the bad ones they do. In the comic books, Superman's archenemy, Lex Luthor, was such an individual. If only such individuals were limited to comic books. Heads of criminal syndicates and especially drug gangs, sometimes try to outdo each other in the evil they do.
7. *To live one's life in a way one considers normal.* Some people, including psychopaths but also others, do not see anything wrong with negative creativity or with harming others. They have no conscience, so it makes little difference to them if their actions cause harm to others.

8. *By accident.* One is seeking to do one thing and accidentally ends up doing another. The other thing proves to be destructive. Amniocentesis was a creative idea to help parents decide whether to proceed with a pregnancy; in some cases, however, it accidentally damaged or killed the baby.

9. *By lack of forethought.* Many negative creative inventions seemed to be good ideas in the short run. The inventors did not think sufficiently about their long-term effects, as in the case of the carbon-emitting vehicles that now clog so many roads and highways around the world.

10. *To do good.* One may believe one is doing good by doing harm. For example, a creator of a new explosive device might believe that they are doing good by creating a weapon that will vanquish an enemy. The problem, of course, is that it is almost always impossible to foresee the long-term consequences of such ideas, such as the idea of nuclear weapons, which now could destroy the world several times over. And how many terrorists and suicide bombers believe they are somehow doing a "good thing" that will take them right to heaven? The inventors may have thought in advance about the long term but simply have underestimated the negative consequences of what they did, as their intentions were positive and honorable.

This last point emphasizes how carefully people have to think about positive creativity in their own lives. It just is so easy to convince ourselves that something we do that is negative is really positive. Without a deep analysis of our own motives, it often is hard to tell just why we are doing what we are doing. Authoritarian governments are cropping up all across the world, including in my own country. Although many supporters of such governments are merely self-serving, others have convinced themselves they need a powerful leader to re-instill order to recover some kind of glorious national past (which of course never really existed).

As noted above, creativity always is judged in a context. Positive creativity is similar in concept to what I have called WICS in the past, or Wisdom-Intelligence-Creativity-Synthesized (Sternberg, 2003, 2009). It is creativity tempered by intelligence – analyzing whether an idea or product is logical, tenable, or sensible – and especially wisdom – assessing whether an idea helps to achieve some kind of common good, by balancing one's own with other interests, over the long term as well as the short term, through the infusion of positive ethical values.

In science as well as in other fields and in society as a whole, we too often have valued creativity in and of itself. We have not adequately considered whether the creativity we are valuing serves a positive, neutral, or even negative purpose. Is a creative idea forwarding science or some other field, or is it merely enhancing our own personal goals? Is it even replicable (Kaufman & Glăveanu, 2018)? Such goals are variable but might include our own eminence, our financial situation, our appearance in a department annual report, our promotion status, or our ego. Indeed, we so easily can get on a scientific treadmill (or an artistic, literary, musical, technological, or other one) that we do not make the time to think about the uses to which our creativity will be put. By the time we have thought things through, it sometimes is too late to put our creativity to optimal use.

An example in science/technology is the invention of ever more powerful weapons of mass destruction. Some of these weapons are enormously creative – novel and effective (in killing people, if that is our goal), assuming our goal is offensive or even to create an effective deterrent. But as Dr. Seuss (1984) recognized in his book *The Butter Battle Book,* such inventions tend to lead to competition where each side is trying to create weapons that out-destroy the others. People tend to view potentially creative acts that are ambiguously bad as more creative than acts that are clearly bad, with the result that in psychological science (or elsewhere), people may view research outcomes that are not unambiguously bad as creative, simply because of the ambiguity.

An outcome of ambiguously valenced technology is social media. Social media take a variety of forms – Facebook, Twitter, and blogs, for example. They serve varied purposes and complement each other in terms of how they function in the world of psychological science, and in the world more generally. Such media can facilitate and speed up communication among people in distant locations, raise awareness of issues facing society, and give people forums for airing debates.

Scholars sometimes have resorted to the use of social media because they have believed that their contributions to the scientific literature have been blocked by editors or referees of journals. For example, articles critiquing work published in a journal may cause anxiety in editors ("Will the critique of authors publishing in my journal make me, as editor, look bad?"), and if the researchers whose work is critiqued serve as reviewers, these researchers sometimes may be able to sabotage publication by writing negative reviews. But truth be told, some scientists and other scholars who have written critiques on social media have never even tried to have their work published in conventional journals. Why? It is easier, less time-consuming, and emotionally less painful to skip the peer-review process. Anyone who publishes knows that this process can be lengthy, frustrating, and, sometimes, simply unsuccessful. One spends a lot of time trying to get one's work published, to no avail (unless one goes to a journal that is perhaps not worth publishing in). The same can happen in any domain – authors of novels or short stories who cannot get their work published; or authors of op-eds who have sent their pieces to one refereed outlet after another with no success.

Social media once seemed like a good and positive idea. When social media first were invented, the inventors likely did not think through and probably could not have anticipated – even if they tried – how social media might later be used for negative purposes: to undermine or at least distort free elections, to spread false and hateful propaganda, to serve as a basis for blatant cyberbullying, or even to undermine and sometimes destroy the careers of people one does not like, for whatever reason.

In the past, if a scientist or other scholar wanted publicly to criticize the work of another, they would have been obliged to have scholarly referees pass their judgment on the criticism. The scholars could not have gone public at the push of a button. But the referees who sometimes are detested also often have saved scientists and other scholars from making foolish and even destructive comments with no basis in fact. With the advent of social media, the push of a button on a phone or a computer can bypass the step of having referees. Echo chambers come to be established consisting of like-minded, and often narrow-minded individuals. These individuals may reinforce what has been said, no matter how obnoxious, damaging, or simply incorrect it may be. Crowd mindlessness–groupthink–takes over, with predictable results.

Some people may come to the viewpoint that anyone in their right mind would share the same "facts" or points of view – namely, their own point of view. Accompanying the increase in use of social media in psychological science and elsewhere (correlationally, not necessarily causally) has been, perhaps, a decrease in the shame people feel in attacking others personally, not just professionally. Falk (2018) has argued that "social media has fouled the virtual public square with bile and menace" (p. 3). Although this comment may seem strong, anyone who has been attacked on social media will understand where Falk was coming from.

Thus, social media present us with great opportunities but also serious challenges. Can we use them to showcase and enhance positive creativity or will our rush to get out our latest half-baked thoughts lead us to use them in a way that fosters negative creativity? And will we recognize what creativity is positive and what creativity is negative?

I believe that there are useful principles for distinguishing between positive and negative creativity. They are the same principles that have contributed, over many centuries, to the generation of wise ideas: honesty, sincerity, transparency, acting toward others the way one would have them act toward oneself, and, of course, reflective analysis of the long-term as well as short-term consequences of one's thoughts and actions.

How would one go about assessing positive creativity, if one indeed wanted to assess it? At a general level, instead of asking questions about things such as unusual uses of a paperclip or what word has something in common with a set of other words, one might ask people challenging questions like "What steps could be taken, which would not bust local or state budgets, to improve our secondary schools?" or "What are some things everyone could do to reduce effects of climate change, even if their individual efforts had only a minor effect?" or in our own field, "What are some ways in which psychological science could be applied to help address the current opioid crisis" (or any other crisis)? Students would be scored for novelty and quality of responses and only separately on the basis of their knowledge of the issue at hand. That is, knowledge is important for creativity, but possession of it does not guarantee creativity and much creative work is done by people who are not necessarily the most knowledgeable (Sternberg, Kaufman, & Pretz, 2002). Expertise can facilitate creativity, but it also can facilitate entrenchment and mental "change blindness." They also would be scored, where applicable, for the potential positivity of their ideas.

It might seem that such assessments would require value judgments, and in testing, at least in many countries, test constructors often try to create measures that are seemingly more "objective." But there are three factors to consider.

First, assessment of creativity, because creativity always occurs in a context (Plucker, 2017), inevitably requires value judgments. Second, when all is said and done, all tests involve value judgments – they often just hide them (Sternberg, 1997, 2016). When, for example, one asks students how to solve challenging math problems on an intelligence test or a college-admissions exam, one is assuming that the skill in solving such problems is important, even for, say, a future English major, stage actor, or pianist. Third, if our students took tests based on the adaptive challenges of other cultures, they might look quite inadequate because their skills in solving such challenges, such as ice fishing or using natural herbal medicines to combat malaria, are lacking (Sternberg & Grigorenko, 2004). That is, *all* tests and their scoring involve value judgments, if not in scoring, then certainly in deciding what to measure, whether implicit or explicit.

The field of psychological science and other scientific fields, even in the face of some notorious examples of negative creativity – manufactured data, massaging of data, serious misinterpretations of data – need to enhance their emphasis on honest and transparent science, but not at the expense of creativity. But there is a risk that we will educate students in ways that enhance their analytical contributions but not their creative ones. Instead, as a field, scientists should simultaneously increase their emphasis both on honest and transparent analysis but also on positive creativity – doing research that not only is career enhancing, but that is field enhancing and potentially even world enhancing. We might ask ourselves what is the research we can do that will truly make a positive and meaningful difference to our field of endeavor?

If we don't always succeed – and we won't – at least we will have tried. The emphasis in the fields of science, on this view, should shift from creativity – which can be positive but also can be neutral or negative – to positive creativity, which will make our fields better, and that, potentially, will make the world a better place, even if just a tiny little bit. There are many examples, but certainly one example would be that of how to lead people to make better decisions in their lives, both for themselves and for others (Kahneman, 2013; Thaler & Sunstein, 2009).

The good thing about the new approaches to science is that they may encourage more transparency and honesty. Because of pressures to publish, difficulties in getting large samples, and the mere fact that underpowered studies could get into good journals, we have been less careful than we needed to be in ensuring that our studies are ones that future researchers can rely on. The cost of such carelessness, on all our parts, has been reliance on results that are "will-o'-the-wisps," setting back the field.

Developing and nurturing creativity in students or anyone else requires instilling particular attitudes toward life and work in those individuals (Sternberg, 2000). These attitudes include three kinds of defiance. The first is willingness to defy the crowd – that is, willingness to act in ways other than the ways in which one's friends and colleagues are acting. The second is willingness to defy oneself and one's past beliefs – that is, willingness to give up on beliefs one has held, perhaps deeply, when those beliefs are no longer justified or shown just to be plain wrong. The third is willingness to defy the ongoing zeitgeist (Sternberg, 2018) – that is, to question the often-unconscious beliefs with which one conducts one's life (such as that creativity is inborn and we can't really do anything to increase it). Creative individuals also need to overcome obstacles, believe in themselves in the face of severe criticism, and realize that their expertise can get in the way of their creativity (Sternberg, Kaufman, & Pretz, 2002). What would it mean to develop positive creativity?

Developing positive creativity would go beyond what is required for developing creativity that can be positive, neutral, or negative. It would mean additionally asking oneself (a) what are the benefits of and positive uses to which my work can be put? (b) What can I do to augment the positive uses and benefits? (c) What are potential harms of my work? (d) What can I do to mitigate the potential harms? (e) What am I not seeing because I do not want to see it, such as long-term effects beyond short-term ones? That is, developing positive creativity would mean developing creativity leavened by intelligence and wisdom (WICS). It would mean thinking about not just coming up with novel and useful ideas, but also what the future implications and uses of these ideas would be. At the same time, we want to ensure the importance of the analytical component – that we assess whether the ideas are truly good ones that work.

There is no way to guarantee that one's ideas will be put to positive use. But one greatly can enhance the probability of this happening if only one gives it some thought. I am doubtful that we scientists are teaching students to give their work that kind of thought (Sternberg & Grigorenko, 2004). We can become so preoccupied with career advancement and sometimes short-range scientific advancement that we may not think about the long term. If we truly want to benefit science as well as education and society, we need to think long term, and we need to foster positive creativity, not merely creativity that may be neutral or negative.

Meanwhile, educators need to move beyond an educational system that heavily emphasizes analytic skills at the expense of positive creative skills. I argued long ago that our educational system tends to produce students who excel in analytical skills but never have much incentive through school to develop their creative skills (Sternberg, 1985a). These are the students who are most heavily rewarded throughout most of schooling, regardless of whether or not they develop their creativity. Historically, students who excel in analytical but not creative skills might come to graduate school and then find that their grade-achieving skills no longer serve them as well as those skills did in grade school, high school, and college. But what if we, as a field, inadvertently made it enough to get by in a career just with analytical skills? If we further push in our educational system the development of analytical skills or even "hyper-analytical" ones, we must make sure not to do so at the expense of pushing the development of positive creative skills. Analytically gifted but uncreative students become who they are not because they are born that way, but because their education makes them that way (Sternberg, 1985a). Education needs today, as it always has needed, to balance the development of positive creative skills with the development of analytical ones.

Being creative is usually uncomfortable and can be potentially dangerous. As noted above, it potentially involves defying the crowd, defying oneself, and defying the zeitgeist (Sternberg, 2018). There is a good reason that people always have been reluctant to be creative. They risk falling prey to the "tall poppy" phenomenon, whereby they end up as the tall poppy in a large field of poppies that gets cut down. The world at large needs *positive creativity* more than ever before. In our push to be transparent, we need to ensure that we encourage positive creative thinking. And, perhaps most of all, we need to encourage simultaneously not only the best science, but also the careful reflection, courtesy, civility, and plain decency that has come to be lacking in so much of contemporary discourse.

## References

Clark, K., & James, K. (1999). Justice and positive and negative creativity. *Creativity Research Journal, 12,* 311–320.

Cropley, D. H., Cropley, A. J., Kaufman, J. C., & Runco, M. A. (Eds.). (2010). *The dark side of creativity.* New York: Cambridge University Press.

Cropley, D. H., Kaufman, J. C., & Cropley, A. J. (2008). Malevolent creativity: A functional model of creativity in terrorism and crime. *Creativity Research Journal, 20,* 105–115.

Cropley, D. H., Kaufman, J. C., White, A. E., & Chiera, B. A. (2014). Layperson perceptions of malevolent creativity: The good, the bad, and the ambiguous. *Psychology of Aesthetics, Creativity, and the Arts, 8,* 400–412.

Csikszentmihalyi, M. (1988). Society, culture, and person: A systems view of creativity. In R. Sternberg (Ed.), *The nature of creativity: Contemporary psychological perspectives* (pp. 325–339). Cambridge: Cambridge University Press.

Csikszentmihalyi, M. (2013). *Creativity: Flow and the psychology of discovery and invention.* New York: HarperCollins.

Falk, W. (2018, February 16). Editor's letter. *The Week,* p. 3.

James, K., Clark, K., & Cropanzano, R. (1999). Positive and negative creativity in groups, institutions, and organizations: A model and theoretical extension. *Creativity Research Journal, 12,* 211–226.

James, K., & Taylor, A. (2010). Positive creativity and negative creativity (and unintended consequences). In D. H. Cropley, A. J. Cropley, J. C. Kaufman, & M. A. Runco (Eds.), *The dark side of creativity* (pp. 33–56). New York: Cambridge University Press.

Kahneman, D. (2013). *Thinking, fast and slow.* New York: Farrar, Straus, & Giroux.

Kaufman, J. C., & Beghetto, R. A. (2009). Beyond big and little: The Four C model of creativity. *Review of General Psychology, 13,* 1–12.

Kaufman, J. C., & Glăveanu, V. (2018). The road to uncreative science is paved with good intentions: Ideas, implementations, and uneasy balances. *Perspectives on Psychological Science, 13*(4), 457–465.

Kaufman, J. C., & Sternberg, R. J. (Eds.). (2010). *Cambridge handbook of creativity.* New York: Cambridge University Press.

Kuhn, T. S. (1970). *The structure of scientific revolutions* (2nd ed.). Chicago, IL: University of Chicago Press.

Lopez, S. J., Pedrotti, J. T., & Snyder, C. R. (2018). *Positive psychology: The scientific and practical explorations of human strengths* (4th ed.). Thousand Oaks, CA: Sage.

Plucker, J. A. (Ed.). (2017). *Creativity and innovation: Theory, research, and practice*. Waco, TX: Prufrock Press.

Runco, M. A. (2017). The dark side of creativity: Potential better left unfulfilled. In J. A. Plucker (Ed.), *Creativity and innovation: Theory, research, and practice* (pp. 49–59). Waco, TX: Prufrock Press.

Seuss, Dr. (Theodore Geisel). (1984). *The butter battle book*. New York: Random House.

Simonton, D. K. (1994). *Greatness*. New York: Guilford Press.

Simonton, D. K. (2004). *Creativity in science: Chance, logic, genius, and zeitgeist*. New York: Cambridge University Press.

Sternberg, R. J. (1985a). *Beyond IQ: A triarchic theory of human intelligence*. New York: Cambridge University Press.

Sternberg, R. J. (1985b). Human intelligence: The model is the message. *Science, 230*, 1111–1118.

Sternberg, R. J. (1986). Inside intelligence. *American Scientist, 74*, 137–143.

Sternberg, R. J. (1997). What does it mean to be smart? *Educational Leadership, 54*(6), 20–24.

Sternberg, R. J. (1999). A propulsion model of types of creative contributions. *Review of General Psychology, 3*, 83–100.

Sternberg, R. J. (2000). Creativity is a decision. In A. L. Costa (Ed.), *Teaching for intelligence II* (pp. 85–106). Arlington Heights, IL: Skylight Training and Publishing.

Sternberg, R. J. (2003). *Wisdom, intelligence, and creativity synthesized*. New York: Cambridge University Press.

Sternberg, R. J. (2009). Wisdom, intelligence, and creativity synthesized: A new model for liberal education. *Liberal Education, 95*(4), 10–15.

Sternberg, R. J. (2010). The dark side of creativity and how to combat it. In D. H. Cropley, A. J. Cropley, J. C. Kaufman, & M. A. Runco (Eds.), *The dark side of creativity* (pp. 316–328). New York: Cambridge University Press.

Sternberg, R. J. (2016). *What universities can be: A new model for preparing students for active concerned citizenship and ethical leadership*. Ithaca, NY: Cornell University Press.

Sternberg, R. J. (2018). A triangular theory of creativity. *Psychology of Aesthetics, Creativity, and the Arts, 12*, 50–67.

Sternberg, R. J. (2020a). FLOTSAM: A theory of the development and transmission of hate. In R. J. Sternberg (Ed.), *Perspectives on hate: How it originates, develops, manifests, and spreads*. Washington, DC: American Psychological Association.

Sternberg, R. J. (2020b). FLOTSAM in practice: Understanding the reawakening of hate in the modern world. In R. J. Sternberg (Ed.), *Perspectives on hate: How it originates, develops, manifests, and spreads*. Washington, DC: American Psychological Association.

Sternberg, R. J. (in press). *Positive creativity*. Cambridge: Cambridge University Press.

Sternberg, R. J., & Grigorenko, E. L. (2004). Successful intelligence in the classroom. *Theory into Practice, 43*(4), 274–280.

Sternberg, R. J., Kaufman, J. C., & Pretz, J. E. (2002). *The creativity conundrum: A propulsion model of kinds of creative contributions*. New York, NY: Psychology Press.

Sternberg, R. J., & Smith, C. (1985). Social intelligence and decoding skills in nonverbal communication. *Social Cognition, 2*, 168–192.

Thaler, R. H., & Sunstein, C. R. (2009). *Nudge: Improving decisions about health, wealth, and happiness*. New York: Penguin Books.

# 4

# Science of Well-Being: Notable Advances

Jessica Kansky and Ed Diener

The interest in the field of subjective well-being has dramatically increased in recent decades. There has been a burst of interest in what makes, keeps, and detracts us from being happy (see the comprehensive Nobascholar.com website for further reading). However, the concept of subjective well-being extends from being simple happiness and refers to how people evaluate their life. It captures how people feel (both positively and negatively) and judge their own life. In this chapter, we will first define the three primary components of our conceptualization of subjective well-being and review the measurements common in well-being research. Perhaps given the technological and scientific advances in the assessments available to measure well-being, we can move on to discuss the hallmark studies and recent trends in both the causes and outcomes associated with subjective well-being. We will describe the primary causes of well-being that researchers have focused on including income, relationships, biology, personality, and important positive behaviors. Subsequently, we will provide an overview of the critical outcomes associated with subjective well-being including the impact on our health, work success, income, relationships, and positive behaviors. Throughout we will pay close attention to discussing the cross-cultural relevancy of these findings and point out discrepancies in the experience and outcomes of well-being across cultures.

*Positive Psychology: An International Perspective*, First Edition.
Edited by Aleksandra Kostić and Derek Chadee.
© 2021 John Wiley & Sons Ltd. Published 2021 by John Wiley & Sons Ltd.

## Relative Independence of Positive Affect, Negative Affect, and Life Satisfaction

There are several definitions of subjective well-being (SWB) that warrant discussion for clarity. Subjective well-being includes the affective components for both positive and negative emotions. Positive emotions include feelings such as enjoyment, contentment, flow, excitement, calmness, and euphoria. Negative emotions include feelings such as sadness, anger, worry, fear, frustration, and depression. Subjective well-being also includes cognitive components, in which individuals judge how content they are with current circumstances to evaluate general life satisfaction. Further, SWB can be broken down into specific domain satisfaction. For example, how satisfied are we within our romantic relationships, our social relationships, with our health, in our career of choice, and so on.

Specifically, according to Diener, Suh, Lucas, and Smith (1999), someone who is high in subjective well-being reports high positive affect, low negative affect, and high life satisfaction. Importantly, all three facets are independently related to key areas of interest and outcomes. Contrary to what some believe, positive and negative affect do not exist on the same continuum, but rather exist as separate entities. Thus, it is possible to report high positive and negative affect, or low positive and negative affect as well as combinations of the two. Simply having low positive affect does not necessarily mean one has lots of negative affect. The independence of these constructs can be seen in prior findings pointing to the relative importance of each for certain outcomes. Specifically, income has been most strongly associated with life satisfaction; social support with positive affect; and neuroticism with negative affect (Diener & Lucas, 1999; Diener & Tay, 2015; Lucas & Diener, 2000, 2001).

## Subjective Well-Being Measurement

It is important to describe the multiple approaches that have been used to study subjective well-being. Perhaps due to the increased interest and empirical demands within this field, measurements have rapidly proliferated, ranging from self-report assessments to physiological measures to daily diary and experience sampling methods.

The simplest way to measure subjective well-being is via self-report on many empirically validated and supported questionnaires. The Satisfaction with Life Scale (SWLS; Diener, Emmons, Larsen, & Griffin, 1985) is a 5-item scale that is used to measure global cognitive judgments about the satisfaction with one's life. Participants indicate the extent to which they agree or disagree with each of the items using a 7-point scale where 1 = strongly disagree and 7 = strongly agree. The SWLS has shown to be a valid and reliable measure of life satisfaction applicable for various age groups and applications. It has demonstrated high convergence with self and other-reported measures of subjective well-being and life satisfaction (Pavot, Diener, Colvin, & Sandvik, 1991). It has shown relative temporal stability, yet remains sensitive to change based on life experiences and events (Pavot & Diener, 1993). Another popular measure to assess the cognitive aspect of well-being is the Flourishing Scale (FS: Diener et al., 2009, 2010). The FS is an 8-item measure of perceived success in key domains such as self-esteem, purpose, optimism, and relationships and has demonstrated good psychometric properties (Diener et al., 2009, 2010).

The SWLS and FS both assess the cognitive and judgmental aspect of subjective well-being, while the Scale of Positive and Negative Experience (SPANE; Diener et al., 2009) primarily assess the affective components. The SPANE is a 12-item measure where six items assess positive feelings and six assess negative feelings. The SPANE has good internal consistency and moderately high temporal reliability, reflecting change across a one-month period based on life events (Diener et al., 2010). This measure has been translated into various languages and deemed appropriate to use cross-culturally with similar validity and reliability estimates (Li, Bai, & Wang, 2013).

Two other, related, measures are important to review: the comprehensive inventory of thriving (CIT) and the brief inventory of thriving (BIT; Su, Tay, & Diener, 2014). The CIT is composed of 54 items that fit into 18 subscales such as accomplishment, self-worth, skill, learning, and community, which covers a diverse range of well-being components. The BIT is comprised of 10 items and provides an assessment of psychological well-being. Both have been primarily used to provide a holistic view of positive functioning. For more information including reliability, validity, translations, and key references on any of the aforementioned measures, visit www.eddiener.com. For a review of the general validity of subjective well-being scales, see Diener and Fujita (1995) and Diener, Inglehart, and Tay (2013).

In addition to using questionnaires such as the ones listed above to assess self-reported subjective well-being, many of these can also be used to gather data from other informants about a particular individual. For example, similar measures can be given to family, friends, spouses, coworkers, or supervisors in which they are asked to report on the well-being of a target individual. The benefit of having multiple informants is that researchers can corroborate reports and identify discrepancies in reporting. In addition, the use of other informants reduces the likelihood of potential bias including self-report bias, in which we may intentionally change what we report to present ourselves in a certain light and memory or recall bias, in which how we remember things may be different than how they actually happened (Park, Upshaw, & Koh, 1988; Schwarz & Strack, 1991). However, prior work found moderate to significant overlap between other informant report and self-report measures (Diener, Smith, & Fujita, 1995; Lucas, Diener, & Suh, 1996). In addition to asking familiar informants to report on a target individual's well-being, expert raters may be used who are trained to observe and record behaviors from interactions with the target individual. Although the use of other informants and expert raters is costly compared to self-reported data, we gain much insight into the broader account of one's well-being.

Beyond questionnaires, subjective well-being can be assessed in more objective, physiological measures including assessing cardiovascular reactivity, skin conductance, and other physical reactions following a controlled stressor (Cacioppo, Berntson, Larsen, Poehlmann, & Ito, 2000; Dinan, 1994). Recent advancements in neuroimaging allow researchers to assess PET or MRI scans of individuals in response to a stressor and link reactivity to well-being (Davidson, 1992; Rutledge, Skandali, Dayan, & Dolan, 2014). Other innovative techniques include coding photographs or texts from myriad print and online sources for positive and negative expressions, events, and words (Danner, Snowdon, & Friesen, 2001; Pavot, Diener, Colvin, & Sandvik, 1991; Thomas & Chambers, 1989). Although we will elaborate later, cross-cultural research has evolved to determine whether there are similar or distinct experiences of well-being in various cultures.

All of the assessments listed above can be utilized at a single time point and provide important correlational and cross-sectional findings. The single time point approach is the fastest way to gather large quantity of data and is often used to assess how current well-being relates to functioning in other domains. Correlational designs can help identify whether two constructs are related to each other as a starting point to then investigate further with more in-depth approaches. Longitudinal research follows up to assess whether one construct can predict change in another measure over time, or how constructs change simultaneously over time. Although longitudinal work helps move us in the direction of identifying which variable predicts another, we still cannot fully determine causality. Experience sampling methods (ESM) or experiential momentary assessments build on the longitudinal study design but typically restrict data collection to a shorter time frame (Kahneman, 1999; Stone, Shiffman, & DeVries, 1999). The typical ESM study asks participants to complete questionnaires several times a day over a multiday period which allows assessment of how the variables change together over time or whether one variable influences change in the other shortterm. Advances in technology, especially mobile technology, has made ESM studies easier via apps or text messaging that are minimally disruptive to individuals' day-to-day activities and thus more representative of naturalistic mood (Reis & Gable, 2000). Daily surveys also provide reductions in certain biases such as the retrospective recall bias (Bolger, Davis, & Rafaeli, 2003).

Although we can see that with increases in complexity of assessments from a single time point to repeated time points, we use experiments as a major method for helping us to understand causality. Experiments manipulate one variable and measure how other constructs subsequently change to understand whether wellbeing is the predictor or outcome of certain constructs. In subjective well-being experiments, mood and affect is often manipulated and then effects can be assessed immediately after the manipulation or via long-term follow-up assessments. Although experiments have many benefits including the ability to understand causal influence more clearly, even experiments face potential bias such as self-fulfilling prophecy effects, demand characteristics, or experimenter bias (Nederhof, 1985; Weber & Cook, 1972). For more in-depth reviews of subjective well-being methodology, please see Diener (2000). Because we now have multiple techniques and approaches to assess well-being, the field continues to grow as well with more complex analyses covering many important facets of life.

## Set Point and Adaptation

One of the long-standing debates in well-being is how much control we have over changing our happiness. There have been many pivotal studies indicating both sides of the debate, and we will discuss each in turn. Historically, the idea that all individuals have a set point of well-being or happiness has dominated. This view suggests that events and experiences can boost or decrease our well-being temporarily, but that over time we will eventually fall back to our baseline, or set point, of happiness. Take, for example, the experience of winning the lottery. Many people imagine winning the lottery will instantly make them happier and that this happiness will have staying power. Alternatively, for a seemingly very negative experience, take, for example, the idea of facing significant injury following an accident. Most people report that such a traumatic experience will have long-lasting negative impact on their well-being. However, Brickman Coates, and Janoff-Bulman (1978) found that lottery winners and paralyzed accident victims were not significantly different in terms of their well-being compared to controls. In other words, these extreme positive and negative events did not have as pervasive an impact on well-being as we might imagine. These findings led to the conclusion that happiness is a hedonic treadmill – we can keep striving for happiness or to avoid unhappiness, but eventually we will revert back to hedonic neutrality.

More recent research has tried to understand why and to what extent such seemingly negative and positive events have little lasting impact on our well-being. Individuals do tend to report a decrease in life satisfaction or positive affect following unfortunate events. However, most report only temporary distress; less than one third report severe or significant distress (Bonanno, Brewin, Kaniasty, & La Greca, 2010). Most people bounce back faster than we might expect. However, it is important to keep in mind that adaptation does not necessarily mean returning to previous level of functioning. Instead, this revised version of adaptation refers to a decrease in well-being immediately following a negative event, but returning to above neutral in happiness over time that is heavily dependent on individual personality (Diener, Lucas, & Scollon, 2006; Headey & Wearing, 1989). Further, there is evidence suggesting that pre-event life satisfaction is important for post-event well-being changes. Specifically, those higher in life satisfaction are more likely to get married and have children and less likely to experience job loss, new job start, and marital separation (Luhmann, Lucas, Eid, & Diener, 2013). This revised notion of the hedonic treadmill model also suggests that an individual may have multiple happiness set points, rather than one global point and that different aspects of well-being can move in different directions independently (Diener et al., 2006). This theory suggests that some people may fully adapt while others may never adapt following significant events, and that individual differences are largely contributing factors.

For example, studies of individuals who are widowed, unemployed, have chronic mental disabilities, or wheelchair bound reported below average positivity, but still above the overall midlevel of happiness (Chwalisz, Diener, & Gallagher, 1988; Clark & Georgellis, 2012; Delespaul & DeVries, 1987). Lucas (2007) found that those who experience a negative event such as widowhood or significant disability report lower subjective well-being post-event compared to pre-event, but they still report more positive feelings compared to negative feelings overall. In more recent work, Clark, Diener, Georgellis, and Lucas (2008) found support for complete adaptation following all (marriage, divorce, widowhood, birth of child, and layoff) but one (unemployment) significant life event, replicating prior findings that unemployment may change one's set point for life satisfaction (Lucas, Clark, Georgellis, & Diener, 2004). Generally, we see that most people do adapt to negative events, but they may not completely revert to their previous level of functioning.

Therefore, more recent research has supported a modified adaptation view. Diener and colleagues (2009) suggested that under this modified adaptation theory, well-being set points can change under certain conditions. This view takes a more optimistic view on well-being in that happiness is malleable and, perhaps with the right skills, one's set point can change over time rather than be doomed to what their current set point might be. Positive psychology interventions have been designed to assess the utility of actively attempting to change the set point of happiness. Interventions have typically been designed to alleviate problematic symptoms for distressed individuals. Positive psychology interventions targeting learning and practicing optimism and flexible thinking, socializing, writing gratitude letters or journals, and engaging in kind activities have been proposed to target anxious and depressive symptoms (Fava et al., 2005; Lyubomirsky, Dickerhoof, Boehm, & Sheldon, 2011; Otake, Shimai, Tanaka-Matsumi, Otsui, & Fredrickson, 2006; Seligman, Rashid, & Parks, 2006; Seligman, Steen, Park, & Peterson, 2005; see also Sin & Lyubomirsky, 2009, for a review). Increases in positive emotions seem to ameliorate depressive symptoms (Geschwind et al., 2010), indicating the possible benefit of positive psychology-based interventions for mental health treatment. However, interventions have also been designed for individuals who are not necessarily in clinical range of mental distress with the goal of changing the set point of well-being.

In recent years, interventions aimed at increasing well-being have proliferated rapidly (see Diener & Biswas-Diener, 2019; Stone & Parks, 2018, for reviews).

These interventions have targeted areas such as meditation (Hofmann, Grossman, & Hinton, 2011), expressing gratitude (Emmons & McCullough, 2003), engaging in kind activities (Otake et al., 2006), identifying personal strengths (Seligman et al., 2005), and writing about emotional experiences (Pennebaker, 1997) to name a few. Furthermore, there is evidence suggesting these interventions may be effective in boosting well-being (Malouff & Schutte, 2016; Sin & Lyubomirsky, 2009; Weiss, Westerhof, & Bohlmeijer, 2016). Interestingly, well-being interventions have been employed across cultures (see Biswas-Diener, Vitters\u00f8, & Diener, 2010; Diener, Diener, Choi, & Oishi, 2018; Diener, Seligman, Choi, & Oishi, 2018) with promising results. Specifically, well-being interventions were associated with decreasing distressing emotions in diverse groups including Kuwait students and a sample in United Arab Emirates (UAE) (Lambert, Passmore, & Joshanloo, 2019; Lambert, Passmore, Scull, Sabah, & Hussain, 2019). Nonetheless, Biswas-Diener and Lyubchik (2013) suggest adapting interventions based on the cultural norms within the intervention group to reduce potential bias and misunderstanding or application of intervention components.

A recent well-being intervention program called ENHANCE is one of the first comprehensive interventions that includes 10 modules covering a wide variety of the above-listed positive interventions (Heintzelman et al., 2020). EHNANCE primarily focuses on psychoeducation regarding happiness, goal setting, changing specific behaviors, and developing habits via tangible, concrete skills. Emerging research suggests the ENHANCE program is associated with higher life satisfaction up to 3-months post-intervention (Heintzelman et al., 2020). Further, participants in the pilot study showed improvements in health (i.e., decreases in body mass index, fewer sick days, and improved cognitive performance) (Lutes et al., 2018, 2019; see also Diener & Biswas-Diener, 2019, for a review). The impact of ENHANCE and other positive interventions on well-being indicates that individuals may be able to change their happiness set point with targeted practice and effort.

## Causes of Well-Being

### Income

It should come as no surprise, given the age-old question, "Can money buy happiness?" that researchers have attempted to disentangle the relationship between finances and subjective well-being. Unfortunately, the answer to this question remains somewhat unclear. When it comes to national income and the relative wealth of a nation, there is evidence suggesting that on a country-wide scale, individuals living in countries with higher national income report greater well-being compared to individuals living in countries with lower national income (De Neve, Diener, Tay, & Xuereb, 2013; Diener, Sandvik, Seidlitz, & Diener, 1993).

The effects for the link between well-being and national income are relatively large. However, when it comes to whether personal income impacts well-being, the image is less clear. The strength of the relationship seems dependent on both individual factors and national factors. For example, overall, there is a small correlation of 0.12 between income and subjective well-being in a United States sample (Diener et al., 1993). However, there is a much stronger correlation between money and happiness for individuals living in disadvantaged countries (i.e., Calcutta slum dwellers; $R = 0.45$) and even stronger for disadvantaged individuals living in disadvantaged countries (i.e., Calcutta sex workers; $R = 0.67$; Biswas-Diener & Diener, 2001). Further, individuals living in societies where there are large disparities between poor and wealth seem to report stronger links between money and well-being, and this disparity may be more important than the role of gross national product on well-being. Specifically, individuals living in societies with high income or wealth inequality report lower happiness (Alesina, Di Tella, & MacCulloch, 2004; Oishi, Kesebir, & Diener, 2011).

The idea that money can buy happiness comes with many caveats, but there is some truth to this classic saying. Unemployed individuals tend to report lower well-being compared to their employed counterparts (Lucas et al., 2004; McKee-Ryan, Song, Wanberg, & Kinicki, 2005). There is a corresponding increase in well-being as income increases up to a certain point (ca. US$60,000) after which more money doesn't equate to similar raises in happiness. This is referred to as the declining marginal utility of finances (Diener et al., 1993) and reflects the idea that money matters for our well-being up to the point where our basic needs are met and fail to deliver similarly potent boosts for our happiness beyond that level. In other words, in the United States, at least, changes in income when already at a higher income level resulted in smaller changes in well-being as compared to changes at lower income levels. Other researchers have argued that income may be linked to life satisfaction but not to the affective aspects of subjective well-being (Kahneman & Deaton, 2010).

Interestingly, aspects of the declining marginal utility of income on happiness have been found in other cultures as well. Jebb and colleagues (2018) found that happiness rises with income to the point of "income satiation" which is US$85,000 for life satisfaction and US$60,000–75,000 for emotional well-being, although this point varies by country. They also found that in certain countries, income beyond this income satiation point resulted in decreases in well-being and was detrimental to happiness. These results were especially strong for the negative effects on enjoying life, rather than for life satisfaction. Perhaps those with significantly higher earnings are taxed with materialism, long hours, arduous tasks, or lacking time for family, all of which may negatively impact life enjoyment. However, much more research is needed to understand the declining marginal of utility of income on happiness. Overall, it remains an unanswered question for who and via which measurements is well-being related to income.

## Social relationships

In addition to the attention that the money-happiness link has received, there are many other important causes of well-being worth considering. One of the strongest links to subjective well-being is one's social relationships, in that supportive relationships are one of the strongest outcomes of well-being (Frisch, 2005; Oishi, Diener, & Lucas, 2007). Those with high positive affect are more social in that they have more friends, closer friends, engage in more social activities, and enjoy spending time in the company of others (Diener & Seligman, 2002; Eid, Riemann, Angleitner, & Borkenau, 2003; Lucas & Fujita, 2000; Lucas, Le, & Dyrenforth, 2008; Mehl, Vazire, Holleran, & Clark, 2010). Overall, happy individuals are reporting higher quality relationships and are also investing their time and energy into social activities that may in turn continue building their relationships.

High subjective well-being has often been found in clusters within social networks, indicating a happiness contagion effect (Fowler & Christakis, 2008). Further, others report higher quality relationships with happy people as well in that they rate time spent together as more rewarding (Harker & Keltner, 2001). Happy people tend to have less small talk and instead fill their conversations with more substantial talking (Mehl et al., 2010). Boehm and Lyubomirsky (2008) found that happy people tend to be rated as more likable and as more popular.

The link between strong social relationships and well-being has been found cross-culturally. Positive feelings are linked to the amount of time spent interacting with others (Lucas, Diener, Grob, Suh, & Shao, 2000). However, cultural differences emerge when assessing the link between positive affect and extraversion specifically. This link in particular was weaker in collectivistic cultures and stronger in individualistic nations (Lucas et al., 2000). Extraversion was also related to higher life satisfaction only when living within an extraverted culture (Fulmer et al., 2010) highlighting the broader context of values within a society.

Beyond the link between general social relationships and well-being, there is also growing support for the benefit of romantic relationships on subjective well-being. Both nonmarital romantic relationships (Campbell, Simpson, Boldry, & Kashy, 2005; Dush & Amato, 2005) and marriage (Diener, Gohm, Suh, & Oishi, 2000; Efklides, Kalaitzidou, & Chankin, 2003) have been associated with subjective well-being. Those high in relationship satisfaction tend to also report higher positive affect and life satisfaction and less negative affect (Adamczyk, 2017; Dyrdal, Røysamb, Nes, & Vittersø, 2011; Love & Holder, 2015).

There is burgeoning evidence that it is not solely relationship status that is related to well-being, but rather satisfaction with current relationship status that impacts our well-being (see Kansky, 2018, for a review). Married individuals report higher levels of happiness compared to those who are cohabitating, casually or exclusively dating, or rarely dating, in descending order of happiness (Dush & Amato, 2005). Married individuals also report greater happiness compared to those who are divorced, separated, or single (Dush, Taylor, & Kroeger, 2008;

Myers, 2000; Proulx, Helms, & Buehler, 2007). In terms of ranking happiness levels and relationship status, marriage is associated with the highest levels of well-being, lending itself to being coined "the marriage benefit"; separation is associated with the lowest levels of well-being while divorce and widowhood fall in between (Helliwell, 2003). Interestingly, the marriage benefit is smaller in collectivist nations and divorce-tolerant nations (Diener et al., 2000), which again points to the importance of contextual factors in assessing specific causes of well-being.

### Genes, biology, and personality

Although money and relationships may be at the forefront of what individuals believe will make them happy, there are myriad other potential sources of well-being. As is the case with most human constructs, our experiences are a result of our innate biology and our experiences with others and with the world. Twin studies can be most helpful in understanding the nature versus nurture debate for well-being. Results indicate that monozygotic twins reared apart (i.e., large nature overlap; little nurture overlap) are more similar in subjective well-being than dizygotic twins reared together (i.e., smaller nature overlap; large nurture overlap) (Haworth, Carter, Eley, & Plomin, 2017; Lykken & Tellegen, 1996). These studies find a heritability of subjective well-being of approximately 0.40, indicating that our genes and biological makeup can be influential in our experience of happiness and well-being (see Røysamb & Nes, 2018, for a review).

Further, specific genes, especially serotonin reuptake genes (5-HTTLPR), may play a role in subjective well-being as well. Historically, serotonin genetic variation has been linked to mental health (Hariri et al., 2002; Heils et al., 1996; Murakami et al., 1999). Specifically, depression has been associated with low serotonin levels and most antidepressant medications (i.e., serotonin reuptake inhibitors) increase the amount of serotonin to decrease depressive symptoms. Variation of the serotonin transporter gene may be linked to susceptibility to optimism or depression. Specifically, the long variant of the 5-HTTLPR allele is related to optimism in that individuals selectively avoided negative information and attune to positive information, while the short variant is associated with a vulnerability to depression (Caspi et al., 2003; Fox, Ridgewell, & Ashwin, 2009; Kendler, Kuhn, Vittum, Prescott, & Riley, 2005). Further, positive mood and life satisfaction may be more strongly linked to serotonin level and variants of the serotonin transporter gene as compared to negative affect (De Neve, 2011; Flory, Manuck, Matthews, & Muldoon, 2004).

Our personality can be influential for our well-being. In particular, extraverts compared to introverts experience more positive feelings while individuals who are more neurotic experience more negative feelings (see Diener & Lucas, 1999; Lucas & Diener, 2000, for reviews). Personality constructs related to social interactions are more strongly linked to positive affect, while those related to emotional states are more strongly associated with negative affect (Emmons & Diener, 1985).

As discussed above, there are caveats to the simple extraversion–happiness link in that for some people and in some cultures this link may be stronger than for others. Perhaps individuals who enjoy spending more time with others get additional boosts to their happiness regardless of where they fall on the extraversion and introversion scale, but it is extraverts who are spending more time with others to get those well-being boosts from social interactions. Diener, Sandvik, Pavot, and Fujita (1992) found that extraverts may select into certain long-term life situations that match their preference for social environments, but that this personality-situation matching effect does not entirely account for the link between extraversion and happiness.

## Strengths and positive behaviors

There are many psychological processes and positive behaviors that may underlie the link between relationships with others and our well-being. Maslow's hierarchy of needs (Maslow, 1943) was designed so that basic needs were necessary to address prior to increasing attention toward more personal, self-actualized goals. However, Tay and Diener (2011) found that, cross-culturally, need fulfillment predicted well-being, but that these needs did not emerge in Maslow's proposed order. Instead, positive feelings were linked to social and respect needs.

Perhaps related to need fulfillment is the idea that goal pursuit and mastery of certain tasks can lead to increases in subjective well-being. Having goals in life provides a sense of meaning and purpose. The ideal goal pursuit process is a balance between individual skill and the challenge of the tasks needed to reach the goal. If the person's skill outreaches the challenge, individuals may experience boredom; if the challenge exceeds the person's skill, then the result may be anxiety. However, if able to correctly balance challenge to skill, individuals may enter a state of flow. Flow is referred to as a state of consciousness in which they are completely and effortlessly absorbed in a particular activity (Csikszentmihalyi, 1997). Flow makes it easier to obtain goals and it is the goal attainment, this mastery of important tasks, that may lead to increases in life satisfaction. In addition, the process of striving to attain goals may be related to well-being. Positive and negative affect related to goal pursuit and perceived success versus failure influences self-esteem and continued engagement in goal striving (Emmons, 1986; Emmons, Diener, & Larsen, 1986).

The AIM model of cognitive processes helps explain many of the relationships between how we think and how we feel as it relates to well-being. The AIM model refers to attention, interpretation, and memory of events (Forgas, 1995). Our mood may lead us to pay attention to different stimuli from the myriad things to which we are exposed at any given time. For example, it may be more likely when we are in a positive mood that we will notice the leaves falling from trees into colorful, beautiful patterns, rather than attend to the wind whipping around us and making us feel cold on a fall morning walk. Our mood may also influence how we interpret ambiguous stimuli. Recall that positive affect is related to optimism such that we may interpret an ambiguous event as more positive and favorable when in a positive mood compared to in a negative mood. Finally, affect may change our memories for certain events or consolidate memories in different ways. The AIM model may be especially powerful for the impact of social interactions and relationships on our well-being (Forgas, 1994; Lyubomirsky, 2001).

However, we are not always accurate in our attention, interpretation, and memory for events as just demonstrated. When we are in negative moods, we tend to believe that the negativity will last for a longer period of time and be more intense than what is typically experienced. Similarly, when we experience a positive life event, we tend to believe that the positivity will be more pervasive and long-lasting than what actually occurs. This phenomenon is coined affective forecasting (Wilson & Gilbert, 2005). In general, our moods may bias our thoughts about how a particular situation is going to affect us in the long run.

## Outcomes of Well-Being

### Health

Subjective well-being has increasingly become a critical aspect of overall health functioning. The way we feel and view ourselves is linked to how we physically feel on a daily basis as well, highlighting the overlap between subjective and objective well-being. Prior research has validated this link between health and subjective well-being as well (Cohen & Rodriguez, 1995; Pressman, Gallagher, & Lopez, 2013; Ryff, Singer, & Dienberg, 2004). Negative affect is associated with more diseases while positive affect is associated with fewer of them (Weiser, 2012). Those who are physically healthy with few physical health complaints tend to also report high subjective well-being and are satisfied with their lives.

Specifically, high life satisfaction is associated with lower inflammatory markers, increased cardiovascular and immune functioning, healthier diet and exercise behaviors, and lower body mass index (Friedman & Ryff, 2012; Grant, Wardle, & Steptoe, 2009; Howell, Kern, & Lyubomirsky, 2007; Steptoe, Dockray, & Wardle, 2009; Uchino, Bowen, & Kent, 2016). Positive affect is associated with lower inflammatory, cardiovascular, and neuroendocrine problems, lower ambulatory heart rate, lower daily cortisol output (i.e., biological marker of stress), lower blood fat and blood pressure, and healthier body mass index (Blanchflower, Oswald, Stewart-Brown, 2013; Steptoe, Wardle, & Marmot, 2005).

It is important to note that we see the positive benefit of positive affect on health cross-culturally. In a study of 142 countries, Pressman and colleagues (2013) found a significant relationship between health and positive emotion. This relationship was stronger in countries with a low gross domestic product. In a study of 16 European nations, life satisfaction was significantly correlated with lower blood pressure, a key marker of physical health as elevated blood pressure is associated with risk for many heart diseases (Blanchflower & Oswald, 2004). In yet another large-scale cross-cultural study, Grant and colleagues (2009) found that high life satisfaction is linked to a greater likelihood of following a healthy diet, exercising regularly, and using sun protection and a lower likelihood of smoking.

There is growing evidence that not only are health and well-being concurrently linked, but well-being may be the driving factor of better health outcomes over time as well. Positive feelings predicted longevity and mortality while negative emotions predicted illness (Diener & Chan, 2011). In a large review, Lyubomirsky, King, and Diener (2005) found that subjective well-being emerges as a predictor of future health and longevity using both cross-sectional and experimental methods. Subsequent large-scale reviews have replicated the finding of positive moods boosting health and longevity (Diener, Pressman, Hunter, & Delgadillo-Chase, 2017; Howell et al., 2007). In an innovative study, Danner and colleagues (2001) coded nuns' diaries for positively valanced words and found that those who had more positive words as young adults lived longer. This effect was replicated in other populations with similar results of positive words associated with living longer (Pressman & Cohen, 2007, 2012). Finally, well-being interventions have been found to improve health and longevity (Diener et al., 2017; Lambert, Moliver, & Thompson, 2015).

Positive affect is linked to a host of health behaviors in addition to physical functioning and diseases. Those with higher positive affect tend to report less sleep problems (Steptoe, O'Donnell, Marmot, & Wardle, 2008), exercise more frequently and eat a balanced, nutritious diet (Blanchflower et al., 2013; Boehm & Kubzansky, 2012; Boehm, Peterson, Kivimaki, & Kubzansky, 2011), and are less likely to engage in risky behaviors including smoking, using other drugs, or not wearing a seatbelt (Goudie, Mukherjee, De Neve, Oswald, & Wu, 2014; Hamer & Chida, 2011). Overall, happy people are choosing to engage in better health habits compared to unhappy people (Kim, Kubzansky, Soo, & Boehm, 2016). Those with negative affect, on the other hand, are more likely to fail to develop healthy behaviors such as beginning a diet or quitting smoking (Haedt-Matt & Keel, 2011; Kassel, Stroud, & Paronis, 2003). Taken together, happier individuals are more likely to choose healthy behaviors and are better able to stick to healthy lifestyle choices over time.

However, happy people are not immune to becoming sick or feeling unwell. Fortunately, positive emotions can be useful in managing an illness. For example, subjective well-being and positive emotions are related to lower reported pain and greater pain tolerance (Howell et al., 2007; Pressman & Cohen, 2005). Positive emotions may also predict faster recovery from certain illnesses. Higher positive affect is linked to faster wound healing (Broadbent & Koschwanez, 2012). A simple positive mood manipulation in which patients were induced to smile after a stress induction was associated with quicker heart rate recovery as well (Kraft & Pressman, 2012). Even for more extreme health concerns, positive affect appears to play a role. For example, stroke patients with more positive emotions were more likely to regain greater functional status (Ostir, Berges, Markides, & Ottenbacher, 2006). One mechanism of the link between positive affect and better prognosis and recovery from illness may be optimism. Optimism predicts longevity, mortality, slower disease progression, decreased stroke incidence, and lower cardiovascular disease risk (Boehm & Kubzansky, 2012; Diener & Chan, 2011; Kim, Park, & Peterson, 2011). Positive affect and optimism may encourage individuals to take preventive health steps, to seek out support and healthcare faster when experiencing a health issue, and to adhere to treatment and medication instructions. All of this may then relate to improved health over time.

## Income and work success

Although the link between income and well-being has already been discussed in terms of the influence that money and financial success has on our happiness, there is also evidence suggesting the opposite pattern. There is growing support that those with higher subjective well-being may earn higher incomes (Peterson, Luthans, Avolio, Walumbwa, & Zhang, 2011). College first-year students who self-reported as more cheerful later earned more money even after controlling for family income (Diener, Nickerson, Lucas, & Sandvik, 2002). However, effects between positive affect and income were strongest for individuals already from high-income households. For those individuals from the lowest income households, having a midlevel of cheerfulness was most predictive of the highest income later. Indeed, other studies that assessed this link in less-advantaged populations have failed to replicate the well-being–income link (Diener et al., 1993; Kansky, Allen, & Diener, 2016).

Beyond potentially impacting income, subjective well-being likely plays a key role in workplace functioning and success. A recent study found that adolescent positive affect predicted higher levels of job competence and career satisfaction a decade later (Kansky et al., 2016). One mechanism that may underlie the link between happiness and job performance is the interactions with others on the job. High subjective well-being is related to positive workplace social relationships, which may in turn promote greater understanding, respect, communication, and trust among coworkers (Simons & Peterson, 2000; Stephens, Heaphy, Carmeli, Spreitzer, & Dutton, 2013; Tenney, Poole, & Diener, 2016). Positive moods boost cooperative behaviors, are linked with greater social support from supervisors, and are associated with greater client satisfaction (Carnevale, 2007; Grandey, Fisk, Mattila, Jansen, & Sideman, 2005; Hennig-Thurau, Groth, Paul, & Gremler, 2006; Staw, Sutton, & Pelled, 1994). Alternatively, poor quality workplace relationships including poor communication, hostility, and incompatible or unclear goals have been associated with higher stress and anxiety, low work commitment, and lower satisfaction and confidence in the workplace all of which can be associated with lower job satisfaction (De Dreu & Weingart, 2003; Tepper, 2000). However, not all negative affect in relationships is detrimental to the workplace. Shared negative affect toward a policy or boss may potentially foster stronger social bonds among coworkers. For example, people who complain about a common issue bond over the shared negative experience and feelings, which can boost social cohesion and connections (Stoverink, Umphress, Gardner, & Miner, 2014). Thus, under certain circumstances both positive and negative emotions may lead to better relationships with coworkers and others within the workplace, which can in turn promote greater job satisfaction and performance.

In addition to the importance of positive workplace relationships, there are many other workplace skills that may be related to well-being. Positive moods help us interpret tasks as being more interesting and satisfying (Isen & Reeve, 2005; Kraiger, Billings, & Isen, 1989). Positive affect is linked to increased patience and perseverance as well (Ifcher & Zarghamee, 2011; Lerner, Li, & Weber, 2013). Further, high well-being and positive affect generate more creativity, motivation, and self-regulation (Amabile, Barsade, Mueller, & Staw, 2005; Tenney et al., 2016), greater curiosity (Jovanovic & Brdaric, 2012; Leitzel, 2000), and increased cognitive flexibility and broader attention (Baas, De Dreu, & Nijstad, 2008; Rowe, Hirsh, & Anderson, 2007; Schmitz, De Rosa, & Anderson, 2009). Interestingly, negative mood and job dissatisfaction may also lead to increase job performance due to increased perseverance and creativity (George & Zhou, 2007; To, Fisher, Ashkanasy, & Rowe, 2012). As is the case with workplace relationships, there is also contradictory evidence suggesting the role of positive and negative moods for work skills.

On an organizational level, there is stronger evidence for the role of employee well-being in predicting positive outcomes. Tenney et al. (2016) found that happy organizations perform better on average across multiple domains. Specifically, happy workplaces have less employee turnover, fewer employee sick days and lower healthcare costs, greater employee citizenship, greater customer loyalty, and more energetic and creative employees.

## Social relationships and behaviors

Findings are starting to point at high quality social relationships, especially romantic relationships, as an important outcome of high subjective well-being. Happy people are more likely to get married, stay married, and report higher satisfaction with their partner (Luhmann et al., 2013; Stutzer & Frey, 2006). Further, those with higher life satisfaction are more likely to remain married and less likely to experience a separation (Luhmann et al., 2013). Even for nonmarried individuals, happiness seems influential in predicting relationship satisfaction (Diener & Seligman, 2002). In an innovative study design in which researchers coded photographs of individuals for positive expressions, results suggested that those with more positive facial expressions have better marital outcomes (Harker & Keltner, 2001; Hertenstein, Hansel, Butts, & Hile, 2009; Seder & Oishi, 2012). In one of the few studies assessing the impact of affect during the teenage years and romantic outcomes in adulthood, Kansky and colleagues (2016) found that positive affect predicted less romantic conflict a decade later in young adulthood according to both the target individual and their partner. When it comes to adult marriages, Gottman (1993) similarly found that positive interactions both in daily life and during times of conflict may predict relationship stability and quality.

Likewise, there is longitudinal and experiments evidence for strong social relationships to predict well-being. Using an ESM design, positive affect and sociability were significantly and consistently correlated across time (Diener, Kanazawa, Suh, & Oishi, 2014). Positive affect during adolescence predicted changes in self-reported sociability and loneliness as well as peer-rated secure attachment during the transition to adulthood (Kansky et al., 2016). Thus, not only did happy individuals themselves indicate better social outcomes over time, but their close friends similarly noted positive benefits.

Most experiments assessing the link between affect and social relationships have manipulated affect and subsequently assessed social behaviors. For example, positive mood inductions were linked to more sociable and cooperative behavior, greater compassion, perspective-taking, and sympathy for someone in distress, increased interested in social activities, increases in self-disclosure, and a preference for social versus isolated situations (Cunningham, 1988a, 1988b; Nelson, 2009; Whelan & Zelenski, 2012). Happy individuals may be more likely to seek out social situations and enjoy their social time more as compared to unhappy individuals. Alternatively, when individuals feel socially disconnected or isolated, they are less likely to self-disclose or be their true selves, which can in turn exacerbate feelings of distress (Lepore, Fernandex-Berrocal, Ragan, & Ramos, 2004). In essence, happy people are creating a positive feedback loop for their social relationships while unhappy people continue to withdraw from others or face unfulfilling relationships.

There are several theoretical accounts for why social relationships are so important for our well-being. One line of research highlights the activities and behaviors associated with interacting with others when we are in good moods. The functional account of emotions posits that affect guides behavior, especially social behavior, by providing informative, evocative, and incentive functions that continue shaping our interactions with others (Keltner & Haidt, 2001; Keltner & Kring, 1998). Positive emotions ranging from contentment and pleasure to enjoyment and excitement inform the individual that their behavior and activity is going well and would be pleasant to repeat in the future. The positive feelings reinforce the behavior so that they are more likely to engage in those behaviors again. The evocative function refers to activities that occur in the presence of others including conversations, games, or play. All of these are shared interactions that build social bonds between people. The incentive function refers to activities that are pleasantly rewarding to individuals due to the positive feelings or behaviors that they receive from their social partner.

A second theoretical account is the broaden-and-build theory by Fredrickson (1998, 2001). Positive emotions help to broaden and build resources for the future that are useful especially in times of future distress. Positive moods allow us to invest in our social relationships and build a supportive social network from which we can pull in the future. Thus, positive emotions allow us to invest in our relationships to build stronger bonds that are useful under future distress. Alternatively, negative moods promote more focused, inward attention, which detracts from investing in relationships or experiences external to us. Happy individuals are more likely to build social capital when experiencing positive affect so that they are less impeded by negative affect and experiences. For further reading on the outcomes associated with well-being, see Kansky & Diener (2017).

## Conclusion

As evidenced in this chapter, there has been an incredible amount of progress on the study of subjective well-being. Technological and methodological advances have allowed researchers to understand the causes and outcomes of well-being in innovative ways. Despite the exciting new research findings, there are countless more endeavors to be undertaken to understand well-being more comprehensively. Future studies would benefit to focus on both the conceptual and theoretical advances of well-being and how it is experienced across the world, as well as on the applied work utilizing what we already know about well-being. The development of interventions and their effectiveness are burgeoning areas of research with the potential for widespread impact on well-being.

## References

Adamczyk, K. (2017). Going beyond relationship status: A cross-sectional and longitudinal investigation of the role of satisfaction with relationship status in predicting Polish young adults' mental health. *Journal of Social and Clinical Psychology, 36*(4), 265–284.

Alesina, A., Di Tella, R., & MacCulloch, R. (2004). Inequality and happiness: are Europeans and Americans different? *Journal of Public Economics, 88*(9–10), 2009–2042.

Amabile, T. M., Barsade, S. G., Mueller, J. S., & Staw, B. (2005). Affect and creativity at work. *Administrative Science Quarterly, 50,* 367–403.

Baas, M., De Dreu, C. K. W., & Nijstad, B. A. (2008). A meta-analysis of 24 years of mood creativity research: Hedonic tone, activation, or regulatory focus? *Psychological Bulletin, 134,* 779–806.

Biswas-Diener, R., & Diener, E. (2001). Making the best of a bad situation: Satisfaction in the slums of Calcutta. *Social Indicators Research, 55*(3), 329–352.

Biswas-Diener, R., & Lyubchik, N. (2013). Microculture as a contextual positive intervention. In T. Kashdan & J. Ciarrochi (Eds.), *Bridging acceptance and commitment therapy and positive psychology: A practitioner's guide to a unifying framework* (pp. 194–214). Oakland, CA: Context Press.

Biswas-Diener, R., Vittersø, J., & Diener, E. (2010). The Danish effect: Beginning to explain high well-being in Denmark. *Social Indicators Research, 97*(2), 229–246.

Blanchflower, D. G., & Oswald, A. J. (2004). Money, sex, and happiness: An empirical study. *The Scandinavian Journal of Economics, 106,* 393–415.

Blanchflower, D. G., Oswald, A. J., & Stewart-Brown, S. (2013). Is psychological well-being linked to the consumption of fruits and vegetables? *Social Indicators Research, 114,* 785–801.

Boehm, J. K., & Kubzansky, L. D. (2012). The heart's content: The association between positive psychological well-being and cardiovascular health. *Psychological Bulletin, 138,* 655–691.

Boehm, J. K., & Lyubomirsky, S. (2008). Does happiness lead to career success? *Journal of Career Assessment, 16,* 101–116.

Boehm, J. K., Peterson, C., Kivimaki, M., & Kubzansky, L. (2011). A prospective study of positive psychological well-being and coronary heart disease. *Health Psychology, 30,* 259–267.

Bolger, N., Davis, A., & Rafaeli, E. (2003). Diary methods: Capturing life as it is lived. *Annual Review of Psychology, 54,* 579–616.

Bonanno, G. A., Brewin, C. R., Kaniasty, K., & La Greca, A. M. (2010). Weighing the costs of disaster: Consequences, risks, and resilience in individuals, families, and communities. *Psychological Science in the Public Interest, 11,* 1–49.

Brickman, P., Coates, D., & Janoff-Bulman, R. (1978). Lottery winners and accident victims: Is happiness relative? *Journal of Personality and Social Psychology, 36*(8), 917–927.

Broadbent, E., & Koschwanez, H. E. (2012). The psychology of wound healing. *Current Opinion in Psychiatry, 25,* 135–140.

Cacioppo, J. T., Berntson, G. G., Larsen, J. T., Poehlmann, K. M., & Ito, T. A. (2000). The psychophysiology of emotion. In M. Lewis & J. M. Haviland-Jones. (Eds.), *Handbook of emotions* (2nd ed., pp. 173–191). New York: Guilford Press.

Campbell, L., Simpson, J. A., Boldry, J. G., & Kashy, D. (2005). Perceptions of conflict and support in romantic relationships: The role of attachment anxiety. *Journal of Personality and Social Psychology, 88,* 510–531.

Carnevale, P. J. (2007). Positive affect and decision frame in negotiation. *Group Decision and Negotiation, 17,* 51–63.

Caspi, A., Sugden, K., Moffitt, T. E., Taylor, A., Craig, I. W., Harrington, H. L., . . . Poulton, R. (2003). Influence of life stress on depression: Moderation

by a polymorphism in the 5-HTT gene. *Science, 301,* 386–389.

Chwalisz, K., Diener, E., & Gallagher, D. (1988). Autonomic arousal feedback and emotional experience: Evidence from the spinal cord injured. *Journal of Personality and Social Psychology, 54,* 820–828.

Clark, A. E., Diener, E., Georgellis, Y., & Lucas, R. E. (2008). Lags and leads in life satisfaction: A test of the baseline hypothesis. *The Economic Journal, 118*(529), F222–F243.

Clark, A. E., & Georgellis, Y. (2012). *Back to baseline in Britain: Adaptation in the BHPS* (IZA Discussion Paper No. 6426). Paris, France: Paris School of Economics.

Cohen, S., & Rodriguez, M. S. (1995). Pathways linking affective disturbances and physical disorders. *Health Psychology, 14,* 374–380.

Csikszentmihalyi, M. (1997). *Finding flow: The psychology of engagement with everyday life.* New York: Basic Books.

Cunningham, M. R. (1988a). What do you do when you're happy or blue? Mood, expectancies, and behavioral interest. *Motivation and Emotion, 12,* 309–331.

Cunningham, M. R. (1988b). Does happiness mean friendliness? Induced mood and heterosexual self-disclosure. *Personality and Social Psychology Bulletin, 14,* 283–297.

Danner, D. D., Snowdon, D. A., & Friesen, W. V. (2001). Positive emotions in early life and longevity: Findings from the nun study. *Journal of Personality and Social Psychology, 80,* 804–813.

Davidson, R. J. (1992). Anterior cerebral asymmetry and the nature of emotion. *Brain and Cognition, 20,* 125–151.

De Dreu, C. K. W., & Weingart, L. R. (2003). Task versus relationship conflict, team performance, and team member satisfaction: A meta-analysis. *Journal of Applied Psychology, 88,* 741–749.

Delespaul, P. A. E. G., & DeVries, M. W. (1987). The daily life of ambulatory chronic mental patients. *Journal of Nervous and Mental Disease, 175,* 537–544.

De Neve, J. E. (2011). Functional polymorphism (5-HTTLPR) in the serotonin transporter gene is associated with subjective well-being: Evidence from a US nationally representative sample. *Journal of Human Genetics, 56*(6), 456–459.

De Neve, J. E., Diener, E., Tay, L., & Xuereb, C. (2013). The objective benefits of subjective well-being. In J. F. Helliwell, R. Layard, & J. Sachs (Eds.), *World Happiness Report 2013* (Vol. 2, pp. 54–79). New York: UN Sustainable Network Development Solutions Network.

Diener, E. (2000). Subjective well-being: The science of happiness, and a proposal for national index. *American Psychologist, 55,* 34–43.

Diener, E., & Biswas-Diener, R. (2019). Well-being interventions to improve societies. In J. Sachs, R. Layard, & J. F. Helliwell (Eds.), *Global happiness and wellbeing: Policy report 2019* (pp. 95–112). New York: Global Happiness Council.

Diener, E., & Chan, M. Y. (2011). Happy people live longer: Subjective well-being contributes to health and longevity. *Applied Psychology: Health and Well-Being, 3,* 1–43.

Diener, E., Diener, C., Choi, H., & Oishi, S. (2018). Revisiting "Most people are happy" – and discovering when they are not. *Perspectives on Psychological Science, 13*(2), 166–170.

Diener, E., Emmons, R. A., Larsen, R. J., & Griffin, S. (1985). The Satisfaction with Life Scale. *Journal of Personality Assessment, 49*(1), 71–75.

Diener, E., & Fujita, F. (1995). Methodological pitfalls and solutions in satisfaction research. In A. C. Samli & M. J. Sirgy (Eds.), *New dimensions in marketing/quality-of-life research* (pp. 27–46). Westport, CT: Greenwood Press.

Diener, E., Gohm, C. L., Suh, E., & Oishi, S. (2000). Similarity of the relations between marital status and subjective well-being across cultures. *Journal of Cross-Cultural Psychology, 31,* 419–436.

Diener, E., Inglehart, R., & Tay, L. (2013). Theory and validity of life satisfaction measures. *Social Indicators Research, 112*(3), 497–527.

Diener, E., Kanazawa, S., Suh, E. M., & Oishi, S. (2014). Why people are in a generally good mood. *Personality and Social Psychology Review, 19,* 235–256.

Diener, E., & Lucas, R. (1999). Personality and subjective well-being. In D. Kahneman, E. Diener, & N. Schwarz (Eds.), *Well-being: The foundations of hedonic psychology* (pp. 213–229). New York: Russell Sage Foundation.

Diener, E., Lucas, R. E., & Scollon, C. N. (2006). Beyond the hedonic treadmill: Revising the adaptation theory of well-being. *American Psychologist, 61*(4), 305–314.

Diener, E., Nickerson, C., Lucas, R. E., & Sandvik, E. (2002). Dispositional affect and job outcomes. *Social Indicators Research, 59,* 229–259.

Diener, E., Pressman, S. D., Hunter, J., & Delgadillo-Chase, D. (2017). If, why, and when subjective well-being influences health, and future needed research. *Applied Psychology: Health and Well-Being, 9,* 133–167.

Diener, E., Sandvik, E., Pavot, W., & Fujita, F. (1992). Extraversion and subjective well-being in a US national probability sample. *Journal of Research in Personality, 26*(3), 205–215.

Diener, E., Sandvik, E., Seidlitz, L., & Diener, M. (1993). The relationship between income and subjective well-being: Relative or absolute? *Social Indicators Research, 28,* 195–223.

Diener, E., & Seligman, M. E. P. (2002). Very happy people. *Psychological Science, 13,* 81–84.

Diener, E., Seligman, M. E. P., Choi, H., & Oishi, S. (2018). Happiest people revisited. *Perspectives on Psychological Science, 13*(2), 176–184.

Diener, E., Smith, H., & Fujita, F. (1995). The personality structure of affect. *Journal of Personality and Social Psychology, 69,* 130–141.

Diener, E., Suh, E. M., Lucas, R. E., & Smith, H. L. (1999). Subjective well-being: Three decades of progress. *Psychological Bulletin, 125*(2), 276–302.

Diener, E., & Tay, L. (2015). Subjective well-being and human welfare around the world as reflected in the Gallup World Poll. *International Journal of Psychology, 50*(2), 135–149.

Diener, E., Wirtz, D., Biswas-Diener, R., Tov, W., Kim-Prieto, C., Choi, D., & Oishi, S. (2009). New measures of well-being. *Social Indicators Research: Assessing Well-Being, 39,* 247–266.

Diener, E., Wirtz, D., Tov, W., Kim-Prieto, C., Choi, D., Oishi, S., & Biswas-Diener, R. (2010). New well-being measures: Short scales to assess flourishing and positive and negative feelings. *Social Indicators Research, 97*(2), 143–156.

Dinan, T. G. (1994). Glucocorticoids and the genesis of depressive illness: A psychobiological model. *British Journal of Psychiatry, 164,* 365–371.

Dush, C. M. K., & Amato, P. R. (2005). Consequences of relationship status and quality for subjective well-being. *Journal of Social and Personal Relationships, 22,* 607–627.

Dush, C. M. K., Taylor, M. G., & Kroeger, R. A. (2008). Marital happiness and psychological well-being across the life course. *Family Relations, 57,* 211–226.

Dyrdal, G. M., Røysamb, E., Nes, R. B., & Vittersø, J. (2011). Can a happy relationship predict a happy life? A population-based study of maternal well-being during the life transition of pregnancy, infancy, and toddlerhood. *Journal of Happiness Studies, 12,* 947–962.

Efklides, A., Kalaitzidou, M., & Chankin, G. (2003). Subjective quality of life in old age in Greece. *European Psychologist, 8,* 178–191.

Eid, M., Riemann, R., Angleitner, A., & Borkenau, P. (2003). Sociability and positive emotionality: Genetic and environmental contributions to the covariations between different facets of extraversion. *Journal of Personality, 71,* 319–346.

Emmons, R. A. (1986). Personal strivings: An approach to personality and subjective well-being. *Journal of Personality and Social Psychology, 51,* 1058–1068.

Emmons, R. A., & Diener, E. (1985). Personality correlates of subjective well-being. *Personality and Social Psychology Bulletin, 11*(1), 89–97.

Emmons, R. A., Diener, E. D., & Larsen, R. J. (1986). Choice and avoidance of everyday situations and affect congruence: Two models of reciprocal interactionism. *Journal of Personality and Social Psychology, 51*(4), 815–826.

Emmons, R. A., & McCullough, M. E. (2003). Counting blessings versus burdens: An experimental investigation of gratitude and subjective well-being in daily life. *Journal of Personality and Social Psychology, 84*(2), 377–389.

Fava, G. A., Ruini, C., Rafanelli, C., Finos, L., Salmaso, L., Mangelli, L., & Sirigatti, S. (2005). Well-being therapy of generalized anxiety disorder. *Psychotherapy and Psychosomatics, 74,* 26–30.

Flory, J. D., Manuck, S. B., Matthews, K. A., & Muldoon, M. F. (2004). Serotonergic function in the central nervous system is associated with daily ratings of positive mood. *Psychiatry Research, 129*(1), 11–19.

Forgas, J. P. (1994). The role of emotion in social judgments: An introductory review and an affect infusion model (AIM). *European Journal of Social Psychology, 24*(1), 1–24.

Forgas, J. P. (1995). Mood and judgment: The affect infusion model (AIM). *Psychological Bulletin, 117*(1), 39–66.

Fowler, J. H., & Christakis, N. A. (2008). Dynamic spread of happiness in a large social network: Longitudinal analysis over 20 years in the Framingham heart study. *The New England Journal of Medicine, 358,* 2249–2258.

Fox, E., Ridgewell, A., & Ashwin, C. (2009). Looking on the bright side: Biased attention and the human serotonin transporter gene. *Proceedings of the Royal Society B: Biological Sciences, 276*(1663), 1747–1751.

Fredrickson, B. L. (1998). What good are positive emotions? *Review of General Psychology, 2,* 300–319.

Fredrickson, B. L. (2001). The role of positive emotions in positive psychology: The broaden-and-build theory of positive emotions. *American Psychologist, 56,* 218–226.

Friedman, E. M., & Ryff, C. D. (2012). Living well with medical comorbidities: A biopsychosocial perspective. *Journals of Gerontology: Series B, Psychological Sciences and Social Sciences, 67,* 535–544.

Frisch, M. B. (2005). *Quality of life therapy.* New York: Wiley.

Fulmer, C. A., Gelfand, M. J., Kruglanski, A. W., Kim-Prieto, C., Diener, E., Pierro, A., & Higgins, E. T. (2010). On "feeling right" in cultural contexts: How person-culture match affects self-esteem and subjective well-being. *Psychological Science, 21*(11), 1563–1569.

George, J. M., & Zhou, J. (2007). Dual tuning in a supportive context: Joint contributions of positive mood, negative mood, and supervisory behaviors to employee creativity. *Academy of Management Journal, 50,* 605–622.

Geschwind, N., Nicolson, N. A., Peeters, F., Van Os, J., Barge-Schaapveld, D., & Wichers, M. C.

(2010). Early improvement in positive rather than negative emotion predicts remission from depression after pharmacotherapy. *European Neuropsychopharmacology, 21,* 241–247.

Gottman, J. M. (1993). Studying emotion in social interaction. In M. Lewis, & J. M. Haviland (Eds.), *Handbook of Emotions* (pp. 475–487). New York: Guilford Press.

Goudie, R. J. B., Mukherjee, S., De Neve, J., Oswald, A. J., & Wu, S. (2014). Happiness as a driver of risk-avoiding behavior: Theory and an empirical study of seatbelt wearing and automobile accidents. *Economica, 81,* 674–697.

Grandey, A. A., Fisk, G. M., Mattila, A. S., Jansen, K. J., & Sideman, L. A. (2005). Is service with a smile enough? Authenticity of positive displays in service encounters. *Organizational Behavior and Human Decision Processes, 96,* 38–55.

Grant, N., Wardle, J., & Steptoe, A. (2009). The relationship between life satisfaction and health behavior: A cross-cultural analysis of young adults. *International Journal of Behavioral Medicine, 16,* 259–268.

Haedt-Matt, A. A., & Keel, P. K. (2011). Revisiting the affect regulation model of binge eating: A meta-analysis of studies using ecological momentary assessment. *Psychological Bulletin, 137,* 660–681.

Hamer, M., & Chida, Y. (2011). Life satisfaction and inflammatory biomarkers: The 2008 Scottish health survey. *Japanese Psychological Research, 53,* 133–139.

Hariri, A. R., Mattay, V. S., Tessitore, A., Kolachana, B., Fera, F., & Goldman, D. (2002). Serotonin transporter genetic variation and the response of the human amygdala. *Science, 297,* 400–403.

Harker, L., & Keltner, D. (2001). Expressions of positive emotion in women's college yearbook pictures and their relationship to personality and life outcomes across adulthood. *Personality Processes and Individual Differences, 80,* 112–124.

Haworth, C. M., Carter, K., Eley, T. C., & Plomin, R. (2017). Understanding the genetic and environmental specificity and overlap between well-being and internalizing symptoms in adolescence. *Developmental Science, 20*(2), 1–9.

Headey, B., & Wearing, A. (1989). Personality, life events, and subjective well-being: Toward a dynamic equilibrium model. *Journal of Personality and Social Psychology, 57,* 731–739.

Heils, A., Teufel, A., Petri, S., Stober, G., Riederer, P., Bengel, D., & Lesch, K. P. (1996). Allelic variation of human serotonin transporter gene expression. *Journal of Neurochemistry, 66*(6), 2621–2624.

Heintzelman, S. J., Kushlev, K., Lutes, L. D., Wirtz, D., Kanippayoor, J. M., Leitner, D., . . . Diener, E. (2020). ENHANCE: Evidence for the efficacy of a comprehensive intervention program to promote durable changes in subjective well-being. *Journal of Experimental Psychology: Applied, 26*(2), 360–383.

Helliwell, J. F. (2003). How's life? Combining individual and national variables to explain subjective well-being. *Economic Modeling, 20,* 331–360.

Hennig-Thurau, T., Groth, M., Paul, M., & Gremler, D. D. (2006). Are all smiles created equal? How emotional contagion and emotional labor affect service relationships. *Journal of Marketing, 7,* 58–73.

Hertenstein, M. J., Hansel, C. A., Butts, A. M., & Hile, S. N. (2009). Smile intensity in photographs predicts divorce later in life. *Motivation and Emotion, 33,* 99–105.

Hofmann, S. G., Grossman, P., & Hinton, D. E. (2011). Loving-kindness and compassion meditation: Potential for psychological interventions. *Clinical Psychology Review, 31*(7), 1126–1132.

Howell, R. T., Kern, M. L., & Lyubomirsky, S. (2007). Health benefits: Meta-analytically determining the impact of well-being on objective health outcomes. *Health Psychology Review, 1,* 83–136.

Ifcher, J., & Zarghamee, H. (2011). Happiness and time preference: The effect of positive affect in a random-assignment experiment. *American Economic Review, 101,* 3109–3129.

Isen, A. M., & Reeve, J. (2005). The influence of positive affect on intrinsic and extrinsic motivation: Facilitating enjoyment of play, responsible work behavior, and self-control. *Motivation and Emotion, 29,* 295–323.

Jebb, A. T., Tay, L., Diener, E., & Oishi, S. (2018). Happiness, income satiation and turning points around the world. *Nature Human Behavior, 2,* 33–38.

Jovanovic, V., & Brdaric, D. (2012). Did curiosity kill the cat? Evidence from subjective well-being in adolescents. *Personality and Individual Differences, 52,* 380–384.

Kahneman, D. (1999). Objective happiness. In D. Kahneman, E. Diener, & N. Schwarz (Eds.), *Well-being: The foundations of hedonic psychology* (pp. 3–25). New York: Russell Sage Foundation.

Kahneman, D., & Deaton, A. (2010). High income improves evaluation of life but not emotional well-being. *Proceedings of the National Academy of Sciences of the United States of American, 107,* 16489–16493.

Kansky, J. (2018). What's love got to do with it? Romantic relationships and well-being. In E. Diener, S. Oishi, & L. Tay (Eds.), *Handbook of well-being.* Salt Lake City, UT: DEF Publishers.

Kansky, J., Allen, J. P., & Diener, E. (2016). Early adolescent affect predicts later life outcomes. *Applied Psychology: Health and Well Being, 8,* 192–212.

Kansky, J., & Diener, E. (2017). Benefits of well-being: Health, social relationships, work, and resilience. *Journal of Positive Psychology and Wellbeing, 1*(2), 129–169.

Kassel, J. D., Stroud, L. R., & Paronis, C. A. (2003). Smoking, stress, and negative affect: Correlation, causation, and context across stages of smoking. *Psychological Bulletin, 129,* 270–304.

Keltner, D., & Haidt, J. (2001). Social functions of emotions. In T. Mayne & G. Bonanno (Eds.), *Emotions: Current issues and future directions* (pp. 192–213). New York: Guilford Press.

Keltner, D., & Kring, A. M. (1998). Emotion, social function, and psychopathology. *Review of General Psychology, 2,* 320–342.

Kendler, K. S., Kuhn, J. W., Vittum, J., Prescott, C. A., & Riley, B. (2005). The interaction of stressful life events and a serotonin transporter polymorphism in the prediction of episodes of major depression: A replication. *Archives of General Psychiatry, 62,* 529–535.

Kim, E. S., Kubzansky, L. D., Soo, J., & Boehm, J. K. (2016). Maintaining healthy behavior: A prospective study of psychological well-being and physi-

cal activity. *Annals of Behavioral Medicine, 51*(3), 337–347.

Kim, E. S., Park, N., & Peterson, C. (2011). Dispositional optimism protects older adults from stroke: The health and retirement study. *Stroke, 42,* 2855–2859.

Kraft, T. L., & Pressman, S. D. (2012). Grin and bear it: The influence of manipulated facial expression on the stress response. *Psychological Science, 23,* 1372–1378.

Kraiger, K., Billings, R. S., & Isen, A. M. (1989). The influence of positive affective states on task perceptions and satisfaction. *Organizational Behavior and Human Decision Processes, 44,* 12–25.

Lambert, L., Moliver, N., & Thompson, D. (2015). Happiness intervention decreases pain and depression, boosts happiness among primary care patients. *Primary Health Care Research and Development, 16*(2), 114–126.

Lambert, L., Passmore, H. A., & Joshanloo, M. (2019). A positive psychology intervention program in a culturally diverse university: Boosting happiness and reducing fear. *Journal of Happiness Studies, 20,* 1141–1162.

Lambert, L., Passmore, H. A., Scull, N., Al Sabah, I., & Hussain, R. (2019). Wellbeing matters in Kuwait: The Alnowair's Bareec education initiative. *Social Indicators Research, 143,* 741–763.

Leitzel, J. D. (2000). *A confirmatory factor analytic investigation of the tripartite model of depression and anxiety in high school adolescents* (Doctoral dissertation number AA19976359, Dissertation Abstracts International, 2000-95024-186).

Lepore, S. J., Fernandez-Berrocal, P., Ragan, J., & Ramos, N. (2004). It's not that bad: Social challenges to emotional disclosure enhance adjustment to stress. *Anxiety, Stress & Coping, 17*(4), 341–361.

Lerner, J. S., Li, Y., & Weber, E. U. (2013). The financial costs of sadness. *Psychological Science, 24,* 72–79.

Li, F., Bai, X., & Wang, Y. (2013). The scale of positive and negative experience (SPANE): Psychometric properties and normative data in a large Chinese sample. *PloS One, 8*(4), Article e61137.

Love, A. B., & Holder, M. D. (2015). Can romantic relationship quality mediate the relation between psychopathy and subjective well-being? *Journal of Happiness Studies, 17,* 2407–2429.

Lucas, R. E. (2007). Long-term disability is associated with lasting changes in subjective well-being: Evidence from two nationally representative longitudinal studies. *Journal of Personality and Social Psychology, 92,* 717–730.

Lucas, R. E., Clark, A. E., Georgellis, Y., & Diener, E. (2004). Unemployment alters the set-point for life satisfaction. *Psychological Science, 15*(1), 8–13.

Lucas, R. E., & Diener, E. (2000). Personality and subjective well-being across the life span. In D. L. Molfese & V. J. Molfese (Eds.), *Temperament and personality development across the life span* (pp. 211–234). Hillsdale, NJ: Lawrence Erlbaum.

Lucas, R. E., & Diener, E. (2001). Understanding extraverts' enjoyment of social situations: The importance of pleasantness. *Journal of Personality and Social Psychology, 81*(2), 343–356.

Lucas, R. E., Diener, E., Grob, A., Suh, E. M., & Shao, L. (2000). Cross-cultural evidence for the fundamental features of extraversion. *Journal of Personality and Social Psychology, 79,* 452–468.

Lucas, R. E., Diener, E., & Suh, E. M. (1996). Discriminant validity of subjective well-being measures. *Journal of Personality and Social Psychology, 71,* 616–628.

Lucas, R. E., & Fujita, F. (2000). Factors influencing the relation between extraversion and pleasant affect. *Journal of Personality and Social Psychology, 79,* 1039–1056.

Lucas, R. E., Le, K., & Dyrenforth, P. S. (2008). Explaining the extraversion positive affect relation: Sociability cannot account for extraverts' greater happiness. *Journal of Personality, 76,* 385–414.

Luhmann, M., Lucas, R. E., Eid, M., & Diener, E. (2013). The prospective effect of life satisfaction on life events. *Social Psychological and Personality Science, 4*(1), 39–45.

Lutes, L. D., Wirtz, D., White, C., Ciszeski, S., Leitner, D., Kanippayoor, J. M., . . . Diener, E. (2018). Increased well-being following a group-based happiness intervention (ENHANCE): 6-month outcomes from a randomized controlled trial.

Lutes, L., Wirtz, D., White, C., Ciszewski, S., Leitner, D., Kanippayoor, J. M., . . . Diener, E. (2019). Is it time for behavioral medicine to start focusing on subjective well-being and happiness? 6-month outcomes from ENHANCE. Society of Behavioral Medicine, Washington, DC (March 6–9).

Lykken, D., & Tellegen, A. (1996). Happiness is a stochastic phenomenon. *Psychological Science, 7*(3), 186–189.

Lyubomirsky, S. (2001). Why are some people happier than others? The role of cognitive and motivational processes in well-being. *American Psychologist, 56*(3), 239–249.

Lyubomirsky, S., Dickerhoof, R., Boehm, J. K., & Sheldon, K. M. (2011). Becoming happier takes both a will and a proper way: Two experimental longitudinal interventions to boost well-being. *Emotion, 11,* 391–402.

Lyubomirsky, S., King, L., & Diener, E. (2005). The benefits of frequent positive affect: Does happiness lead to success? *Psychological Bulletin, 131,* 803–855.

Malouff, J. M., & Schutte, N. S. (2016). Can psychological interventions increase optimism? A meta-analysis. *Journal of Positive Psychology, 12*(6), 594–604.

Maslow, A. H. (1943). A theory of human motivation. *Psychological Review, 50*(4), 370–396.

McKee-Ryan, F., Song, Z., Wanberg, C. R., & Kinicki, A. J. (2005). Psychological and physical well-being during unemployment: A meta-analytic study. *Journal of Applied Psychology, 90*(1), 53–76.

Mehl, M. R., Vazire, S., Holleran, S. E., & Clark, C. S. (2010). Eavesdropping on happiness: Well-being is related to having less small talk and more substantive conversations. *Psychological Science, 21,* 539–541.

Murakami, F., Shimomura, T., Kotani, K., Ikawa, S., Nanba, E., & Adachi, K. (1999). Anxiety traits associated with a polymorphism in the serotonin transporter gene regulatory region. *Journal of Human Genetics, 44*(1), 15–17.

Myers, D. (2000). The funds, friends and faith of happy people. *American Psychologist, 55,* 56–67.

Nederhof, A. J. (1985). Methods of coping with social desirability bias: A review. *European Journal of Social Psychology, 15*(3), 263–280.

Nelson, D. W. (2009). Feeling good and open-minded: The impact of positive affect on cross cultural empathic responding. *Journal of Positive Psychology, 4,* 53–63.

Oishi, A., Diener, E., & Lucas, R. E. (2007). The optimum level of well-being: Can people be too happy? *Perspectives on Psychological Science, 2,* 346–360.

Oishi, S., Kesebir, S., & Diener, E. (2011). Income inequality and happiness. *Psychological Science, 22*(9), 1095–1100.

Ostir, G. V., Berges, I. M., Markides, K. S., & Ottenbacher, K. J. (2006). Hypertension in older adults and the role of positive emotions. *Psychosomatic Medicine, 68,* 727–733.

Otake, K., Shimai, S., Tanaka-Matsumi, J., Otsui, K., & Fredrickson, B. L. (2006). Happy people become happier through kindness: A counting kindness intervention. *Journal of Happiness Studies, 131,* 925–971.

Park, K. B., Upshaw, H. S., & Koh, S. D. (1988). East Asians' responses to Western health items. *Journal of Cross-Cultural Psychology, 19*(1), 51–64.

Pavot, W., & Diener, E. (1993). The affective and cognitive context of self-reported measures of subjective well-being. *Social Indicator Research, 28*(1), 1–20.

Pavot, W., Diener, E. D., Colvin, C. R., & Sandvik, E. (1991). Further validation of the satisfaction with life scale: Evidence for the cross-method convergence of well-being measures. *Journal of Personality Assessment, 57*(1), 149–161.

Pennebaker, J. W. (1997). Writing about emotional experiences as a therapeutic process. *Psychological Science, 8*(3), 162–166.

Peterson, S. J., Luthans, F., Avolio, B. J., Walumbwa, F. O., & Zhang, Z. (2011). Psychological capital and employee performance: A latent growth modeling approach. *Personnel Psychology, 64,* 427–450.

Pressman, S. D., & Cohen, S. (2005). Does positive affect influence health? *Psychological Bulletin, 131,* 925–971.

Pressman, S. D., & Cohen, S. (2007). The use of social words in autobiographies and longevity. *Psychosomatic Medicine, 69,* 262–269.

Pressman, S. D., & Cohen, S. (2012). Positive emotion words and longevity in famous deceased psychologists. *Health Psychology, 31,* 297–305.

Pressman, S. D., Gallagher, M. W., & Lopez, S. J. (2013). Is the emotion-health connection a "first-world problem"? *Psychological Science, 24,* 544–549.

Proulx, C. M., Helms, H. M., & Buehler, C. (2007). Marital quality and personal well-being: A meta-analysis. *Journal of Marriage and Family, 69,* 576–593.

Reis, H. T., & Gable, S. L. (2000). Event-sampling and other methods for studying everyday experience. In H. T. Reis & C. M. Judd (Eds.), *Handbook of research methods in social and personality psychology* (pp. 190–222). Cambridge: Cambridge University Press.

Rowe, G., Hirsh, J. B., & Anderson, A. K. (2007). Positive affect increases the breadth of attentional selection. *Proceedings of the National Academy of Sciences, 104,* 383–388.

Røysamb, E., & Nes, R. B. (2018). The genetics of wellbeing. In E. Diener, S. Oishi, & L. Tay (Eds.), *Handbook of well-being.* Salt Lake City, UT: DEF Publishers.

Rutledge, R. B., Skandali, N., Dayan, P., & Dolan, R. J. (2014). A computational and neural model of momentary subjective well-being. *Proceedings of the National Academy of Sciences of the United States of America, 111,* 12252–12257.

Ryff, C. D., Singer, B. H., & Dienberg Love, G. (2004). Positive health: Connecting well-being with biology. *Philosophical Transactions of the Royal Society B: Biological Sciences, 359*(1449), 1383–1394.

Schmitz, T. W., De Rosa, E., & Anderson, A. K. (2009). Opposing influences of affective state valence on visual cortical encoding. *Journal of Neuroscience, 29,* 7199–7207.

Schwarz, N., & Strack, F. (1991). Context effects in attitude surveys: Applying cognitive theory to social research. *European Review of Social Psychology, 2*(1), 31–50.

Seder, J. P., & Oishi, S. (2012). Intensity of smiling in Facebook photos predicts future life satisfaction. *Social Psychological and Personality Science, 3,* 407–413.

Seligman, M. E. P., Rashid, T., & Parks, A. C. (2006). Positive psychotherapy. *American Psychologist, 61,* 774–788.

Seligman, M. E. P., Steen, T. A., Park, N., & Peterson, C. (2005). Positive psychology progress: Empirical validation of interventions. *American Psychologist, 60,* 410–421.

Simons, T. L., & Peterson, R. S. (2000). Task conflict and relationship conflict in top management teams: The pivotal role of intragroup trust. *Journal of Applied Psychology, 85,* 102–111.

Sin, N. L., & Lyubomirsky, S. (2009). Enhancing well-being and alleviating depressive symptoms with positive psychology interventions: A practice-friendly meta-analysis. *Journal of Clinical Psychology, 65,* 467–487.

Staw, B. M., Sutton, R. I., & Pelled, L. H. (1994). Employee positive emotion and favorable outcomes at the workplace. *Organization Science, 5,* 51–71.

Stephens, J. P., Heaphy, E. D., Carmeli, A., Spreitzer, G. M., & Dutton, J. E. (2013). Relationship quality and virtuousness: Emotional carrying capacity as a source of individual and team resilience. *Journal of Applied Behavioral Science, 49,* 13–41.

Steptoe, A., Dockray, S., & Wardle, J. (2009). Positive affect and psychobiological processes relevant to health. *Journal of Personality, 77,* 1747–1776.

Steptoe, A., O'Donnell, K., Marmot, M., & Wardle, J. (2008). Positive affect, psychological well-being and good sleep. *Journal of Psychosomatic Research, 64,* 409–415.

Steptoe, A., Wardle, J., & Marmot, M. (2005). Positive affect and health-related neuroendocrine, cardiovascular, and inflammatory processes. *Proceedings of the National Academy of Sciences, USA, 102,* 6508–6512.

Stone, A. A., Shiffman, S. S., & DeVries, M. W. (1999). Ecological momentary assessment. In D. Kahneman, E. Diener, & N. Schwarz (Eds.), *Well-being: The foundation of hedonic psychology* (pp. 26–39). New York: Sage.

Stone, B. M., & Parks, A. C. (2018). Cultivating subjective well-being through positive psychological interventions. In E. Diener, S. Oishi, & L. Tay (Eds.), *Handbook of well-being.* Salt Lake City, UT: DEF Publishers.

Stoverink, A. C., Umphress, E. E., Gardner, R. G., & Miner, K. N. (2014). Misery loves company: Team dissonance and the influence of supervisor-focused interpersonal justice climate on team cohesiveness. *Journal of Applied Psychology, 99,* 1059–1073.

Stutzer, A., & Frey, B. (2006). Does marriage make people happy, or do happy people get married? *Journal of Behavioral and Experimental Economics, 35,* 326–347.

Su, R., Tay, L., & Diener, E. (2014). The development and validation of comprehensive inventory of thriving (CIT) and brief inventory of thriving (BIT). *Applied Psychology: Health and Well-Being, 6*(3), 251–279.

Tay, L., & Diener, E. (2011). Needs and subjective well-being. *Journal of Personality and Social Psychology, 101,* 354–365.

Tenney, E. R., Poole, J. M., & Diener, E. (2016). Does positivity enhance work performance? Why, when, and what we don't know. *Research in Organizational Behavior, 36,* 27–46.

Tepper, B. J. (2000). Consequences of abusive supervision. *Academy of Management Journal, 43,* 178–190.

Thomas, L. E., & Chambers, K. O. (1989). Phenomenology of life satisfaction among elderly men: Qualitative and quantitative views. *Psychology and Aging, 4,* 284–289.

To, M. L., Fisher, C. D., Ashkanasy, N. M., & Rowe, P. A. (2012). Within-person relationships between mood and creativity. *Journal of Applied Psychology, 97,* 599–612.

Uchino, B. N., Bowen, K., & Kent, R. (2016). Social support and mental health. In H. Friedman & K. Fingerman (Eds.), *Encyclopedia of mental health* (2nd ed., pp. 189–195). Oxford: Elsevier.

Weber, S. J., & Cook, T. D. (1972). Subjects effects in laboratory research: An examination of subject roles, demand characteristics, and valid inference. *Psychological Bulletin, 77,* 273–295.

Weiser, E. B. (2012). Associations between positive and negative affect and 12-month physical disorders in a national sample. *Journal of Clinical Psychology in Medical Settings, 19,* 197–210.

Weiss, L. A., Westerhof, G. J., & Bohlmeijer, E. T. (2016). Can we increase psychological well-being? The effects of interventions on psychological well-being: A meta-analysis of randomized controlled trials. *Plos One, 11*(6), Article e0158092.

Whelan, D. C., & Zelenski, J. M. (2012). Experimental evidence that positive moods cause sociability. *Social Psychological and Personality Science, 3,* 430–437.

Wilson, T. D., & Gilbert, D. T. (2005). Affective forecasting: Knowing what to want. *Current Directions in Psychological Science, 14*(3), 131–134.

5

# Positive Psychology: Coaching Leadership Tensions

Ilona Boniwell and Wendy-Ann Smith

## Introduction

Leaders nowadays must live their business lives facing volatile, uncertain, complex, and ambiguous market conditions, often summarized as VUCA environment (Horney, Passmore, & O'Shea, 2010). They are required to be highly agile in order to assimilate, manage, and develop information from global markets, economies, media, shareholders, suppliers, employees, peers, superiors, and other stakeholders. As before, leaders are faced with the need to achieve ambitious business results, yet are engaged in new forms of relationships that are complex, global, and very often virtual. With hierarchical structures breaking down, and Generation Y arriving to the workplace, containing, managing, and leveraging so many different elements effectively, call for a different mindset, as well as new skills and competencies to generate the collective energy and engagement toward a demanding goal.

Leadership has been shown to be a key factor in worker engagement (Shuck & Herd, 2012). Teams led by leaders who focus on strengths, giving frequent recognition, encouragement, and maintaining a positive perspective are more engaged and have higher project performance (Arakawa & Greenberg, 2007). A review of studies on the relationship between leadership and employee engagement concluded that transformational, authentic, ethical, and charismatic leadership styles all have a positive relationship with employee engagement at an individual level (Carasco-Saul, Kim, & Kim, 2014). Furthermore, in a Gallup survey employee engagement was found to be increased when corporate goals are well communicated, and goals are aligned to corporate vision at all levels of the organization. Additionally, employees experience a sense of autonomy and accountability to

*Positive Psychology: An International Perspective*, First Edition.
Edited by Aleksandra Kostić and Derek Chadee.
© 2021 John Wiley & Sons Ltd. Published 2021 by John Wiley & Sons Ltd.

achieve their workplace goals when they are aligned with corporate goals (Amabile & Kramer, 2012).

We prefer to broadly describe the mindset that responds to complex political and economic demands with novel strategies adapted to the changing world as *positive leadership*. Facing the challenges of global competition, mechanistic approaches to development of organizations have their limitations. To overcome these limitations, organizations must identify and nurture new sources of creativity, autonomy, and initiative in their teams. This can be achieved by placing the human being at the center of the value creation process, so that companies can hope to regain room for maneuver and reduce pressure on their employees. Positive leadership can be defined as *the ability to mobilize, facilitate and develop a community of exceptional performers, using individual strengths, positive emotions, motivation, and vision as drivers.* Importantly, we do not necessarily view positive leadership as a distinct leadership style, but rather as an umbrella construct encompassing several leadership styles with similar characteristics.

*Positive psychology,* or otherwise called the science of flourishing, is a discipline that has challenged the field of human sciences to reconsider the positive aspects of life. Instead of drawing on a "disease model," it encourages empirical research into factors that enable individuals and communities to thrive and focus on finding the best in oneself. Areas of study include well-being and its determinants, neuropsychological bases of positive emotions, resilience, creativity, economics of happiness, and positive institutions. The basic premise of positive psychology is that human flourishing cannot be achieved simply through curing pathology and eliminating behavioral and emotional problems, but requires building and capitalizing on strengths and capacities. Since its creation in 1998, the field has grown dramatically, judging by the research output, widespread popularity, and recognition by business, educational, and governmental institutions.

*Positive organizational scholarship* investigates positive deviance, or the ways in which organizations and their members flourish and prosper in especially favorable ways. Positive refers to an affirmative bias focused on the elevating processes and dynamics in organizations. Organizational refers to the processes and conditions that occur in and through organizations, especially taking into account the context in which positive phenomena occur. Scholarship refers to the scientific, theoretically based, and rigorous investigation of positive phenomena (Cameron, Bright, & Caza, 2004).

*Positive organizational behavior* is the study and application of positively orientated human resource strengths and psychological capacities that can be measured, developed, and effectively managed for performance improvement in today's workplace (Luthans & Youssef, 2004).

*Positive leadership* is a study of what elevates individuals and organizations (in addition to what challenges them), what goes right in organizations (in addition to what goes wrong), what is life-giving (in addition to what is problematic or life-depleting), what is experienced as good (in addition to what is objectionable), what is extraordinary (in addition to what is merely effective), and what is inspiring (in addition to what is difficult or arduous) (Cameron, 2008a).

Inclusive leadership is defined by Moss, Sims, Dodds, and David (2016) as a dynamic blend of transformational and servant leadership. They describe an inclusive leader as "someone who is aware of their own biases and preferences; actively seeks out and considers different views and perspectives to inform better decision-making; sees diverse talent as a source of competitive advantage; and inspires diverse people to drive organizational and individual performance towards a shared vision."

## Workplace Coaching

Coaching in the workplace has been in practice for at least the past 30 years, under various professional guises, such as mentoring, training, and coaching, moreover coaching in the workplace has predominantly focused on coaching at the top end of the organization as "executive coaching." However, the tensions experienced by leaders impact the workplace as a whole at all levels, hence it can be argued "workplace coaching" be the term and practice a more widely accepted and practiced stance of leaders with their teams.

Grant (2001) defines workplace coaching as "a solution-focused, result-orientated systematic process in which the coach facilitates the enhancement of work performance and the self-directed learning and personal growth of the coachee" (p. 8) to more effectively "regulate and direct their interpersonal and intrapersonal resources to better attain their goals" (Grant, 2006, p. 153), and cooperatively work to elucidate common values and goals among the competing organizational forces. Having found common ground through the processes of workplace coaching, it is argued increased engagement, decreasing the negative impact of leadership and organizational tensions will result.

Positive psychology coaching for the workplace (PPCW) is the blend of positive psychology theory and practices grounded in evidence-based coaching with a focus on all internal and external organizational stakeholders. PPCW "has the potential to enable the best of human functioning to be present and active at both the individual level and within teams" (Boniwell & Smith, 2018, p. 161).

## Leadership Tensions

How can one, as a coach, help their coachee in the position of responsibility lead an effective team in which engagement, meaning, and tangible results outweigh the stress of conflicting values, goals, motives, and emotional states? How do we enable this leader to confidently understand and deploy their strengths and their potential for innovation, and these of others? How to support them in achieving tangible positive results and enabling well-being in their employees?

The capacity to mobilize, facilitate, and develop a community of exceptional performers using positive drivers may be achieved with ease, or at least we would like to imagine so. More frequently, however, it is a struggle – sometimes at a cost to the leader's psychological state. Yet, the very fact that it is a struggle may also be the sign of a leader working toward a positive leadership sphere.

Robert Quinn, one of the fathers of positive organizational scholarship talks of positive leadership as a capacity to hold and integrate contrasting or paradoxical tensions of two positive opposites, such as change and stability, for example, or growth focus and cost control (Quinn, 2015). His approach is informed by the competing values framework (CVF), one of the most influential and extensively researched models in the area of organizational culture research (Cameron & Quinn, 2011). In our own research, four such tensions have been identified as characteristics of positive leadership: (1) happiness versus performance, (2) openness to emotions versus emotion management, (3) vision clarifying versus alignment, and (4) humility versus audacity (Boniwell, in preparation). This chapter is organized around these principle tensions of positive leadership. The presentation of each of the tensions will involve some limited theoretical underpinnings, leadership citations offering illustrations, and tangible coaching tools and questions enabling progression within each of the four tensions.

## (1) Coaching for Happiness at Work: Well-Being and Performance

If you are an employee, chances are that you already believe that well-being at work is important, even without considering the evidence. According to a recent French report, 67% of workers consider well-being imperative, in comparison to a significantly smaller number of HR managers (55%). When it comes to business leaders, the number drops still – this time down to 32% (Hirigoyen, 2008). We may be surprised to discover such discrepancy between the numbers, but what are the possible explanations behind them? Is this because the leaders are too far removed from the reality of employees' life and work to understand? Or can this finding be explained by the awareness of the tension between the necessity of both well-being and performance?

Mike is a recently retired vice-chancellor of Anglia Ruskin University, the third largest university in the United Kingdom with over 35,000 students. Even though to an innocent reader, running the university may not be quite akin to running a business, the annual turnover figure of 170 million put this doubt into perspective. Mike puts it this way:

> I think any leader; you have a tension, don't you? Because you have to take as much out of people as you humanly can in a context where, whatever line of work you're in, you'll never have enough resources to go around. So you are probably going to be asking people to do more than is reasonable. To give more commitment than it is reasonable. So you've got to get people working as hard as they possibly can and

sometimes economics means you have to ask for even more. So the more rewarding people find the workplace, then the more they will contribute to it. That for me is about the quality of ideas and feeling you are a part of something which is exiting, vibrant, going places that you're proud, that you have a stake there. I think well-being is so important.

Studies in positive psychology have provided ample evidence that frequent positive affect and subjective well-being lead to several outcomes indirectly associated with performance, such as generating better and more creative ideas, interacting better with colleagues and bosses, receiving more help and support, enjoying better health, and taking less sick days (Lyubomirsky, King, & Diener, 2005). Many of the companies on the Fortune 500's list have already prioritized well-being investments. We have all heard about Googleplex with its array of healthy restaurants open 24 hours per day, offering massages, haircuts, medical services, sport centers, heated toilet seats, and foreign language courses (all free of charge). Facebook is not far behind with its provision of dry cleaning and hairdresser services, free candy shops and dentists, US$4,000 in cash for new parents, and childcare reimbursements.

Yet, not all leaders are the decision makers when it comes to well-being investments comparable to those of banks or high-tech companies. The tension between getting people to perform and getting them to feel well in their work or personal life may rise to the surface, either implicitly or explicitly. Some of the possible coaching questions to start exploring the issue may first center on the client's own representation of happiness/well-being, before proceeding to examining the tension itself.

How do you define happiness?
What is happiness for you?
What makes you happy? How do you know?
When you are happiest, who are you with?
How important does it feel for you to be happier?
How important is happiness for your own performance?
What comes to your mind if you are asked to compare two questions; "How can I get the most out of my people?" with "How can I get people to perform at their best?"

With regard to the last question, we can note subtle but significant differences. The first question brings up images of sucking every last drop of energy out of employees, while the second results in an energy-producing work environment where employees want to do their very best and will go that extra mile to accomplish their work.

If the client is willing to explore the question further, a coach may propose the *integrated well-being dashboard* exercise, building up a composite picture of their current happiness/well-being (Boniwell, 2016). The integrated well-being dashboard has been designed to give the user a brief overview of their well-being using well-established, scientifically validated one or multiple-items indicators presented in an easy-to-grasp, visually appealing manner (sample questions below).

If life was a ladder, on which of the stairs would you position yourself?

What is your current level of satisfaction concerning your health, work, and relationships?

How would you rate your current level of positive emotions? Negative emotions?

What is your current energy level?

Taking everything into consideration, do you view the activities of your life as truly chosen by yourself?

Importantly, the dashboard is only ever a conversation springboard:

What indicator appears as particularly relevant/important for you today?

What other questions would you ask to get a snapshot picture of your happiness?

If you were to design your own dashboard, to capture your daily states the way that *you* see them, what indicators would you include?

Among multiple interventions that can be used to promote well-being in the workplace, simple physical and relational actions may be quite impactful. *Relatively inexpensive benefits* that have a substantial impact on happiness and engagement may range from a high-end espresso machine, snacks in the fridge, and delivered homemade meals to complementary passes to a nearby gym. Nike workers now have access to nap-friendly *quiet rooms* that can also be used for meditation. Google, a forerunner in employee perks, has a number of futuristic napping pods scattered throughout its campus, and NASA as expected is at the forefront of design with their *napping pods*. Even if investing in a napping pod may not suit everyone's budget, encouraging power naps on any chair can positively affect the well-being and personal performance of employees.

One simple way to build relational well-being is to offer *free lunch* once in a while (weekly or monthly). A catered meal for all employees is not a dramatic expense, but it encourages people to spend time together and exchange in an informal atmosphere. Keeping a *table of birthdays* of all company employees and inviting the head manager or director to wish happy birthday on the day allows everyone to feel recognized and valued as an individual within the company. Depending on the size of the structure, it may be possible to organize money pots (per team or service) to buy a little present.

## (2) Coaching for Emotions at Work: Going to, Going through

Emotional awareness and experience of self and others are imperative to leadership to help forge real, empathic, and flourishing relationships, and additionally to aid commitment and engagement to the organizational and leadership vision.

Emotions  are a driving force, however, left unchecked they also have the ability to overwhelm, dent confidence in decision-making, and negatively affect the overall emotional sphere of a team. This is why this tension revolves around being open to emotional information on the one hand (going to the emotion) and, on the other hand, being able to deal with the emotion when and where necessary (going through).

The starting point to developing a constructive relationship with emotions is to understand that these are data and they provide important information about ourselves, the way we feel *and* think, and about others. Emotions are not good or bad per se, it is just information. The emotional centers of the brain are designed to scan our environment and react based on perceptions and past experiences, usually without conscious thought. Their primary function is to mobilize us to deal quickly with important interpersonal or threatening events. These emotions give us early warning signs to pay attention and respond quickly. Our cognitive systems then make sense of the situation and, if necessary, we adjust our behavior. This is why emotions play a far greater role in determining business outcomes than many professionals think. In a study of 358 managers at Johnson & Johnson, researchers found that the managers who demonstrated the highest performance had significantly more emotional competences (Cavallo & Brienza, 2001).

Emotional Intelligence, or EQ as commonly known, is the capacity to recognize and manage our emotions and those of others. Salovey, Caruso, and Mayer's (2004) EQ model postulates four major branches or facets to the emotional intelligence concept: perceiving, understanding, using, and managing emotions. These branches can serve as a helpful framework for considering major tools and questions in coaching leaders.

## Perceiving emotions

Awareness of and knowledge of their own emotional states and triggers as well as their teams are integral to regulation of emotions, therein impacting one's leadership thought repertoires and behaviors. Deliberately focusing attention, mindfully, to become more aware of the current emotional climate of one's team and one's own emotional reactions helps the development of this ability. Additionally, *mood apps* such as Niko Niko are a valuable tool, to help build awareness and track mood according to activity. Coaching questions may include:

What is happiness to you? What happens when you are happy?
What is sadness/unhappiness for you? What happens when you are sad/
  unhappy?
What was your emotional reaction?
How did you feel?
What are your thoughts about this emotion?
What have you learned from this experience of this emotion?
What are you experiencing right now?
What do you think your colleague felt?
How do you think the team might be feeling about this?

## Understanding emotions

Stress and anxiety are commonplace issues that many of us will face at some point in our lifetime; but denial of these conditions is still widespread, particularly in the workplace. For example, a recent British survey found that 42% of workers felt that work stress and anxiety was regarded as a sign of weakness, meaning that they go unrecognized, undiagnosed, and untreated. Yet, accepted or not, depression, anxiety, and other mental health problems are hard to ignore, especially as many of these underlie both absenteeism and presenteeism. According to the Organisation for Economic Co-operation and Development (OECD), the total cost of mental health problems to businesses is estimated at nearly €80 billion each year. In addition to that, stress is responsible for 40% of all work-related illnesses.

The capacity to understand one's emotional reactions and trace these back to the underlying causes, as well as being able to predict the eventual consequences, is important in analyzing emotional climate, emotional pressures, and psychosocial difficulties. Acknowledging the "whole" person through concern for other areas of life that are not work related, for example, enquiring about an employee's spouse, children, and/or parents, as well as their nonwork time helps the leader to develop a more complete understanding of the individual. Including an emotional culture component to the development of the vision is likely to result in a "sticky" vision that is accepted emotionally, intellectually, and to increase motivation.

> What emotion are you experiencing now? To what event or thought is this emotion related?
> What could have led to this change in feeling?
> What is the emotion telling you?
> What are the likely consequences of such an emotional state?
> How can you help your competitor to save face so that you negotiate the best possible deal for the company? (this is an example of a contextual question)

## Using emotions to facilitate thinking

Try walking into a room happy, smiling, making eye contact; what is the response? Then try walking into another room tense, hurried with no eye contact, what is the response? How are your colleagues likely to be feeling *and* thinking as a result of exposure to your mood? You will have spread your mood to those you interacted with through your behavior and subsequent neurological changes, a phenomenon known as emotional contagion (Barsade, 2002).

Positive *and* negative emotions affect our thinking and behavior in different ways. The work of Barbara Fredrickson and others, has shown that positive emotions "open our hearts and minds, making us more receptive and more creative" (Fredrickson, 2009, p. 21). Kashdan and Biswas-Diener (2014) speak of the whole emotional self, and the potential that all emotions, whether positive or negative, have a beneficial function. With awareness and support, negative emotions such as anger, sadness, shame, guilt, and so on, can be used toward a positive outcome, for example, anger can fuel creative problem solving:

> How does your mood influence your thinking right now?
> How does your employee's mood influence their thinking right now?
> Is the way you are feeling about this situation helping you to manage it and to move forward?
> What feeling and thoughts would serve you better?
> Based on our discussion about the feelings involved here, how might these be affecting your team's attitude?

## Managing emotions

As already mentioned, emotions are contagious, especially if one is a leader. Managing a positive emotional tone by exercising, getting enough sleep, taking time to emotionally disconnect, listening to relaxing music, or practicing mindfulness won't just sustain your client's own psychological health, but would also help them to get the most out of their team (Boniwell, 2012; Lewis, 2011; Salovey et al., 2004):

> What mood would you like your team to have during XY scenario?
> What can you do to achieve this outcome?
> What stress reduction activity could you try right now?
> Rating emotional intensity pre- and postintervention using a Likert scale of 0–10.
> What is the difference from your first rating? Have you noticed anything different in yourself? What are these differences?
> How is this learning useful to you?
> How can you help your team to manage this disappointment?

*Expressing gratitude,* either by letter, email, or telling someone how much you appreciate them, and why, focusing on the behavior only, is one of the ways to manage emotions. Gratitude is "useful when two parties have had a falling out. It's a way of realigning emotions and thinking to the positive, healthy spectrum after negative emotions are expressed" (Fredrickson, 2009; Moss et al., 2016; Van Nieuwerburgh, 2014, p. 105).

After working through the four-quadrant EQ model above, you could also explore the interactions between your client's emotions and their strengths:

> What virtuous strength/s have been prominent in the past when experiencing this emotion in a similar situation (label it – e.g., anger, guilt, sadness)?
> What was the outcome – negative or positive?
> Looking to virtuous strengths (as detailed in Vision Alignment below), what strength was used?

Was this the most appropriate strength for the best outcome? Could you recapture and identify the emotion experienced when utilizing the identified strength and plan a course of action using this strength or use the identified appropriate strength for the current scenario?

## (3) Coaching for Vision at Work: Clarifying and Aligning

Although the creating, communicating, and driving to completion one's vision is often seen as the capacity of positive leadership, in reality, it is often a struggle to achieve both the sharing of one's core ideology (values and core purpose) and aligning others with the leader's envisioned future. This part will focus on the clarification of one's vision, examining the reality of the lived vision in an organization and introducing tools for aligning the strengths of employees with the organizational vision.

Vision alignment in organizations and teams is the foundation for striving and success. A leaders' ability to align themselves and their team to a common vision is often fraught with competing/differing values, goals, personalities, strengths, talents, and motivations hindering vision congruence. However, these differences when accepted and harnessed provide a wealth of possibility for increased creative thinking, new perspectives to problem solving, therein having the potential to increase engagement, satisfaction, and success. It is how these differences are harnessed that is the key. Moss and colleagues (2016), in their inclusive leadership model, have identified various leadership competencies such as listening, growth, and awareness, among others, that help create a culture of leadership based on virtuous strengths and values identification to acknowledge the "whole" self within a diverse structure in order to form collective transformational visions in line with the overarching organizational vision.

Values are the drivers of decisions and behaviors in all facets of life, including the workplace. An ongoing tension for a leader is to have their own values and those of their team align with the organization values and vision. Without appropriate attention to awareness, development, and implementation, values are unlikely to have a positive impact to workplace behaviors and practices and may even be detrimental to the individual and organization as a whole (Thomas, 2013).

Due to differing personal histories, personalities, and multiple other life factors, value congruence is often difficult to attain. There are numerous reports in the media of what can be, at times, devastating effects of misaligned values. For example, it could be argued that the 2005 BP oil spill was in part due to decisions by executives that were not in-line with BP's corporate values about safety, "Safety is good business. Everything we do relies upon the safety of our workforce and the communities around us. We care about the safe management of the environment. We are committed to safely delivering energy to the world" (BP, 2016). While the BP example is extreme, it highlights the importance of value alignment for the success of leaders, employees, and organizations.

Coaching for values calls for recalling key moments of success/experiences, looking for the patterns to determine the stronger more prominent values, and examining previous actions where your team members/coachees have a sense that come what may you have made decisions fully aligned with themselves. Posing the following questions will help bring your clients values to awareness and aid vision alignment:

What are you consistently drawn to and why?
What truly matters to you and does your job enables you to fulfill this?
What do both yourself and your organization gain from what you are doing?
Who are you working with and what larger tasks are you doing in a collective sense?
Where are the misalignments between your values and your organizations values/mission?
What are the similarities? What part of the end product or service do you see value alignment?

In practice, achieving alignment may be far harder than it sounds. L'Oréal, a leading affordable luxury goods partner, with a turnover in excess of €17 billion and a culturally diverse employee base of around 98,000 exemplifies positive leadership practices with the organizations vision and ethical charter being available in 65 languages for ease of accessibility for all employees worldwide. David, a deputy learning director of L'Oreal Group stated, "We want to regain agility though a higher level of cooperation. We have identified, thanks to an in-depth diagnosis, that having leaders setting a clear strategic frame as a basis for a shared vision is key for enabling alignment within teams and across functions at all levels of the organization, of course, starting with the Group ExCom."

L'Oreal have had a strong coaching culture for many years with mixed results. David explains

"A number of coaching assignments have developed over the last five years, but we haven't seen a higher level of alignment happening as a result. It has reinforced each individual capability to engage but no collective benefit with a higher level of cooperation. We are now developing more of a team coaching approach, both for intact teams and for project or ecosystem-based teams. The results in terms of collective intelligence are amazing, resulting in speed, creativity, mutual adjustment, engagement, and pleasure at work."

Strengths interventions are ways to help align organizational and leadership vision. There is mounting evidence for the strengths-based approach to leadership and team development; top performing leaders have been shown to have a strengths approach (Clifton & Harter, 2003), experience greater engagement (Rath, 2007), and an increase in collaboration and inclusiveness toward a common organizational vision (White & Waters, 2015), and a sense of "this is my calling" when engaging four or more of one's strengths (Harzer & Ruch, 2012). Additionally, it has been observed that all team members tend to naturally and autonomously assume a leadership role at various stages of a project according to their strengths when in a strengths-focus working culture (Cameron, 2008b). Labeling, identifying or, as it is commonly known, "spotting," and developing strengths engenders a positive culture of appreciation and working with greater meaning, therein increasing engagement (Biswas-Diener, 2010).

Coaching to bring awareness of one's unique combination of strengths has the potential to mediate any gaps alignment between one's authentic self, the team, and organizational vision. Some of the possible strengths tools and interventions are suggested below.

1. *Strengths cards* are an interactive tool for learning what strengths are and engaging in strengths identification. The cards provide explanations and questions for how each of the strengths might be used. A Google search will show a variety of strengths cards available for purchase (see Boniwell, 2015, as an example).

2. There are various online *assessments* to determine strengths (VIA, Strengthscope, Realize2, StrengthFinder), each offering a comprehensive report. Some are free others are paid. It is helpful to review them to determine which would suit your clients' needs best.

3. Conducting *strengths conversations* is performed by recalling scenarios where your client and their team performed particularly well, were enthusiastic (noted in tone of voice, behavior, positive mood), and highly engaged. Identify what it was that they performed well and label it. Record the strengths in a bubble chart and explore these with further questions (Biswas-Diener, 2010, p. 254):

   > Which situations bring out this strength in you?
   > Which situations block you from using this strength?
   > When might you want to tone down this strength?
   > What could you change that would give you an opportunity to use this strength more?
   > How might you use two or more of these strengths in conjunction with one another?
   > Name instances in which two strengths together produced a superior result than either alone might have?
   > How this strength is instrumental in achieving your vision?

4. Keeping strengths *visible*. Brainstorm how your client could symbolize their strengths. For example, they could create a storyboard with their strengths labeled in text or in pictures.

5. Having built a bank of knowledge of values and strengths your clients are now well placed to create their own and transformational "Everest" vision/goal (Cameron, 2013):

   > What is the highest aspiration you can achieve?
   > What colorful and inspirational language can exemplify what you believe in?

What do you care most deeply about that should be pursued?

What symbols capture the objectives you wish to attain?

What strengths will you use to achieve your Everest vision?

## (4) Coaching the Self at Work: Humility and Audacity

A recent study of more than 1,500 employees from six different countries identi-fied audacity/courage and humility as two of the four critical leadership factors for creating an environment where employees from different demographic back-grounds feel included (Prime & Salib, 2014). This tension, or should we say, an inte-gration between these two seemingly contradictory characteristics also emerged from the qualitative interviews with positive leaders (Boniwell, in preparation). Humility, modesty, openness to learning from criticism, and admitting mistakes appears to coexist with the strength of courage and audacity, such as taking per-sonal risks for the greater good, in positive leaders.

Anthony, the former headmaster of the Wellington College, and the current Vice-Chancellor of a well known university is a telling example of embracing humility:

> My model of leadership is very much that of the undefended leader. This kind of leadership comes not from the ego, but from the suspension of the ego. If we want to be, we can all be much more authentic, because the ego is only ever a personality construction. It, the ego is a contingent structure that is accumulated in a series of responses to what happens in the world, the authentic self is something that is unique to a person, it is not an intellectual construct and it can be lived to an experience from a position of stillness and so what I try and do is to lead as much as I can from this undefended, authentic place, where there is only me. This isn't something I've learned in this or that leadership or management, or went on this course or have an MBA, which I do have, it is coming out from deep inside me. The subtitle is called leading out of who you are.

Mike, whom we already met earlier in the chapter, started conducting orches-tras from the age of 18 (that's in addition to his academic career, of course).

> "There were pieces of music I wanted to do that no one else was doing and the way to do those was to get an orchestra together and wave my arms at them. So this was intellectually motivating. I wished to do the music and the only way to do it was that. For me, a weak manager will want to have people less good than themselves. Back to my orchestra, I was an amateur musician but I had professional players that were obviously, musically, much better than me. But what that allowed me to do was to do really ambitious, difficult and exciting things."

How can a selfless/modest person be audacious? How can we coach for humility or audacity as the prominent positive leadership strengths? Indeed, how can we coach for egoless-ness? The traditions of developmental, existential, and narrative coaching may offer some insights that could be potentially extended and integrated into positive psychology coaching. Bachkirova (2011) inspires us to consider some of the common coaching issues that may be addressed when coaching "beyond the ego":

1.  Helping the client to anticipate and prevent potential internal blockages to the needed changes.
2.  Challenging the client's conception of "the best" in their task of being the best they can be.
3.  Helping the client to untangle their own views on authenticity.
4.  Helping the client to explore a way of living with the existential paradoxes and dichotomies that affect their life.
5.  Challenging nontraditional ways of falling into the trap of expected leadership behaviors.
6.  Exploring client's relationship to taking courageous action.
7.  Supporting the client in their attempt at reconsidering the nature of the self.

Interventions around working with mistakes and failure and integrating these into one's own representation of personality may be helpful for this tension. For instance, the Failure CV, developed by the software development company HCL Technologies, invites leaders to list some of their biggest career blunders and mistakes, and then explain what they have learned from this experience. This intervention develops both courage/risk taking *and* humility.

Bachkirova (2011) mentions a Native Americans tradition of assimilating new knowledge or learning new skills gradually through "medicine wheels." For instance, one's attitude toward mistakes may go through different stages (see Figure 5.1).

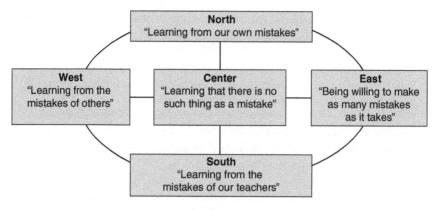

**Figure 5.1**    Varying attitudes toward mistakes.

# Conclusion

In this chapter we have examined some of the common tensions experienced by those in leadership positions, in particular, leaders whose approaches may potentially or currently fall under the broad umbrella of positive leadership. In Robert Quinn's (2015) vision of a positive organization he sees it not as a static entity, but as a system of multiple tensions. In a similar vein, we have proposed to see the task of leadership as the integration between positive opposites that could each become a negative when taken as standalone or to the extreme. Coaching for positive leadership requires helping, supporting, and challenging the client to move beyond either/or choices toward both/and dynamics, bringing together happiness *and* performance, emotional going to *and* going through, clarifying one's vision *and* aligning other with it, humility *and* audacity.

# References

Amabile, T., & Kramer, S. (2012). To give your employees meaning, start with mission. *Harvard Business Review*.

Arakawa, D., & Greenberg, M. (2007). Optimistic managers and their influence on productivity and employee engagement in a technology organization: Implications for coaching psychologists. *International Coaching Psychology Review, 2*(1), 78–89.

Bachkirova, T. (2011). *Developmental coaching: Working with the self*. Maidenhead: McGraw-Hill Education.

Barsade, S. G. (2002). The ripple effect: Emotional contagion and its influence on group behavior. *Administrative Science Quarterly, 47*(4), 644–675.

Biswas-Diener, R. (2010). *Practicing positive psychology coaching: Assessment, activities, and strategies for success*. Hoboken, NJ: Wiley.

Boniwell, I. (2012). *Positive psychology in a nutshell*. Maidenhead: Open University Press.

Boniwell, I. (2015). *The strengths cards*. Paris: Positran.

Boniwell, I. (2016). *Integrated well-being dashboard*. Paris: Positran.

Boniwell, I. (in preparation). Positive leadership through dynamic tensions: using thematic analysis to explore dilemmas of leadership experience.

Boniwell, I., & Smith, W.-A. (2018). Positive psychology coaching for positive leadership. In S. Green & S. Palmer (Eds.), *Positive psychology coaching in practice* (pp. 159–178). New York: Routledge.

BP. (2016). Our values and code of conduct. Retrieved from http://www.bp.com/en/global/corporate/who-we-are/our-values-and-code-of-conduct.html.

Cameron, K. S. (2008a). Positively deviant organizational performance and the role of leadership values. *The Journal of Values-Based Leadership, 1*(1), Article 8.

Cameron, K. (2008b). A process for changing organization culture. In T. G. Cummings (Ed.), *Handbook of organization development* (pp. 429–445). Thousand Oaks, CA: Sage.

Cameron, K. S. (2013). *Practicing positive leadership: Tools and techniques that create extraordinary results*. San Francisco, CA: Berret-Koehler.

Cameron, K. S., Bright, D., & Caza, A. (2004). Exploring the relationships between organizational virtuousness and performance. *American Behavioral Scientist, 47*(6), 766–790.

Cameron, K. S., & Quinn, R. E. (2011). *Diagnosing and changing organizational culture: Based on the competing values framework*. Hoboken, NJ: Wiley.

Carasco-Saul, M., Kim, W., & Kim, T. (2014). Leadership and employee engagement: Proposing research agendas through a review of literature. *Human Resource Development Review, 14*(1), 38–63.

Cavallo, C., & Brienza, M. A. (2001). *Emotional competence and leadership excellence at Johnson & Johnson: The emotional intelligence and leadership study*. Corporate Consulting Group.

Clifton, D. O., & Harter, J. K. (2003). Investing in strengths. In K. S. Cameron, J. E. Dutton, & R. E. Quinn (Eds.), *Positive organizational scholarship: Foundations of a new discipline* (pp 111–121). San Francisco, CA: Berrett-Koehler.

Fredrickson, B. L. (2009). *Positivity: Top-notch research reveals the 3-to-1 ratio that will change your life*. New York: Random House.

Grant, A. M. (2001). *Towards a psychology of coaching (Unpublished doctoral dissertation)*. University of Sydney, Australia.

Grant, A. (2006). An integrated goal-focused approach to executive coaching. In D. Stober & A. Grant (Eds.), *Evidence based coaching handbook: Putting best practices to work for your clients* (pp. 153–192). Hoboken, NJ: Wiley.

Harzer, C., & Ruch, W. (2012). When the job is a calling: The role of applying one's signature strengths at work. *The Journal of Positive Psychology, 7*(5), 362–371.

Hirigoyen, M. F. (2008). La souffrance au travail et les pathologies émergentes. *L'information psychiatrique, 84*(9), 821–826.

Horney, N., Pasmore, B., & O'Shea, T. (2010). Leadership agility: A business imperative for a VUCA world. *People & Strategy, 33*(4), 32–38.

Kashdan, T., & Biswas-Diener, R. (2014). *The upside of your dark side: Why being your whole self – not just your "good" self – drives success and fulfillment*. New York: Plume.

Lewis, S. (2011). *Positive psychology at work: How positive leadership and appreciative inquiry create inspiring organizations*. New York: Wiley.

Luthans, F., & Youssef, C. M. (2004). Human, social, and now positive psychological capital management: Investing in people for competitive advantage. *Organizational Dynamics, 33*(2), 143–160.

Lyubomirsky, S., King, L., & Diener, E. (2005). The benefits of frequent positive affect: Does happiness lead to success? *Psychological Bulletin, 131*(6), 803–855.

Moss, G. (2016). Inclusive leadership: A miracle cure. *Changeboard*. Retrieved from http://www.changeboard.com/content/5963/inclusive-leadership-a-miracle-cure.

Moss, G., Sims, C., Dodds, I., & David, A. (2016). Inclusive leadership: Boosting engagement, productivity and organizational diversity. *Equal Opportunities Review, 268*.

Prime, J., & Salib, E. R. (2014). *Inclusive leadership: The view from six countries*. Catalyst.

Quinn, R. E. (2015). *The positive organization: Breaking free from conventional cultures, constraints, and beliefs*. Oakland, CA: Berrett-Koehler.

Rath, T. (2007). *Strengthsfinder 2.0*. New York: Gallup Press.

Salovey, P., Caruso, D., & Mayer, J. D. (2004). Emotional intelligence in practice. In P. A. Linley & S. Joseph (Eds.), *Positive psychology in practice* (pp. 447–463). Hoboken, NJ: Wiley.

Shuck, B., & Herd, A. M. (2012). Employee engagement and leadership: Exploring the convergence of two frameworks and implications for leadership development in HRD. *Human Resource Development Review, 11*(2), 156–181.

Sims, C. (2016). *Inclusive leadership: The sign of a thriving organization*. Poster presentation at Positive Psychology Conference, Angers.

Thomas, T. P. (2013). *The effect of personal values, organizational values, and person-organization fit on ethical behaviors and organizational commitment outcomes among substance abuse counselors: A preliminary investigation (Doctoral thesis)*. University of Iowa.

Van Nieuwerburgh, C. (2014). *An introduction to coaching skills: A practical guide*. London: Sage.

White, M. A., & Waters, L. E. (2015). A case study of "The Good School": Examples of the use of Peterson's strengths-based approach with students. *Journal of Positive Psychology, 10*(1), 69–76.

# 6

# Positive Cyberpsychology: A Conceptual Framework

Jolanta Burke

The fields of positive and cyberpsychology, although largely independent from each other, have been growing exponentially in the last two decades making a substantial contribution to the social sciences research (Hart & Sasso, 2011; Smahel, Dedkova, Daneback, Walrave, & Schouten, 2019). Many of the studies carried out in cyberpsychology have been influenced by the positive psychological movement (e.g., Horwood & Anglim, 2019) and vice versa (e.g., Hughes & Burke, 2018).

Furthermore, there have been attempts to combine both fields in a form of a *positive technology* approach (Riva, Baños, Botella, Wiederhold, & Gaggioli, 2012) according to which technology can be used to foster well-being at various levels, such as emotional, engagement, or throughout connectedness. Calvo and Peters (2014) extends this collaboration of two fields into more components of well-being. As it stands, positive technology is making an impact with almost 40% of its peer-reviewed articles published in the past five years. However, a more systematic and comprehensive approach is required to align both fields, thus prompting more substantial cross-fertilization of their concepts, which this chapter advocates.

Positive psychology is "a science of positive subjective experience, positive individual traits, and positive institutions" (Seligman & Csikszentmihalyi, 2000, p. 5). It aims to examine the conditions and processes contributing to individuals', groups', and institutions' optimal human functioning (Gable & Haidt, 2005). At a meta-psychological level, it refocuses researchers on studying positive aspects of human functioning, such as well-being, hope, or optimism; at a pragmatic level, it examines the processes, which lead individuals to achieve positive aspects of functioning (Linley, Joseph, Harrington, & Wood, 2006). Therefore,

*Positive Psychology: An International Perspective*, First Edition.
Edited by Aleksandra Kostić and Derek Chadee.
© 2021 John Wiley & Sons Ltd. Published 2021 by John Wiley & Sons Ltd.

positive psychology advocates to view humans, their emotions, thoughts, behaviors, and outcomes from a positive perspective.

Cyberpsychology, however, is the study of humans' interaction with technology and, specifically, it is research on how human behavior and emotional states are affected by technologies (Kirwan & Power, 2014). It researches "the psychological processes, motivations, intentions, behavioral outcomes, and effects on both our online and offline worlds, associates with any form of technology" (Attrill, 2015, p. 2). Therefore, it is a field that examines individuals in a specific environment, that is, when interacting with technology, such as smartphones, internet, artificial intelligence, or surveillance.

Kirwan (2016a) divides the topics of cyberpsychology into three themes: (a) how humans interact with technology; (b) how to develop technology that addresses human needs and desires; and (c) how technology affects human behavior. The cyberpsychology topics most frequently applied in the context of positive psychology focus on the author's second point of developing technology that addresses human needs, specifically, developing well-being programs, which are delivered via technological vehicle, instead of face-to-face. However, there is significantly less research on the positive impact of humans interacting with technology and the way in which technology affects human behavior.

Furthermore, the third industrial revolution that saw electronics and information technology used to automate production, and the current, fourth industrial revolution which is focused on such areas as cloud and mobile computing, big data, and machine learning, or advanced robotics (Ghislieri, Molino, & Cortese, 2018), are not well represented in the research that combines positive psychology and cyberpsychology. Kirwan (2016b, 2016c) suggests other, underrepresented technologies that can be used, such as virtual reality or artificial intelligence. This is yet another reason as to why creating a field of positive cyberpsychology may prove beneficial to researchers and practitioners.

The topics in positive psychology are vast. A study that aimed to empirically map out the themes discussed in positive psychology lists such areas of research as (a) positive subjective experience, well-being, flourishing, happiness, the good life; (b) virtues, character strengths, talents; (c) interpersonal, for example, gratitude, forgiveness; (d) health; (e) meaning, self-efficacy, perceived control; (f) optimal or adaptive behavior, that is, resilience and coping; (g) religion and spirituality; (h) application of positive psychology in real world; and (i) process of becoming authentic, actualization of potential, and growth (Hart & Sasso, 2011). Another study that aimed to trace the size and breadth of positive psychology showed 233 key positive psychology terms which included such topics as autonomy, optimism, self-efficacy, engagement, self-determination, love, creativity, altruism, and many more (Rusk & Waters, 2013). Therefore, when compared to the current content of positive technology research, which is often based on the Riva et al. model (2012), the emerging field of positive cyberpsychology should offer wider-reaching research that expands beyond the well-being topics.

The view of the impact of technology on individuals is predominately pejorative (e.g., Friedman & Currall, 2003) and often overexaggerated (e.g., Gaggioli, 2014; Olweus & Limber, 2018), which is why a more balanced perspective, including both negative and positive impact of the human–technology interaction is required, hence the call for positive cyberpsychology. Positive cyberpsychology is herewith defined as the science of positive psychology in the cyberenvironment, which aims to study (a) the positive impact of technology assisting in direct improvement of individual's and group's well-being and optimal human functioning online; (b) the positive subjective experiences and impact of technology on individuals and groups; and (c) the positive subjective experiences and impact of online content on individuals and groups. With this in mind, the forthcoming sections will delve deeper into each one of the aspects of positive cyberpsychology.

## Technology in Experiencing Well-being and Optimal Human Functioning

There is an explosion of interventions delivered via technology aimed to diagnose and reduce pathologies (e.g., Neuman, 2016; Sharma, Achuth, Deb, Puthankattil, & Acharya, 2018). They are often referred to as e-health, i-health or tele-health and include both interactive and noninteractive interventions reminding participants to take their medication, or carry out other routine remedial tasks throughout the day, with a view to reduce their symptoms of ill health (Krishna, Boren, & Balas, 2009). In addition to this, more creative technologies, such as virtual reality therapies, neuroimaging for pain management, diabetes, depression, and similar pathologies (Thomas, 2014; Williams et al., 2018), are introduced to help individuals manage their ill-being. However, while these technologies often refer to "health" and "well-being," they do not always focus on enhancing well-being in the context of positive psychology.

Well-being is a concept independent from ill-being (see Burke, 2016, for a review). In a study with over 6,000 participants in the United Kingdom, 34% of them demonstrated both symptoms of mental health issues (ill-being)and well-being (Huppert & Whittington, 2003). Thus, they may coexist in an individual and contribute to their well-being differently.

There are many theories of well-being, which range from separate hedonic and eudaimonic perspectives, such as subjective well-being theory (SWB: Diener, 2000), and psychological well-being theory (PWB: Ryff & Keyes, 1995), through to more complex theories of psychological flourishing, such as the well-being theory (Seligman, 2011), flourishing (Huppert & So, 2013), flourishing scale (Diener et al., 2010), or the mental health continuum (MHC: Keyes, 2002).

Most of the well-being and flourishing theories are componential, meaning that they assume that well-being constitutes a sum of elements, the increase of which will escalate an individual's overall levels of well-being (Burke, 2020). Well-being includes such elements as self-acceptance, positive emotions, meaning and purpose, autonomy, positive relationship, self-esteem, to mention a few (Burke, 2018b). Research that measures the impact of interventions or environment on the well-being elements is therefore deemed as positive psychological research (Burke, 2018a). Equally, when the impact of interventions delivered via the technological vehicle is measured using "positive" measures, the cyberpsychology research may be categorized as belonging to the positive cyberpsychology.

To date, the concept of positive measure (Gallagher & Lopez, 2019), as a requirement for a positive–psychological study was not strictly adhered to. For example, when positive psychology interventions have been used along with a nonpositive measure, it was deemed a positive psychology study (e.g., Carlson, Speca, Faris, & Patel, 2007; Stanton et al., 2002; Van der Lee & Garssen, 2012). However, the definition of positive psychology intervention is that (a) its goal is to build positive variables, (b) the empirical evidence exists yielding it a scientifically based intervention, and (c) empirical evidence demonstrates positive outcomes (Parks & Biswas-Diener, 2013), which is measured using positive measures.

It this context, positive cyberpsychology research may promote more rigorous adherence to the positive measure principles. In an overview of randomized control trials testing online positive psychology interventions, it was found that while an intervention might reduce illness, it does not necessarily increase well-being (Mitchell, Vella-Brodrick, & Klein, 2010). Therefore, both concepts need to be measured separately and establishing positive cyberpsychology research angle may increase the number of studies carried out in cyberpsychology, which apply positive measures.

To date, many interventions have been applied to participants online (e.g., Mitchell et al., 2010; Proyer, Gander, Wellenzohn, & Ruch, 2015; Woodworth, O'Brien-Malone, Diamond, & Schüz, 2018). The effect of the interventions varies depending on the media through which they are introduced. For example, *expressive writing* is an intervention created prior to the commencement of the positive psychological movement, however, the positive outcomes of expressive writing have been assessed showing that it increases the effective coping behavior in the face of adversity (Spera, Buchfeind, & Pennebaker, 1994), enhances mood (Pennebaker, 1997), and results in a long-term improvement of immune system functioning (Pennebaker, Kiecolt-Glaser, & Glaser, 1988). Furthermore, the initial intervention has been tweaked creating a more positive approach to writing (King, 2001), thus firmly placing it in the group of positive psychology interventions. While Smyth and Pennebaker (2008) found that the topics which individuals write about do not seem very significant, typing participants' deeper thoughts and feelings appears to be less beneficial than handwriting them (Brewin & Lennard, 1999). At the same time, interviews with bloggers and video bloggers, whose content is deeply personal, thus similar to the expressive writing intervention, shows that blog writing has a positive effect on their well-being (Huh, Liu, Neogi, Inkpen, & Pratt, 2014; Watson, 2018). Further studies need to be carried out to identify the effectiveness of positive psychology interventions applied via technological medium, and an establishment of a positive cyberpsychology movement can aid in this endeavor.

When studying participants completing positive psychology interventions online, researchers need to enquire into not only the effectiveness of the well-being interventions, but also the optimal ease of use, which is the cyberpsychology domain (Munson, Lauterbach, Newman, & Resnick, 2010; Parks, Della Porta, Pierce, Zilca, & Lyubomirsky, 2012). Therefore, cyberpsychology research can inform the positive psychology researchers and practitioners on the most optimal methods to present positive psychology interventions online and via other technological media.

Ironically, in a paper about the future of cyberpsychology, and specifically positive technology, Botella et al. (2012) note that despite the extent of technology in human lives and the impact of it on their daily life experiences, none of the existing positive psychology texts mention the importance of cyberpsychology. This is an oversight and it is crucial that more collaboration is seen between these two rapidly emerging fields.

The field of cyberpsychology offers an array of findings that may be used to best present positive psychology content. They range from single theories, such as the online disinhibition effect, dissociative anonymity, through to the effect of asynchronicity of online resources, gender-bending, as well as evidence-based tools on how to make online communities work, use most effective ways to communicate via e-mail, the application of avatars in mental health interventions, the amount of time users spend online, and many more relevant topics (Attrill, 2015; Suler, 2016; Torniainen-Holm et al., 2016). All these findings can serve well when designing a well-being improvement program online.

Overall, the amalgamation of positive psychology and cyberpsychology in the context of technology assisting in the improvement of well-being can be particularly beneficial. Increased knowledge of positive psychology can help cyberpsychologists create programs and interventions that measure positive outcomes in their participants and go beyond well-being into other areas of optimal human functioning. Likewise, cyberpsychology knowledge can help positive psychology researchers and practitioners to apply ample methods in presenting positive psychology content online.

## Impact of Technology on Well-Being

Technology is an integral part of life and the interaction with it may have either positive or negative impact. For example, some individuals experience technostress when dealing with novel technology, which indicates an unhealthy approach to coping with it (Brod, 1984). In order to reduce the negative effect of new technology, Brivio and colleagues (2018) encourage programmers and other online creators to apply positive psychology findings and specifically the positive technology model (Riva et al., 2012) to ensure end users are positively impacted by it. However, more research is required to identify what can be done in order to both ensure the end-users' positive experiences of technology and measure its effectiveness using rigorous psychological measurements. The example of this will be provided by analyzing the impact of smartphones on individuals.

Smartphones are open operating systems that are constantly connected to the internet (Moore, 2018). They are fitted with artificial intelligence structures (Wajcman & Rose, 2011) and used by almost 3 billion people worldwide (GSMA, 2018; Statista, 2019). Therefore, the extent of the impact it has on individuals, societies, and even generations is considerable.

The cyberpsychology research about negative effects of smartphones is significantly greater than studies indicating the positive aspects of these hand-held devices. The use of smartphones is associated with headaches, sleep disorder, anxiety, irritation, migraine, to mention a few (Söderqvist, Carlberg, & Hardell, 2008; Szyjkowska, Gadzicka, Szymczak, & Bortkiewicz, 2014; Zheng et al., 2015). Smartphones are often blamed for instigating technology overload, which comes in three forms, that is, information overload, communication overload, and system features overload (Karr-Wisniewski & Lu, 2010). The information overload refers to the easy access of data available on smartphones; the communication overload is associated with various social networking apps such as WhatsApp, Facebook, Viber, WeChat, Handouts, and many more (Google Play, 2019); whereas the system features overload is associated with a variety of unstandardized characteristics of health apps (Van Velsen, Beaujean, & Van Gemert-Pijnen, 2013).

The consequences of technology overload are significant with some researchers contributing it to work–family conflict (Harris, Marett, & Harris, 2011). However, other researchers disagree claiming that while the use of a laptop outside of work is associated with work–family conflict, no such correlation was found when participants used their smartphone outside of work (Gadeyne, Verbruggen, Delanoeije, & De Cooman, 2018).

In addition to the technology overload, a significant number of studies about the impact of smartphones on individuals focus on their problematic use, addiction, dependence, or compulsion to use them (Jain, Gedam, & Patil, 2019). Using phones is often associated with negative outcomes such as engaging with it for longer periods of time than intended (65%), procrastination (58%), and distraction (40%) (Horwood & Anglim, 2018). Interventions aimed to reduce the use of a phone yielded positive effects on the individuals' quality of sleep and their well-being (Hughes & Burke, 2018).

While there is a great amount of research about the negative effects of smartphones, there is significantly less research focusing on the positive aspects of smartphones, on which the positive cyberpsychology field may expand. For example, research indicates that using a phone helps individuals feel better when they are feeling down (Horwood & Anglim, 2018), it is treated as a reward for good behavior among youth, makes them feel safer, and is considered as the most useful device to maintain contact with social networks (Ahad & Anshari, 2017). Furthermore, the impact of aesthetics of smartphones has been measured indicating an important hedonic effect of phone screen size (Kim & Sundar, 2014). Also, individuals are more likely to adopt new technological features of smartphones when they are perceived as "cool" (Kim, Shin, & Park, 2015). These are just some of the studies showing a positive effect of smartphones, however, significantly more are required to redress the imbalance in research.

In an attempt to identify potential smartphone well-being scale questions, the author surveyed 130 adults, 55.4% males and 44.6% females, in Ireland, aged 19–29 (28.5%), 40–49 (35.4%), and the remaining were 50 and over (19.3%). They were asked about the frequency with which they have used their smartphone and, while most used it between 2 and 6 hours a day (36.9%), 23.1% of participants used it less than 2 hours and the remaining 24.6% used it for more than 9 hours in a 24-hour period.

Questions were based on the PERMA theory of well-being (Seligman, 2011), and tweaked to make them relevant to smartphone use. For example, instead of being asked a generic question about feeling supported by others, participants were asked to rate their agreement with a statement: "Using my smartphone enables me to receive help and support from others"; or instead of being asked to what extent do they lead a purposeful and meaningful life, they were asked to rate an agreement to a statement: "Using my smartphone helps me lead a purposeful and meaningful life." Additional statements have been included, which were informed by the current research on the potential benefits of using smartphones, for example, curiosity (Hochberg, Kuhn, & Mueller, 2018; Moon & Kim, 2001; Pan, Chang, & Sun, 2014) and safety (Trub & Barbot, 2016). The questionnaire consisted of 13 statements, which participants were asked to agree with using a 5-point Likert scale that ranged from strongly disagree to strongly agree. The mean and standard deviation came from the participants' direct responses, whereas the frequencies for each group came from an aggregated groups of strongly *disagree* and *disagree* which created group 1 (disagree); *neither agree nor disagree*, which created group 2 (ambivalent); and *agree* and *strongly agree* which created group 3 (agree). The details of the questionnaire can be found in Table 6.1. The Cronbach alpha in the current study was high at $\alpha = 0.90$.

The mean and standard deviation (Table 6.2) indicated that the highest level of agreement came from statements about a smartphone helping participants to satisfy their sense of curiosity (M = 3.91, SD = 0.79), to allow them accomplish their goals (M = 3.48; SD = 1.07), to make their life more enjoyable (M = 3.18; SD = 0.95), to make them feel they belong to a community, for example, social network (M = 3.11; SD = 1.19), and to help them feel more interested and engaged in life (M = 3; SD = 1.02). The lowest level of agreement was found in the statements about a smartphone helping participants to flourish in life (M = 2.45; SD = 0.93), followed by aiding them to lead a purposeful and meaningful life (M = 2.63; SD = 1.06), and

**Table 6.1**    Smartphone well-being scale.

Please read each statement carefully and think about the impact your smartphone has on you. Using the scale provided, report how much you agree with each statement.

| *Using my smartphone* | *Strongly disagree* | *Disagree* | *Neither agree nor disagree* | *Agree* | *Strongly agree* |
| --- | --- | --- | --- | --- | --- |
| 1. Makes my life more enjoyable | | | | | |
| 2. Helps me feel more interested and engaged in life | | | | | |
| 3. Makes me feel more satisfied with life | | | | | |
| 4. Allows me to grow as a person | | | | | |
| 5. Improves my relationships with people | | | | | |
| 6. Makes me feel I belong to a community (e.g., social network) | | | | | |
| 7. Satisfies my sense of curiosity | | | | | |
| 8. Enables me to receive help and support from others | | | | | |
| 9. Helps me lead a purposeful and meaningful life | | | | | |
| 10. Contributes to my wellbeing | | | | | |
| 11. Allows me to accomplish my goals | | | | | |
| 12. Makes me feel safe | | | | | |
| 13. Helps me flourish in life | | | | | |

**Table 6.2**    Descriptive results for each item of the questionnaire.

| Item | N | M | SD |
| --- | --- | --- | --- |
| Enjoyment | 130 | 3.18 | 0.95 |
| Interest | 130 | 3 | 1.02 |
| Satisfaction | 130 | 2.9 | 1.03 |
| Growth | 130 | 2.95 | 1.11 |
| Relationships | 130 | 2.86 | 1.13 |
| Belonging | 130 | 3.11 | 1.19 |
| Curiosity | 130 | 3.91 | 0.79 |
| Support | 130 | 3.20 | 0.98 |
| Meaning and purpose | 130 | 2.63 | 1.06 |
| Wellbeing | 130 | 2.84 | 1.10 |
| Goals | 130 | 3.48 | 1.07 |
| Safety | 130 | 2.94 | 1.10 |
| Flourishing | 82 | 2.45 | 0.93 |

contributing to their well-being (M = 2.84; SD = 1.10). Therefore, some components of PERMA, for example, accomplishment, enhancement of some positive emotions, and a sense of belonging, scored highly, yet when asked about the smartphone contribution to participants' overall well-being and flourishing, their scores indicated higher levels of disagreement with these statements. Interestingly, the statement about smartphones helping participants flourish yielded 48 missing answers, suggesting the confusion that some respondents felt about the impact of smartphones on their well-being, therefore they might have chosen not to select any of the responses. This may be due to the general, negative view of the impact of smartphones on well-being and participants' cognitive dissonance associated with responding to the well-being questions about it.

Furthermore, the frequency of participants' agreement and disagreement with the statements was analyzed in aggregated groups, the findings of which can be seen in Table 6.3. Despite well-being and flourishing means showing higher levels of participants' disagreement, almost a third of them agreed with the statement that using a smartphone contributes to their well-being and just over 5% agreed that it helps them flourish. This indicates that technology can not only have a positive impact on individuals, but it can also aid in enhancing their levels of well-being.

The highest number of participants agreed with a statement that smartphone use helps them satisfy their sense of curiosity (78.5%), allows them to accomplish their goals (56.2%), enhances their experiences of positive emotions (enjoyment: 39.2%; interest: 33.1%), makes them feel that they are supported by others (43.1%), belongs to a community (43.1%) and helps them improve relationships (30.8%). Furthermore, the results indicate that for a third of participants, using a smartphone is associated with feeling safe, therefore, it has an impact on some of the basic human needs (Maslow, 1969).

**Table 6.3**  Frequency of agreement with each statement.

| Item | Disagree | Ambivalent | Agree |
| --- | --- | --- | --- |
| Enjoyment | 23.8% | 36.9% | 39.2% |
| Interest | 33.8% | 33.1% | 33.1% |
| Satisfaction | 34.6% | 40% | 25.4% |
| Growth | 35.4% | 33.1% | 31.5% |
| Relationships | 40.8% | 28.5% | 30.8% |
| Belonging | 32.3% | 24.6% | 43.1% |
| Curiosity | 6.2% | 15.4% | 78.5% |
| Support | 23.1% | 33.8% | 43.1% |
| Meaning and purpose | 44.6% | 37.7% | 17.7% |
| Wellbeing | 35.4% | 36.9% | 27.7% |
| Goals | 16.9% | 26.9% | 56.2% |
| Safety | 32.3% | 36.9% | 30.8% |
| Flourishing | 28.5% | 29.2% | 5.4% |

While over 30% of participants agreed that a smartphone improves their relationships, over 40% of them disagreed with this statement suggesting the different ways in which participants use their phone and the psychological impact it may have on them. Further research into this could shed a light as to the circumstances in which a phone improves participants' relationships, that is, whether it is due to the device itself and its ownership or specific apps participants use.

Taking all the findings from the study into consideration, they provide evidence that technology has a capacity to enhance some participants' self-reported well-being. Following from Botella et al.'s (2012) call to positive psychologist to pay more attention to cyberpsychology, especially given the emerging evidence of the positive effects of technology on individuals, more research needs to be carried out into using technology in a form of a positive psychology intervention and not only as a vehicle for introducing positive psychology interventions. If, indeed, some types of technology are able to enhance an individual's well-being, then providing participants with them may serve as a route to happiness.

In another, ongoing study carried out by the author, an initial sample of 48 participants from Ireland completed a survey in order to identify how much of the variance in smartphone well-being can be explained by the frequency of participants using their smartphones for taking or viewing pictures, instant messaging, health or other apps, personal and work e-mail, news, YouTube, Kindle, music, games, and social networks. According to the preliminary data, most of the participants (47.9%) were aged 18–25, 29.2% were aged 26–29, and the remaining were aged over 30. The vast majority of participants used their phones for 2–6 hours a day (68.8%), 20.8% for 6–8 hours, and the remainder for less than 2 hours or more than 9 hours.

Participants received the potential questions from the previously mentioned smartphone well-being scale (SWS) and a demographic scale, which included the frequency with which participants used different apps or phone features. The internal reliability of the SWS scale was $\alpha = 0.90$. Standard multiple regression was used to assess the ability of the frequency with which participants used their smartphone to predict their smartphone well-being. Preliminary analyses were carried out to ensure no violation of the assumptions of normality, linearity, multicollinearity and homoscedasticity. The results can be found in Table 6.4.

The variance explained by the model was 44%, $F (13, 48) = 2.07$, $p < 0.05$. Three measures, in particular, were statistically significant, with work mail recording the highest value (*beta* = −0.72), followed by personal main (*beta* = 0.67) and finally other apps (*beta* = −0.38).

The results are showing that frequent checking of work e-mail had a negative effect on participants' smartphone well-being, however, their personal e-mail had an opposite effect. Also, using some apps predicted lower levels of well-being, but there were no statistically significant results for any other features.

**Table 6.4**    Standard multiple regression for predicting smartphone well-being, N = 48.

| Variable | B | SE B | $\beta$ |
|---|---|---|---|
| Taking pictures | −0.05 | 0.20 | −0.04 |
| Viewing pictures | 0.14 | 0.22 | 0.12 |
| Instant messaging | 0.78 | 0.86 | 0.13 |
| Health apps | 0.37 | 0.23 | 0.28 |
| Other apps | −0.46 | 0.20 | −0.38* |
| Personal main | 1.07 | 0.33 | 0.67* |
| Work mail | −0.88 | 0.25 | −0.72** |
| News | −0.04 | 0.28 | −0.04 |
| YouTube | −0.07 | 0.18 | −0.06 |
| Kindle, podcasts, audible and similar | 0.15 | 0.16 | 0.15 |
| Music | −0.17 | 0.21 | −0.13 |
| Games | 0.19 | 0.21 | 0.14 |
| Social networking sites | 0.14 | 0.21 | 0.11 |
| $R^2$ | | | 0.44 |
| F for change in $R^2$ | | | 2.07 |

*$p < 0.05$; **$p < 0.001$.

These results are in line with other studies that considered the impact of work e-mail on individuals and used other than SWB measures to assess well-being (R. Brown, Duck, & Jimmieson, 2014; Pignata, Lushington, Sloan, & Buchanan, 2015; Waller & Ragsdell, 2012). Future studies, both qualitative and quantitative, should aim to identify other reasons for some participants scoring highly on their smartphone well-being, as the reason for higher levels of smartphone well-being might be yet unknown.

These studies are a starting point for discussing how technology can enhance individuals' well-being. The creation of a positive cyberpsychology movement might prompt more such studies and scales. Apart from smartphones, other types of technology should be researched as well as their effect on users' well-being. However, as in the previous section of this chapter, the correct measures that measures positive outcomes should be used (e.g., Gallagher & Lopez, 2019). This will enrich the current research and redress the imbalance that exists in cyberpsychology skewed toward the negative.

## Impact of Online Content on Well-Being

In addition to the interventions provided to masses via technology to enhance well-being, as well as the technological devices themselves, another important research that ought to be considered by the field of positive cyberpsychology is measuring the incidents of positive outcomes of viewing and engaging with online content. That engagement comes in a form of apps and text available to participants. It differs from the first category of research in so far as their interventions are consciously set up to improve well-being and a different type of health, whereas in this category of positive cyberpsychology research, the content has an indirect impact on individuals' well-being.

An example of such content is Instagram, which has 500 million users daily (Clarke, 2018) and the number of users is expected to double over the next few years (McCormick, 2018). Instagram is a social networking site that encourages users to capture their daily experiences and share it online in a picture form (Stapleton, Luiz, & Chatwin, 2017). Photographic psychology refers to the psychology of creating, sharing, and reacting to images in the cyberspace (Suler, 2013). To date, most research in this area, thus a lot of research relating to Instagram, is negative.

Instagram is found to impact individuals negatively, affecting both their satisfaction with their bodies and their mood (Harper & Tiggemann, 2008). Specifically, their dissatisfaction occurs as a result of internalization of beauty ideals created by society (Fardouly, Willburger, & Vartanian, 2018). Given that the edited images are often removed from reality, they become propagators of unrealistically thin or fit bodies (Cohen, Irwin, Newton-John, & Slater, 2019).

On a positive side, however, "likes" on Instagram have the power to reduce dissatisfaction (Tiggemann, Hayden, Brown, & Veldhuis, 2018). Furthermore, over the last few years hashtags such as #self-compassion, #loveyourself, and #body-positive have grown exponentially (Z. Brown & Tiggemann, 2016; Cohen et al., 2019; Slater, Varsani, & Diedrichs, 2017) helping individuals cope with a less than ideal body image. In addition to this, positive comments have found to enhance Instagram users' confidence and improve their self-evaluation (Feltman & Szymanski, 2018).

These studies suggest a positive move toward providing a balanced view of the internet content. Furthermore, given the negative image that the internet content creates, positive psychology interventions may be used in future studies to help individuals bounce back from negative experiences online. This is why more such studies are required in which positive cyberpsychology may play an important role.

## Positive versus Negative Cyberpsychology

Bad events, emotions, and information is often stronger than good (Baumeister, Bratslavsky, Finkenauer, & Vohs, 2001), which is partially the reason why research usually focuses more on the negative rather than positive aspects of human beings. When studies about depression are compared to those about happiness, pathological studies are significantly more prevalent (Myers, 2000). Achor (2010) claims that the prevalence is as great a ratio of 17 studies about abnormalities to one study about well-being. The same is true for other fields. For example, Randolph (2013) examined 10 years of publication trends in clinical neuropsychology and found that only 6% of empirical studies examined normalities, whereas the majority focused on cognitive deficits.

Cyberpsychology follows a similar trend in focusing on negative outcomes. There are many studies with the objective of enhancing well-being via technology. However, when the research is considered, which focuses primarily on the positive impact of technology and online content on well-being, the ratio is 16 : 1, meaning that 16 studies focus on addiction and problematic use of technology in comparison to one study focusing on the health benefits of it. For research to offer a more balanced perspective on the impact of technology on human beings, the positive psychological shift needs to happen. Thus, creating a positive cyberpsychology angle may serve as a great starting point for a change.

The current chapter is a call to all positive psychologists to consider the robust research carried out in the field of cyberpsychology when designing positive psychology interventions using technology. Furthermore, it is a call to measure the effectiveness of technology to enhance well-being and the positive impact of online content, so that findings from that can be used in deepening the researchers' knowledge on what is the good life and how to experience it. Finally, it is also a call to all cyberpsychologists to begin using more positive psychology in their work. Only when the two fields collaborate effectively together can greater inroads be made in positive cyberpsychology.

## References

Achor, S. (2010). *The happiness advantage: The seven principles of positive psychology that fuel success and performance at work*. New York: Crown Business/Random House.

Ahad, A. D., & Anshari, M. (2017). Smartphone habits among youth: Uses and gratification theory. *International Journal of Cyber Behavior, Psychology and Learning, 7*(1), 65–75.

Attrill, A. (2015). Introduction. In A. Attrill (Ed.), *Cyberpsychology* (pp. 1–6). Oxford: Oxford University Press.

Baumeister, R. F., Bratslavsky, E., Finkenauer, C., & Vohs, K. D. (2001). Bad is stronger than good. *Review of General Psychology, 5*(4), 323–370.

Botella, C., Riva, G., Gaggioli, A., Wiederhold, B. K., Alcaniz, M., & Baños, R. M. (2012). The present and future of positive technologies. *Cyberpsychology, Behavior, and Social Networking, 15*(2), 78–84.

Brewin, C. R., & Lennard, H. (1999). Effects of mode of writing on emotional narratives. *Journal of Traumatic Stress, 12*, 355–361.

Brivio, E., Gaudioso, F., Vergine, I., Mirizzi, C. R., Reina, C., Stellari, A., & Galimberti, C. (2018). Preventing technostress through positive technology. *Frontiers in Psychology, 9*, 1–5.

Brod, C. (1984). *Technostress: The human cost of the computer revolution*. Reading, MA: Addison-Wesley.

Brown, R., Duck, J., & Jimmieson, N. (2014). E-mail in the workplace: The role of stress appraisals and normative response pressure in the relationship between e-mail stressors and employee strain. *International Journal of Stress Management, 21*(4), 325–347.

Brown, Z., & Tiggemann, M. (2016). Attractive celebrity and peer images on Instagram: Effect on women's mood and body image. *Body Image, 19*, 37–43.

Burke, J. (2016). *Happiness after 30: The paradox of aging.* Dublin, Ireland: Jumpp Publishing.

Burke, J. (2018a). Conceptual framework for a positive psychology coaching practice. *Coaching Psychologist, 14*(1), 16–25.

Burke, J. (2018b). The languishing limbo: Coaching for wellbeing. *Coaching Today, 26,* 12–17.

Burke, J. (2020). *The ultimate guide to implementing wellbeing programmes for school.* London: Routledge.

Burke, J., & Minton, S. J. (2019). Well-being in post-primary schools in Ireland: The assessment and contribution of character strengths. *Journal of Irish Educational Studies, 38*(2), 177–192.

Calvo, R. A., & Peters, D. (2014). *Positive computing: Technology for wellbeing and human potential.* Cambridge, MA: MIT Press.

Carlson, L. E., Speca, M., Faris, P., & Patel, K. D. (2007). One year pre–post intervention follow-up of psychological, immune, endocrine and blood pressure outcomes of mindfulness-based stress reduction (MBSR) in breast and prostate cancer outpatients. *Brain, Behavior & Immunity, 21*(8), 1038–1049.

Clarke, T. (2018). 24+ Instagram statistics that matter to marketers in 2019 [online]. Retrieved from https://blog.hootsuite.com/instagram-statistics.

Cohen, R., Irwin, L., Newton-John, T., & Slater, A. (2019). #bodypositivity: A content analysis of body positive accounts on Instagram. *Body Image, 29,* 47–57.

Diener, E. (2000). Subjective well-being: The science of happiness and a proposal for a national index. *American Psychologist, 55*(1), 34–43.

Diener, E., Wirtz, D., Tov, W., Kim-Prieto, C., Choi, D., Oishi, S., & Biswas-Diener, R. (2010). New well-being measures: Short scales to assess flourishing and positive and negative feelings. *Social Indicators Research, 97,* 143–156.

Fardouly, J., Willburger, B. K., & Vartanian, L. R. (2018). Instagram use and young women's body image concerns and self-objectification: Testing mediational pathways. *New Media & Society, 20*(4), 1380–1395.

Feltman, C. E., & Szymanski, D. M. (2018). Instagram use and self-objectification: The roles of internalization, comparison, appearance commentary, and feminism. *Sex Roles, 78*(5–6), 311–324.

Friedman, R. A., & Currall, S. C. (2003). Conflict escalation: Dispute exacerbating elements of e-mail communication. *Human Relations, 56*(11), 1325–1347.

Gable, S. L., & Haidt, J. (2005). What (and why) is positive psychology? *Review of General Psychology, 9*(2), 103–110.

Gadeyne, N., Verbruggen, M., Delanoeije, J., & De Cooman, R. (2018). All wired, all tired? Work-related ICT-use outside work hours and work-to-home conflict: The role of integration preference, integration norms and work demands. *Journal of Vocational Behavior, 107,* 86–99.

Gaggioli, A. (2014). CyberSightings. *Cyberpsychology, Behavior, and Social Networking, 17*(6), 423.

Gallagher, M. W., & Lopez, S. J. (Eds.). (2019). *Positive psychological assessment: A handbook of models and measures* (2nd ed.). Washington, DC: American Psychological Association.

Ghislieri, C., Molino, M., & Cortese, C. G. (2018). Work and organizational psychology looks at the fourth industrial revolution: How to support workers and organizations? *Frontiers in Psychology, 9,* Article 2365.

Google Play. (2019). Top communication apps. Retrieved August 16, 2020, from https://play.google.com/store/apps/category/COMMUNICATION?hl=en.

GSMA. (2018). The mobile economy report 2018 [online]. Retrieved August 16, 2020, from https://www.gsma.com/asia-pacific/resources/the-mobile-economy-report-2018.

Harper, B., & Tiggemann, M. (2008). The effect of thin ideal media images on women's self-objectification, mood, and body image. *Sex Roles: A Journal of Research, 58*(9–10), 649–657.

Harris, K. J., Marett, K., & Harris, R. B. (2011). Technology-related pressure and work–family conflict: Main effects and an examination of moderating variables. *Journal of Applied Social Psychology, 41*(9), 2077–2103.

Hart, K. E., & Sasso, T. (2011). Mapping the contours of contemporary positive psychology.

*Canadian Psychology/Psychologie Canadienne*, *52*(2), 82–92.

Hochberg, K., Kuhn, J., & Mueller, A. (2018). Using smartphones as experimental tools-effects on interest, curiosity, and learning in physics education. *Journal of Science Education and Technology*, *27*(5), 385–403.

Horwood, S., & Anglim, J. (2018). Personality and problematic smartphone use: A facet-level analysis using the five factor model and HEXACO frameworks. *Computers in Human Behavior*, *85*, 349–359.

Horwood, S., & Anglim, J. (2019). Problematic smartphone usage and subjective and psychological well-being. *Computers in Human Behavior*, *97*, 44–50.

Hughes, N., & Burke, J. (2018). Sleeping with the frenemy: How restricting "bedroom use" of smartphones impacts happiness and wellbeing. *Computers in Human Behavior*, *85*, 236–244.

Huh, J., Liu, L. S., Neogi, T., Inkpen, K., & Pratt, W. (2014). Health vlogs as social support for chronic illness management. *ACM Transactions on Computer-Human Interaction*, *21*(4), Article 23.

Huppert, F. A., & So, T. T. C. (2013). Flourishing across Europe: Application of a new conceptual framework for defining well-being. *Social Indicators Research*, *110*(3), 837–861.

Huppert, F. A., & Whittington, J. E. (2003). Evidence for the independence of positive and negative well-being: Implications for quality of life assessment. *British Journal of Health Psychology*, *8*(1), 107–122.

Jain, P., Gedam, S. R., & Patil, P. S. (2019). Study of smartphone addiction: Prevalence, pattern of use, and personality dimensions among medical students from rural region of central India. *Open Journal of Psychiatry & Allied Sciences*, *10*(2), 133–138.

Karr-Wisniewski, P., & Lu, Y. (2010). When more is too much: Operationalizing technology overload and exploring its impact on knowledge worker productivity. *Computers in Human Behavior*, *26*(5), 1061–1072.

Keyes, C. L. M. (2002). The mental health continuum: From languishing to flourishing in life. *Journal of Health and Social Behavior*, *43*(2), 207–222.

Kim, K. J., Shin, D.-H., & Park, E. (2015). Can coolness predict technology adoption? Effects of perceived coolness on user acceptance of smartphones with curved screens. *Cyberpsychology, Behavior, and Social Networking*, *18*(9), 528–533.

Kim, K. J., & Sundar, S. S. (2014). Does screen size matter for smartphones? Utilitarian and hedonic effects of screen size on smartphone adoption. *CyberPsychology, Behavior and Social Networking*, *17*(7), 466–473.

King, L. A. (2001). The health benefits of writing about life goals. *Personality and Social Psychology Bulletin*, *27*(7), 798–807.

Kirwan, G. (2016a). Introduction to cyberpsychology. In I. Connolly, M. Palmer, H. Barton, & G. Kirwan (Eds.), *An introduction to cyberpsychology* (pp. 3–13). New York: Routledge.

Kirwan, G. (2016b). Psychological applications of virtual reality. In I. Connolly, M. Palmer, H. Barton, & G. Kirwan (Eds.), *An introduction to cyberpsychology* (pp. 271–285). New York: Routledge.

Kirwan, G. (2016c). The psychology of artificial intelligence. In I. Connolly, M. Palmer, H. Barton, & G. Kirwan (Eds.), *An introduction to cyberpsychology* (pp. 286–298). New York: Routledge.

Kirwan, G., & Power, A. (2014). What is cyberpsychology? In A. Power & G. Kirwan (Eds.), *Cyberpsychology and new media: A thematic reader* (pp. 3–14). New York: Psychology Press.

Krishna, S., Boren, S. A., & Balas, E. A. (2009). Healthcare via cell phones: A systematic review. *Telemedicine & E-Health*, *15*(3), 231–240.

Linley, P. A., Joseph, S., Harrington, S., & Wood, A. M. (2006). Positive psychology: Past, present, and (possible) future. *Journal of Positive Psychology*, *1*(1), 3–16.

Maslow, A. H. (1969). The farther reaches of human nature. *Journal of Transpersonal Psychology*, *1*(1), 1–9.

McCormick, E. (2018). Instagram is estimated to be worth more than $100 Billion. [online] Bloomberg. Retrieved from https://www.bloomberg.com/news/articles/2018-06-25/value-of-facebook-s-instagram-estimated-to-top-100-billion.

Mitchell, J., Vella-Brodrick, D., & Klein, B. (2010). Positive psychology and the internet: A mental health opportunity. *E-Journal of Applied Psychology*, *6*(2), 30–41.

Moon, J.-W., & Kim, Y.-G. (2001). Extending the TAM for a World-Wide-Web context. *Information & Management, 38*(4), 217–230.

Moore, A. (2018). Combat the distraction. *TD: Talent Development, 72*(7), 11.

Munson, S., Lauterbach, D., Newman, M., & Resnick, P. (2010). Happier together: Integrating a wellness application into a social network site. In T. Ploug, P. Hasle, & H. Oinas-Kukkonen (Eds.), *Persuasive Technology* (pp. 27–39). Berlin: Springer.

Myers, D. G. (2000). The funds, friends, and faith of happy people. *American Psychologist, 55*(1), 56–67.

Neuman, Y. (2016). Artificial intelligence in public health surveillance and research. In D. D. Luxton (Ed.), *Artificial intelligence in behavioral and mental health care* (pp. 231–254). San Diego, CA: Elsevier Academic Press.

Olweus, D., & Limber, S. P. (2018). Some problems with cyberbullying research. *Current Opinion in Psychology, 19*, 139–143.

Pan, L.-Y., Chang, S.-C., & Sun, C.-C. (2014). A three-stage model for smart phone use antecedents. *Quality & Quantity: International Journal of Methodology, 48*(2), 1107–1115.

Parks, A. C., & Biswas-Diener, R. (2013). Positive interventions: Past, present, and future. In T. B. Kashdan & J. Ciarrochi (Eds.), *Mindfulness, acceptance, and positive psychology: The seven foundations of well-being* (pp. 140–165). Oakland, CA: Context Press/New Harbinger.

Parks, A. C., Della Porta, M. D., Pierce, R. S., Zilca, R., & Lyubomirsky, S. (2012). Pursuing happiness in everyday life: The characteristics and behaviors of online happiness seekers. *Emotion, 12*(6), 1222–1234.

Pennebaker, J. W. (1997). Writing about emotional experiences as a therapeutic process. *Psychological Science, 8*, 162–166.

Pennebaker, J. W., Kiecolt-Glaser, J., & Glaser, R. (1988). Disclosure of traumas and immune function: Health implications for psychotherapy. *Journal of Consulting and Clinical Psychology, 56*, 239–245.

Pignata, S., Lushington, K., Sloan, J., & Buchanan, F. (2015). Employees' perceptions of email communication, volume and management strategies in an Australian university. *Journal of Higher Education Policy and Management, 37*(2), 159–171.

Proyer, R. T., Gander, F., Wellenzohn, S., & Ruch, W. (2015). Strengths-based positive psychology interventions: A randomized placebo-controlled online trial on long-term effects for a signature strengths- vs. a lesser strengths-intervention. *Frontiers in Psychology, 6*, 456.

Randolph, J. J. (2013). Positive neuropsychology: Synthesis and future directions. In J. J. Randolph (Ed.), *Positive neuropsychology: Evidence-based perspectives on promoting cognitive health* (pp. 161–170). New York: Springer Science + Business Media.

Riva, G., Baños, R. M., Botella, C., Wiederhold, B. K., & Gaggioli, A. (2012). Positive technology: Using interactive technologies to promote positive functioning. *CyberPsychology, Behavior and Social Networking, 15*(2), 69–77.

Rusk, R. D., & Waters, L. E. (2013). Tracing the size, reach, impact, and breadth of positive psychology. *Journal of Positive Psychology, 8*(3), 207–221.

Ryff, C. D., & Keyes, C. L. M. (1995). The structure of psychological well-being revisited. *Journal of Personality and Social Psychology, 69*(4), 719–727.

Seligman, M.P. (2011). *Flourish*. New York: Free Press.

Seligman, M. P., & Csikszentmihalyi, M. (2000). Positive psychology: An introduction. *American Psychologist, 55*(1), 5–14.

Sharma, M., Achuth, P. V., Deb, D., Puthankattil, S. D., & Acharya, U. R. (2018). An automated diagnosis of depression using three-channel bandwidth-duration localized wavelet filter bank with EEG signals. *Cognitive Systems Research, 52*, 508–520.

Slater, A., Varsani, N., & Diedrichs, P. C. (2017). #fitspo or #loveyourself? The impact of fitspiration and self-compassion Instagram images on women's body image, self-compassion, and mood. *Body Image, 22*, 87–96.

Smahel, D., Dedkova, L., Daneback, K., Walrave, M., & Schouten, A. (2019). A breakthrough year for cyberpsychology: More citations, more submissions – and more impact. *Cyberpsychology, 13*(1), 1–5.

Smyth, J. M., & Pennebaker, J. W. (2008). Exploring the boundary conditions of expressive writing: In search for the right recipe. *British Journal of Health Psychology*, *13*, 1–7.

Söderqvist, F., Carlberg, M., & Hardell, L. (2008). Use of wireless telephones and self-reported health symptoms: A population-based study among Swedish adolescents aged 15–19 years. *Environmental Health: A Global Access Science Source*, *7*, 1–10.

Spera, S. P., Buchfeind, E. D., & Pennebaker, J. W. (1994). Expressive writing and coping with job loss. *Academy of Management Journal*, *37*, 722–733.

Stanton, A. L., Danoff-Burg, S., Sworowski, L. A., Collins, C. A., Branstetter, A. D., Rodriguez-Hanley, A., ... Austenfeld, J. (2002). Randomized, controlled trial of written emotional expression and benefit finding in breast cancer patients. *Journal of Clinical Oncology*, *20*(*20*), 4160–4168.

Stapleton, P., Luiz, G., & Chatwin, H. (2017). Generation validation: The role of social comparison in use of Instagram among emerging adults. *CyberPsychology, Behavior and Social Networking*, *20*(3), 142–149.

Statista. (2019). Number of smartphone users worldwide 2014–2020 [online] Retrieved from https://www.statista.com/statistics/330695/number-of-smartphone-users-worldwide.

Suler, J. R. (2013). *Photographic psychology: Image and psyche*. True Centre Publishing. Retrieved from http://truecenterpublishing.com/photopsy/article_index.htm.

Suler, J. R. (2016). *Psychology of the digital age: Humans become electric*. Cambridge: Cambridge University Press.

Szyjkowska, A., Gadzicka, E., Szymczak, W., & Bortkiewicz, A. (2014). The risk of subjective symptoms in mobile phone users in Poland: An epidemiological study. *International Journal of Occupational Medicine & Environmental Health*, *27*(2), 293–303.

Thomas, D. A. (2014). Virtual reality research continues to progress at the National Institutes of Health. *Cyberpsychology, Behavior, and Social Networking*, *17*(6), 334.

Tiggemann, M., Hayden, S., Brown, Z., & Veldhuis, J. (2018). The effect of Instagram "likes" on women's social comparison and body dissatisfaction. *Body Image*, *26*, 90–97.

Torniainen-Holm, M., Pankakoski, M., Lehto, T., Saarelma, O., Mustonen, P., Joutsenniemi, K., & Suvisaari, J. (2016). The effectiveness of email-based exercises in promoting psychological well-being and healthy lifestyle: A two-year follow-up study. *BMC Psychology*, *4*, Article 21.

Trub, L., & Barbot, B. (2016). The paradox of phone attachment: Development and validation of the young adult attachment to phone scale (YAPS). *Computers in Human Behavior*, *64*, 663–672.

Van der Lee, M. L., & Garssen, B. (2012). Mindfulness-based cognitive therapy reduces chronic cancer-related fatigue: A treatment study. *Psycho-Oncology*, *21*(3), 264–272.

Van Velsen, L., Beaujean, D. J. M. A., & Van Gemert-Pijnen, J. E. W. C. (2013). Why mobile health app overload drives us crazy, and how to restore the sanity. *BMC Medical Informatics & Decision Making*, *13*(1), 1–5.

Wajcman, J., & Rose, E. (2011). Constant connectivity: Rethinking interruptions at work. *Organization Studies*, *32*, 941–961.

Waller, A. D., & Ragsdell, G. (2012). The impact of e-mail on work-life balance. *Aslib Proceedings*, *64*(2), 154–177.

Watson, B. R. (2018). "A window into shock, pain, and attempted recovery": A decade of blogging as a coping strategy in New Orleans. *New Media & Society*, *20*(3), 1068–1084.

Williams, L. M., Pines, A., Goldstein-Piekarski, A. N., Rosas, L. G., Kullar, M., Sacchet, M. D., ... Ma, J. (2018). The ENGAGE study: Integrating neuroimaging, virtual reality and smartphone sensing to understand self-regulation for managing depression and obesity in a precision medicine model. *Behaviour Research and Therapy*, *101*, 58–70.

Woodworth, R. J., O'Brien-Malone, A., Diamond, M. R., & Schüz, B. (2018). Data from "Web-based positive psychology interventions: A reexamination of effectiveness." *Journal of Open Psychology Data*, *6*(1).

Zheng, F., Gao, P., He, M., Li, M., Tan, J., Chen, D., ... Zhang, L. (2015). Association between mobile phone use and self-reported well-being in children: A questionnaire-based cross-sectional study in Chongqing, China. *BMJ Open*, *5*(5), Article e007302.

# 7

# Earth to Humans: Get with It or Get Out!: Adaptive Intelligence in the Age of Human-Induced Catastrophes

Robert J. Sternberg

An online humor magazine, *The Onion*, once carried an article, "Planet Earth doesn't know how to make it any clearer it wants everyone to leave" (*The Onion*, 2011). The story pointed out how, even after increased "natural catastrophes" of all kinds, people do not seem to be getting the message that the planet does not want them.

The article was meant to be humorous, but, in the time of coronavirus, it might seem that the Earth really is trying to send us a message. Actually, in a sense, it has been trying to send us a message since long before the advent of COVID-19 and before 2011. But the message is not about "natural catastrophes" but rather about human-induced ones. The message is to stop doing what we are doing before it is too late.

The large majority of catastrophes facing humans (and other species) today are not natural, but rather human-induced. Increased hurricane, tornado, typhoon, and other weather-related events have been caused at least in part by global climate change, which in turn has been largely or entirely caused by human activity (Carbon Brief, 2017), which at this point should surprise practically no one. Air pollution and water pollution also do not come out of nowhere – they derive from human activity as well – plastics, factory emissions, vehicle emissions, dumping of waste, and so on.

What does all of this have to do with intelligence? The sad thing is that in typical contemporary conceptions of intelligence, the answer is "practically nothing." That does not tell us that these issues are not problematical; rather, it tells us that our contemporary notions of intelligence, in a word, stink. They are as polluting of the intellectual atmosphere as unfiltered factory emissions are of the physical atmosphere.

*Positive Psychology: An International Perspective*, First Edition.
Edited by Aleksandra Kostić and Derek Chadee.
© 2021 John Wiley & Sons Ltd. Published 2021 by John Wiley & Sons Ltd.

Right now, I, like millions of others in the world, am stuck in my home because of the novel coronavirus. In my case, there is no law or regulation (yet) preventing me from leaving and going to any establishment I please that is still open. There are three problems, however. First, very few places are open for shopping. Supermarkets, fortunately, are still open, but they are poorly stocked. Second, we all are strongly discouraged from going near other people, so many of the places we might want to go – shopping centers, movie houses, sports stadiums – are either closed or off-limits. Third, I live in the part of the United States with, by far, the largest number of novel coronavirus cases, so it would be very hard not to take public- health recommendations seriously. Add to that my advancing age and the greater seriousness of coronavirus for older people, and, basically, I'm stuck.

The situation would not be so bad were it not for the fact that epidemiologists and other experts have been warning us about a pandemic for many years (Friedman, 2020), at least back to 2012 (by the Rand Corporation), and much earlier by anyone who saw what happened in the Spanish Flu of 1918. That's over a century to prepare. Was the world prepared? No. Was the United States prepared? No. Did politicians, including the US president, lie through their teeth until even many of their own unthinking supporters no longer believed the lies (Westbrook & Dosani, 2020)? Yes. But then, former President Trump lied about almost everything, having told, at least publicly, as of the end of 2019, over 15,000 lies (Mindock, 2019). Is anyone even bothering to count anymore? The problem is that his lies killed people. Until he changed his story, he was telling people that novel coronavirus was nothing to worry about (Rogers, 2020). So, he told people to go on with their lives, and some of those who were as credulous as to believe him paid the price by becoming seriously or fatally ill. That's not being a "very stable genius" (Diaz, 2018). It's not even intelligent. If intelligence is about adaptation – helping people to survive and even thrive in their environment–it's stupid.[1] Why is this scenario a serious problem for current conceptions and tests of intelligence?

In an intelligence test or one of its proxies, the test-taker is given problems to solve and then is expected to provide or, in the case of multiple-choice, choose the correct answer. If the test-taker provides the correct answer, they get credit. If they provide an incorrect answer, there is generally no credit, although a few tests allow partial credit. But basically, the test-taker is scored for being able to distinguish what is correct from what is incorrect – or what is true from what is false.

Suppose, though, that a person is able to distinguish what is correct from what is incorrect, or true from what is false, on a test of academic and not very important problems, at the same time that the person is unable to make this distinction for serious real-world problems with real consequences. Suppose even that the person is far more able to make such a distinction on a test than would be their great-grandparents, but is less able to make the distinction in real life than the great-grandparents. Who would be smarter, the person who was better at taking the tests, or the person who was better at solving real-world problems?

This question is not hypothetical. During the twentieth century, IQs around the world rose an average of 30 points (Flynn, 1987). People became *much* better at solving IQ-test problems. The difference, for example, between an IQ of 100 and an IQ of 130 is the difference between someone who is intellectually average and someone who is, in terms of IQ, at the borderline of being intellectually gifted; it is also the difference between someone who is intellectually average (IQ = 100) and someone who, with an IQ of 70, is borderline intellectually challenged. The only reason that the average IQ remained 100 during the extent of the twentieth century is that test publishers re-normed the tests to keep the average IQ at 100.

The world was not necessarily doing a super job of solving its problems during the beginning of the twentieth century. For example, the so-called Spanish flu of 1918 is estimated to have affected more than a quarter of the world's population at the time and to have killed over 50 million people worldwide (CDC, n.d.). But people in 1918, including medical professionals, knew much less about viruses and the mechanisms of transmission than they do today. They had no time to prepare. In contrast, the world, having been warned repeatedly of the danger of a pandemic (which was expected to be, but is not a strain of flu), had plenty of time to prepare contingency plans.

What country was truly prepared when the pandemic hit in full force in 2020? None. Intelligence certainly involves the "ability to learn" (Intelligence and Its Measurement: A Symposium, 1921). What exactly did the world learn from the earlier pandemic? What has it learned, really, about controlling proliferation of nuclear weapons, combating global climate change, or anything else of importance? Leaders of the major nations, such as, but not limited to the United States and Australia, actually have acted in ways to worsen climate change (Dennis, 2019). It is time for us to think of intelligence as adaptive – as adaptive intelligence – rather than just as general intelligence that does little, nothing, or negative things with regard to the future of humanity and the world (Sternberg, 2019, in press).

The paradox of modern psychology is that it values the predictor over the criterion. The predictor, of course, is IQ and scores on related proxy tests. The criterion is performance on whatever it is that IQ is supposed to predict. For all our high IQs, people are doing a lousy job of managing the world. The current pandemic of novel coronavirus shows how lousy the job is in real time, but, regrettably, future generations will have to learn the truly awful consequences of the stupidity of early twenty-first century humans in allowing climate change to pass multiple danger points and reacting either by doing nothing or by acting in ways that have made the situation much worse. Nations today are *not* acting in ways to preserve a future for their own future generations.

In psychology, it is common to distinguish between competence and performance (Davidson & Sternberg, 1985). Competence refers to what a person is capable of; performance refers to what a person actually does. Competence predicts performance, but very imperfectly. At best, IQ tests would be competence tests. They might show what a person is capable of. As tests of real-world competence, they are highly flawed, for reasons that have been discussed in many venues (see, e.g., Hedlund, 2020; Sternberg et al., 2000). For example, real-world problems usually do not have unique correct answers; they are not presented in multiple-choice format; they are for high stakes rather than low stakes; they are emotionally fraught; and there are constraints that other people impose on solutions, including constraints that lead people to choose bad solutions. As Jean-Claude Juncker said in reference to political decisions, "We all know what to do, we just don't know how to get re-elected after we've done it" (Juncker, 2007, quoted in Buti, Turrini, Van den Noord, and Biroli, 2008, p. 2). Often, in the real world, the problem is how to do the right thing and to have it rewarded rather than punished – the opposite of the situation with standardized tests.

In the everyday world, practical intelligence consists in large part of workarounds. How can one accomplish what one knows needs to be accomplished, despite the constraints working against doing whatever it is? In ethical decision-making, a problem typically is that acting ethically will result in negative rather than positive consequences, as Alexander Vindman and almost anyone who has stood up to Donald Trump learned (Sheth, 2020). Although the level of corruption in the Trump administration likely broke all records in US history for a presidential administration – what other president publicly pardoned officials who committed treason, thieves, and assorted miscreants, while punishing loyal Americans? – the problem is not limited to corrupt administrations in any one particular country. The world operates in a context very different from that of a multiple-choice test, whether with honorable politicians and business people or with corrupt ones.

## Social Psychology and Intelligence

One of the most meaningful books ever to have been written on intelligence as adaptation (or, to be exact, maladaptation) is a book that was written as a social-psychological treatise (Festinger, Riecken, & Schachter, 1956). The book is about a cult that believes the world is about to end. Only true believers in the teachings of the cult will be saved. These true believers have given up everything – homes, possessions, family ties – to prepare for their escape together.

A spaceship from the planet Clarion will come to take away and save the true believers. The rest of the world will be destroyed by a great flood to take place before dawn on a particular date, namely, December 21, 1954. The date comes; the group waits for the alien spaceship to arrive at midnight. It does not come. The time is changed to later in the night; the spaceship still does not come. The followers are totally confused until a message arrives. God has decided to spare the world because of the group's devotion. In other words, the group has single-handedly saved the world from destruction. (The world's faith was tested, much as Abraham's was when he offered up Isaac for a sacrifice and only spared Isaac because of a last-minute intervention by an angel.) The group becomes even more firm in its belief than it was before. In other words, the counterfactual evidence that one would expect to disabuse the group of its illusions, for the most part, strengthened an even more absurd set of illusions.

The study was undertaken to test the predictions of Leon Festinger's cognitive-dissonance theory (later published by Festinger, 1957). In particular, creating a cognitively inconsistent event – the failure of the spaceship to arrive from Clarion – might have resulted in the revelation that the beliefs the group held were erroneous. But another way to react to dissonance is to double down on the belief, thereby resolving the dissonance simply by lying to oneself about what is true or plausible. Put another way, facts no longer matter.

Why would many (but not all) people reaffirm false beliefs in the face of cognitive dissonance between reality and their beliefs, no matter how flimsy the evidence for those beliefs? According to Festinger, five conditions needed to be met.

First, the belief has to have been held with deep conviction and must be relevant to the actions that the individual is taking and potentially will take. If someone gives up their life as they have known it to await the arrival of an alien spaceship, it is a fair guess that the person takes the belief very seriously!

Second, the individual must have committed themself to the belief through action that is difficult to undo. Moving to a community of cultists certainly would qualify as an action representing serious commitment.

Third, the belief has to be specific enough and sufficiently oriented toward events in the real world, that such events could firmly, indeed unequivocally, refute the belief.

Fourth, the disconfirming event must occur and be recognized as such by the believer.

Fifth and finally, the believer must have a group that provides cohesive social support for reinterpreting the event as consistent with their original belief and even as a stronger basis than before for convincing others of the correctness of their beliefs, and perhaps of proselytizing others to join in those beliefs.

What does all this have to do with intelligence as adaptation or lack of intelligence as maladaptation? Through an unfortunate isolation of disciplines within psychology and the building of imaginary barriers between these disciplines, different disciplines of psychology often have grown up disconnected from, and have been seen as irrelevant to, each other. Real-world problem solving and decision making of any consequence almost always occurs in a sociocultural context that, at times, is highly fraught emotionally, such as in the extreme case of waiting to be rescued by aliens. In that case, all five of Festinger's constraints applied.

But wait! It does not take extreme cases like awaiting alien rescue for the five constraint to be met. Cognitive-dissonance theory was not intended merely for extreme events, but for the events that confront us every day. So, no matter that many Republicans and others in the United States for many years vehemently argued against high levels of government spending and bailouts. They changed their minds when it was convenient.

There are other theories of why people react as they do to cognitively dissonant information. For example, Bem and Allen (1974) suggested that what Festinger viewed as cognitive dissonance is actually self-perception. That is, people see themselves behaving in strange ways – perhaps ways they never would have predicted they would behave – and conclude that, if they are behaving that way, they must believe in whatever the basis for their actions is. Thus, instead of seeing actions merely emanating from thoughts, Bem and Allen suggested that people's thoughts emanate from their actions. They feel that what their actions imply to them they must feel, given the way they are acting. For the most part, the implications of the two theories are the same (although not identical).

Mitch McConnell, the Republican leader of the Senate, revealed a trillion-dollar spending package in response to coronavirus, the kind of package that he and his colleagues almost certainly would have vehemently opposed had it been released by a Democrat (Stein, DeBonis, Werner, & Kane, 2020). Although perhaps nothing would embarrass McConnell, his colleagues for the most part lined up behind him, having gone from being spending scolds, before former President Trump, to being the biggest spenders in the history of the United States, under former President Trump.

The utter lack of embarrassment is not limited to the amazingly hypocritical members of McConnell's party. Senator Bernie Sanders, a Democratic candidate for president in the election of 2020, released public-assistance programs that would have cost roughly $50 trillion if they were costed out (Samuelson, 2020). Where would the money come from, even for a small fraction of this massive social-spending program? Increased taxation, of course. But Sanders never gave a clue as to how increases in taxation would yield anything close to the levels of funding that would be needed for his programs. That doesn't seem to have bothered him any more than McConnell's about-face bothered him. Sanders, to his credit, remained consistent in this political philosophy. But he also remained consistent in his inability to get any of his proposed programs through Congress, leading him to be, essentially, utterly ineffectual as a Senator, at least in terms of getting his legislative ideas passed (Brodey, 2020; Dovere, 2016). He never said how he would get his ideas into practice as a president – why would things change under a Sanders presidency? He did not know; neither did his supporters. Did they care? I have no idea.

What is clear is that people at different points on a political spectrum are not only willing but eager to follow leaders who are like the emperor with no clothes. The leaders say one thing, do another, and retain their support. They retain their support, at least in part, because tribalism and ideology are stronger than rational thinking (Packer, 2018). People follow the crowd and the crowd follows the authorities (see Chapter 2, Positive Creativity).

## Role of Rational Thinking

Keith Stanovich and his colleagues (Stanovich, 2010; Stanovich, West, & Toplak, 2016) have studied rational thinking and even built a test of rational thinking. They have found rational thinking to be, at best, weakly related to the cognitive skills measured by IQ tests and their proxies. This finding should not be terribly surprising. There is a big difference between recognizing flaws in the clarity of our thinking and answering multiple-choice questions on an IQ test or proxy.

Consider just five of the informal logical fallacies committed on pretty much a daily basis.

1. *Begging the question.* Asked a question they cannot answer, they answer a different question or provide a woefully incomplete answer to the question they've received. Politicians probably let scarcely a day pass by without committing this fallacy.
2. *False dichotomy.* People assume that two options are dichotomous – mutually exclusive – when they are just two of a number of alternative options. For example, people may ask themselves whether they are going to protect themselves from coronavirus or not. But there is a whole continuum of steps in-between complete protection (e.g., isolation on an island; Marchetti, 2020) and no protection at all (Roberts, 2020).
3. *Ad hominem argument.* This is an argument that appears only at the most superficial level to be about an issue, when it is actually a personal attack on an individual or group of individuals who disagree with you. President Trump has blamed pretty much everyone except himself for the problems associated with the coronavirus (Smith, 2020).
4. *Straw person argument.* One accuses an opponent, often unnamed, of a position in an argument that neither they nor, likely, anyone else takes. In other words, one defends one's position against an imaginary counter-position, falsely ascribing that position to people who don't hold it. Politicians, of course, do this all the time, creating imaginary enemies to make themselves look good. They are especially susceptible to doing this in times of crisis, seeking a scapegoat to blame for their own failings. But we all can do it. It happens in academia frequently, with scholars accusing others of taking positions that the others don't take.
5. *Appeal to authority.* This obvious cognitive error has become especially invidious during the reign of former President Trump, as he seemed to believe himself to be an authority about nearly everything, including the coronavirus, certainly more so than recognized experts in the medical profession (Lopez, 2020). This may have been part of an effort to confuse people about who the real experts are so that people would listen to Trump about anything and everything (Lutz, 2020).

## Role of Personality

Avoidance of informal logical fallacies and of irrational thinking, in general, is not just a matter of abilities. It is also a matter of personality. Many studies have been done relating personality to intelligence. The findings are not always completely consistent, but one finding that is consistent is that the personality trait of openness to experience is moderately correlated with intelligence, almost without regard to how intelligence is measured (DeYoung, 2020). Openness to experience includes attributes such as intellectual curiosity, willingness to take on complex intellectual challenges, interest in intellectual matters, imaginativeness, elaborated fantasy life, aesthetic appreciation, and the like.

Although people might think that personality attributes are etched in stone, of course they are not. Anyone can develop intellectual interests, willingness to undertake intellectual challenges, and the like. As Walter Mischel (1996) pointed out years ago, personality is at least in part situational. If one is in an intellectually exciting environment, for example, one is more likely to develop openness to experience than if one is in an intellectually stultifying environment. Children and adults alike will benefit from the environment that encourages rather than discourages openness to experience.

## The Role of Positive Psychology

Positive psychology focuses on people's strengths and on possible ways to help them to flourish (Lopez, Pedrotti, & Snyder, 2018). Flourishing in life, however, is not, or at least, should not be about excelling on tests that have modest ecological validity for the kinds of challenges people will face in their lives. Rather, the focus should be on helping people to flourish in the problems they will encounter in their professional and personal lives – problems that are often vaguely formulated, complex, emotionally arousing, perplexing, and unsusceptible to being solved in a multiple-choice format.

Intelligence should help people solve not only relatively trivial and meaningless test problems, but also help them to solve complex, high-stakes real-world problems. Yet, decade after decade, many and probably most societies emphasize in schooling problems that stretch a kind of intelligence that will be of little use, and arguably, worse than useless in solving real-world problems. The stunning failure of the world's leaders to prepare for coronavirus should dispel any myth that, at least in the United States, the schools are doing what needs fully to be done. Indeed, incredibly, during the Trump administration, the government did a comprehensive simulation of what would happen if there were an unexpected pandemic of the kind the world is having right now. The predictions for what was called the "crimson contagion" were right on target with what is happening.

What happened to the simulation? In typical incompetent and maladaptive governmental fashion, the Trump team marked the report "not to be disclosed" (Sanger, Lipton, Sullivan, & Crowley, 2020). If that is not a terrific example of "negative psychology," what is? The government did the simulation and then covered it up so that it could not be used before millions of people would become ill, and many of them, dead. Of course, the perpetrators will pay no cost. President Trump crowed about his perfect response to the pandemic. Would the world expect any more from him?

Societies could be teaching positive and useful lessons, if they chose to. For the most part, they don't. Rather, they teach students lots of stuff that the students never will need and then assess them on this largely useless information. Is that the best we can do? Can we afford to teach and test in such a misguided way in a time when the world is facing such dire threats? The answer has to be no. We already are paying the steep price of global climate change, air pollution, water pollution, terrorism, and now, neglect of public health. How long can this go on? Students need to learn about and be tested on real problems – or simulation problems that, at the least, have the characteristics of real problems (Sternberg, 2019, in press). We all can do this. *Have students address and try to solve real problems with real constraints.* That's what schools should teach; that's what schools should assess. It's as simple as that. That is the positive-psychological message. Prepare students for the real world, not for an invented world of academic schooling and tests. The future of the world depends on it.

The Earth is not telling us to leave. It is begging us to stay. Will we listen – before it is too late?

## Note

1   There are a number of political examples in this chapter. Please note that they include both US parties. This is not a political essay, but it does cover how political decisions can be adaptively intelligent or unintelligent. Regrettably, many such decisions in recent years have been adaptively unintelligent, at best, and adaptively stupid, at worst.

## References

Bem, D. J., & Allen, A. (1974). On predicting some of the people some of the time: The search for cross-situational consistencies in behavior. *Psychological Review, 81*(6), 506–520.

Brodey, S. (2020). What Bernie Sanders really got done in his 29 years in Congress. *Daily Beast*. Retrieved from https://www.thedailybeast.com/what-bernie-sanders-really-got-done-in-his-29-years-in-congress.

Buti, M., Turrini, A., Van den Noord, P., & Biroli, P. (2008). Defying the "Juncker curse": Can reformist governments be re-elected? Economic paper 324, European Economy. Retrieved August 19, 2020, from https://ec.europa.eu/economy_finance/publications/pages/publication_summary12588_en.htm.

Carbon Brief. (2017). Analysis: Why scientists think that 100% of global warming is due to humans.

Retrieved from https://www.carbonbrief.org/analysis-why-scientists-think-100-of-global-warming-is-due-to-humans.

Centers for Disease Control and Prevention (CDC). (n.d.). 1918 pandemic (H1N1 virus). https://www.cdc.gov/flu/pandemic-resources/1918-pandemic-h1n1.html.

Davidson, J. E., & Sternberg, R. J. (1985). Competence and performance in intellectual development. In E. Neimark, R. de Lisi, & J. H. Newman (Eds.), *Moderators of competence* (pp. 43–76). Hillsdale, NJ: Lawrence Erlbaum.

Dennis, B. (2019). In bleak report, UN says drastic action is only way to avoid worst effects of climate change. *The Washington Post*. Retrieved from https://www.washingtonpost.com/climate-environment/2019/11/26/bleak-report-un-says-drastic-action-is-only-way-avoid-worst-impacts-climate-change.

DeYoung, C. G. (2020). Intelligence and personality. In R. J. Sternberg (Ed.), *Handbook of intelligence* (Vol. 2, 1011–1047). New York: Cambridge University Press.

Diaz, D. (2018). Trump: I'm a "very stable genius." CNN. Retrieved from https://www.cnn.com/2018/01/06/politics/donald-trump-white-house-fitness-very-stable-genius/index.html.

Dovere, E. I. (2016). Sanders had big ideas but little impact on Capitol Hill. *Politico*. Retrieved from https://www.politico.com/story/2016/03/bernies-record-220508

Festinger, L. (1957). *A theory of cognitive dissonance*. Stanford, CA: Stanford University Press.

Festinger, L., Riecken, H. W., & Schachter, S. (1956). *When prophecy fails: A social and psychological study of a modern group the predicted the destruction of the world*. New York: Harper & Row.

Flynn, J. R. (1987). Massive IQ gains in 14 nations. *Psychological Bulletin, 101,* 171–191.

Friedman, U. (2020). We were warned. *The Atlantic*. Retrieved from https://www.theatlantic.com/politics/archive/2020/03/pandemic-coronavirus-united-states-trump-cdc/608215

Hedlund, J. (2020). Practical intelligence. In R. J. Sternberg (Ed.), *Cambridge handbook of intelligence* (Vol. 2, pp. 736–755). New York: Cambridge University Press.

Intelligence and its Measurement: A symposium. (1921). *Journal of Educational Psychology, 12,* 123–147, 195–216, 271–275.

Juncker, J.-P. (2007). Quoted in European Commission. Retrieved from https://ec.europa.eu/economy_finance/publications/pages/publication_summary12588_en.htm.

Lopez, G. (2020). Trumpe's expert urged caution about a coronavirus treatment: Trump hyped it up anyway. Vox. Retrieved from https://www.vox.com/policy-and-politics/2020/3/20/21188397/coronavirus-trump-press-briefing-covid-19-anthony-fauci.

Lopez, S. J., Pedrotti, J. T., & Snyder, C. R. (2018). *Positive psychology: The scientific and practical explorations of human strengths* (4th ed.). Thousand Oaks, CA: Sage.

Lutz, E. (2020). Coronavirus: Trump's mixed messages "undeermines public trust," experts say. *The Guardian*. Retrieved from https://www.theguardian.com/us-news/2020/mar/01/trump-science-coronavirus-public-trust.

Marchetti, S. (2020). Italian hermit living alone on an island says self-isolation is the ultimate journey. CNN. Retrieved from https://www.cnn.com/travel/article/Italy-hermit-coronavirus/index.html.

Mindock, C. (2019). Trump has made over 15,000 false or misleading statements since becoming president, report says. *Independent*. Retrieved from https://www.nytimes.com/video/opinion/100000007038780/trump-lies-about-coronavirus.html?action=click&module=Opinion&pgtype=Homepage.

Mischel, W. (1996). *Personality and assessment*. Mahwah, NJ: Lawrence Erlbaum. *The Onion*. (2011, June 1). Planet Earth doesn't know how to make it any clearer it wants everyone to leave. Retrieved from https://www.theonion.com/planet-earth-doesnt-know-how-to-make-it-any-clearer-it-1819572679.

Packer, G. (2018). A new report offers insights into tribalism in the age of Trump. *The New Yorker*. Retrieved from https://www.newyorker.com/news/daily-comment/a-new-report-offers-insights-into-tribalism-in-the-age-of-trump

Roberts, C. (2020, March 13). How to protect yourself from coronavirus. *Consumer Reports*.

Retrieved from https://www.consumerreports. org/coronavirus/how-to-protect-yourself-from-coronavirus.

Rogers, K. (2020). Trump now claims he always knew the coronavirus would be a pandemic. *The New York Times*. Retrieved from https://www. nytimes.com/2020/03/17/us/politics/trump-coronavirus.html.

Samuelson, R. J. (2020). Here's how much a Bernie Sanders presidency would cost. *The Washington Post*. Retrieved from https://www.washingtonpost. com/opinions/the-sanders-bill-for-democracy-50-trillion/2020/02/26/c6963114-58dc-11ea-9b35-def5a027d470_story.html.

Sanger, D. E., Lipton, E., Sullivan, E., & Crowley, M. (2020, March 20). Before virus outbreak, a cascade of warnings went unheeded. *The New York Times*. Retrieved from https://www.nytimes.com/2020/03/19/us/politics/trump-coronavirus-outbreak.html.

Sheth, S. (2020). "I'm not happy with him": Impeachment witness Lt. Col. Alexander Vindman was escorted from the White House on Friday. *Business Insider*. Retrieved from https://www.businessinsider.com/trump-considering-ousting-alexander-vindman-impeachment-witness-ukraine-report-2020-2.

Smith, D. (2020). "I don't take responsibility": Trump shakes hands and spreads blame over coronavirus. *The Guardian*. Retrieved from https:// www.theguardian.com/us-news/2020/mar/13/donald-trump-coronavirus-national-emergency-sketch.

Stanovich, K. E. (2010). What intelligence tests miss: The psychology of rational thought. New Haven, CT: Yale University Press.

Stanovich, K. E., West, R. F., & Toplak, M. E. (2016). *The rationality quotient: Toward a test of rational thinking*. Cambridge, MA: MIT Press.

Stein, J., DeBonis, M., Werner, E., & Kane, E. (2020). Senate Republicans release massive economic stimulus bill for coronavirus response. *The Washington Post*. Retrieved from https://www. washingtonpost.com/business/2020/03/19/trump-coronavirus-economic-plan-stimulus.

Sternberg, R. J. (2019). A theory of adaptive intelligence and its relation to general intelligence. *Journal of Intelligence, 7*(4), Article 23.

Sternberg, R. J. (in press). *Adaptive intelligence*. New York: Cambridge University Press.

Sternberg, R. J., Forsythe, G. B., Hedlund, J., Horvath, J., Snook, S., Williams, W. M., . . . Grigorenko, E. L. (2000). *Practical intelligence in everyday life*. New York: Cambridge University Press.

Westbrook, A., & Dosani, S. (2020). The president is lying. *The New York Times*. Retrieved from https:// www.nytimes.com/video/opinion/100000007038780/trump-lies-about-coronavirus.html?action=click&module=Opinion&pgtype=Homepage

# 8

# Time Perspective and Good Feelings

Aleksandra Kostić, Derek Chadee,
and Marija Pejičić

## Introduction

Psychological research on time indicates that the attitude toward time has a strong, and even powerful influence on the way lives are modeled (Zimbardo & Boyd, 1999, 2008). The way we relate to different time intervals and the way in which we separate and connect them, and then separate again, thus creating smaller units which, sometimes, require a more careful analysis, determine our feelings, observations, behaviors, and the entire experience (Gonzalez & Zimbardo, 1985). This is important for understanding personal attitude toward time, which an individual sometimes does not recognize or is not aware of enough, but it is important to identify that attitude so that its positive effects could be strengthened and deepened and the negative ones weakened (Zimbardo & Boyd, 2008, p. 6). Accordingly, there is utility in analyzing the characteristics of a personal attitude toward time: its direction (positive or negative), then, extremeness (very pronounced, moderate or weak), and its inner balance. The subjective experience of time should make time work for an individual and make their life happier, better, and more meaningful (Kostić & Nedeljković, 2013; Zimbardo & Boyd, 1999). The ability of humans to think about their past, present ,and future, and the meanings and values they ascribe to them, as well as the feelings that they experience (as cited in Baumeister, 2018, p. 24, Suddendorf, 2013), enables the inflow of new information about the attitude toward time and its effects.

As Rosenzweig, Breedlove, and Watson (2005) point out, emotions have several dimensions, including feelings, action tendencies, physiological arousal, and motivational programs. Our emotions, therefore, are quite directly associated with

*Positive Psychology: An International Perspective*, First Edition.
Edited by Aleksandra Kostić and Derek Chadee.
© 2021 John Wiley & Sons Ltd. Published 2021 by John Wiley & Sons Ltd.

the formation of time perspectives. Stolarski, Matthews, Postek, Zimbardo, and Bitner (2014) suggest that our personality and emotions and emotional experiences are factors that influence the formation of our time perspective. The emotions associated with one time perspective to another may have a suppression or incitement effect to the dominance of that one time perspective in relation to another. However, there is a circular relationship between emotions and time perspective in that our time perspectives are associated emotions that would have, to some extent, determined their formation. As Stolarski et al. (2014, p. 809) reported: "Findings confirmed that time perspective appears to influence both recall and anticipation of mood. For example, past negative time perspective is associated with anticipation of negative moods, and past positive perspective relates to both recall and anticipation of energy. Time perspective may structure the individual's affective experience."

In this chapter, our interest is directed toward the analysis of the connection between the subjective experience of time and an individual's positive affective experience. Therefore, an important question to ask is whether a certain preferred temporal orientation implies a higher number of positive, and another one implies a higher number of negative effects. Can a positive attitude toward the past, the present, or the future provide the impression of a good life, with which an individual is mostly content and which gives them more positive than negative feelings, and allows them to have emotional stability and balance and the feeling of happiness, that is, the experience of subjective well-being (Baumeister, Vohs, Aaker, & Garbinsky, 2013, p. 505)?

Sometimes unnoticeably, and sometimes with intrusion, time *crawls into* all pores of life, thus shaping our observations, thoughts, feelings, plans, decisions, and behaviors (Kostić & Chadee, 2017; Zimbardo & Boyd, 1999). During a conversation, when we mention experiences that happened a few days or a few years ago, we rely on our recent or remote memories, on the images of those experiences which are lively and full of details, or the lack of all that, while being wrapped in either pleasant or unpleasant emotions. Talking about what we have previously experienced can reveal the attitude toward time which we have left behind, while we are aware that the current experiences of fulfillment and pleasure, or indifference and boredom, or painful resignation, will also soon become a part of the past, just like the recently finished conversation (Kostić, Pejičić, & Chadee, 2017).

Most people experience time as something that has essential value to them, something that is by itself available and provided, and something that should always be available to them. In their book, *The Time Paradox*, Zimbardo and Boyd (2008, p. 10) make an observation that, even though time is certainly of great importance and it has incomparably higher significance in relation to some other values, such as economic, it is often spent automatically, recklessly, and too lightly. The authors believe that this happens only because people have not learned to think about time, about its special value, sense, and the meaning it has for them.

However, different time frameworks can be filled with both positive and negative effects, as well as indifference. They can become the center of increased activity, motivation and achievement, the area for new solutions and transformations, but also, the framework which is filled by passivity, helpless waiting for an outcome, and conviction that everything is set in advance. Most certainly, the reflections of past and present experiences model the way in which an individual thinks about the future, full of hope and belief that they will achieve all important desires and significant goals, that the time which has yet to come will be better, or, on the contrary, that the future will be uncertain, insecure, and will not depend on their actions. Boniwell (2005) states that time has *a unique sense and meaning for each individual.* This meaning is, according to Hendricks and Peters (1986), deeply connected with an individual's activities, thoughts, and feelings as well as the changes which they observe while going through different life stages. However, the events which occur sequentially in a row, and the measuring of their duration, do not determine the subjective experience of an individual.

Time provides us with many opportunities to feel happiness. This is confirmed by our memories of beautiful moments that we have previously experienced, the enjoyment of current experiences, and the optimistic expectation of future joyful events. Our personal, and sometimes exaggerated, attitude toward certain time perspectives is connected with the experience of both positive and negative emotions. It is clear that the positive attitude toward the past as well as the hedonistic attitude toward the present represent a good framework for the occurrence of positive emotions. We wonder whether a positive attitude toward the future, through planning, prediction, and the control of possible positive outcomes, can also be the source of our happiness.

## Time Perspective

Time cannot be explained as an exclusively realistic and objectively given physical entity which we experience with the help of our senses and certain sensory processes. The perception of time is not analogous to the observation of a physical object, its color, shape, and firmness. Time is also a psychological entity (Block, 1990; Block & Zakay, 1996), because it cannot be understood without taking into consideration the personal traits of an individual, their individual experiences, and their subjective interpretations. This is reflected in the terms which are mentioned by Boniwell (2009, p. 296): *lived time* (Gorman & Wessman, 1977), *psychological time* (Golovakina & Kronick, 1989), or *subjective experience of time* (Levin & Zakay, 1989), all of which clearly point to time being treated within the subjective paradigm. Research shows (Husman & Hilpert, 2017; Kazakina, 1999; Kostić, Pejičić, & Chadee, 2017; Seginer, 2005, 2017; Zimbardo & Boyd, 1999, 2008) that the subjective interpretations of past and present, as well as the attitude toward future goals, plans, and organization of activities, have a great influence on the individual and their social functioning. People subjectively evaluate and interpret their memories, remote and current experiences, expectations and desires, and forms attitudes toward them. During the evaluation of different periods in life, individuals recognize a change in relation to what they have experienced by comparing it with what they currently experience or expect to experience later. They realize that despite a close connection between the change and time, these two phenomena cannot be perceived as equal.

*Time perspective* is one of the key areas in the research of psychological time (Zimbardo & Boyd, 1999). The observed connection between the attitude toward time and one's behavior has increased the interest of researchers in studying this relation, leaving aside the observations of some other phenomena, such as the subjective estimation of the duration of a certain time interval or the individual way of using time (Boniwell, 2009).

If we reflect on the beginnings of the scientific interest in the study of time and the attitude toward it (Stolarski, Fieulaine, & Van Beek, 2015, pp. 3–4), two very important publications can be singled out: "The Perception of Time" by William James (1890/1950) and "Time Perspective and Morale" by Kurt Lewin (1942). The former publication shows that the scientific study of time and its duration received a significant place in psychology, while the latter publication connects us directly to the theoretical foundation of time perspective. In his observation on the nature of morality and hope as its significant component, Lewin (1942) emphasized the importance of the individual's subjective view of time. In his opinion, a personal attitude toward the future "controls" not only an individual's morale and decisions, but also their feelings, actions, and chosen and achieved goals. Lewin also pointed out that everyone should focus on what they currently experience, which was always significantly related to what they had previously experienced or would experience in the future. Believing that he was one of the first researchers who realized the true significance of time perspective for studying and understanding human behavior, Zimbardo and Boyd (2008, p. 51) cite Lewin's definition of time perspective (1942), which he reduced to "one's overall psychological view of the future and the past which is reflected in the present moment." Boniwell notices (2009, p. 296) that Lewin's point of view on the interconnectedness of past, present, and future time has also been acceptable to some other researchers of time in psychology (Lennings, 1996; Lennings, Burns, & Cooney, 1998; Nuttin, 1985; Zimbardo & Boyd, 1999).

Zimbardo and Boyd (2008, p. 51) state that traditional definitions of time perspective and the analysis of the aforementioned definitions suggest that there is a similarity in the concept of time with the scientists who lived and operated in different epochs.

As a fundamental dimension of time, time perspective can be understood in several ways: as the knowledge about something that has passed, which occurs now and which has yet to come (James, 1950/1890); as a type of behavior which results not only from the present experience but also from what has been experienced before or can be expected to be experienced in the future (Fraisse, 1963), and as a dominant orientation of an individual toward a specific course of time, which makes and shapes their world of motivation, experience, and behavior (De Volder, 1980). Also, time perspective can be viewed as a construct made of cognitive and affective components which collectively determine the attitude toward the past, the present, and the future (Lennings, 1996) and as an individually cognitive approach which represents the determinant of the way in which an individual observes, thinks, and behaves (Boniwell, 2009).

Zimbardo and Boyd (2008, p. 51) define this construct in the following way: "Time perspective is the often nonconscious personal attitude that each of us holds toward time and the process whereby the continual flow of existence is bundled into time categories that help to give order, coherence, and meaning to our lives." They state that the attitude toward time can be positive or negative, specifically oriented toward the past, the present, or the time that is coming, and it can also be balanced among the aforementioned temporal frameworks. A large step toward a deeper understanding of time perspective has been made by constructing and developing the instrument labeled as the Zimbardo time perspective inventory (ZTPI; Zimbardo & Boyd, 1999). The instrument was developed with the aim of measuring a personal attitude toward time, and it contains 56 statements and five subscales, which include five time factors: future, past-positive, past-negative, present-hedonism, and present. Taking into consideration the length of the questionnaire, Zimbardo and Boyd have developed a unique scale for measuring the transcendental-future orientation (TFTPI). Over the last decades, TFTPI has been widely accepted, adapted, and applied in different countries (the United States, Spain, Portugal, Sweden, Croatia, Serbia, Trinidad, Russia, Brazil, Italy, France, Germany, the Czech Republic, China, and Japan).

According to the theory and 30 years of research by Zimbardo and Boyd (2008, p. 52), there are six main time perspectives. Time perspectives are labeled in the following manner: past-negative, past-positive, present-hedonistic, present-fatalistic, future, and transcendental-future. The past-negative perspective (PN) is characterized by a predominantly negative attitude toward the events from the past, which is also reflected in the frequent mentioning of failure, traumatic experiences, and frustrations of an individual. On the contrary, the past-positive orientation (PP) is characterized by a warm and sentimental view on what one has experienced before, also including the negative experiences which they are trying to perceive from a more positive angle. The present-hedonistic attitude (PH) guides and "pushes" an individual toward enjoyment and different immediate pleasures, without taking into consideration the consequences of current activities on the future. The present-fatalistic attitude (PF) is characterized by experiencing general helplessness, hopelessness, surrendering of oneself to whatever comes in the future, for which an individual believes to be predetermined, already set and not favorable for them. That individual thinks that their effort is not worth it, which reduces their personal efficiency and active engagement. The future orientation (F) is characterized by thinking about that which is yet to come, setting future goals and planning activities, which usually implies the prevalence of the principle of reality and the existence of control. An individual is capable of postponing little pleasures if they expect to get a bigger one in the future, as a reward for the invested effort and commitment. The transcendental-future is the sixth time perspective of *time psychology* by Zimbardo and Boyd. As it has been mentioned, with the aim of determining the level of presence of this dimension, a special instrument (TFTPI) has been created. The individual expects to go to heaven after death and believes in the afterlife and reincarnation. They have good impulse control and rethink each activity due to the consequences it might have on the future.

The time perspective of an individual or a group reveals, first of all, the dominant way of thinking about the past, the present, or the future time, which is based on the existing system of values and related cultural patterns, which are internalized during socialization (Zimbardo & Boyd, 2008). The attitude toward time which can become a stable characteristic of behavior is accompanied by certain feelings, beliefs, and approaches, which is the reason that it can provide answers to many questions which arise from different situations and areas of life.

Having observed that there was a research tendency to focus only on one time orientation, Kazakina (1999, 2015, p. 503), in her study, included all three time orientations by analyzing them along different dimensions (density, emotional valence, and extension). Her results pointed to two variables to which the researchers did not pay much attention. First, this refers to the *temporal continuity*, that is, the experience of an intrinsic connection of the past, the present, and the future of an individual. Second, when it comes to the feelings and thoughts of an individual, Kazakina also revealed the possibility of establishing a certain balance – *temporal balance* – within the aforementioned time frameworks. These are very important discoveries because they give a new image of time perspective which is not shattered, divided but integrated, and harmonious and meaningfully connected through one's own experience.

The research by Zimbardo and Boyd (1999, p. 1285) indicates that the profile of balanced time perspective (BTP) implies moderate to high scores on past-positive, present-hedonistic, and future perspectives, and relatively low scores on past-negative and present-fatalistic perspectives. The basic characteristic of this balanced attitude toward different time frameworks is flexibility, that is, the ability and motivation to take different time perspectives depending on the demands of a situation, personal needs, personality traits, and the properties of the given assignment (Boniwell & Zimbardo, 2004; Zimbardo, 2002; Zimbardo & Boyd, 1999, p. 1285). The focus on one specific time dimension usually limits an individual to adapt to the conditions in which they currently find themself (Zimbardo & Boyd, 1999), whereby being flexible allows for the most adequate time dimension to be in the temporary foreground while the other dimensions are in the background. The balance and continuity of time perspectives are related to high productivity and the feeling of well-being. Namely, it has been shown that being satisfied with one's past, present, and future makes people significantly more successful at work, at achieving and developing their careers, as well as establishing satisfactory relationships with their friends and family (Boniwell, Osin, Linley, & Ivanchenko, 2010).

## Positive Affective Experiences

Although scientists may differ in their attempts to define happiness and other categories of positive emotions, one thing is quite certain: people want a life filled with pleasant experiences which awaken positive emotions, regardless of what their antecedents are. Compliant to this hedonistic goal, a life which brings positive affective experiences to a person can be viewed as *good* (eudaimonia). For many people, to live a *good life* is an important goal toward which they aspire while equating the assessment of the quality of their entire life with the positive feelings that they are currently experiencing. Keyes and Annas (2009) argue that there are significant differences between a person's experience of happiness and the good life that they are living. Thus hedonism is "one of the options within eudaimonism," whereby "our eudaimonic well-being definitions and the hedonic well-being definitions hinge on two key constructs: feeling and functioning" (2009, p. 198). In attempting to differentiate between a happy and a meaningful life – which despite certain overlaps cannot be reduced to one and the same for a happy life is not necessarily a meaningful life and vice versa – Baumeister et al. (2013) state that *meaningfulness*, that is, an assessment of purpose of one's life, could be observed as "more central to eudaimonia than to simply feeling good" (Baumeister et al., 2013, p. 506; see also Baumeister, 2018, p. 21).

Positive affect states, including pride, concern, interest, and engagement, encourage risk-taking behavior to sustain and increase positive affect in the present. These are characteristic of the present-hedonistic time perspective and approached behavior associated with the future time perspective (Sailer et al., 2014; Sirois, 2014). Noteworthy, is the dominant effect of past-negative over past-positive time perspective on psychological well-being. Baumeister, Catanese, and Vohs (2001) suggest that negative life events have a stronger psychological impact than positive. However, focusing on both negative and positive experiences can result in happiness, in that focusing on negative life events may lead to avoidance of mistakes while focusing on positive life events can motivate to achieve important goals (Iranpour, Erfani, & Ebrahimi, 2018).

In their article on the measurement and the structure of happiness, Linley, Maltby, Wood, Osborne, and Hurling (2009) state that this emotion, in a general sense, can be understood and measured in two ways within the subjective experience of well-being (*subjective well-being*). They argue that the structure of the subjective experience of well-being consists of two components – affective and cognitive. The first one is based on the established balance of the influence of positive and negative affects (*affect balance*), with a tendency of the positive affects to prevail, while the second component relates to the assessment of satisfaction with life overall (*satisfaction with life*). And while the affective component indicates a person's current emotional state, the cognitive component attests to the creation of a person's value proposition of satisfaction with their life hitherto. Independently from all differences in the nature and the structure of these components, Baumeister et al. (2013, p. 506) argue that *affective balance* and *satisfaction with life* are closely linked to a person's ability to gratify their basic and other needs and to reach what they had wanted, what they had considered worthy, and to which they had aspired. If their various needs are gratified, it is clear that this will affect the occurrence of positive emotions.

Considering the *enjoyable emotions* category, Ekman states that there are "more than a dozen" (2003, p. 190) of these emotions, that they are universal in nature, that they are emotions which we enjoy, which are pleasant, which please us, and which are different from one another in their properties (sensory pleasures, excitement, relief, ecstasy, gratitude, happiness, wonderment, ecstasy, elevation, contentment, and more), although they are adorned with the same facial sign – a *smile*. Ekman (2003, p. 204) states that the smiles which express different enjoyment emotions differ in duration and volume. It is difficult to identify which emotion is portrayed based on this facial configuration, however, listening carefully to a person's voice can be a good and reliable source of information about what the person is feeling.

Unfortunately, the term *enjoyment of emotions* is not distinctive enough and, in commenting on this fact, Ekman states: "The problem with the words *enjoyment* and *happiness* is that they're not specific enough; they imply a single state of mind and feeling, in the same way in which the terms *upset* and *negative* don't reveal whether someone is sad, angry, afraid, or disgusted." Hence, Ekman deems that the term *happiness* does not adequately explicate "which kind of happiness was occurring," which sometimes creates confusion for it is also used to denote different experiences and subjective assessments (Ekman, 2003, p. 202).

Ekman discusses (2003, p. 203) the existence of a certain personal predisposition to experience enjoyable emotions. Thus, it turns out that people with more pronounced extraversion and greater emotional stability are more likely to report being happier, which is correlated to their lower sensitivity to social rejection and better adaptation to the demands of the culture in which they live. It has not been specifically investigated whether some specific personality traits can be predictors of experiencing the different types of enjoyment emotions mentioned by Ekman. However, it has been indicated that an optimistic attitude, especially one that permeates the whole outlook on life, can be a predictor of the occurrence of positive feelings and good moods, achievements, and physical health of a person (Peterson, 2000).

Some other research (Lyubomirsky, 2007) also indicates differences in the behavior of people who claim to be happy compared to those who say that they are not. It can be observed that people who place themselves in the category of happy people are very optimistic about creating an idea of the future including clearly setting goals whereby they preplan activities and steps to be taken. When faced with difficulties in achieving their set goals, they are able to undertake adequate strategies and successfully cope with obstacles. They usually pay attention to the building of stable and high-quality friendly, family, and professional relationships, trying to *sense* other people's states and help them when they are in need. They aspire to gratifications, they enjoy them, portraying that they are aware of the present moment in which they live. They feel and express gratitude for everything that they have.

Taking into account the aforementioned behavioral tendencies characteristic of people who consider themselves happy (Lyubomirsky, 2007), Zimbardo and Boyd (2008, pp. 252–253) argue that it is easy to notice the correlation of these approaches with certain time perspectives. Thus, gratitude fits well within the frame of positive attitude toward the past (PP), and an orientation toward gratifications fits well within the frame of hedonistic experience of the present (HP), whereby an optimistic view of the future is in line with the time perspective of the future (F).

In his book, *The Other Side of Happiness*, Brock Bastian (2018, p. 7) makes an interesting observation about the way in which the we may *view* both a happy and a sad person. For some observers, the expression of happiness is not only an indicator of a person's internal state but it is also a signal that they are successful, accomplished, healthy, that everything is all right with them. On the contrary, a sad person may be viewed as someone who is missing something, as someone who is ill, as a person with whom there is something wrong. Nevertheless, unpleasant experiences and negative affects are a part of a person's overall real experience and they are difficult to avoid. Therefore, we cannot deny or reject them. Does this mean that a person should learn to mitigate their painful experiences, reinterpret them, direct their attention to positive contents, or find useful influences of some other factors without questioning the realization of their dream of a good life? This is not about not recognizing the existence of different affective experiences, but rather it is about ways for a person to cope with them, to combine them in a way which will ensure their satisfaction with life.

## Time Perspective and Subjective Positive Affects

Within the concept of positive psychology, developed by Martin Seligman, time perspective occupies a significant place (Seligman & Csikszentmihalyi, 2000). One of the dimensions of this model implies positive subjective experiences (the remaining two are: positive individual traits and positive institutions), whereby well-being and pleasure are analyzed as constructs which are related to the past, hope and optimism as constructs which refer to the future, and flow and happiness are most often related to the present. Thus, this model has provided the context for the study of the relations between time perspectives, on one side, and positive subjective experiences, on the other.

There are differences among these categories of positive subjective experiences which are similar in content, but, nevertheless, different, which will also enable a more differentiated view of the relations between these constructs and the afore-mentioned time perspectives. Thus, Diener, Shuh, Lucas, and Smith (1999) believe that the subjective well-being is a complex term which includes four lower terms, such as the presence of positive (pleasant) affect, the absence of negative (unpleasant) affect, life satisfaction, and domain satisfaction. The first component comprises emotions, such as "joy, elation, contentment, pride, affection, happiness, ecstasy" (p. 277). The most important negative affects are: "guilt and shame, sadness, anxiety and worry, anger, stress, depression, envy" (p. 277). When it comes to global judgments, that is, cognitive evaluation of life satisfaction, this component refers to "the desire to change life, satisfaction with current life, satisfaction with past, satisfaction with future, and significant others' views of one's life" (p. 277). Finally, the fourth component is related to the satisfaction in different domains, such as: "work, family, leisure, health, finances, self or one's group" (p. 277).

Simons, Peeters, Janssens, Lataster, and Jacobs (2016) found that age was a moderator between time perspective and well-being. Their study found that age decreased the strengthening of the negative association between the past-negative time perspective and happiness. The authors note that the "results of the final regression analyses performed separately in the two different age groups, support this moderation effect: the negative association between the past-negative time perspective was weaker in the older group than in the younger group. In addition, the older group showed a weaker association between a present-fatalistic time perspective and happiness than the younger group did." However, it should be noted that there is an inverse relationship between age and savoring, that is "attending to, appreciating, and enhancing positive experiences through either volitional attempts or more automatic processes that occur in response to positive events" (Palmer & Gentzler, 2019). Palmer and Gentzler's (2019) study suggests that the relationship between these two factors is mediated by a reduction in hedonic motivation as a result of aging together with a drive to have high positive affect arousal. These factors, as the authors suggest, help us to appreciate the dynamics between positive emotions, emotional regulation, and time perspective.

In the following, this chapter will present the relation between time perspectives and some of the most frequently studied positive subjective experiences.

Regarding the orientation toward the past, the empirical data have shown that those individuals who have a dominant past-negative time perspective tend to report less expressed happiness (Boniwell et al., 2010; Drake, Duncan, Sutherland, Abernethy, & Henry, 2008; Jones, 2014; Zimbardo & Boyd, 1999), lower satisfaction with life (Boniwell et al., 2010; Desmyter & De Raedt, 2012; Gao, 2011; Jones, 2014; Kostić & Nedeljković, 2013; Naeger, 2001; Nedeljković & Kostić, 2018; Tseferidi, Griva, & Anagnostopoulos, 2017; Zhang & Howell, 2011), less expressed positive affect (Boniwell et al., 2010; Desmyter & De Raedt, 2012; Nedeljković & Kostić, 2018), lower evaluation of the purpose in life (Boniwell et al., 2010), lower positivity (Nedeljković & Kostić, 2018), lower levels of positive mood states (energy and hedonic tone) (Stolarski et al., 2014), lower degree of mindfulness (Drake et al., 2008), and lower optimism, observed as a personality trait (Naeger, 2001) or attribution style (Boniwell et al., 2010). On the contrary, past-positive oriented individuals show higher optimism, measured as a personality trait (Naeger, 2001), higher prevalence of the optimistic attribution style (Boniwell et al., 2010), higher satisfaction with life (Boniwell et al., 2010; Desmyter & De Raedt, 2012; Gao, 2011; Jones, 2014; Kazakina, 1999; Kostić & Nedeljković, 2013; Naeger, 2001; Tseferidi et al., 2017; Zhang & Howell, 2011), higher level of happiness (Boniwell et al., 2010; Drake et al., 2008; Jones, 2014; Zimbardo & Boyd, 1999), prevalence of the positive affect (Boniwell et al., 2010; Nedeljković & Kostić, 2018), purpose in life (Boniwell et al., 2010), higher levels of energy and hedonic tone (Stolarski et al., 2014), and mindfulness (Drake et al., 2008). In the research conducted by Naeger (2001), both of these perspectives have been the predictors of subjective well-being (whose score has been obtained by summing up the scores from the scales which measured subjective life satisfaction and happiness). In accordance with the aforementioned understanding of Diener et al. (1999), in one study, satisfaction with life was examined through three scales which measured past satisfaction with life, concurrent life satisfaction, and future expectation of life satisfaction (Boniwell et al., 2010). Both past-positive and past-negative time perspectives were in correlation with all satisfaction with life scales. These two time orientations were the only ones distinguished in the mentioned study (Jones, 2014) as significant predictors of life satisfaction and happiness. Past-negative time perspective has, in another study (Ortuño et al., 2013), confirmed its predictive power when it comes to satisfaction with life, as a criterion. Furthermore, along with present-hedonistic TP and past-negative TP, it was the most stable predictor of current mood (Stolarski et al., 2014). Therefore, people who are inclined to evoke negative memories are indeed less satisfied with their lives as well as less happy in the present moment. A sentimental and warm attitude toward the past, however, makes a person happier and more satisfied with their life. From the aforementioned it can be seen that the way in which a person interprets past events gives context to their evaluation of their own life in general, thus permeating the estimated level of happiness as well, which is dominantly bound to the present moment. Boniwell et al. (2010) draw further attention to the strong correlation between satisfaction with past and satisfaction with present, which requires additional research.

According to empirical data, the fatalistic present is negatively correlated with satisfaction with life (Boniwell et al., 2010; Gao, 2011; Jones, 2014; Kostić & Nedeljković, 2013; Nedeljković & Kostić, 2018; Tseferidi et al., 2017; Zhang & Howell, 2011), happiness (Boniwell et al., 2010; Jones, 2014; Zimbardo & Boyd, 1999), positive mood states (energy and hedonic tone) (Stolarski et al., 2014), positive affect and positivity (Nedeljković & Kostić, 2018), mindfulness (Drake et al., 2008), optimism (as a personality trait) (Naeger, 2001), optimistic attribution style, and purpose in life (Boniwell et al., 2010). In the mentioned research (Naeger, 2001), this perspective was distinguished as a significant predictor of subjective well-being in general, but in another study, where it was combined with other dimensions of time perspectives, it was the only perspective that did not make an independent contribution to the explanation of the score on the satisfaction with life scale (Kostić & Nedeljković, 2013). It can be assumed that the attitude of helplessness and experiencing lack of control over one's own life, which is characteristic of persons with a fatalistic view on the present, partly determine their evaluation of the present moment as well as their entire life, giving them a negative direction. On the contrary, while entailing indulging in the present moment and instant gratifications, the hedonistic present positively correlates with happiness (Boniwell et al., 2010; Drake et al., 2008; Zimbardo & Boyd, 1999), life satisfaction (Gao, 2011; Kazakina, 1999; Kostić & Nedeljković, 2013; Naeger, 2001; Nedeljković & Kostić, 2018; Tseferidi et al., 2017; Zhang & Howell, 2011), positive affect (Desmyter & De Raedt, 2012; Nedeljković & Kostić, 2018), positivity (Nedeljković & Kostić, 2018), energy and hedonic tone (Stolarski et al., 2014), and optimism as an attribution style (Boniwell et al., 2010), but negatively correlates with mindfulness (Drake et al., 2008). In one of the studies (Naeger, 2001), it was also distinguished as a predictor of subjective well-being in general. However, no correlation of this time perspective with life satisfaction and happiness was obtained in Jones's study (2014). It seems that the relation between this perspective and the subjective experiences examined is not so simple. As Naeger (2001) states, such a carefree attitude toward the present, while neglecting the consequences of present choices and behaviors which might affect their future, "needs to be cultivated in order to enhance SWB [subjective well-being] and happiness in the present tense" (p. 48). Thus, it can be assumed that in this relation there is also a certain moderator variable, the inclusion of which would allow for a more complete interpretation of their relation.

In one study (Wills, Sandy, & Yaeger, 2001), individuals oriented toward future time perspective perceived a higher sense of control and well-being, while other authors have furthermore determined its positive correlation with satisfaction with life (Boniwell et al., 2010; Gao, 2011; Kostić & Nedeljković, 2013; Nedeljković & Kostić, 2018; Tseferidi et al., 2017; Zhang & Howell, 2011), presence of positive affect and positivity (Nedeljković & Kostić, 2018), as well as with purpose in life and optimism (Boniwell et al., 2010). In some other studies, no correlation has been found between future time perspective, on the one hand, and life satisfaction (Jones, 2014; Naeger, 2001), happiness (Drake et al., 2008; Jones, 2014; Naeger, 2001; Zimbardo & Boyd, 1999) and positive mood states (energy and hedonic tone) (Stolarski et al., 2014), on the other hand. The results of the regression analysis suggest somewhat different conclusions – when considering the effects of other time perspectives on energy, this time perspective has become its significant predictor (Stolarski et al., 2014). Furthermore, Naeger (2001) found that this time perspective significantly contributes to an increase of subjective well-being in general, and Desmyter and De Raedt (2012) found that it also contributes to an increase in the representation of positive affect. This inconsistency of results once again points to the complexity of relations between taken time perspectives and positive subjective experiences, where orientation toward the future, involving careful and conscientious planning of goal-directed activities, can lead to positive outcomes, but also reduce spontaneity and increase anxiety and hurriedness and thus reduce the enjoyment of the present moment (Boniwell & Zimbardo, 2003).

Based on the results reviewed so far, it can be concluded that the relation between the two past time perspectives, on the one hand, and positive affective experiences, on the other hand, has found the greatest empirical confirmation, while other relations require further research. Furthermore, inconsistent findings of correlations and regression analyses suggest that instead of examining the relations between individual time perspectives and different positive subjective experiences, one should consider a person's position on all the examined dimensions of a time perspective, as well as their interaction. Thus, Stolarski et al. (2014, p. 823) found that "the hypothesized adaptive self-regulative effect of Future is countered by the lower level of hedonic striving of future-oriented individuals." This kind of direction of the researcher requires taking a holistic approach in dealing with these phenomena, *bringing to the scene* a balanced time perspective.

Empirical findings show that individuals with a balanced time perspective, in comparison to all other time perspective profiles, generally report higher levels of well-being (Boniwell et al., 2010), higher levels of happiness (Drake et al., 2008; Zhang, Howell, & Stolarski, 2013), mindfulness (Drake et al., 2008), higher satisfaction with life (Gao, 2011; Zhang et al., 2013), positive affect, psychological need satisfaction, self-determination, vitality, and gratitude (Zhang et al., 2013), as well as higher levels of positive mood states, for example, energy and hedonic tone (Stolarski et al., 2014).

The aforementioned data show that orientation toward a particular time perspective can be important for the subjective experience of a person's well-being. However, since the dominant time perspective is a product of experience, it can be worked on towards building a balanced time perspective which can generally advance a person's daily life, their achievements, and their stable sense of happiness.

## References

Bastian, B. (2018). *The other side of happiness: Embracing a more fearless approach to living.* London: Penguin Books.

Baumeister, R. F. (2018). Happiness and meaningfulness as two different and not entirely compatible versions of the good life. In J. P. Forgas & R. F. Baumeister (Eds.), *The social psychology of living well* (pp. 21–33). Abingdon: Routledge.

Baumeister, R. F., Catanese, K. R., & Vohs, K. D. (2001). Bad is stronger than good. *Review of General Psychology, 5*, 323–370.

Baumeister, R. F., Vohs, K. D., Aaker, J. L., & Garbinsky, E. N. (2013). Some key differences between a happy life and a meaningful life. *Journal of Positive Psychology, 8*(6), 505–516.

Block, R. A. (1990). *Cognitive models of psychological time.* Hillsdale, NJ: Lawrence Erlbaum.

Block, R. A., & Zakay, D. (1996). Models of psychological time revisited. In H. Helfrich (Ed.), *Time and mind* (pp. 171–195). Kirkland, WA: Hogrefe & Huber.

Boniwell, I. (2005). Beyond time management: How the latest research on time perspective and perceived time use can assist clients with time-related concerns. *International Journal of Evidence-Based Coaching and Mentoring, 3*(2), 61–74.

Boniwell, I. (2009). Perspectives on time. In S. J. Lopez & C. R. Snyder (Eds.), *Oxford handbook of positive psychology* (pp. 295–302). Oxford: Oxford University Press.

Boniwell, I., Osin, E., Linley, P. A., & Ivanchenko, G. V. (2010). A question of balance: Time perspective and well-being in British and Russian samples. *The Journal of Positive Psychology, 5*(1), 24–40.

Boniwell, I., & Zimbardo, P. G. (2003). Time to find the right balance. *The Psychologist, 16*(3), 129–131.

Boniwell, I., & Zimbardo, P. G. (2004). Balancing one's time perspective in pursuit of optimal functioning. In P. A. Linley & S. Joseph (Eds.), *Positive psychology in practice* (pp. 165–178). Hoboken, NJ: Wiley.

Desmyter, F., & De Raedt, R. (2012). The relationship between time perspective and subjective well-being of older adults. *Psychologica Belgica, 52*(1), 19–38.

De Volder, M. L. (1980). *Motivation and FTP as possible determinants of study behavior and academic achievement (in Dutch).* (Unpublished doctoral dissertation). University of Louvain, Belgium.

Diener, E., Shuh, E. M., Lucas, R. E., & Smith, H. L. (1999). Subjective wellbeing: Three decades of progress. *Psychological Bulletin, 125*(2), 276–302.

Drake, L., Duncan, E., Sutherland, F., Abernethy, C., & Henry, C. (2008). Time perspective and correlates of wellbeing. *Time and Society, 17*(1), 47–61.

Ekman, P. (2003). *Emotion revealed: Recognizing faces and feelings to improve communication and emotional life.* New York: Times Books/Henry Holt.

Fraisse, P. (1963). *The psychology of time.* New York: Harper & Row.

Gao, Y. J. (2011). Time perspective and life satisfaction among young adults in Taiwan. *Social Behavior and Personality, 39*(6), 729–736.

Golovakina, E. I., & Kronick, A. A. (1989). *Psihologicheskoje vryemya lichnostyi [Psychological time of personality].* Kiev, Ukraine: Naukova Dumka.

Gonzalez, A., & Zimbardo, P. G. (1985). Time in perspective. *Psychology Today, 19*(3), 20–26.

Gorman, B. S., & Wessman, A. E. (1977). Images, values, and concepts of time in psychological research. In B. Gorman & A. Wessman (Eds.), *The personal experience of time* (pp. 217–263). New York: Plenum.

Hendricks, J., & Peters, C. B. (1986). The times of our lives. *American Behavioral Scientist, 29*(6), 662–678.

Husman, J., & Hilpert, J. C. (2017). Extending future time perspective theory through episodic future thinking research: A multidisciplinary approach to thinking about the future. In A. Kostić & D. Chadee (Eds.), *Time perspective – theory and practice* (pp. 267–280). London: Palgrave Macmillan.

Iranpour, S. M., Erfani, N., & Ebrahimi, M. E. (2018). Determining the relationship between time perspective and student happiness. *Journal of Research in Medical and Dental Sciences, 6*(3), 212–219.

James, W. (1950). *The principles of psychology* (Vol. 1). New York: St. Martin's Press. (Original work published 1890).

Jones, M. (2014). *The Zimbardo time perspective inventory: Exploring the relationships between time perspective and measures of wellbeing (Doctoral dissertation).* California State University, Chico.

Kazakina, E. (1999). *Time perspective of older adults: Relationships to attachment style, psychological well-being, and psychological distress (Doctoral dissertation).* Columbia University, New York.

Kazakina, E. (2015). The uncharted territory: Time perspective research meets clinical practice: Temporal focus in psychotherapy across adulthood and old age. In M. Stolarski, N. Fieulaine, & W. van Beek (Eds.), *Time perspective theory: Review, research and application: Essays in honor of Philip G. Zimbardo* (pp. 499–516). Switzerland: Springer.

Keyes, C. L. M., & Annas, J. (2009). Feeling good and functioning well: Distinctive concepts in ancient philosophy and contemporary science. *Journal of Positive Psychology, 4*(3), 197–201.

Kostić, A., & Chadee, D. (2017). Time for time perspective. In A. Kostić & D. Chadee (Eds.), *Time perspective – theory and practice* (pp. 1–8). London: Palgrave Macmillan.

Kostić, A., & Nedeljković, J. (2013). *Studije vremenskih perspektiva u Srbiji. [Studies of time perspectives in Serbia].* Niš, Serbia: Punta.

Kostić, A., Pejičić, M., & Chadee, D. (2017). Hugging the past: The way we were and the way we are. In A. Kostić & D. Chadee (Eds.), *Time perspective – theory and practice* (pp. 143–165). London: Palgrave Macmillan.

Lennings, C. J. (1996). Drug use and risk behavior: Queensland and national data. *Youth Studies Australia, 15*(2), 29–36.

Lennings, C. J., Burns, A. M., & Cooney, G. (1998). Profiles of time perspective and personality: Developmental considerations. *Journal of Psychology, 132*(6), 629–641.

Levin, I., & Zakay, D. (Eds.). (1989). *Time and human cognition: A life-span perspective.* Amsterdam: North-Holland.

Lewin, K. (1942). Time perspective and morale. In G. W. Lewin (Ed.), *Resolving social conflicts* (pp. 103–124). New York: Harper.

Linley, P. A., Maltby, J., Wood, A. M., Osborne, G., & Hurling, R. (2009). Measuring happiness: The higher order factor structure of subjective and psychological well-being measures. *Personality and Individual Differences, 47*(8), 878–884.

Lyubomirsky, S. (2007). *The how of happiness.* London, UK: Sphere.

Naeger, M. (2001). *Temporal perspectives, dispositional styles, and subjective well-being (Master's thesis).* Western Kentucky University, Bowling Green.

Nedeljković, J., & Kostić, A. (2018). *Time perspective and positive affects.* Unpublished raw data.

Nuttin, J. M. (1985). Narcissism beyond gestalt and awareness: The name–letter effect. *European Journal of Social Psychology, 15*(3), 353–361.

Ortuño, V., Gomes, C., Vásquez, A., Belo, P., Imaginário, S., Paixão, M. P., & Janeiro, I. (2013). Satisfaction with life and college social integration: A time perspective multiple regression model. In M. P. Paixão, J. T. da Silva, V. Ortuño, & P. Cordeiro (Eds.), *International studies on time perspective* (pp. 101–106). Coimbra, Portugal: University of Coimbra Press.

Palmer, C. A., & Gentzler, A. L. (2019). Age-related differences in savoring across adulthood: The role of emotional goals and future time perspective. *Journal of Happiness Studies, 20*(4), 1281–1304.

Peterson, C. (2000). The future of optimism. *American Psychologist, 55*(1), 44–56.

Rosenzweig, M. R., Breedlove, S. M., & Watson, N. V. (2005). *Biological psychology: An introduction to behavioral and cognitive neuroscience.* Sunderland, MA: Sinauer.

Sailer, U., Rosenberg, P., Nima, A. A., Gamble, A., Garling, T., Archer, T., & Garcia, D. (2014). A happier and less sinister past, a more hedonistic and less fatalistic present and a more structured future: Time perspective and well-being. *PeerJ, 2*, Article e303.

Seginer, R. (2005). Adolescent future orientation: Intergenerational transmission and intertwining tactics in cultural and family settings. In W. Friedlmeier, P. Chakkarath, & B. Schwarz (Eds.), *Culture and human development: The importance* of cross-cultural research to the social sciences (pp. 208–226). Hove: Psychology Press.

Seginer, R. (2017). Future orientation and psychological well-being in adolescence: Two multiple-step models. In A. Kostić & D. Chadee (Eds.), *Time perspective – theory and practice* (pp. 339–363). London: Palgrave Macmillan.

Seligman, M. E., & Csikszentmihalyi, M. (2000). Positive psychology: An introduction. *American Psychologist, 55*(1), 5–14.

Simons, M., Peeters, S., Janssens, M., Lataster, J., & Jacobs, N. (2016). Does age make a difference? Age as moderator in the association between time perspective and happiness. *Journal of Happiness Studies, 19*(1), 57–67.

Sirois, F. M. (2014). Out of sight, out of time? A meta-analytic investigation of procrastination and time perspective. *European Journal of Personality, 28*(5), 511–520.

Stolarski, M., Fieulaine, N., & Van Beek, W. (2015). Time perspective theory: The introduction. In M. Stolarski, N. Fieulaine, & W. van Beek (Eds.), *Time perspective theory: Review, research and application: Essays in honor of Philip G. Zimbardo* (pp. 1–13). Switzerland: Springer.

Stolarski, M., Matthews, G., Postek, S., Zimbardo, P. G., & Bitner, J. (2014). How we feel is a matter of time: Relationships between time perspectives and mood. *Journal of Happiness Studies, 15*(4), 809–827.

Suddendorf, T. (2013). *The gap: The science of what separates us from other animals.* New York: Basic Books.

Tseferidi, S. I., Griva, F., & Anagnostopoulos, F. (2017). Time to get happy: Associations of time perspective with indicators of well-being. *Psychology, Health & Medicine, 22*(5), 618–624.

Wills, T. A., Sandy, J. M., & Yaeger, A. M. (2001). Time perspective and early onset substance use: A model based on stress-coping theory. *Psychology of Addictive Behaviors, 15*(2), 118–125.

Zhang, J. W., & Howell, R. T. (2011). Do time perspectives predict unique variance in life satisfaction beyond personality traits? *Personality and Individual Differences, 50*(8), 1261–1266.

Zhang, J. W., Howell, R. T., & Stolarski, M. (2013). Comparing three methods to measure a balanced time perspective: The relationship between a balanced time perspective and subjective well-being. *Journal of Happiness Studies, 14*(1), 169–184.

Zimbardo, P. G. (2002). Just think about it: Time to take out time. *Psychology Today, 35*(2), 62.

Zimbardo, P. G., & Boyd, J. N. (1999). Putting time in perspective: A valid, reliable individual-difference metric. *Journal of Personality and Social Psychology, 77*(6), 1271–1288.

Zimbardo, P. G., & Boyd, J. N. (2008). *The time paradox: The new psychology of time that will change your life.* New York: Free Press.

# 9

# Physiological and Epigenetic: Implications of Positive Emotions

Massimo Agnoletti and Sandro Formica

## Introduction

The aim of this chapter is to explore the relationships between positive emotions and the epigenetic dynamics that promote physiological and cellular health. Its main goal is to deepen the study of the positive emotions' processes improving the psychophysical well-being in the absence of psychological pathologies or deviations from a normal condition. The underlying assumption of this chapter is that positive psychology will continue to be validated as a new field of study by scholars as well as by society owing to the support offered by the increasing body of knowledge related to the physiological mechanisms of emotions. The nature of the scientific inquiry is fundamentally rooted in the exploration of cause and effect relationships. Inevitably, as we deepen our understanding of the physiological and cellular implications of positive emotions, we are likely to increase the quality of life of human beings. This introduction serves as a guideline to define positive emotions and to highlight the paradigmatic transformation occurring in the scientific community as it relates to psychology and biomedical sciences. The sections that follow deal with key mechanisms related to processes triggered by positive emotions that foster good health.

Despite ongoing debate (Diener, 1999; Ekman & Davidson, 1994), most scholars agree that emotions are a subset of the broader class of affective phenomena that develop over relatively short time spans (Ekman, 1994; Rosenberg, 1998; Russell & Feldman Barrett, 1999). The psychological process of emotions may be either conscious or unconscious and it triggers a number of complex response systems, such as subjective experiences, facial expressions, cognitive processing,

*Positive Psychology: An International Perspective*, First Edition.
Edited by Aleksandra Kostić and Derek Chadee.
© 2021 John Wiley & Sons Ltd. Published 2021 by John Wiley & Sons Ltd.

and physiological changes (Fredrickson, 2001). Most emotion theorists link the functions of an emotion to specific action tendencies (Frijda, Kuipers, & Schure, 1989; Lazarus, 1991; Oatley & Jenkins, 1996; Tooby & Cosmides, 1990). For example, fear is linked with the need to escape, anger with the urge to attack, disgust with the impulse to expel, and so on. In the case of positive emotions, it seems hard to find this kind of two-way correspondence specificity between action tendency and matching positive emotion (Fredrickson & Levenson, 1998). Moreover, when individuals experience mild positive affect, even in neutral contexts (Diener & Diener, 1996; Ito & Cacioppo, 1999), they tend to continue any line of thinking or action that they have initiated (Clore, 1994).

The broaden-and-build theory proposed by Barbara Fredrickson (1998) states that certain discrete positive emotions share the ability to broaden people's momentary thought-action repertoires and build their enduring personal resources, ranging from physical and intellectual to social and psychological resources. Fredrickson's perspective on positive emotions is aligned with the three physiological processes – the dopaminergic neural pathways, the anti-inflammatory cholinergic pathway, and interoceptive information – illustrated in this chapter. These processes and the positive emotions associated with them trigger a wide range of behaviors, unlike the limiting behavioral responses to negative emotions, such as quick and decisive actions finalized to solve threatening situations. Specifically, the dopaminergic neural pathways explain our level of motivation, the anti-inflammatory cholinergic pathway plays a critical role in modulating the immune system, and the interoceptive information manages the inflow and outflow of information to and from our organism. All three physiological processes reflect complex systems affecting positive emotions and regulating the biological well-being of human beings.

Positive emotions are the outcome of hedonistic experiences that entail a pleasurable aspect, such as enjoying a tasty meal, being entertained by a videogame, or being in a state of flow. Thus, pleasure is a necessary component of positive emotions and must be considered within the context in which it triggers the positive and health-promoting physiological and cellular changes of a given behavior or experience. Not all pleasurable experiences are providing health-promoting changes. For example, smoking a cigarette, despite its perceived short-term pleasurable experience due to the activation of endorphins, is likely to generate negative health consequences. Positive emotions and pleasure can be triggered not only by hedonistic but also by eudaimonic experiences. The experiential emotional states defined as eudaimonic are characterized by a positive state that involves growth, meaning, and self-realization and defines well-being in terms of the degree to which a person is fully functioning (Delle Fave, Massimini, & Bassi, 2011; G. J. Lewis, Kanai, Rees, & Bates, 2014; Seligman & Csikszentmihalyi, 2000; Ryan & Deci, 2001) and in psychophysical health (Davidson, 2000; Fredrickson et al., 2013).

Until the 1980s, biological and psychological scientific studies focused almost exclusively on the exploration and betterment of pathologies. Because the science of biology preceded that of psychology, clinical progress in the treatment of illnesses, pathologies, and traumatic events became the benchmark and focus within the context of psychological sciences. As a consequence, research and education funding related to psychology revolved around the cure, treatment, and prevention of mental illnesses. Within this scientific paradigm, researchers focused their attention on minimizing psychological disturbances, while no consideration was given to those people who, in the absence of pathologies, were interested in feeling better. Norman Cousins, a well-known journalist and expert in psycho-neuro-immunology, after curing his ankylosing spondylitis with nontraditional techniques, wrote in the *New England Journal of Medicine* and in a later book with the same title: "The inevitable question arose in my mind: what about the positive emotions? If negative emotions produce negative chemical changes in the body, wouldn't the positive emotions produce positive chemical changes? Is it possible that love, hope, faith, laughter, confidence, and the will to live have therapeutic value? Do chemical changes occur only on the downside?" (Cousins, 1979, p. 5). Since then, the biomedical sciences have opened up to the possibility that positive emotions are bound to produce positive changes in the human body.

Biomedical research focuses on the knowledge and application of physical and chemical processes to remedy acute illnesses and traumas requiring immediate attention. The goal of this research was, and still is, to ensure the survival of the patient. By achieving this goal, human beings healed bone fractures and were saved from cardiac arrest, traumatic lesions, and other conditions that would, in most cases, cause death. The effectiveness and efficiency of this emergency intervention research approach was mostly due to three factors. The first relates to the accuracy of an immediate diagnosis, based on the knowledge of the physical and chemical processes occurring in a specific traumatic event or acute illness. The second points at eliminating the imminent danger caused by the acuity of an illness or trauma. The third refers to the lack of cognitive and/or psychological engagement of the patient. These three factors are grounded on sophisticated and complex medical discoveries not necessarily related to human species – for example, the advancement in the understanding of the cardiovascular system of humans generated from animal studies – and do not require the patient's direct involvement in terms of cognition, emotions, and motivation. It was considered normal, therefore, that psychology and, specifically, positive psychology was not regarded as a relevant field of study in the context of urgent medical procedures (Agnoletti, 2004; Deacon & Mckay, 2015; Farre & Rapley, 2017; Johnson, 2013). The success of the biomedical model in addressing pathology and traumatology is based on two factors: the in-depth knowledge of physical and chemical dynamics of nonhuman physiology and the lack of consideration of how the human mind operates, its complexity and heterogeneity. For example, anesthesiological procedures eliminate at the core the problems that might be caused by anxiety, bypassing pain and consciousness during surgery.

If, on one hand, psychological sciences have not been necessarily effective in protecting a person who is suicidal without the assumption of drugs; on the other hand, biomedical sciences that involve medium to long-term psychological processes show limited success, especially when compared to their effectiveness in dealing with emergency aid. Recently, we have assisted to a gradual convergence between the two – psychological and biomedical sciences – to conceive and apply successful integrated intervention systems, especially in the oncological and immunological fields of medicine (Andersen et al., 2008; Küchler, Bestmann, Rappat, Henne-Bruns, & Wood-Dauphinee, 2007; Rosenkranz et al., 2003; Witek-Janusek et al., 2008). In the last few decades, owing to advanced biometric technologies, neural, physiological, and cellular processes have been linked to psychological processes. One example of that is the development of a branch of neurosciences made possible by the progress in neuroimaging technologies, referred to as behavioral neuroscience. Progressively, the scientific community has minimized the separation between mind and body thanks to the integration of studies focusing on psychological, neural, and cellular systems. The dichotomy between body and mind is mostly based on linguistics and the boundaries between the two are increasingly blurred and lacking compelling scientific support. As proof of this claim stands the seminal work of molecular biologist and Nobel laureate Elizabeth Blackburn and psychologist Elissa Epel (Epel et al., 2004; Epel, Daubenmier, Moskowitz, Folkman, & Blackburn, 2009; O'Donovan et al., 2009). When analyzing telomeres – DNA structures used as indicators to determine potential and residual longevity and quality of life – those two researchers demonstrated that cellular aging depends, among other factors, on mental attitudes.

While advancements in technology opened the door to correlations between physiology and psychology, new studies on molecular biology started to branch out from the old paradigm based on genetic determinism to embrace the field of epigenetics. This field supports the theory that parts of the DNA can be activated or silenced as a consequence of extragenetic constructs, such as thoughts, feelings, and lifestyle. It is thanks to the field of epigenetics that we are currently investigating the dynamics occurring in neuroplasticity (Berlucchi & Buchtel, 2009; Hölzel et al., 2010; Maguire, Woollett, & Spiers, 2006) as they relate to the experience-dependent neural plasticity construct. Future advancements in positive psychology will be not only possible but inevitable, because the field of epigenetics will foster the body of knowledge on cellular physiological dynamics. The "telomere's funnel effect" or "telomere's bottleneck effect" is a successful example of that. It is the outcome of the convergent nature of multiple independent or partially independent constructs, in terms of domains of relevance and causal pathways – nutrition, motor activity, sleep quality, social relationships, and psychological well-being – in influencing the telomeres' structure, a fundamental indicator of psychophysical well-being and longevity (Agnoletti, 2019).

Overall, the convergence of advanced technological tools, such as functional magnetic resonance imaging, tomography, positron emissions, molecular biology tests; new scientific paradigms in biomedicine, such as epigenetics; and psychology, has provided the opportunity to investigate new research areas.

For example, epigenetic psychology (Agnoletti, 2018a), a field of study unexplored in the past, focuses on physiological and cellular implications of positive and negative emotions and their consequences on overall health and well-being (Agnoletti, 2018b; Bhasin et al., 2013; Conklin et al., 2015; Fredrickson et al., 2013; Jacobs et al., 2011; Lavretsky et al., 2012; Schutte & Malouff, 2014). The integration of knowledge coming from biomedical and psychological sciences is also bringing a new and valuable understanding of the physiological and cellular dynamics of positive emotions.

The purpose of this chapter is to highlight the advantages that physiological and cellular epigenetic effects have on positive emotions. To achieve this purpose, three elements are presented and explored: the dopaminergic neural pathway, the cholinergic anti-inflammatory pathway, and the interoceptive information. The dopaminergic neural pathway deepens the understanding of motivational influences leading to behaviors aimed at repeating positive emotional experiences and promoting better health. There are two types of behavioral experiences that can potentially trigger positive emotions: hedonistic, which could lead to behavioral dependency, and eudaimonic, which has demonstrated to strengthen humans' well-being in the long term. The cholinergic anti-inflammatory pathway, instead, helps emphasize positive over negative emotions, within the context of the immune system, so critical to our psychophysical health. Finally, the interoceptive information plays an essential role in managing stress and helps minimize negative stress while stimulating emotions that support positive stress.

## Dopaminergic Neural Pathway

Since the beginning of the new millennium, scientific research about neural dopaminergic pathways has helped shape the understanding and purpose of these unique neurons and their influence on motivation and human behavior. For example, the relationship between the dopamine molecule and positive emotions depends on behaviors seeking or promoting rewards and gratification (Badgaiyan, Fischman, & Alpert, 2009; Chaillou, Giersch, Hoonakker, Capa, & Bonnefond, 2017; Chiew & Braver, 2014; DeYoung, 2013). Dopamine is a complex molecule, acting as a neurotransmitter in neural networks of most vertebrate and invertebrate animal species, humans included. In addition to being a critical element of hedonistic pleasure, the dopamine molecule is also actively involved in influencing attention, arousal, movement control, reward, and gratification (Björklund & Dunnett, 2007; Björklund & Lindvall, 1984; Floresco, Magyar, Ghods-Sharifi, Vexelman, & Tse, 2006; Klanker, Feenstra, & Denys, 2013; Robinson, Fischer, Ahuja, Lesser, & Maniates, 2016). In the past, it was wrongly believed that neural dopaminergic pathways served as "pleasure molecules" and were only activated in hedonistic experiences (Kringelbach & Berridge, 2010; K. S. Smith, Berridge, & Aldridge, 2011; K. S. Smith, Mahler, Peciña, & Berridge, 2010). Recently, the scientific community has understood the complexity of these neural pathways and the multiple functions they perform. A new study (Raghanti et al., 2018) has found that humans are characterized by a massive presence of neurons when compared with primates.

Through epigenetics processes, the dopamine neural pathway connected with reward and gratification is a learning prediction system that depends on past experience and drives human behavior. In particular, the function of the reward system is to detect and monitor the proper neural associations leading to the pursuit of evolutionary meaningful behaviors (Agnoletti, 2019; Kobayashi & Hsu, 2019; Saunders, Richard, Margolis, & Janak, 2018). Once the reward system considers a neural association as stable and reliable, the neurons that were previously energized gradually decrease their activation to signal the completion of that specific learning process. It is, therefore, clear that peak activations of dopamine neurons are associated with a novelty effect. As the novelty effect subsides, the perceptive stimuli processed by the dopaminergic neurons connected to the reward pathway flatten.

The activation of the dopaminergic neurons – defined as "want" – occurs just before the activation of a separate group of neurons stimulated by hedonistic experiences – defined as "like." The neural reward pathways facilitate the associative learning between perceptive stimuli – named cues – and the reward or gratification information by epigenetically altering the neurons activated in the process. It is the neurotransmitter dopamine that triggers this chain of transformative events. The dopamine neural pathway connected with reward and gratification is functional to the pathways leading to the experience of pleasure associated with positive emotions. However, the focus of the first pathway – connected with reward and gratification – is on the experience, while the second pathway – leading to feeling pleasure – activates the hedonistic emotion linked to the expected reward. Researchers have been testing the probability that the activation of the dopaminergic pathways related to gratification is more associated with the sensation of control, as a result of the relationship between expectations and perceived stimuli, than with the sensation of pleasure (Ott & Nieder, 2019). It is worth noting that the sensations of control and pleasure are not mutually exclusive and can be experienced simultaneously in ecological contexts, such as when eating a desired meal (Volkow, Wang, & Baler, 2011).

The sensation of pleasure is not only limited to the time in which we are involved in a pleasurable event. We can, and do, feel pleasure before the event itself by anticipating the experience of it. Robert Sapolsky, a stress researcher from Stanford University, explains that the role of dopamine is not necessarily linked with the sensation of pleasure. Instead it relates to the excitement that comes from predicting a future event that involves pleasure. To use his words: "Dopamine is not about pleasure, it's about the anticipation of pleasure. It's about the pursuit of happiness rather than happiness itself" (Sapolsky, 2011, 1:01). To support that, research has demonstrated that we are willing to renounce to a hedonistic reward, activated via the neural pathway defined as "like," if and when we obtain relevant information about that specific reward (Bromberg-Martin & Hikosaka, 2009). Renunciation to hedonistic rewards may also occur when receiving information regarding future scenarios (Niv & Chan, 2011) or when satisfying a need for curiosity by receiving even marginally meaningful or trivial information (Kobayashi & Hsu, 2019). Somehow, the sensation of control fulfilled by obtaining information directly or indirectly related to a future event spikes a dopaminergic reward pathway leading to a positive emotion.

The role of dopaminergic reward pathways is more extensive than what is commonly understood. Their activation is not only limited to their association with hedonistic behaviors linked to addictions, such as smoking, drinking, overeating, gambling, and so on. Literature (Basso & Suzuki, 2017; Kjaer et al., 2002) shows that an increased activation of dopaminergic neurons triggered by hedonistic positive emotions is also associated with positive habits leading to better health, such as physical activities, healthy nutrition, meditative practices, and flow experiences (Manzano et al., 2013; Volkow et al., 2011).

A deeper understanding of the neuro-functional mechanism of the dopaminergic pathway helps discriminate between the behavioral dynamics connected to healthy hedonistic positive emotions and those connected to unhealthy hedonistic positive emotions. When we engage in desired activities in all aspects of life – intimate partnerships, travel, spirituality, friendships, family, and so on – and are in a state of flow, our brain releases dopamine in the mesolimbic section of the dopaminergic pathway (Ottenheimer, Richard, & Janak, 2018; K. S. Smith, Tindell, Aldridge, & Berridge, 2009). This section emphasizes the immediate gratification of conditioned stimuli based on the "here and now" and constructs a neural communication link with the executive system, which is part of the prefrontal cortex (PFC), the area of the brain that helps transcend our focus on the here and now. The ongoing interactions of the mesolimbic and prefrontal cortex pathways can be captured by epigenetic "experience-dependent" variations; one of the causes of neural plasticity. When a person feels balanced and experiences psychophysical well-being as a result of healthy behavioral choices, the activation of the PFC and the mesolimbic pathways are stable, counterbalancing the attention on the "here and now" with the attention on possible future consequences of those behavioral choices. If, instead, the mesolimbic system shows a functional dominance over the PCF, a clinical addiction is likely to occur. This specific functional dominance reflects, from a phenomenological perspective, a polarization where priority is given to the present moment as opposed to the possible negative scenarios caused by current decisions. Warren Bickel and his colleagues describe the functional power struggle between the PFC and mesolimbic dopaminergic systems by pointing out the negative health consequences of a dominating mesolimbic system, which fosters the supremacy of immediate gratification (Bickel et al., 2018).

As illustrated earlier in this chapter, positive emotions are also elicited by eudaimonic experiences. Eudaimonic experiences show a heightened complexity, when compared with the hedonistic experiences (Delle Fave et al., 2011; Lewiset al., 2014; Ryan & Deci, 2001; Seligman & Csikszentmihalyi, 2000). Complexity differences between the eudaimonic and hedonistic experiences are not only recorded from a psychological perspective (Ryan & Deci, 2001; Vázquez, Hervás, Rahona, & Gómez, 2009), but also from a neurophysiological structural perspective (Castro & Berridge, 2014; Davidson, 2000; Heller et al., 2013; G. J. Lewis et al., 2014) and from a functional epigenetic perspective (Fredrickson et al., 2013). Unlike hedonistic experiences, eudaimonic experiences are achieved through commitment and dedication, while providing meaning and purpose to increase the overall state of well-being and quality of life (Delle Fave et al., 2011; Ryan & Deci, 2001; Seligman & Csikszentmihalyi, 2000). Eudaimonic well-being protects from psychopathologies and predicts an overall physical well-being, in addition to being inversely associated with cortisol levels (Davidson, 2000; Heller et al., 2013). Those individuals who enjoy psychophysical well-being after experiencing positive events, show lower levels of cortisol and present a high activation in the striatum and PFC; both areas are involved in turning on the neurophysiological circuit of reward (Heller et al., 2013). It has been hypothesized that a sustained activation of the reward system as a response to positive events represents the basis of well-being and stimulates the adaptive regulation of the hypothalamic–pituitary–adrenal (HPA) axis (Heller et al., 2013). Conversely, as a consequence of negative events, PFC and amygdala are not activated (Urry et al., 2006).

Being in a state of flow is considered an eudaimonic experience and carries a specific psycho-neuro-physiological configuration (Nakamura & Csikszentmihalyi, 2009; Ullén et al., 2011). By activating the dopaminergic pathway of reward, researchers found a direct relationship between the inclination to have flow experiences and the perception of control (Mosing et al., 2012). To support this correlation, there is scientific evidence linking the degree of difficulty by people in generating optimal flow experiences with the lack of availability of the dopamine receptor D2, which is found in the dorsal striatum (Manzano et al., 2013). Overall, when we feel positive emotions as a result of eudaimonic experiences, there is a positive epigenetic impact on the immune system cells as they become more effective in managing stress and fighting inflammation (Fredrickson et al., 2013). Inflammation, among other negative consequences, creates lack of motivation by producing more inflammatory cytokines (Treadway, Cooper, & Miller, 2019).

From a psychological perspective, scientific evidence related to the dopaminergic circuit of reward presented in this section points at eudaimonic, as opposed to hedonistic, experiences as precursors to positive emotions. Even though eudaimonic experiences require a higher level of engagement and commitment at both the individual and social level compared to hedonistic experiences, they bring about sustainable and long-term health and well-being. This recommendation is particularly significant within the context of a society that promotes activities and experiences geared toward immediate gratification. Ultimately, the most desirable approach is to reach a balance between hedonistic and eudaimonic experiences to foster an integrated and mutually beneficial psychological and cellular well-being. From a neural perspective, it is the interaction between the dopaminergic pathways "want" and the pleasure pathways "like" that determines the degree of well-being experienced. The activation of the dopaminergic pathway of reward in association with eudai-monic states is one of the most effective ways to promote psychosocial well-being through a more efficient stress management, better health, and positive emotions.

## Cholinergic Anti-Inflamatory Pathway

The goal of this section is to provide a guideline on how to strengthen the immune system and, consequently, people's health by better understanding the relationship between positive emotions and the cholinergic anti-inflammatory pathway (CAP). This goal is now achievable thanks to the most recent technological biomedical advances and by applying a scientific paradigm reflecting appropriate cultural and mental perspectives. In 1981, the immunologist Robert Good explained what is meant by this scientific paradigm:

> Immunologists are often asked whether the state of mind can influence the body's defenses. Can positive attitude, a constructive frame of mind, grief, depression, or anxiety alterability resist infections, allergies, autoimmunities, or even cancer? Such questions leave me with a feeling of inadequacy because I know deep down that such influences exist, but I am unable to tell how they work, nor can I in any scientific way prescribe how to harness these influences, predict, or control them. Thus they cannot usually be addressed in scientific prospective. (Good, 1981, xvii)

Metal'nikov and Chorine (1926) successfully tested 55 years earlier the immune response of a pavlovian conditioning of a dog. They succeeded in demonstrating a relationship between cognitive learning and the immune system. That experiment challenged the status quo of the paradigm of that time, which was based on sepa-rating the causal dynamics of the mind and the biological-physiological processes. In other words, that paradigm did not consider the interaction between the pro-cesses of learning leading to neuroplasticity and changes in the immune system. Back then, the biomedical scientific community decided to ignore Metal'nikov and Chorine's study. Decades later, Ader and Cohen (1975) demonstrated that conditioning the brain would affect the immune system. Furthermore, Blalock (1989) discovered that the nervous and immunity systems communicate by using the same molecules. It was, therefore, consequential that psychological dynamics and the immune system were somehow linked by a reciprocal interaction through the nervous system. In addition, Besedovsky documented how the brain receives information about the immune system through molecules, named inflammatory cytokines, capable of activating the hypothalamic–pituitary–adrenal (HPA) axis (Besedovsky, Del Rey, & Sorkin, 1981; Besedovsky, Del Rey, Sorkin, & Dinarello, 1986), which is the endocrine branch of the stress system.

CAP brings about a new understanding of the interaction between psychology and the immune system because it connects complex physiological and molecular processes to mental states. Specifically, CAP plays a pivotal role in regulating the immune dynamics in the body. The regulation of the immune processes is also influenced by the specific emotions experienced and by their frequency. To better understand CAP's purpose and function, selected processes of the immune system are presented and discussed here. When a pathogenic foreign body – antigen – enters the organism through the skin, it causes a reaction by macrophages, dendritic, and mast cells, which are receptors in charge of recognizing and identifying possible exogenous threats (Abbas, Lichtman, & Pillai, 2017). Those receptors are activated owing to an epigenetic mechanism – gene expression – that causes the first specific immune response through cytokines (Abbas et al., 2017). If this first response is not effective, the immune system activates the adaptive or learned response, which stems from cellular, immunological memory (Fricchione, Yeung, & Ivkovic, 2016). Cytokines are part of complex protein molecules, including interleukins, chemokines, and interferons. Interleukins are in charge of white blood cells, chemokines promote the flow of immune cells, and interferons are dedicated to fight viruses. Cytokines coordinate communication among immune cells, neurons, muscular cells, and endothelial cells. In coordination with other molecules, cytokines are activated in the area where the pathogen is identified to eliminate it and rebuild the damaged cells and tissues (Abbas et al., 2017). In performing this defensive and reconstructive function, the inflammatory function is activated, thus increasing the inflow of blood in the affected area through redness, swelling, heat, and pain. Because the inflammatory activation of cytokines is localized and concentrated, the immunity system is generally effective in contrasting pathogens. Humans are usually unaware of the activation of cytokines because this process does not cause any physical pain. It is possible, however, that the production of cytokines could be far superior to the number of antigens they are fighting against. This could potentially cause death because the excessive presence of cytokines ends up damaging not only the antigens but also the healthy cells. The immunologist Thomas Lewis wrote about the cytokines that "we are in more danger from them than from the invaders" (1974, p. 554). For example, the protein molecules tumor necrosis factor (TNF) are among the most powerful cytokines, particularly effective in fighting tumors when their activity is localized and selective. By the same token, their activity can cause a highly damaging reaction when not localized, harming healthy cells, tissues, and organs (Tracey et al., 1986). Septic shocks represent such an occurrence.

The CNI-1493 molecule found by Bianchi et al. (1996) has an anti-inflammatory function capable of minimizing the excessive production of TNF. When injected directly in the brain of lab mice, CNI-1493 was about 300,000 times more effective than intravenous injection (Tracey, 2006). The brain, therefore, plays a critical role in fighting inflammation through the vagus nerve (VN) of the autonomic nervous system, by quickly and effectively blocking the TNF cytokine production by macrophages. As a result of Tracey's work (2006) it was demonstrated that inflammatory conditions are controlled through a communication system going from the brain to the immune system using the VN pathway. Further studies, however, demonstrated that the opposite way of communication is also true. Watkins et al. (1995) and Hansen, O'Connor, Goehler, Watkins, and Maier (2001), found that one of the functions of the VN is that of informing the brain about active inflammations in any organ of the body, thus proving that communication can also move from the periphery to the brain. Furthermore, Tracey (2002) showed the process by which the efferent branch of the VN controls the inflammation detected by its afferent fibers. Specifically, this process is activated by a network of neurons that intercepts the VN and induces it to release acetylcholine in the organ targeted by the inflammation, epigenetically inducing a suppression of TNF cytokine production by macrophages, after the T-cells are activated in the immune system. Tracey labeled this process cholinergic anti-inflammatory pathway (CAP). CAP is, therefore, a process that makes use of the VN to optimize the immune system and control inflammation by fighting harmful bacterial or viral activities and by blocking the destructive consequences of the excessive production of cytokines.

The VN used by CAP to control inflammations is the main and most extensive parasympathetic nerve of the autonomous nervous system. It connects the central nervous system and all organs with a bidirectional communication using 80% of afferent fibers and 20% efferent fibers. From a biological point of view, the VN contrasts oxidative stress and inflammation. The functioning of the VN can be indexed by the activation of the frontal cortex and the amygdala, both instrumental in regulating emotions (Urry et al., 2006). Also, the VN's activity was found to be linked with the neuro-endocrine stress axis (Thayer, Ahs, Fredrikson, Sollers, & Wager, 2012). Fundamentally, the VN activation and functions are inextricably related with human behavior, including lifestyle (Gidron, Deschepper, De Couck, Thayer, & Velkeniers, 2018). When the VN is particularly active, it results in a high VN index, which predicts a low risk and a more accurate prognosis of cardiovascular, cancer, and pulmonary diseases (Thayer et al., 2012). A low VN index is associated with a slower and less effective healing of cardiovascular, endocrine, and immune diseases (Weber et al., 2010).

In understanding and explaining how the brain controls the immune system, researchers started exploring the brain activation caused by negative emotional states and how those states might affect the immune system and the consequent health of human beings (Tracey, 2006). Additional research has demonstrated a relationship between positive emotional experiences and a more effective functioning of the VN, psychological well-being, and overall health. This research stems from positive psychology and its primary objective is to shed light on the psychophysical processes affecting positive emotions (Fredrickson, 2001, 2013).

It appears that negative and positive emotions run through neural pathways in different areas of the brain. Specifically, the left-half brain hosts the majority of positive emotions, the parasympathetic VN connection, and the nervous connections to the heart. The right-half brain hosts most of the negative emotions and the sympathetic system connections (Craig, 2005; Oppenheimer, Gelb, Girvin, & Hachinski, 1992; Wittling, 1995). Taggart, Boyett, Logantha, and Lambiase (2011) pointed out that when the right brain is activated by negative emotions and at the same time in the left brain there is an absence of positive emotions, the sympathetic nervous system takes over the autonomic nervous system, triggering negative health consequences.

Emotion regulation, the ability to effectively manage and respond to an emotional experience and adapt to solicitations coming from the external environment, was found to be correlated to heart rate variability (HRV) (Appelhans & Luecken, 2006; Thayer & Brosschot, 2005). HRV is a functioning index of the autonomic nervous system, which includes VN, and measures the interaction of complex systems, including cardio-circulatory, nervous, and respiratory systems (Agostoni, Chinnock, De Burgh Daly, & Murray 1957; Bonaz, Bazin, & Pellissier, 2018; Thayer et al., 2012; Weber et al., 2010).

The function of emotion regulation is to generate and nurture positive emotions while effectively managing negative emotions. Individuals with a high emotion regulation have high levels of HRV at rest (Appelhans & Luecken, 2006; Thayer & Lane, 2009). Correspondingly, during tasks that activate emotion regulation the HRV values associated with the VN increase (T. W. Smith et al., 2011). HRV is inversely correlated with perceptions linked to threatening or dangerous events while directly correlated with perceptions of contexts and events perceived as safe and secure. This specific correlation results from the activation of the ventral medial prefrontal cortex (Buchanan et al., 2010; Thayer et al., 2012). Current literature acknowledges that this specific area of the brain, the ventral medial prefrontal cortex, plays a critical role in performing cognitive evaluations finalized to emotional regulations (Eippert et al., 2007; Urry et al., 2006).

The vagal tone indexed by HRV is positively associated with positive emotions, such as cheerfulness and calmness. It is also associated with life satisfaction, which supports the claim that the level of HRV is an effective index of self-regulatory strength and stress management (Geisler, Vennewald, Kubiak, & Weber, 2010). Martens et al. (2010) explored the relationship between vagal tone and self-esteem, demonstrating that positive feedback elicits positive emotions which, in turn, increases the HRV index. The positive relationship between self-esteem and vagal tone HRV was proven even when at rest (Martens et al., 2010). Literature supports a positive relationship between HRV level and both perceived social connectedness (Kok & Fredrickson, 2010) and nurturing positive emotions (Eisenberg et al., 1995; Fabes & Eisenberg, 1997; Kok et al., 2013; Oveis et al., 2009). Positive emotions such as compassion (Stellar, Cohen, Oveis, & Keltner, 2015; Stellar & Keltner, 2017) have been associated with a higher activation of the VN, while predicting a low production of pro-inflammatory cytokines (Stellar, John-Henderson, et al., 2015). Fredrickson and Levenson (1998) also found that positive emotions allow for a more effective and efficient recovery from cardiovascular sequelae of negative emotions. Fredrickson et al. (2013) have also found an inverse relationship between hedonistic experiences and production of pro-inflammatory molecules. After a meditation session, Bhasin et al. (2013) have documented an epigenetic change of the genes in charge of energy metabolism, insulin secretion and inflammatory pathways.

The research results presented in this section explain that life experiences affect the cellular information of the immunity system through epigenetic processes mediated by CAP.

Overall, current scientific evidence shows that the cholinergic anti-inflammatory pathway plays a fundamental role in activating a two-way communication and integrating mental states, neuro-physiological, endocrine, and cellular structures through "experience-dependent" epigenetic changes that cause neuroplasticity, behavioral flexibility, and adaptation. The quality and quantity of life experiences, be them conscious or unconscious, psychological, physiological or cellular, trigger epigenetic changes, which in turn affect our quality of life and the perception of our personal identity.

## Interoception Information

The third psychophysiological process related to the experience of positive emotions and their neurophysiological activation is that of interoception. It operates within a context of a highly integrated organism and it is characterized by a continuous bidirectional communication between emotions and endogenous sensorial exchanges (Ader, Felten, & Cohen, 2006). When we focus our attention in a way that promotes a flow of specific interoceptive information, positive emotions are triggered and psychological well-being enhanced. Therefore, understanding the physiological and cellular mechanisms regulating interoceptive information is critical in the pursuit of improving the quality of life of individuals, regardless of their status of being affected or not by psychological pathologies.

Interoception is a complex concept, first labeled by the Nobel laureate Charles Scott Sherrington who defined it as the body-to-brain axis of sensation concerning the state of the internal body and its visceral organs (Sherrington, 1948). Its definition has been refined with time, to become more articulated and inclusive (Cameron, 2001; Craig, 2016; Vaitl, 1996). Interoception is the process through which the central nervous system perceives, integrates, and interprets the endogenous communication, providing an overall conscious or unconscious representation of perceived reality, constantly updated by multiple functions (Craig, 2002, 2003, 2016; Khalsa et al., 2018; Vaitl, 1996). Among the principal functions carried on by the interoceptive processes there are homeostasis, survival, stress management, adaptive behaviors, and the capacity to generate cognitive and emotive experiences. The conscious interoceptive information can be triggered by answering simple questions, such as "How are you feeling right now?" (Craig, 2016). The answer we offer to such a question is the result of an assessment of our inner state of being. The degree of accuracy, sensibility, and awareness of the interoceptive information varies, thus affecting many critical aspects of our health and quality of life. The improper functionality of the interoceptive processes contributes to the generation of mental disorders, like anxiety, mood swings, food disorders, addictions, autism spectrum disorder, attention disorders, and psychosomatic problems (Du Bois, Ameis, Lai, Casanova, & Desarkar, 2016; Hatfield, Brown, Giummarra, & Lenggenhager, 2019; Khalsa et al., 2018; Paulus & Stein, 2010; Quadt, Critchley, & Garfinkel, 2018; Schauder, Mash, Bryant & Cascio, 2015; Schulz & Vogele, 2015; Stern, 2014; Wiersema & Godefroid, 2018).

In the last decade, the psychological academic community has grown more interested in the concept of interoception, especially as it relates to emotions, self-regulation, decision making, and conscience (Critchley & Garfinkel, 2017; Garfinkel & Critchley, 2013). Researchers in the biomedical field have intensified their studies on interoception to better understand the heart function, gut microbiota, and immune responses (Herbert et al., 2012; Herbert & Pollatos, 2014; Herbert, Pollatos, Flor, Enck, & Schandry, 2010), and have shed some light on neuroanatomic features of interoceptive information influencing emotions (Craig, 2016; Khalsa, Rudrauf, Feinstein, & Tranel, 2009; Seth & Critchley, 2013). Specifically, interoceptive information relevant to homeostatic control, physiological needs, pain, and organ integrity signals is carried centrally by the unmyelinated and lightly myelinated afferents spinal laminar 1 spinothalamic tract. From a central nervous system perspective, we now understand that there is a hierarchical and convergent organization of information in the spinal tract, which springs from the vagus nerve toward the cortical representations within the insular cortex (Craig, 2016; Critchley & Garfinkel, 2017).

Existing literature on physiological health shows that interoceptive mechanisms play a fundamental role through the management and coordination of homeostatic reflexes and allostatic responses related to the emotive, cognitive, and motivational information system of our mind (Quadt et al., 2018). The constant flow of interoceptive information in time and space helps define a sense of self, our unique experiences, and our own sense of identity (Quadt et al., 2018).

There are three dimensions pertaining to the interoceptive information, when perceived consciously: interoceptive accuracy (performance on objective behavioral tests of heartbeat detection), interoceptive sensibility (self-evaluated assessment of subjective enteroception), and interoceptive awareness (metacognitive awareness of interoceptive accuracy) (Garfinkel, Seth, Barrett, Suzuki, & Critchley, 2015). Interoceptive awareness includes the ability of accurately detecting and evaluating cues related to physiological activations and it is associated with the emotive information necessary to effectively regulate emotions (Agnoletti, 2019; Farb et al., 2015; Füstös, Gramann, Herbert, & Pollatos, 2013; Price &

Hooven, 2018). Scholars have explained the reason why a poor quality of interoceptive information, in terms of interoceptive accuracy, interoceptive sensibility, or interoceptive awareness, might occur: (a) the endogenous communication is not balanced, (b) a disfunction is underdiagnosed and a partial count of pro-inflammatory cytokines is considered, and (c) the information relative to a physiological improvement is not accurately assessed, for example, by understating an improvement in cardiac variability (HRV). When the interoceptive accuracy, interoceptive sensibility, or interoceptive awareness are not correctly recognized and assessed, it is likely that we experience anxiety and depression (Hartmann, Schmidt, Sander, & Hegerl, 2019; Paulus & Stein, 2010). The continuous, integrated, bidirectional communication that generates neural activation and endocrinal production, was successfully tested when, through the heart rate variability (HVR), researchers were able to measure the association between positive emotions and the level of activation of the VN (Eisenberg et al., 1995; Fabes & Eisenberg, 1997; Oveis et al., 2009; Stellar & Keltner, 2017). Other experiments tested the relation of positive emotions and the (low) level of pro-inflammatory cytokines and demonstrated an improved state of the immune system (Stellar, John-Henderson, et al., 2015). The understanding and application of the scientific evidence discussed so far must be interpreted within the context of a broader view and must take into account the interplay, complexity, and wholeness of the human organism. In this context, we understand that the vagus nerve (VN) is the main neural axis of efferent and afferent communication of the central nervous system and all internal organs (Thayer et al., 2012; Tracey, 2002) and inflammatory cytokines influence the motivational and emotive dopaminergic system (Treadway et al., 2019).

There are several behavioral practices that are associated with positive interoceptive information when carried on selectively, persistently, and with intention. Among them, there are meditation, yoga, Thai Chi, relaxation response, practicing most sports, and eudaimonic flow experiences. They all embed common traits and characteristics, such as focus and concentration on the here and now (Benson, Beary, & Carol, 1974; Farb, Segal, & Anderson, 2013; Garland, 2016; Nakamura & Csikszentmihalyi, 2009). The higher the frequency of those practices, the more actively we stimulate the neural structures and the positive interoceptive information leading to the efficacy and efficiency optimization of positive experiences and emotions. This hypothesis is supported by evidence coming from the practice of mindfulness meditation, which is associated with an increase of cortical thickness in the brain regions of the prefrontal cortex and right anterior insula. These two are key brain areas involved in the attention, interoception, sensory processing (Lazar et al., 2000; Lazar et al., 2005), and cortical representations of interoceptive attention (Farb et al., 2013). Epigenetic changes also occur when meditating, via cellular metabolism energetic genes, by affecting energy metabolism, insulin secretion, and inflammatory pathways (Bhasin et al., 2013). Another proof that we can consciously and positively affect the interoceptive information process is offered by Fischer, Messner, and Pollatos (2017), in measuring the successful results of eight weeks of "body scan" intervention (Fischer et al., 2017). Further support was described by De Jong et al. (2016) after testing the positive effect of mindfulness-based cognitive therapy on the interoceptive information processes of patients with chronic pain and comorbid depression. There is little doubt that interoceptive information processes are linked to our health and psychophysical well-being and add value to positive psychology research as they can be effectively measured, analyzed, and altered to improve our lives.

## Conclusion

The purpose of this chapter is to deepen the understanding of the physiological and cellular mechanisms that relate to psychology and, specifically, positive psychology. By matching the body of knowledge coming from biomedics and positive psychology, ample evidence was presented to emphasize that the health and quality of the life of human beings can be improved as we become aware of our thoughts, words, deeds, and lifestyle. As a new scientific field, positive psychology has been borrowing from other disciplines to withstand the scientific inquiry and to become a platform from which to promote well-being of individuals and society at large.

As the biomedical and psychological functional dynamics of positive emotions and their effect on human health are tested and understood, positive psychology will increase its credibility within the scientific community. Technological advancements in the biomedical field, particularly in the field of neuroimaging, combined with epigenetic testing are bringing together mind and body to point at a more holistic and integrated approach toward health and well-being. As we deepen our understanding of positive psychology within the context of biomedical examination, we come to the realization of the complex and highly coordinated integration of the systems making up our being. As much progress is required to fully understand the physiological processes explored in this chapter, current knowledge related to the dopaminergic neural pathways, cholinergic anti-inflammatory pathway and interoceptive information, sets the stage for future advancements in understanding the effect of human behavior on health and well-being.

## References

Abbas, A., Lichtman, A., & Pillai, S. (2017). *Cellular and molecular immunology* (9th ed.). Amsterdam: Elsevier.

Ader, R., & Cohen, N. (1975). Behaviorally conditioned immunosuppression. *Psychosomatic Medicine, 37*, 333–340.

Ader, R., Felten, D. L., & Cohen, N. (2006). *Psychoneuroimmunology* (4th ed.). Cambridge, MA: Academic Press.

Agnoletti, M. (2004). Il modello bio-psico-culturale [The bio-psycho-cultural model]. *Dipav, 11*, 11–33.

Agnoletti, M. (2018a). Psicologia Epigenetica: La nuova frontiera della Psicologia[Epigenetic psychology: The new frontier of psychology]. *State of Mind*, *10*. Retrieved from https://www.stateofmind.it/2018/10/psicologia-epigenetica.

Agnoletti, M. (2018b). L'Asse psiche-telomeri: Ecco come la mente influenza l'invecchiamento [The psycho-telomeres axis: How the mind affects aging]. *PNEINEWS, 5*, 4–8.

Agnoletti, M. (2019). "L'Effetto imbuto" o "effetto collo di bottiglia" dei telomeri [Telomere's "funnel effect" or Telomere's "bottleneck effect"]. *Medicalive Magazine, 5*, 18–21. Retrieved from https://www.medicalive.it/leffetto-imbuto-o-effetto-collo-di-bottiglia-dei-telomeri.

Agostoni, E., Chinnock, J. E., De Burgh Daly, M., & Murray, J. G. (1957). Functional and histological studies of the vagus nerve and its branches to the heart, lungs and abdominal viscera in the cat. *Journal of Physiology, 135*, 182–205.

Andersen, B. L., Yang, H.-C., Farrar, W. B., Golden-Kreutz, D. M., Emery, C. F., Thornton, L. M., . . . Carson, W. E. (2008). Psychologic intervention improves survival for breast cancer patients: A randomized clinical trial. *Cancer, 113*(12), 3450–3458.

Appelhans, B. M., & Luecken, L. J. (2006). Heart rate variability as an index of regulated emotional responding. *Review of General Psychology, 10*, 229–240.

Badgaiyan, R. D., Fischman, A. J., & Alpert, N. M. (2009). Dopamine release during human emotional processing. *Neuroimage, 47*(4), 2041–2045.

Basso, J. C., & Suzuki, W. A. (2017). The effects of acute exercise on mood, cognition, neurophysiology, and neurochemical pathways: A review. *Brain Plasticity, 2*(2), 127–152.

Benson, H., Beary, J. F., & Carol, M. P. (1974). The relaxation response. *Psychiatry, 37*(1), 37–46.

Berlucchi, G., & Buchtel, H. A. (2009). Neuronal plasticity: Historical roots and evolution of meaning. *Experimental Brain Research, 192*, 307–319.

Besedovsky, H. O., Del Rey, A., & Sorkin, E. (1981). Lymphokine-containing supernatants from con A-stimulated cells increase corticosterone blood levels. *Journal of Immunology, 126*, 385–387.

Besedovsky, H. O., Del Rey, A., Sorkin, E., & Dinarello, C. A. (1986). Immunoregulatory feedback between interleukin-1 and glucocorticoid hormones. *Science, 233*, 652–654.

Bhasin, M., Dusek, J., Chang, B., Joseph, M., Denninger, J., Fricchione, G., . . . Libermann, T. (2013). Relaxation response induces temporal transcriptome changes in energy metabolism, insulin secretion and inflammatory pathways. *PLoS One, 8*(5), Article e62817.

Bianchi, M., Bloom, O., Raabe, T., Cohen, P. S., Chesney, J., Sherry, B., . . . Tracey, K. J. (1996). Suppression of proinflammatory cytokines in monocytes by a tetravalent guanylhydrazone. *The Journal of Experimental Medicine, 183*(3), 927–936.

Bickel, W. K., Mellis, A. M., Snider, S. E., Athamneh, L. N., Stein, J. S., & Pope, D. A. (2018). 21st century neurobehavioral theories of decision making in addiction: Review and evaluation. *Pharmacology Biochemistry and Behavior, 164*, 4–21.

Björklund, A., & Dunnett, S. B. (2007). Dopamine neuron systems in the brain: An update. *Trends Neurosciences, 30*(5), 194–202.

Björklund, A., & Lindvall, O. (1984). Dopamine-containing systems in the CNS. In A. Björklund & T. Hökfelt (Eds.), *Handbook of chemical neuroanatomy. Vol. 2: Classical transmitters in the CNS, Part I* (pp. 55–122). Amsterdam: Elsevier.

Blalock, J. E. (1989). A molecular basis for bidirectional communication between the immune and neuroendocrine systems. *Physiological Reviews, 69*, 1–32.

Bonaz, B., Bazin, T., & Pellissier, S. (2018). The vagus nerve at the interface of the microbiota-gut-brain axis. *Frontiers in Neuroscience, 12*, Article 49.

Bromberg-Martin, E., & Hikosaka, O. (2009). Midbrain dopamine neurons signal preference for advance information about upcoming rewards. *Neuron, 63*(1), 119–126.

Buchanan, T. W., Driscoll, D., Mowrer, S. M., Sollers, J. J., Thayer, J. F., Kirschbaum, C., & Tranel, D. (2010). Medial prefrontal cortex damage affects physiological and psychological stress responses differently in men and women. *Psychoneuroendocrinology, 35*, 56–66.

Cameron, O. G. (2001). *Visceral sensory neuroscience: Interoception.* New York: Oxford University Press.

Castro, D. C., & Berridge, K. C. (2014). Advances in the neurobiological bases for food "liking" versus "wanting." *Physiology & Behavior, 136*, 22–30.

Chaillou, A.-C., Giersch, A., Hoonakker, M., Capa, R. L., & Bonnefond, A. (2017). Differentiating motivational from affective influence of performance-contingent reward on cognitive control: The wanting component enhances both proactive and reactive control. *Biological Psychology, 125*, 146–153.

Chiew, K., & Braver, T. (2014). Dissociable influences of reward motivation and positive emotion on cognitive control. *Cognitive, Affective, & Behavioral Neuroscience, 14*(2), 509–529.

Clore, G. L. (1994). Why emotions are felt. In P. Ekman & R. Davidson (Eds.), *The nature of emotion: Fundamental questions* (pp. 103–111). New York: Oxford University Press.

Conklin, Q., King, B., Zanesco, A., Pokorny, J., Hamidi, A., Lin, J., . . . Saron, C. (2015). Telomere lengthening after three weeks of an intensive insight meditation retreat. *Psychoneuroendocrinology, 61*, 26–27.

Cousins, N. (1979). *Anatomy of an Illness as perceived by the patient.* New York: W. W. Norton.

Craig, A. D. (2002). How do you feel? Interoception: The sense of the physiological condition of the body. *Nature Reviews Neuroscience, 3*, 655–666.

Craig, A. D. (2003). Interoception: The sense of the physiological condition of the body. *Current Opinion in Neurobiology, 13*, 500–505.

Craig, A. D. (2005). Forebrain emotional asymmetry: A neuroanatomical basis? *Trends in Cognitive Sciences, 9*, 566–571.

Craig, A. D. (2016). *How do you feel? An interoceptive moment with your neurobiological self.* Princeton, NJ: Princeton University Press.

Critchley, H. D., & Garfinkel, S. N. (2017). Interoception and emotion. *Current Opinion in Psychology, 17*, 7–14.

Davidson, R. J. (2000). Affective style, psychopathology, and resilience: Brain mechanisms and plasticity. *American Psychologist, 55*(11), 1196–1214.

Deacon, B., & Mckay, D. (2015). The biomedical model of psychological problems: A call for critical dialogue. *Behavior Therapist, 38*, 231–235.

De Jong, M., Lazar, S. W., Hug, K., Mehling, W. E., Hölzel, B. K., Sack, A. T., . . . Gard, T. (2016). Effects of mindfulness-based cognitive therapy on body awareness in patients with chronic pain and comorbid depression. *Frontiers in Psychology, 7*, Article 967.

Delle Fave, A., Massimini, F., & Bassi, M. (2011). *Psychological selection and optimal experience across cultures: Social empowerment through personal growth.* Dordrecht: Springer.

DeYoung, C. G. (2013). The neuromodulator of exploration: A unifying theory of the role of dopamine in personality. *Frontiers in Human Neuroscience, 7*, Article 762.

Diener, E. (1999). Introduction to the special section on the structure of emotion. *Journal of Personality and Social Psychology, 76*(5), 803–804.

Diener, E., & Diener, C. (1996). Most people are happy. *Psychological Science, 7*, 181–185.

Du Bois, D., Ameis, S. H., Lai, M.-C., Casanova, M. F., & Desarkar, P. (2016). Interoception in autism spectrum disorder: A review. *International Journal of Developmental Neuroscience, 52*, 104–111.

Eippert, F., Veit, R., Weiskopf, N., Erb, M., Birbaumer, N., & Anders, S. (2007). Regulation of emotional responses elicited by threat-related stimuli. *Human Brain Mapping, 28*, 409–423.

Eisenberg, N., Fabes, R. A., Murphy, B., Maszk, P., Smith, M., & Karbon, M. (1995). The role of emotionality and regulation in children's social functioning: A longitudinal study. *Child Development, 66*, 1360–1384.

Ekman, P. (1994). All emotions are basic. In P. Ekman & R. J. Davidson (Eds.), *The nature of emotion: Fundamental questions* (pp. 15–19). New York: Oxford University Press.

Ekman, P., & Davidson, R. J. (Eds.). (1994). *The nature of emotion: Fundamental questions.* New York: Oxford University Press.

Epel, E., Blackburn, E., Lin, J., Dhabhar, F. S., Adler, N. E., Morrow, J. D., & Cawthon, R. M. (2004). Accelerated telomere shortening in response to life stress. *Proceedings of the National Academy of Sciences, 101*(49), 17312–17315.

Epel, E., Daubenmier, J., Moskowitz, J., Folkman, S., & Blackburn, E. (2009). Can meditation slow rate of cellular aging? Cognitive stress, mindfulness, and telomeres. *Annals of the New York Academy of Sciences, 1172,* 34–53.

Fabes, R. A., & Eisenberg, N. (1997). Regulatory control and adults' stress-related responses to daily life events. *Journal of Personality and Social Psychology, 73,* 1107–1117.

Farb, N. A., Daubenmier, J., Price, C., Gard, T., Kerr, C., Dunn, B., . . . Mehling, W. E. (2015). Interoception, contemplative practice, and health. *Frontiers in Psychology, 6,* Article 763.

Farb, N. A., Segal, Z. V., & Anderson, A. K. (2013). Mindfulness meditation training alters cortical representations of interoceptive attention. *Social Cognitive and Affective Neuroscience, 8*(1), 15–26.

Farre, A., & Rapley, T. (2017). The new old (and old new) medical model: Four decades navigating the biomedical and psychosocial understandings of health and illness. *Healthcare, 5*(4), Article 88.

Fischer, D., Messner, M., & Pollatos, O. (2017). Improvement of interoceptive processes after an 8-week body scan intervention. *Frontiers in Human Neuroscience, 11,* Article 452.

Floresco, S., Magyar, O., Ghods-Sharifi, S., Vexelman, C., & Tse, M. T. L. (2006). Multiple dopamine receptor subtypes in the medial prefrontal cortex of the rat regulate set-shifting. *Neuropsychopharmacology, 31,* 297–309.

Fredrickson, B. L. (1998). What good are positive emotions? *Review of General Psychology, 2,* 300–319.

Fredrickson, B. L. (2001). The role of positive emotions in positive psychology: The broaden-and-build theory of positive emotions. *American Psychologist, 56*(3), 218–226.

Fredrickson, B. L. (2013). Positive emotions broaden and build. *Advances in Experimental Social Psychology, 47,* 1–53.

Fredrickson, B. L., Grewen, K. M., Coffey, K. A., Algoe, S. B., Firestine, A. M., Arevalo, J. M. G., . . . Cole, S. W. (2013). A functional genomic perspective on human well-being. *Proceedings of the National Academy of Sciences, 110*(33), 13684–13689.

Fredrickson, B. L., & Levenson, R. W. (1998). Positive emotions speed recovery from the cardiovascular sequelae of negative emotions. *Cognition and Emotion, 12*(2), 191–220.

Fricchione, G., Yeung, A., & Ivkovic, A. (2016). *The science of stress: What it is, why we feel it, how it affects us.* Brighton: Ivy Press.

Frijda, N. H., Kuipers, P., & Schure, E. (1989). Relations among emotion, appraisal, and emotional action readiness. *Journal of Personality and Social Psychology, 57,* 212–228.

Füstös, J., Gramann, K., Herbert, B., & Pollatos, O. (2013). On the embodiment of emotion regulation: Interoceptive awareness facilitates reappraisal. *Social Cognitive and Affective Neuroscience, 8*(8), 911–917.

Garfinkel, S. N., & Critchley, H. D. (2013). Interoception, emotion and brain: New insights link internal physiology to social behavior. Commentary on: "Anterior insular cortex mediates bodily sensibility and social anxiety" by Terasawa et al. (2012). *Social Cognitive and Affective Neuroscience, 8,* 231–234.

Garfinkel, S. N., Seth, A., Barrett, A. B., Suzuki, K., & Critchley, H. (2015). Knowing your own heart: Distinguishing interoceptive accuracy from interoceptive awareness. *Biological Psychology, 104,* 65–74.

Garland, E. L. (2016). Restructuring reward processing with mindfulness-oriented recovery enhancement: Novel therapeutic mechanisms to remediate hedonic dysregulation in addiction, stress, and pain. *Annals of the New York Academy of Sciences, 1373*(1), 25–37.

Geisler, F., Vennewald, N., Kubiak, T., & Weber, H. (2010). The impact of heart rate variability on subjective well-being is mediated by emotion regulation. *Personality and Individual Differences, 49,* 723–728.

Gidron, Y., Deschepper, R., De Couck, M., Thayer, J. F., & Velkeniers, B. (2018). The vagus nerve can predict and possibly modulate non-communicable chronic diseases: Introducing a neuroimmunological paradigm to public health. *Journal of Clinical Medicine, 7*(10), Article 371.

Good, R. A. (1981). Foreword: Interactions of the body's major networks. In R. Ader (Ed.), *Psychoneuroimmunology* (pp. xvii–xx). New York: Academic Press.

Hansen, M. K., O'Connor, K. A., Goehler, L. E., Watkins, L. R., & Maier, S. F. (2001). The contribution of the vagus nerve in interleukin-1beta–induced fever is dependent on dose. *American Journal of Physiology-Regulatory, Integrative and Comparative Physiology, 280,* 929–934.

Hartmann, R., Schmidt, F. M., Sander, C., & Hegerl, U. (2019). Heart rate variability as indicator of clinical state in depression. *Frontiers in Psychiatry, 9,* Article 735.

Hatfield, T. R., Brown, R. F., Giummarra, M., & Lenggenhager, B. (2019). Autism spectrum disorder and interoception: Abnormalities in global integration? *Autism, 23*(1), 212–222.

Heller, A. S., Van Reekum, C. M., Schaefer, S. M., Lapate, R. C., Radler, B. T., Ryff, C. D., & Davidson, R. J. (2013). Sustained striatal activity predicts eudaimonic well-being and cortisol output. *Psychological Science, 24*(11), 2191–2200.

Herbert, B. M., Herbert, C., Pollatos, O., Weimer, K., Enck, P., Sauer, H., & Zipfel, S. (2012). Effects of short-term food deprivation on interoceptive awareness, feelings and autonomic cardiac activity. *Biological Psychology, 89,* 71–79.

Herbert, B. M., & Pollatos, O. (2014). Attenuated interoceptive sensitivity in overweight and obese individuals. *Eating Behaviors, 15,* 445–448.

Herbert, B. M., Pollatos, O., Flor, H., Enck, P., & Schandry, R. (2010). Cardiac awareness and autonomic cardiac reactivity during emotional picture viewing and mental stress. *Psychophysiology, 47,* 342–354.

Hölzel, B., Carmody, J., Evans, K., Hoge, E., Dusek, J., Morgan, L., . . . Lazar, S. (2010). Stress reduction correlates with structural changes in the amygdala. *Social Cognitive and Affective Neuroscience, 5*(1), 11–17.

Ito, T. A., & Cacioppo, J. T. (1999). The psychophysiology of utility appraisals. In D. Kahneman, E. Diener, & N. Schwartz (Eds.), *Well-being: The foundations of hedonic psychology* (pp. 470–488). New York: Russell Sage Foundation.

Jacobs, T. L., Epel, E. S., Lin, J., Blackburn, E. H., Wolkowitz, O. M., Bridwell, D. A., . . . Saron, C. D. (2011). Intensive meditation training, immune cell telomerase activity, and psychological mediators. *Psychoneuroendocrinology, 36*(5), 664–681.

Johnson, S. B. (2013). Increasing psychology's role in health research and health care. *American Psychologist, 68*(5), 311–321.

Khalsa, S. S., Adolphs, R., Cameron, O. G., Critchley, H. D., Davenport, P. W., Feinstein, J. S., . . . Paulus, M. P. (2018). Interoception and mental health: A roadmap. *Biological Psychiatry: Cognitive Neuroscience and Neuroimaging, 3*(6), 501–513.

Khalsa, S. S., Rudrauf, D., Feinstein, J., & Tranel, D. (2009). The pathways of interoceptive awareness. *Nature Neuroscience, 12*(12), 1494–1496.

Kjaer, T., Bertelsen, C., Piccini, P., Brooks, D., Alving, J., & Lou, H. (2002). Increased dopamine tone during meditation-induced change of consciousness. *Cognitive Brain Research, 13,* 255–259.

Klanker, M., Feenstra, M., & Denys, D. (2013). Dopaminergic control of cognitive flexibility in humans and animals. *Frontiers in Neuroscience, 7,* 201.

Kobayashi, K., & Hsu, M. (2019). Common neural code for reward and information value. *Proceedings of the National Academy of Sciences, 116*(26), 13061–13066.

Kok, B. E., Coffey, K., Cohn, M., Catalino, L., Vacharkulksemsuk, T., Algoe, S., . . . Fredrickson, B. (2013). How positive emotions build physical health: Perceived positive social connections account for the upward spiral between positive emotions and vagal tone. *Psychological Science, 24,* 1123–1132.

Kok, B. E., & Fredrickson, B. L. (2010). Upward spirals of the heart: Autonomic flexibility, as indexed by vagal tone, reciprocally and prospectively predicts positive emotions and social connectedness. *Biological Psychology, 85*(3), 432–436.

Kringelbach, M. L., & Berridge, K. C. (2010). *Pleasures of the brain.* New York: Oxford University Press.

Küchler, T., Bestmann, B., Rappat, S., Henne-Bruns, D., & Wood-Dauphinee, S. (2007). Impact of psychotherapeutic support for patients with gastrointestinal cancer undergoing surgery: 10-year survival results of a randomized trial. *Journal of Clinical Oncology, 25*(19), 2702–2708.

Lavretsky, H., Epel, E. S., Siddarth, P., Nazarian, N., Cyr, N. S., Khalsa, D. S., . . . Irwin, M. R. (2012). A pilot study of yogic meditation for family dementia caregivers with depressive symptoms: Effects on mental health, cognition, and telomerase activity. *International Journal of Geriatric Psychiatry, 28*(1), 57–65.

Lazar, S. W., Bush, G., Gollub, R. L., Fricchione, G. L., Khalsa, G., & Benson, H. (2000). Functional brain mapping of the relaxation response and meditation. *Neuroreport, 11*, 1581–1585.

Lazar, S. W., Kerr, C. E., Wasserman, R. H., Gray, J. R., Greve, D. N., Treadway, M. T., . . . Fischl, B. (2005). Meditation experience is associated with increased cortical thickness. *Neuroreport, 16*(17), 1893–1897.

Lazarus, R. S. (1991). *Emotion and adaptation.* New York: Oxford University Press.

Lewis, G. J., Kanai, R., Rees, G., & Bates, T. C. (2014). Neural correlates of the "good life": Eudaimonic well-being is associated with insular cortex volume. *Social, Cognitive, and Affective Neuroscience, 9*, 615–618.

Lewis, T. (1974). *The lives of a cell: Notes of a biology watcher.* New York: Viking Press.

Maguire, E. A., Woollett, K., & Spiers, H. J. (2006). London taxi drivers and bus drivers: A structural MRI and neuropsychological analysis. *Hippocampus, 16*(12), 1091–1101.

Manzano, Ö., Cervenka, S., Jucaite, A., Hellenäs, O., Farde, L., & Ullén, F. (2013). Individual differences in the proneness to have flow experiences are linked to dopamine D2-receptor availability in the dorsal striatum. *Neuroimage, 67*, 1–6.

Martens, A., Greenberg, J., Allen, J., Hayes, J., Schimel, J., & Johns, M. (2010). Self-esteem and autonomic physiology: Self-esteem levels predict cardiac vagal tone. *Journal of Research in Personality, 44*(5), 573–584.

Metal'nikov, S., & Chorine, V. (1926). Role des reflexes conditionells darts l'immunite'. *Annales de l'Institut Pasteur, 40*, 893–900.

Mosing, M. A., Pedersen, N. L., Cesarini, D., Johannesson, M., Magnusson, P. K. E., Nakamura, J., . . . Ullén, F. (2012). Genetic and environmental influences on the relationship between flow proneness, locus of control and behavioral inhibition. *PLoS One, 7*(11), Article e47958.

Nakamura, J., & Csikszentmihalyi, M. (2009). Flow theory and research. In C. R. Snyder & S. J. Lopez (Eds.), *Oxford handbook of positive psychology* (pp. 195–206). Oxford: Oxford University Press.

Niv, Y., & Chan, S. (2011). On the value of information and other rewards. *Nature Neuroscience, 14*(9), 1095–1097.

Oatley, K., & Jenkins, J. M. (1996). *Understanding emotions.* Cambridge, MA: Blackwell.

O'Donovan, A., Lin, J., Tillie, J., Dhabhar, F. S., Wolkowitz, O. M., Blackburn, E., & Epel, E. (2009). Pessimism correlates with leukocyte telomere shortness and elevated interleukin-6 in post-menopausal women. *Brain, Behavior and Immunity, 23*(4), 446–449.

Oppenheimer, S. M., Gelb, A. W., Girvin, J. P., & Hachinski, V. C. (1992). Cardiovascular effects of human insular cortex stimulation. *Neurology, 42*, 1727–1732.

Ott, T., & Nieder, A. (2019). Dopamine and cognitive control in prefrontal cortex. *Trends in Cognitive Sciences, 23*(3), 213–234.

Ottenheimer, D. J., Richard, J. M., & Janak, P. H. (2018). Ventral pallidum encodes relative reward value earlier and more robustly than nucleus accumbens. *Nature Communications, 9*(1), 4350.

Oveis, C., Cohen, A. B., Gruber, J., Shiota, M. N., Haidt, J., & Keltner, D. (2009). Resting respiratory sinus arrhythmia is associated with tonic positive emotionality. *Emotion, 9*, 265–270.

Paulus, M. P., & Stein, M. B. (2010). Interoception in anxiety and depression. *Brain Structure and Function, 214*, 451–463.

Price, C., & Hooven, C. (2018). Interoceptive awareness skills for emotion regulation: Theory and approach of mindful awareness in body-oriented therapy (MABT). *Frontiers in Psychology, 9*, Article 798.

Quadt, L., Critchley, H. D., & Garfinkel, S. N. (2018). The neurobiology of interoception in health and disease. *Annals of the New York Academy of Sciences, 1428*(1), 112–128.

Raghanti, M. A., Edler, M. K., Stephenson, A. R., Munger, E. L., Jacobs, B., Hof, P. R., . . . Lovejoy, C. O. (2018). A neurochemical hypothesis for the origin of hominids. *Proceedings of the National Academy of Sciences, 115*(6), E1108–E1116.

Robinson, M. J., Fischer, A. M., Ahuja, A., Lesser, E. N., & Maniates, H. (2016). Roles of "wanting" and "liking" in motivating behavior: Gambling, food, and drug addictions. In E. Simpson & P. Balsam (Eds.), *Behavioral neuroscience of motivation* (*Current topics in behavioral neurosciences, 27*, pp. 105–136). Cham: Springer.

Rosenberg, E. L. (1998). Levels of analysis and the organization of affect. *Review of General Psychology*, 2, 247–270.

Rosenkranz, M. A., Jackson, D. C., Dalton, K. M., Dolski, I., Ryff, C. D., Singer, B. H., . . . Davidson, R. J. (2003). Affective style and *in vivo* immune response: Neurobehavioral mechanisms. *Proceedings of the National Academy of Sciences*, 100(19), 11148–11152.

Russell, J. A., & Feldman Barrett, L. (1999). Core affect, prototypical emotional episodes, and other things called emotion: Dissecting the elephant. *Journal of Personality and Social Psychology*, 76, 805–819.

Ryan, R., & Deci, E. (2001). On happiness and human potentials: A review of research on hedonic and eudaimonic well-being. *Annual Review of Psychology*, 52, 141–166.

Sapolsky, R. (2011, March). Dopamine jackpot! *Sapolsky on the science of pleasure*. Retrieved from https://www.youtube.com/watch?v=axrywDP9Ii0

Saunders, B. T., Richard, J. M., Margolis, E. B., & Janak, P. H. (2018). Dopamine neurons create Pavlovian conditioned stimuli with circuit-defined motivational properties. *Nature Neuroscience*, 21(8), 1072–1083.

Schauder, K., Mash, L., Bryant, L., & Cascio, C. (2015). Interoceptive ability and body awareness in autism spectrum disorder. *Journal of Experimental Child Psychology*, 131, 193–200.

Schulz, A., & Vögele, C. (2015). Interoception and stress. *Frontiers in Psychology*, 6, 993.

Schutte, N. S., & Malouff, J. M. (2014). A meta-analytic review of the effects of mindfulness meditation on telomerase activity. *Psychoneuroendocrinology*, 42, 45–48.

Seligman, M. E. P., & Csikszentmihalyi, M. (2000). Positive psychology: An introduction. *American Psychologist*, 55(1), 5–14.

Seth, A. K., & Critchley, H. D. (2013). Extending predictive processing to the body: Emotion as interoceptive inference. *Behavioral and Brain Sciences*, 36, 227–228.

Sherrington, C. S. (1984). *The integrative action of the nervous system*. Cambridge: Cambridge University Press.

Smith, K. S., Berridge, K. C., & Aldridge, J. W. (2011). Disentangling pleasure from incentive salience and learning signals in brain reward circuitry. *Proceedings of the National Academy of Sciences*, 108(27), E255–E264.

Smith, K. S., Mahler, S. V., Peciña, S., & Berridge, K. (2010). Hedonic hotspots: Generating sensory pleasure in the brain. In M. L. Kringelbach & K. C. Berridge (Eds.), *Pleasures of the brain* (pp. 27–49). New York: Oxford University Press.

Smith, K. S., Tindell, A., Aldridge, W., & Berridge, K. (2009). Ventral pallidum roles in reward and motivation. *Behavioural Brain Research*, 196(2), 155–167.

Smith, T. W., Cribbet, M. R., Nealey-Moore, J. B., Uchino, B. N., Williams, P. G., Mackenzie, J., & Thayer, J. F. (2011). Matters of the variable heart: Respiratory sinus arrhythmia response to marital interaction and associations with marital quality. *Journal of Personality and Social Psychology*, 100, 103–119.

Stellar, J. E., Cohen, A., Oveis, C., & Keltner, D. (2015). Affective and physiological responses to the suffering of others: Compassion and vagal activity. *Journal of Personality and Social Psychology*, 108(4), 572–585.

Stellar, J. E., John-Henderson, N., Anderson, C. L., Gordon, A., McNeil, G. D., & Keltner, D. (2015). Positive affect and markers of inflammation: Discrete positive emotions predict lower levels of inflammatory cytokines. *Emotion*, 15(2), 129–133.

Stellar, J. E., & Keltner, D. (2017). Compassion in the autonomic nervous system: The role of the vagus nerve. In P. Gilbert (Ed.), *Compassion: Concepts, research and applications*. New York: Routledge.

Stern, E. (2014). Neural circuitry of interoception: New insights into anxiety and obsessive-compulsive disorders. *Current Treatment Options in Psychiatry*, 1(3), 235–247.

Taggart, P., Boyett, M. R., Logantha, S. J., & Lambiase, P. (2011). Anger, emotion, and arrhythmias: From brain to heart. *Frontiers in Physiology*, 2, Article 67.

Thayer, J. F., Ahs, F., Fredrikson, M., Sollers, J. J., & Wager, T. D. (2012). A meta-analysis of heart rate variability and neuroimaging studies: Implications for heart rate variability as a marker of stress and health. *Neuroscience & Biobehavioral Reviews*, 36(2), 747–756.

Thayer, J. F., & Brosschot, J. F. (2005). Psychosomatics and psychopathology: Looking up and down from the brain. *Psychoneuroendocrinology*, 30, 1050–1058.

Thayer, J. F., & Lane, R. D. (2009). Claude Bernard and the heart–brain connection: Further elaboration of a model of neurovisceral integration. *Neuroscience & Biobehavioral Reviews*, 33, 81–88.

Tooby, J., & Cosmides, L. (1990). The past explains the present: Emotional adaptations and the structure of ancestral environments. *Ethology and Sociobiology*, 11, 375–424.

Tracey, K. J. (2002). The inflammatory reflex. *Nature*, 420, 853–859.

Tracey, K. J. (2006). *Fatal sequence: The killer within.* New York: Dana Press.

Tracey, K. J., Beutler, B., Lowry, S. F., Merryweather, J., Wolpe, S., Milsark, I. W., . . . Albert, J. D. (1986). Shock and tissue injury induced by recombinant human cachectin. *Science*, 234(4775), 470–474.

Treadway, M., Cooper, J., & Miller, A. (2019). Can't or won't? Immunometabolic constraints on dopaminergic drive. *Trends in Cognitive Sciences*, 23(5), 435–448.

Ullén, F., De Manzano, O., Almeida, R., Magnusson, P. K. E., Pedersen, N. L., Nakamura, J., . . . Madison, G. (2011). Proneness for psychological flow in everyday life: Associations with personality and intelligence. *Personality and Individual Differences*, 52, 167–172.

Urry, H. L., Van Reekum, C. M., Johnstone, T., Kalin, N. H., Thurow, M. E., Schaefer, H. S., . . . Davidson, R. J. (2006). Amygdala and ventromedial prefrontal cortex are inversely coupled during regulation of negative affect and predict the diurnal pattern of cortisol secretion among older adults. *Journal of Neuroscience*, 26, 4415–4425.

Vaitl, D. (1996). Interoception. *Biological Psychology*, 42(1–2), 1–27.

Vázquez, C., Hervás, G., Rahona, J. J., & Gómez, D. (2009). Psychological well-being and health: Contributions from positive psychology. *Annuary of Clinical and Health Psychology*, 5, 15–28.

Volkow, D., Wang, G., & Baler, R. (2011). Reward, dopamine and the control of food intake: Implications for obesity. *Trends in Cognitive Sciences*, 15(1), 37–46.

Watkins, L. R., Goehler, L. E., Relton, J. K., Tartaglia, N., Silbert, L., Martin, D., & Maier, S. F. (1995). Blockade of interleukin-1 induced hyperthermia by subdiaphragmatic vagotomy: Evidence for vagal mediation of immune-brain communication. *Neuroscience Letters*, 183, 27–31.

Weber, C. S., Thayer, J. F., Rudat, M., Wirtz, P. H., Zimmermann-Viehoff, F., Thomas, A., . . . Deter, H. C. (2010). Low vagal tone is associated with impaired post stress recovery of cardiovascular, endocrine, and immune markers. *European Journal of Applied Physiology*, 109(2), 201–211.

Wiersema, J. R., & Godefroid, E. (2018). Interoceptive awareness in attention deficit hyperactivity disorder. *PLoS One*, 13(10), Article e0205221.

Witek-Janusek, L., Albuquerque, K., Chroniak, K. R, Chroniak, C., Durazo-Arvizu, R., & Mathews, H. L. (2008). Effect of mindfulness based stress reduction on immune function, quality of life and coping in women newly diagnosed with early stage breast cancer. *Brain, Behavior, and Immunity*, 22(6), 969–981.

Wittling, W. (1995). Brain asymmetry in the control of autonomic-physiologic activity. In R. J. Davidson & K. J. Hugdahl (Eds.), *Brain asymmetry* (pp. 305–357). Cambridge, MA: MIT Press.

# 10

# Youth Civic Engagement: Exploring Micro and Macro Social Processes

Laura Wray-Lake, Burkhard Gniewosz, Celina Benavides, and Sara Wilf

On Fridays around the world starting in September 2018, millions have gathered to demand action to combat climate change. In March 2019, #FridaysforFuture mobilized 1.6 million people across 13 countries, and the majority of protesters were 14 to 19 years old (Wahlström et al., 2019). In *Time for Outrage: Indignez-vous!,* French resistance leader Stepháne Hessel (2011) urged youth to act on their outrage about injustice, saying "Our capacity for freedom is indispensable, as is our freedom to engage" (p. 12). Sociologists have long recognized that youth have a "fresh take" on society, meaning that they view society's issues with a new lens and create new generations with their visions for social change (Mannheim, 1952). Social and political movements in our current history – such as #FridaysforFuture, March for Our Lives, Black Lives Matter, and the Women's March – showcase youth as integral civic leaders. Through social media platforms like Twitter and Facebook, youth are creating new forms of civic engagement to respond to global social and political issues (Bennett, Wells, & Freelon, 2011; Boulianne, 2015; Jenkins, Shresthova, Gamber-Thompson, Kligler-Vilenchik, & Zimmerman, 2018; Xenos, Vromen, & Loader, 2014). Globalization has made an international perspective on youth civic engagement more relevant than ever, and the field needs more cohesive conceptual views on youth civic engagement and its developmental correlates.

Democracies need their members to be actively civically engaged in order to thrive. Much like living organisms that need energy to exist, no complex human society can long survive unless it is able to capture the energies of new generations. Adolescence is a critical time for youth to explore worldviews, find their place in society, and feel connected to something larger than themselves. Thus, adolescents

*Positive Psychology: An International Perspective*, First Edition.
Edited by Aleksandra Kostić and Derek Chadee.
© 2021 John Wiley & Sons Ltd. Published 2021 by John Wiley & Sons Ltd.

are capable of making their own unique contributions to society. It is a society's responsibility to provide structures, role models, and experiences that prepare young people to become responsible adults, and societies should be responsive to youths' input. This symbiosis of societies' need for engaged young people and youth's need for a supportive developmental environment is fulfilled through youth civic engagement. Youth are society's future leaders and relevant participants in society's present. Through civic engagement, youth can uphold a society's stability and can also engage in critique of a society's status quo.

In this chapter, we draw on extant theory and research to define civic engagement in a way that captures the diverse orientations and expressions of youth internationally. As elaborated below, we define civic engagement as behaviors, values and attitudes, knowledge, and efficacy that result from interactions between individuals and their communities and are focused on community-relevant issues. Communities can range from local to global, depending on individuals' perspectives. Taking a developmental perspective, we examine the nature of opportunities that manifest through interactions with others, take place in the micro- or proximal, everyday contexts, and encourage youth to develop into actively engaged citizens. Social interactions within micro-contexts are embedded in larger cultural or macrosocial contexts that affect the development of adolescent civic engagement in various ways. Understanding these macro-contextual opportunities and constraints is relevant for cross-cultural work and for culturally situating any investigation of youth civic engagement.

## Conceptualizing Youth Civic Engagement

Research on civic engagement is inherently multidisciplinary, and various definitions of civic engagement have been offered (Adler & Goggin, 2005; Amnå, 2012; Sherrod, Torney-Purta, & Flanagan, 2010; Wray-Lake, Metzger, & Syvertsen, 2017). It behooves civic scholars to begin reaching consensus in defining civic engagement. The definition we offer above is broad and inclusive enough to be relevant to youth around the world. To dissect our definition, civic engagement is *fundamentally based on interactions* between individuals and their community, is *contextually based* in the sense that community is a context and the nature of this context varies across individuals, and is *multidimensional* (comprised of behaviors, values and attitudes, knowledge, and efficacy). Moreover, civic engagement can be distinguished from citizenship. Citizenship is a formal, legal designation of membership to a society, with rights and responsibilities that go with it (Hyman, 2002; Walzer, 1989). Civic engagement is the subjective representation of citizenship that entails psychological or tangible interactions with a group of others where individuals express rights and act on responsibilities, yet formal membership is not required. An example of this distinction is the civic engagement of undocumented immigrants in the United States (e.g., Perez, Espinoza, Ramos, Coronado, & Cortes, 2010).

### Interactions with community

We argue that civic engagement cannot occur without interactions between an individual and their community. These person–community interactions can be measurable, tangible relationships or can be conceptual, abstract, and ideological. For example, youth participate in online communities that are both virtual and global in scope (Pathak-Shelat & Bhatia, 2019). Essentially, civic engagement requires understanding the self in relation to a larger group of others in the public sphere. The ability to distinguish self from others starts developing very early in life (Hart & Fegley, 1995) – it is from this view of the self in relation to others that civic engagement takes root and grows (Flanagan, 2013). The relationship between self and society can be positive, based in social trust and reciprocity among community members: such positive bonds are at the heart of social capital (Coleman, 1988; Putnam, 2000). The association between social trust and civic engagement is mutually reinforcing, and has been described as a virtuous circle (Uslaner, 2002). When individuals feel connected to a group, they are more likely to act in ways that benefit the group (Stürmer & Simon, 2004). Views about community and government begin developing in early childhood (Patterson et al., 2019), and as youth develop emotional and cognitive skills during adolescence, views of broader others continue to evolve (Metzger & Smetana, 2010). Thus, opportunities to participate in groups and interact with others are particularly critical for civic development during childhood and adolescence. These interactions help youth develop a sense of who they are, what they value, and their perceptions of society.

As some community connection is a necessary precursor to civic engagement, it follows that civic engagement is inherently contextually based. In becoming civically engaged, youth have agency to determine the scope of their community, and thus community can refer to local, national, international, or virtual groups of others. An accumulation of interactions with others likely determines how broadly youth define their communities and thus, in what ways they choose to engage. Civic engagement is typically directed toward a public sphere (i.e., not just toward a group of family or friends), although some youth from socioeconomically disadvantaged communities consider their care, support, and help toward family as contributing to improving their larger communities (McBride, Sherraden, & Pritzker, 2006; Wray-Lake & Abrams, 2020).

Civic engagement should also be conceptualized as contextually based to account for micro- and macrosocial contexts. In other words, civic engagement in a particular community, nation, or region is shaped by the opportunities and constraints for engagement in that context. This fact must be recognized in conceptualizing youth civic engagement across cultures.

### Multiple dimensions of civic engagement

Civic engagement should be defined multidimensionally to account for diverse ways in which individuals can express their relationship and commitments to community (Amnå, 2012; Haste & Hogan, 2006; Wray-Lake et al., 2017; Youniss et al., 2002). For example, helping the homeless, protecting the environment, politically campaigning, protesting, and blogging or tweeting about social issues are legitimate forms of civic engagement. Studying youth civic engagement requires a multidimensional perspective, as not all forms of civic behaviors are systematically available to younger members of society – including electoral politics, organizational membership, or civic leadership. Behaviors alone cannot capture civic engagement, as opportunities for civic action are vastly unequal across settings, and attitudes, interests, and other psychological commitments are key ingredients of civic engagement (Sherrod & Lauckhardt, 2009). We highlight behaviors, values and attitudes, knowledge, and efficacy as dimensions of civic engagement.

*Behaviors.* Many have attempted to categorize civic behaviors (e.g., Ekman & Amnå, 2012; Haste & Hogan, 2006; Teorell, Torcal, & Montero, 2007; Verba & Nie, 1972; Westheimer & Kahne, 2004). The most basic form of civic behavior involves being socially responsible by avoiding criminal behaviors that are detrimental to others and performing basic duties such as paying taxes or obtaining a driver's license (Westheimer & Kahne, 2004). These law-abiding behaviors are important for the stability and function of society, yet they are not heavily emphasized in the civic engagement literature because of their passive nature and high prevalence. A common distinction between civic actions is whether they are political or nonpolitical (Amnå, 2012). Political actions are defined by exerting power or influencing people or institutions with power on decisions about social issues; these behaviors can be formal or informal, legal or illegal, online or offline, and can involve exerting influence inside or outside of political and government systems (Wray-Lake, 2019). Nonpolitical civic action falls in the realm of volunteering, helping others, and community problem-solving in ways that do not directly interact with government or larger systems.

Different types of civic actions may be explained by distinct developmental patterns, precursors, and individual difference factors; unfortunately, this issue is understudied. Studies of Italian adolescents have suggested different developmental correlates for volunteering versus political behavior (Crocetti, Jahromi, & Meeus, 2012; Marzana, Marta, & Pozzi, 2012): For example, Crocetti and colleagues (2012) showed that identity status and processes were more strongly related to adolescents' volunteering than their political behavior. Thus, there is merit in studying a broad range of youth civic behaviors – and related developmental processes – to understand youth's relationship to the polity across time and contexts.

*Values and attitudes.* Diverse motives undergird civic behavior, such as personal, instrumental, helping, or social justice intentions (Ballard, Malin, Porter, Colby, & Damon, 2015). Values and attitudes can motivate behavior and result from civic actions, highlighting important reciprocal associations between dimensions of civic engagement. For example, service experiences in adolescence prospectively predict more positive values and attitudes toward engagement

(Metz & Youniss, 2005). In the aggregate, values and attitudes can provide insight into public opinion both nationally and internationally; youth's views on social issues are less studied and underappreciated, but give insight into social change (Oosterhoff, Wray-Lake, Palmer, & Kaplow, 2020). Youth civic engagement research tends to avoid the study of particular political worldviews and ideologies, yet various views such as authoritarianism (Sibley & Duckitt, 2013), system justification (Godfrey & Cherng, 2016), and social justice orientations (Ginwright & Cammarota, 2002) shape the nature of civic engagement.

*Knowledge.* Most studies of youth civic knowledge focus on facts about government and political processes (e.g., Attar-Schwartz & Ben-Arieh, 2012; Campbell, 2008; Finkel & Ernst, 2005; McDevitt & Chaffee, 2000). Scholars emphasize youth civic knowledge because of its association with later voting (Cohen & Chaffee, 2013; Galston, 2007); this link between knowledge and voting is consistently found across cultures (Schulz, Ainley, Fraillon, Kerr, & Losito, 2010; Torney-Purta, Lehmann, Oswald, & Schulz, 2001). Civic knowledge has also been positively linked to other civic engagement dimensions, such as attitudes and efficacy (Cohen & Chaffee, 2013; Torney-Purta, Wilkenfeld, & Barber, 2008). Civic knowledge has important implications for civic education, as assessing youth civic knowledge is a way to evaluate the effectiveness of civic education curricula within and across nations (Torney-Purta, 2002; Villegas-Reimers, 1994). Civic knowledge can extend beyond traditional factual knowledge measures and include children's knowledge about one's rights or knowledge about oppression, inequality, and structural roots of problems (Kassimir & Flanagan, 2010). Recognizing structural roots of problems is a component of critical consciousness, and this knowledge and awareness of inequality is thought to lead to civic efficacy and justice-oriented civic actions (Watts, Diemer, & Voight, 2011). We encourage the field to continue expanding views on and measures of diverse forms of civic knowledge.

*Efficacy.* Civic efficacy is a dimension of civic engagement known by other terms including agency, empowerment, voice, and sociopolitical control (Christens, 2019; Lerner, Wang, Champine, Warren, & Erickson, 2014; Wray-Lake & Abrams, 2020). Defined as feelings of personal mastery in addressing social, political, or community issues, civic efficacy is a well-known precursor to civic participation (Diemer & Li, 2011; Verba, Schlozman, & Brady, 1995), and civic action also builds efficacy (Christens, Peterson, & Speer, 2011; Christoph, Gniewosz, & Reinders, 2014). Some consider youth efficacy or agency to be a central driver of civic development; in other words, youth can actively chart their own course of civic development (Amnå, Ekström, Kerr, & Stattin., 2009; Lerner et al., 2014). Civic efficacy contributes to well-being and growth in personal identity (Christens & Peterson, 2012) and is paramount to striving for liberation and equality and resisting oppression (Watts & Guessous, 2006).

In sum, a multidimensional definition of civic engagement means that we must acknowledge that any given civic behavior or attitude is but one component of a larger whole. A multidimensional view offers an inclusive way of studying civic engagement that can be applied across cultures and settings. Dimensions of civic engagement influence each other in dynamic ways, and studying these dynamic links can give further insights into how youth become civically engaged and the factors that lead to different expressions of civic engagement.

## Civic engagement and positive psychology

According to Aristotle, civic engagement is a key part of eudaimonia, or a life well lived (Aristotle, 2009). Contemporary scholars similarly argue that positive contributions to community and society are markers of individual well-being that extend beyond personal happiness and consider the greater good (Keyes, 2007; Rossi, 2001). Empirically, certain types of civic engagement – like community service and helping behavior – are associated with traditional markers of well-being including positive affect, life satisfaction, and lower depressive symptoms (Ballard, Hoyt, & Pachucki, 2019; Kim & Pai, 2010; Musick & Wilson, 2003; Weinstein & Ryan, 2010; Wray-Lake, DeHaan, Shubert, & Ryan, 2019). Helping behavior and social responsibility values have also been linked to increased cardiovascular health (Schreier et al., 2013) and lower health-risk behavior (Ballard et al., 2019; Wray-Lake et al., 2012). Civic engagement may promote well-being through several mechanisms, such as by (a) strengthening individuals' social capital (e.g., Mahatmya & Lohman, 2012; Putnam, 2000); (b) satisfying psychological needs for autonomy, competence, and relatedness (Wray-Lake et al., 2019); (c) developing identity, purpose, and meaning in life (Flanagan & Bundick, 2011); and (d) directly stimulating physiological processes of reward processing, mental health functioning, and stress regulation (e.g., Piliavin & Siegl, 2015). However, not all types of civic engagement result in heightened health and well-being. Certain types of civic engagement, such as political activism, can come with social, physical, and personal risks (McAdam, 1986), and individuals who are part of racial/ethnic, immigrant, or sexual minority groups may bear the burdens of civic engagement at disproportionate rates (Ballard & Ozer, 2016; Santos & VanDaalen, 2018). At the same time, political activism may serve as an active coping strategy and buffer the negative effects of discrimination on well-being for youth of color (Hope & Spencer, 2017). Research should continue to build empirical evidence for how, for whom, and under what conditions civic engagement is good for the individuals who choose to engage.

*Contextualizing the greater good.* Many definitions of youth civic engagement hinge on the function of promoting *the greater good*. Indeed, there is broad agreement that contexts and opportunities should be designed worldwide to encourage youth's positive contributions to community and society (Lerner et al., 2014; Petersen, Koller, Motti-Stefanidi, & Verma, 2016). However, conceptions of the greater good differ, both within and across societies (Gruman, Lumley, & González-Morales, 2018; Kassimir, 2006; Levine & Higgins-D'Alessandro, 2010). In a cross-cultural context, where some nations face complex intergroup strife or have unstable political systems, the greater good is likely to be in dispute. Thus, in our definition of civic engagement, promoting the "greater good" is conspicuously absent because we believe that individuals' values and community norms dictate the precise nature of the greater good for a given context. Defining the greater good is a value judgment made by individuals; and societies determine desirable states of engagement for its members. There can be a "dark side" to civic engagement (Fiorina, 1999; Theiss-Morse & Hibbing, 2005); youth who engage in civic activities that are destructive or intolerant may be advancing the "greater good" of their counter-cultural group (Boehnke & Hadjar, 2006) but counteracting the greater good of broader society. Civic engagement certainly does not always advance democracy and can perpetuate authoritarianism, xenophobia, racism, sexism, and other forms of oppression in democratic and nondemocratic societies (Ciftci & Bernick, 2015; Sibley & Duckitt, 2013).

Thus, there is variation within and between cultures in definitions of the greater good. Researchers make their own value judgments with respect to the civic dimensions they study and term desirable. Regarding this issue, we offer three reflections. First, researchers can advance understanding of civic engagement by explicitly recognizing their own values and ways of conceptualizing the greater good. The vast majority of published studies on youth civic engagement aim to understand contributions to the greater good, but often the nature of the "greater good" is implicit and unnamed. Second, as a field, investigating the full range of ways that youth can engage in civic life without limiting studies to researchers' conceptualizations of the desirable can advance developmental and cultural understandings of which types of civic engagement build which kinds of greater goods. Similarly, a definition of civic engagement that avoids specification of one particular greater good may be best poised to generate knowledge about civic engagement that is comparable across cultural contexts.

## A developmental perspective

Civic engagement is based on interactions with others, and youth are continually developing along multiple civic dimensions as these interactions become more frequent, diverse, and complex. Thus, the people and institutions that surround young people in their daily lives necessarily shape youth's civic behaviors, values and attitudes, knowledge, and efficacy over time (Flanagan, 2013). As noted above, youth are agents of their own civic development and influence the settings and relationships that, in turn, shape their lives (Amnå et al., 2009; Lerner et al., 2014). A developmental perspective is useful for understanding the origins of civic engagement, processes related to change in civic engagement over time, and growth or change in other domains that result from civic engagement.

To be applicable globally, studying youth civic development should integrate a cultural perspective. Bronfenbrenner's ecological theory of human development is relevant for understanding variation across micro- and macrolevels of youth's environments. Proximal processes – enduring interactions between individuals and their immediate, microlevel environments that occur over time – are presumed to be the "primary mechanisms producing human development" (Bronfenbrenner & Morris, 2006, p. 795). We highlight microlevel processes including interactions with positive role models, communication about values and politics, and democratic climates that encourage youth civic development. We also review research showing the importance of macrosocial dimensions, such as a nation's social contract with its members, cultural orientation, and macrosocial changes.

## Role of Microsocial Processes

Building on an ecological and developmental systems approach, the positive youth development (PYD) perspective describes civic engagement in adolescence as a result of individuals' mutually beneficial interactions with their proximal developmental contexts (Lerner et al., 2014). When developmental opportunities nurture capacities in youth, contributions to civil society are likely to result (Lerner, Dowling, & Anderson, 2003; Zaff, Boyd, Li, Lerner, & Lerner, 2010). Proximal contexts such as families, schools, peer groups, and communities both online and offline – and particularly the interactions with *people* in these everyday contexts – can provide developmental opportunities for adolescents that lead to civic engagement. We highlight role modeling, communication, and democratic climates as mechanisms by which micro-contexts promote youth civic engagement.

### Role modeling

Research consistently finds that parents who are civically engaged tend to have civically engaged children. Studies around the world have found positive correlations between parents' and adolescents' reports of political interest, political participation, and community service (e.g., Cicognani, Zani, Fournier, Gavray, & Born, 2012; Quaranta & Dotti Sani, 2016; Schulz et al., 2010). A range of studies, including two meta analyses, have illustrated parent–adolescent congruence on civic attitudes such as tolerance, equality, and views on immigrants (Degner & Dalege, 2013; Gniewosz & Noack, 2015; Grob, 2005; Heinemann, 2012; Ter Bogt, Meeus, Raaijmakers, & Vollebergh, 2001). Qualitative studies in Chile (Martínez, Peñaloza, & Valenzuela, 2012), Italy (Marta, Pozzi, & Marzana, 2010), and the United States (McAdam, 1988) have found that adolescents are inspired by their parents to become civically active. Beyond the extensive research on parents, research has also found that friends' social responsibility, political interest, political engagement, protest behavior, and attitudes toward immigrants prospectively predict adolescents' engagement on these same indicators (e.g., Schmid, 2012; Van Zalk, Kerr, Van Zalk, & Stattin, 2013).

Parent–child and peer–adolescent similarity in civic behaviors, values, and attitudes are often interpreted as indicative of modeling processes. According to social learning theory (Bandura, 1977), children observe and adopt the behaviors of individuals who they respect or value, such as when seeing their parents being active in the community. Observing role models' behaviors may also be important for developing attitudes: A German study found that teachers' attitudes toward immigrants were positively associated with students' attitudes if teachers' attitudes matched their own behaviors in the classroom (Bovier & Boehnke, 1995). Adults who work with youth in community-based organizations can also inspire youth to become civically engaged through their own civic engagement (Lerner, Alberts, Jelicic, & Smith, 2006). However, role modeling is often assumed, rather than explicitly studied. In fact, some research has attributed parent–child similarity in political attitudes in part to genetic similarity (Hufer, Kornadt, Kandler, & Riemann, 2019), and others have described an active child-driven process whereby youth first perceive (accurately or not) and then choose whether to adopt their parents' political views (Ojeda & Hatemi, 2015). Thus, modeling appears important for youth civic engagement but needs to be more rigorously studied to rule out competing hypotheses.

## Communication

Communication about values and political issues is a valuable aspect of civic socialization. In a seven-nation study (Australia, United States, Sweden, Hungary, Bulgaria, Czech Republic, Russia), Flanagan, Bowes, Jonsson, Csapó, and Sheblanova (1998) showed that family values of social responsibility consistently predicted adolescents' civic commitments across nations. These parental value messages are also related to adolescents' social trust (Wray-Lake & Flanagan, 2012). In addition, one of the strongest predictors of youth civic engagement is political and social issue discussions with parents. Cross-national evidence indicates that parent–child discussions about political and social issues predicts higher civic interest, knowledge, and political participation (e.g., Ekström & Östman, 2013; McIntosh, Hart, & Youniss, 2007; Schulz et al., 2010; Wray-Lake & Shubert, 2019). Importantly, adolescents can also drive discussions with parents and shape their civic views and behaviors (Hooghe & Stiers, 2020; Kim & Stattin, 2019; Miklikowska, 2016).

Within and across societies, teachers communicate civic messages to youth. Classroom social and political discussions relate to higher youth civic knowledge, efficacy, and action (e.g., Torney-Purta et al., 2008; Wray-Lake & Sloper, 2016). Classroom discussions may directly motivate youth civic development or indirectly promote civic participation through sparking civic interests outside of the classroom (Lee, Shah, & McLeod, 2013). Some argue that civics classes more strongly influence the civic engagement of youth with fewer civic socialization opportunities at home (Neundorf, Niemi, & Smets, 2016). Teachers may also transmit civic values. Portuguese adolescents perceived their teachers as transmitting values of respect, tolerance, solidarity, and equality and teaching them how to behave in society (Nogueira & Moreira, 2011). Similarly, students who perceive their teachers as more knowledgeable, inspiring, and confident were more likely to internalize democratic attitudes, trust in government, and a sense of social responsibility (B. Özdemir, Stattin, & Özdemir, 2016; Finkel & Ernst, 2005). Unfortunately, classroom civic opportunities are vastly unequal across youth and cultures (Levinson, 2012), and often teachers prefer to avoid controversial topics (Hess & McAvoy, 2014), leading to wide variability in civic education.

Although communication with peers is not frequently studied, Klofstad (2009) reported evidence from a random assignment study that political discussions with college roommates led to higher civic participation. Several studies suggest that sociopolitical discussions with peers can be important socializers of youth civic engagement (Ekström & Östman, 2013; Erentaitė, Žukauskienė, Beyers, & Pilkauskaitė-Valickienė, 2012; Levinsen & Yndigegn, 2015; Quintelier, 2013; Šerek & Umemura, 2015). Thus, clearly communication about civic values and sociopolitical issues from multiple socialization agents is important for youth civic development. Yet, further research is needed to explore how these socialization methods shape adolescents' civic engagement, as some scholarship has shown that not all civic discussions are created equally and the content and context matter considerably (Oosterhoff & Metzger, 2016; Wray-Lake & Shubert, 2019).

## Democratic climates

Across families, schools, and communities, democratic climates in which youth feel respected and have opportunities for egalitarian relationships and decision-making can foster youth civic engagement. Although power differentials are inevitable in adult–youth relationships because adults have more authority and responsibility in most contexts, minimizing hierarchical structures within families, schools, and community organizations can serve to empower youth to express their own views, take initiative, and build civic competencies (Mitra & Serriere, 2012; Zeldin, Camino, & Mook, 2005). Democratic parenting, where parents respect adolescents' opinions and offer opportunities for egalitarian discussions, has been associated with more positive attitudes toward immigrants (Kracke, Noack, Hofer, & Klein-Allermann, 1993), less political alienation (Gniewosz, Noack, & Buhl, 2009), higher levels of social trust (Wray-Lake & Flanagan, 2012), higher levels of social responsibility (Schmid, 2012), and community service and activism (Lauglo & Øia, 2006). However, intriguing patterns in recent research suggest that parental warmth is related to lower youth political behavior years later (Pavlova, Silbereisen, Ranta, & Salmela-Aro, 2016).

Similarly, within and across nations, open classroom climates in schools can shape adolescents' civic development, relating to higher civic knowledge, critical consciousness, likelihood of voting, political efficacy, and political interest (Amadeo, Torney-Purta, Lehmann, Husfeldt, & Nikolova, 2002; Godfrey & Grayman, 2014; Jagers, Lozada, Rivas-Drake, & Guillaume, 2017; Lauglo & Øia, 2006; Schulz et al., 2010, Šerek & Machackova, 2017; White & Mistry, 2019).

Transparent and democratic teaching practices were linked to more tolerant attitudes (Almond & Verba, 1963; Diedrich, 2006; Gniewosz & Noack, 2008), lower levels of political alienation (Gniewosz et al., 2009), and higher social trust (Damico, Conway, & Damico, 2000). The key aspect of democratic climates may be feeling a sense of belongingness to a collective (Flanagan, 2013) and feeling heard and valued (Wray-Lake & Abrams, 2020).

Although this chapter does not provide an exhaustive review of the proximal contexts that shape youth civic engagement, clearly people in adolescents' everyday lives can play a direct role in civic development, and existing research offers tangible implications for civic practice. Unfortunately, families, schools, and neighborhoods differ dramatically in their social capital resources and thus in adolescents' access to civic experiences (e.g., Bourdieu & Passeron, 1977; Kahne & Middaugh, 2008; Schlozman, Verba, & Brady, 2012). Within societies, these inequalities must be remedied in order to offer equal opportunity for civic voice and participation.

Additionally, it is beyond the scope of this chapter to review the various characteristics of individuals that predict civic engagement or moderate the role of contextual effects on civic engagement. For example, personality (such as extraversion or conscientiousness), coping style, moral reasoning, empathy, perspective-taking, self-regulation abilities, and communication skills may be precursors to youth civic engagement (Astuto & Ruck, 2017; Bekkers, 2005; Marzana et al., 2012; Metzger et al., 2018; Mueller et al., 2011; Šerek, Lacinova, & Macek, 2012; Van Goethem et al., 2012). In line with the concept of active person–environment interactions (Scarr & McCartney, 1983), individuals with certain characteristics may seek out the kinds of environments that are most likely to cultivate civic engagement, or these characteristics may determine which adolescents benefit most from civic socialization in their proximal contexts. Person–environment interactions have received relatively little attention in the civic engagement literature, but represent an important area for understanding heterogeneity in developmental pathways to civic engagement.

## Role of Macro-Societal Contexts

The structure of and opportunities within a society, also known as macrosocial contexts, define the boundaries within which civic engagement can be expressed. Youth's civic behaviors, values and attitudes, knowledge, and efficacy vary across nations. Flanagan and colleagues (Flanagan, Martínez, & Cumsille, 2011; Kassimir & Flanagan, 2010) have identified several cultural elements that take specific forms in relation to youth civic engagement. Following their model, we discuss the role of the social contract, the independent-collectivistic continuum, and groupways, or subgroup differences in youth's relationships to the nation-state. We also note social changes that can affect nations and shape youth civic engagement.

## Social contract

Through constitutions and laws, nations define citizenship and identify the rights and responsibilities associated with membership. This agreement between a nation and its citizens has been described as the social contract (Rousseau, 1762/1987). There are obvious national differences in the rights afforded to citizens that affect youth civic engagement. Nations vary in the legally specified voting age: for example, the voting age is 18 in many places around the world, yet is 16 or 17 for at least 16 countries (Wray-Lake et al., 2020). Sometimes, rights are restricted in order to silence opposition to the nation-state. For example, during military rule in Chile, student council groups were banned to restrict the youth voice (Flanagan et al., 2011). Saudi Arabia bans all forms of protests and demonstrations (Chen, 2012). Some places such as China, Russia, and parts of the Middle East control knowledge and information through restricting internet access or, in the case of Hong Kong's Umbrella Movement, constrain protests through violent police tactics (Chen, 2011; Human Rights Watch, 2019; Singh, 2012), likely because knowledge, access to new ideas, and use of social media can help youth in authoritarian countries mobilize to challenge national policies. The extent to which the social contract specifies the responsibilities of citizenship also varies across countries; some countries require military service or mandate voting. Some argue that civic engagement through social media opens new avenues for civic development globally, particularly for youth in countries with more restricted civic opportunities (Chan & Guo, 2013). In summary, a nation's political structure and laws set objective opportunities and barriers for youth civic engagement.

As part of civic development, youth form lay theories of the social contract, meaning individuals' understandings of how the system works and how they fit into it (Flanagan & Campbell, 2003). For example, youth in long-standing democracies reported higher trust in government-related institutions compared to youth from recently transitioned democracies (Amadeo et al., 2002). Youth in Australia and the United States, societies that promote capitalism and free market principles, supported the belief that success is earned based on merit and hard work, and were less likely than the youth from other countries to expect the government to play a role in people's lives (Flanagan & Campbell, 2003). Thus, the structure and systems in place in a country can fundamentally shape youth's views of government, public institutions, and others in society. Understandings of a society's structure and norms are likely passed down to youth through mediating institutions such as family and school (Flanagan et al., 2011).

## Independent versus collectivist societies

Cultural psychologists have long noted that societies exist on a continuum from independence to interdependence or collectivism (Kagitçibasi, 1997; Markus &

Kitayama, 1991; Triandis, 1995). When cultural practices encourage individuals to integrate the goals of others as part of oneself, collective civic action may be achieved more easily (Flanagan et al., 2011). Youth in more independent cultures may have to make a more concerted effort to connect personal goals with goals of the common good, and thus may show more individual variability in civic engagement. Given cultural variability in autonomy values, there are likely cultural differences in the extent to which microsocial environments encourage youth to construct and exercise civic efficacy. Adolescents from socialist (more collectivist) countries more strongly endorse government responsibility for the economy compared to peers from free market (individualist) countries (Amadeo et al., 2002; Baldi, Perie, Skidmore, Greenberg, & Hahn, 2001). In another study, youth from collectivist-oriented societies (i.e., Bulgaria, Czech Republic, and Hungary) were more likely to engage in household chores and caring for younger siblings or grandparents without expecting compensation (Bowes, Flanagan, & Taylor, 2001); these kinds of views about responsibility and helping others are core civic values. Thus, the cultural orientation of the nation appears to be influential in the process of civic development, likely transmitted through everyday contexts.

## Groupways

Flanagan and colleagues (2011) used the idea of "groupways" to capture the notion that individuals' lay theories about the social contract vary based on social group membership. Individuals' relationships with the nation-state look different depending on one's status in society, as often rights are unequally distributed across groups. Pathways and opportunities for civic engagement vary depending on social status, as shown by decades of research on socioeconomic disparities in civic engagement across ages and cultures (e.g., Schlozman et al., 2012). Experiences of exclusion and discrimination are systematically higher for racial/ethnic minority groups, immigrants, sexual and gender minority groups, individuals in poverty, and other marginalized groups within and across nations (Sanchez-Jankowski, 2002; Vogt, Bormann, & Cederman, 2016; Wrench, Rea, & Ouali, 2016). Experiences of exclusion can damage physical and mental health, damper feelings of belonging, create barriers to traditional forms of civic engagement, and heighten awareness of injustice (Barrett & Brunton-Smith, 2014; Carter, Lau, Johnson, & Kirkinis, 2017; Hope & Spencer, 2017). Youth who experience exclusion based on social status may respond by disengaging from civic life, and others may respond through increased political action, particularly when they are aware of injustice, have civic efficacy, and feel connected to a collective (Diemer, Rapa, Voight, & McWhirter, 2016; Jemal, 2018; Wray-Lake & Abrams, 2020). Research should continue to identify cross-cultural similarities in the groupways of marginalized groups, as well as identify specific, contextualized civic pathways based on social statuses within cultures.

## Macrosocial changes

Youth often rally together in times of great need, such as natural disasters, or in pivotal moments in history, such as national elections. Singular events, gradual social change movements, and political climate can mobilize youth involvement (Davis, 2004; Schwadel & Garneau, 2014; Sears & Valentino, 1997). Exposure to prolonged conflict, including civil war, ethnic conflict, or regime change could prompt a variety of youth reactions, including limited civic engagement due to psychological or physical trauma, greater feelings of empowerment to engage in social change, or heightened prosocial responses to help others. For example, Bosnian and Palestinian youth who were exposed to political violence reported caring for the wounded, exemplifying empathy and prosocial skills (Barber, 2008). Globalization and the digital age have greatly altered the abilities of youth to organize, communicate locally and globally, and be agents of social change in times of societal upheaval. Examples of large-scale cross-national youth-led movements include the Arab Spring (Kuhn, 2012), #FridaysforFuture (Wahlström et al., 2019), as well as numerous localized examples, such as a Twitter-based campaign against institutional racism at the University of Cape Town among South African students (Bosch, 2017). Singular events, due to natural or environmental disasters, have also sparked youth engagement, such as Japanese youth who joined the collective in rebuilding their country after Japan's 2011 tsunami (Mavros, 2012). After the 9/11 terrorist attacks, many US youth responded by volunteering and making charitable donations (Phillips & Gershoff, 2006). As unique social moments arise, such as today's global COVID-19 pandemic, we need research that can rapidly respond to capture how these macro forces shape youth civic development.

## Mediation and moderation of microprocesses

Proximal processes in the micro-environment and broad factors from the macrosocial context are interconnected in relation to youth civic engagement. Proximal processes can be moderated by larger cultural forces, as indicated by research finding that particular microsocial processes predict youth civic engagement only in certain countries and contexts (e.g., Flanagan et al., 1998; Flanagan & Campbell, 2003; Schulz et al., 2018; Torney-Purta, Richardson, & Barber, 2005). For example, Torney-Purta and colleagues (2005) reported that teachers' education and confidence in teaching civics classes related to civic knowledge in certain countries only. Additionally, micro-contexts may play a mediating role, passing down cultural norms and beliefs about the social contract through everyday interactions with youth (Flanagan et al., 2011). In other words, micro-contexts can be a "transmission belt" of macrosocial effects in which families, schools, and communities serve as settings for transmitting society's values, political and social philosophies, and norms. This mediational process can be illustrated through indirect effects of the media (a marker of macrosocial influence) on youth civic engagement. One study found that news media influence youth civic engagement indirectly through discussions with parents (Boyd, Zaff, Phelps, Weiner, & Lerner, 2011). Other work includes an agentic role for youth, such that national and international events spark youth's political interests, who then seek discussions and socialization opportunities to act on these interests (Stattin, Hussein, Özdemir, & Russo, 2017). Discussions with parents, teachers, and peers may help adolescents make sense of current events and solidify their civic values, attitudes, and behavioral responses.

## Future Directions

In this chapter, we offer a definition of youth civic engagement that is multidimensional, contextualized, and thus applicable across international contexts. We encourage more definitional conversations among scholars across disciplines and cultures in an effort to ultimately build consensus, identify contrasts, and bring cohesion to this field of study. Researchers should be more explicit about their assumptions about what forms of civic engagement are studied, why, and how they contribute to the greater good or not. For example, given the global rise of right-wing authoritarianism (Mounk, 2018), more research is needed on youth civic engagement in the context of right-wing movements. Additionally, research should be open to new forms of civic engagement that youth create and apply, such as ways of challenging oppression using social media tools. Future research that embraces a multidimensional view of civic engagement and simultaneously examines multiple civic indicators can advance a more comprehensive understanding of youth civic engagement, its developmental roots, and the benefits and costs of civic engagement.

Unfortunately, most of the published research on youth civic engagement comes from the United States and Europe. We need more research on youth civic engagement from other nations, such as in the Global South, where we know less about youth civic engagement but youth obviously have strong capacity for positively contributing to society and leading movements for social change (Abdou & Skalli, 2017; Flores, 2019; Peñafiel & Doran, 2018). In addition to the several landmark cross-national studies of youth civic engagement conducted decades ago (Flanagan et al., 1998; Torney-Purta et al., 2001), more cross-cultural work is needed, especially given that youth continue to create new ways of engaging with society, often faster than can be documented through research. Cross-cultural studies would be particularly useful when driven by theoretical questions about the youth's diverse expressions of civic engagement, proximal processes, macrosocial influences, and interactions among micro- and macrosocial factors.

Our literature review of the proximal processes related to civic development only scratches the surface. Rather than giving an exhaustive list, we highlighted prominent examples of developmental opportunities that can lead to civic engagement in family, school, and community contexts. Research must contend with the mechanisms by which young people develop distinct forms of civic engagement.

Longitudinal research is essential to add clearer insight into the sequence and directionality of developmental processes. Furthermore, despite research from the 1960s indicating that civic development begins considerably prior to adolescence (e.g., Easton & Dennis, 1969; R. D. Hess & Torney, 1967), very little contemporary research on civic engagement examines childhood. Although costly and time-consuming, longitudinal studies spanning childhood and adolescence, and that consider the cultural context, have the potential to provide incredible insights into civic developmental pathways.

In future research on civic development, the study of interactions should be paramount. Bronfenbrenner (1979) suggested that in ecological research, "the principal main effects are likely to be interactions" (p. 38). We briefly highlighted person–context interactions as they help us understand civic engagement, and there is considerable room for continued exploration of such interactions. Interactions between micro-contexts, termed meso-system effects, are also not sufficiently studied in relation to youth civic engagement, but it is highly plausible that one micro-context could reinforce or counteract the effect of another. We outlined the nature of macrosocial contexts in relation to youth civic engagement and suggested interactive effects between micro- and macrosocial contexts. More research on cross-level interactions would illuminate the extent to which proximal developmental processes vary across cultures and would inform culturally sensitive practices of socializing civic engagement. Finally, institutions with which youth interact in their everyday lives play a mediating role of transmitting broader social norms and values to youth (Flanagan et al., 2011). Research that examines these transmission belts in more depth would generate more knowledge about cultural transmission, allowing for individual and collective reflection on these efforts.

Continued scholarship on developmental and cultural processes related to youth civic engagement is important for building civic theory to address the fundamental question of how and why youth become engaged in society. Research is accumulating that can readily inform policy and practices to help youth around the world harness their potential via civic engagement.

## References

Abdou, E. D., & Skalli, L. H. (2017). Egyptian youth-led civil society organizations: Alternative spaces for civic engagement? In E. Oinas, H. Onodera, & L. Suurpää (Eds.), *What politics?* (pp. 75–94). Boston, MA: Brill.

Adler, R. P., & Goggin, J. (2005). What do we mean by "civic engagement"? *Journal of Transformative Education, 3*(3), 236–253.

Almond, G. A., & Verba, S. (1963). *The civic culture: Political attitudes and democracy in five nations.* Princeton, NJ: Princeton University Press.

Amadeo, J. A., Torney-Purta, J., Lehmann, R., Husfeldt, V., & Nikolova, R. (2002). *Civic knowledge and engagement: An IEA study of upper secondary students in sixteen countries.* Amsterdam: International Association for the Evaluation of Educational Achievement.

Amnå, E. (2012). How is civic engagement developed over time? Emerging answers from a multidisciplinary field. *Journal of Adolescence, 35*(3), 611–627.

Amnå, E., Ekström, M., Kerr, M., & Stattin, H. (2009). Political socialization and human agency:

The development of civic engagement from adolescence to adulthood. *Statsvetenskaplig Tidskrift*, *111*(1), 27–40.

Aristotle. (2009). *The Nicomachean ethics* (D. Ross, Trans., L. Brown, rev. and intro.). Oxford: Oxford University Press.

Astuto, J., & Ruck, M. (2017). Growing up in poverty and civic engagement: The role of kindergarten executive function and play predicting participation in 8th grade extracurricular activities. *Applied Developmental Science*, *21*(4), 301–318.

Attar-Schwartz, S., & Ben-Arieh, A. (2012). Political knowledge, attitudes and values among Palestinian and Jewish youth in Israel: The role of nationality, gender and religiosity. *Children and Youth Services Review*, *34*(4), 704–712.

Baldi, S., Perie, M., Skidmore, D., Greenberg, E., & Hahn, C. (2001). *What democracy means to ninth-graders: US results from the IEA Civic Education Study*. Washington, DC: National Center for Educational Statistics, US Department of Education.

Ballard, P. J., Hoyt, L. T., & Pachucki, M. C. (2019). Impacts of adolescent and young adult civic engagement on health and socioeconomic status in adulthood. *Child Development*, *90*(4), 1138–1154.

Ballard, P. J., Malin, H., Porter, T. J., Colby, A., & Damon, W. (2015). Motivations for civic participation among diverse youth: More similarities than differences. *Research in Human Development*, *12*(1–2), 63–83.

Ballard, P. J., & Ozer, E. J. (2016). The implications of youth activism for health and well-being. In J. Conner & S. M. Rosen (Eds.), *Contemporary youth activism: Advancing social justice in the United States* (pp. 223–243). Santa Barbara, CA: Praeger.

Bandura, A. (1977). *Social learning theory*. Englewood Cliffs, NJ: Prentice Hall.

Barber, B. K. (2008). Contrasting portraits of war: Youths' varied experiences with political violence in Bosnia and Palestine. *International Journal of Behavioral Development*, *32*(4), 298–309.

Barrett, M., & Brunton-Smith, I. (2014). Political and civic engagement and participation: Towards an integrative perspective. *Journal of Civil Society*, *10*(1), 5–28.

Bayram Özdemir, S., Stattin, H., & Özdemir, M. (2016). Youth's initiations of civic and political discussions in class: Do youth's perceptions of teachers' behaviors matter and why? *Journal of Youth and Adolescence*, *45*(11), 2233–2245.

Bekkers, R. (2005). Participation in voluntary associations: Relations with resources, personality, and political values. *Political Psychology*, *26*, 439–454.

Bennett, W. L., Wells, C., & Freelon, D. (2011). Communicating civic engagement: Contrasting models of citizenship in the youth web sphere. *Journal of Communication*, *61*(5), 835–856.

Boehnke, K., & Hadjar, A. (2006). Xenophobia. In L. R. Sherrod, C. A. Flanagan, R. Kassimir, & A. K. Syvertsen (Eds.), *Youth activism: An international encyclopedia* (pp. 684–687). Westport, CT: Greenwood Press.

Bosch, T. (2017). Twitter activism and youth in South Africa: The case of# RhodesMustFall. *Information, Communication & Society*, *20*(2), 221–232.

Boulianne, S. (2015). Social media use and participation: A meta-analysis of current research. *Information, Communication & Society*, *18*(5), 524–538.

Bourdieu, P., & Passeron, J.-C. (1977). *Reproduction in education, society and culture*. London: Sage.

Bovier, E., & Boehnke, K. (1995). Linke Lehrer – rechte Schüler? Zu Einflüssen von Lehrerwerthaltungen und Unterrichtsstil auf Fremdenfeindlichkeit und Gewaltbereitschaft von Schülern in Ost- und Westberlin [Left-wing teachers – right-wing students? The impact of teacher values and teaching style on hostility toward foreigners and propensity for violence in eastern and western Berlin students]. In R. Arbinger & R. S. Jäger (Eds.), *Zukunftsperspektiven empirisch-pädagogischer Forschung* (pp. 28–35). Landau: Verlag Empirische Pädagogik.

Bowes, J. M., Flanagan, C., & Taylor, A. J. (2001). Adolescents' ideas about individual and social responsibility in relation to children's household work: Some international comparisons. *International Journal of Behavioral Development*, *25*, 60–68.

Boyd, M. J., Zaff, J. F., Phelps, E., Weiner, M. B., & Lerner, R. M. (2011). The relationship between adolescents' news media use and civic engagement: The indirect effect of interpersonal communication with parents. *Journal of Adolescence*, 34(6), 1167–1179.

Bronfenbrenner, U. (1979). *The ecology of human development*. Cambridge, MA: Harvard University Press.

Bronfenbrenner, U., & Morris, P. A. (2006). The bioecological model of human development. In R. M. Lerner (Ed.), *Handbook of child psychology. Vol. 1: Theoretical models of human development* (6th ed., pp. 793–828). Hoboken, NJ: Wiley.

Campbell, D. E. (2008). Voice in the classroom: How an open classroom climate fosters political engagement among adolescents. *Political Behavior*, 30, 437–454.

Carter, R. T., Lau, M. Y., Johnson, V., & Kirkinis, K. (2017). Racial discrimination and health outcomes among racial/ethnic minorities: A meta-analytic review. *Journal of Multicultural Counselling and Development*, 45(4), 232–259.

Chan, M., & Guo, J. (2013). The role of political efficacy on the relationship between Facebook use and participatory behaviors: A comparative study of young American and Chinese adults. *Cyberpsychology, Behavior, and Social Networking*, 16(6), 460–463.

Chen, S. (2011, May 4). China tightens internet censorship controls. *BBC News*. Retrieved August 2, 2012, from http://www.bbc.co.uk/news/world-asia-pacific-13281200.

Christens, B. D. (2019). *Community power and empowerment*. New York: Oxford University Press.

Christens, B. D., & Peterson, N. A. (2012). The role of empowerment in youth development: A study of sociopolitical control as mediator of ecological systems' influence on developmental outcomes. *Journal of Youth and Adolescence*, 41(5), 623–635.

Christens, B. D., Peterson, N. A., & Speer, P. W. (2011). Community participation and psychological empowerment: Testing reciprocal causality using a cross-lagged panel design and latent constructs. *Health Education & Behavior*, 38(4), 339–347.

Christoph, G., Gniewosz, B., & Reinders, H. (2014). How does community service promote prosocial behavior? Examining the role of agency and ideology experience. *International Journal of Behavioral Development*, 38(6), 499–508.

Cicognani, E., Zani, B., Fournier, B., Gavray, C., & Born, M. (2012). Gender differences in youths' political engagement and participation: The role of parents and of adolescents' social and civic participation. *Journal of Adolescence*, 35(3), 561–576.

Ciftci, S., & Bernick, E. M. (2015). Utilitarian and modern: Clientelism, citizen empowerment, and civic engagement in the Arab world. *Democratization*, 22(7), 1161–1182.

Cohen, A. K., & Chaffee, B. W. (2013). The relationship between adolescents' civic knowledge, civic attitude, and civic behavior and their self-reported future likelihood of voting. *Education, Citizenship and Social Justice*, 8(1), 43–57.

Coleman, J. S. (1988). Social capital in the creation of human capital. *The American Journal of Sociology*, 94, S95–S121.

Crocetti, E., Jahromi, P., & Meeus, W. (2012). Identity and civic engagement in adolescence. *Journal of Adolescence*, 35(3), 521–532.

Damico, A. J., Conway, M. M., & Damico, S. B. (2000). Patterns of political trust and mistrust: Three moments in the lives of democratic citizens. *Polity*, 32(3), 377–400.

Davis, J. A. (2004). Did growing up in the 1960s leave a permanent mark on attitudes and values? *Public Opinion Quarterly*, 68, 161–183.

Degner, J., & Dalege, J. (2013). The apple does not fall far from the tree, or does it? A meta-analysis of parent–child similarity in intergroup attitudes. *Psychological Bulletin*, 139(6), 1270–1304.

Diedrich, M. (2006). Connections between quality of school life and democracy in German schools. In A. Sliwka, M. Diedrich, & M. Hofer (Eds.), *Citizenship education* (pp. 121–134). Münster: Waxmann.

Diemer, M. A., & Li, C. H. (2011). Critical consciousness development and political participation among marginalized youth. *Child Development*, 82(6), 1815–1833.

Diemer, M. A., Rapa, L. J., Voight, A. M., & McWhirter, E. H. (2016). Critical consciousness: A developmental approach to addressing marginalization and oppression. *Child Development Perspectives, 10*(4), 216–221.

Easton, D., & Dennis, J. (1969). *Children in the political system: Origins of political legitimacy.* New York: McGraw-Hill.

Ekman, J., & Amnå, E. (2012). Political participation and civic engagement: Towards a new typology. *Human Affairs, 22*(3), 283–300.

Ekström, M., & Östman, J. (2013). Family talk, peer talk and young people's civic orientation. *European Journal of Communication, 28*(3), 294–308.

Erentaitė, R., Žukauskienė, R., Beyers, W., & Pilkauskaitė-Valickienė, R. (2012). Is news media related to civic engagement? The effects of interest in and discussions about the news media on current and future civic engagement of adolescents. *Journal of Adolescence, 35*(3), 587–597.

Finkel, S. E., & Ernst, H. R. (2005). Civic education in post-apartheid South Africa: Alternative paths to the development of political knowledge and democratic values. *Political Psychology, 26*(3), 333–364.

Fiorina, M. P. (1999). Extreme voices: A dark side of civic engagement. In T. Skocpol & M. P. Fiorina (Eds.), *Civic engagement in American democracy* (pp. 395–426). Washington, DC: Brookings Institution.

Flanagan, C. A. (2013). *Teenage citizens: The political theories of the young.* Cambridge, MA: Harvard University Press.

Flanagan, C. A., Bowes, J. M., Jonsson, B., Csapó, B., & Sheblanova, E. (1998). Ties that bind: Correlates of adolescents' civic commitments in seven countries. *Journal of Social Issues, 54*(3), 457–475.

Flanagan, C., & Bundick, M. (2011). Civic engagement and psychosocial well-being in college students. *Liberal Education, 97*(2), 20–27.

Flanagan, C. A., & Campbell, B. (with Botcheva, L., Bowes, J., Csapó, B., Macek, P., & Sheblanova, E.). (2003). Social class and adolescents' beliefs about justice in different social orders. *Journal of Social Issues, 59*(4), 711–732.

Flanagan, C. A., Martínez, M. L., & Cumsille, P. (2011). Civil societies as cultural and developmental contexts for civic identity formation. In L.

Jensen (Ed.), *Bridging cultural and developmental approaches to psychology* (pp. 113–137). New York: Oxford University Press.

Flores, W. (2019). Youth-led anti-corruption movement in post-conflict Guatemala: "Weaving the future?" *IDS Bulletin, 50*(3), 37–51.

Galston, W. A. (2007). Civic knowledge, civic education, and civic engagement: A summary of recent research. *International Journal of Public Administration, 30*(6–7), 623–642.

Ginwright, S., & Cammarota, J. (2002). New terrain in youth development: The promise of a social justice approach. *Social Justice, 29*(4), 82–95.

Gniewosz, B., & Noack, P. (2008). Classroom climate indicators and attitudes towards foreigners. *Journal of Adolescence, 31*(5), 609–624.

Gniewosz, B., & Noack, P. (2015). Parental influences on adolescents' negative attitudes toward immigrants. *Journal of Youth and Adolescence, 44*(9), 1787–1802.

Gniewosz, B., Noack, P., & Buhl, M. (2009). Political alienation in adolescence: Associations with parental role models, parenting styles, and classroom climate. *International Journal of Behavioral Development, 33*(4), 337–346.

Godfrey, E. B., & Cherng, H. Y. S. (2016). The kids are all right? Income inequality and civic engagement among our nation's youth. *Journal of Youth and Adolescence, 45*(11), 2218–2232.

Godfrey, E. B., & Grayman, J. K. (2014). Teaching citizens: The role of open classroom climate in fostering critical consciousness among youth. *Journal of Youth and Adolescence, 43*(11), 1801–1817.

Grob, U. (2005). Kurz- und langfristige intergenerationale Transmission von Ausländerablehnung [Short- and long-term intergenerational transmission of hostility toward foreigners]. *Zeitschrift für Soziologie der Erziehung und Sozialisation, 25*(1), 32–51.

Gruman, J. A., Lumley, M. N., & González-Morales, M. G. (2018). Incorporating balance: Challenges and opportunities for positive psychology. *Canadian Psychology/psychologie canadienne, 59*(1), 54.

Hart, D., & Fegley, S. (1995). Altruism and caring in adolescence: Relations to moral judgment and self-understanding. *Child Development, 66*(5), 1346–1359.

Haste, H., & Hogan, A. (2006). Beyond conventional civic participation, beyond the moral-political divide: Young people and contemporary debates about citizenship. *Journal of Moral Education*, *35*(4), 473–493.

Heinemann, K. S. (2012). Wodurch wird die Vorurteilsentwicklung im Kindes- und Jugendalter beeinflusst? Eine Meta-Analyse zu individuellen und sozialen Einflussfaktoren [What influences prejudice development in childhood and adolescence? A meta-analysis of individual and social factors] (Doctoral thesis). University of Jena, Germany.

Hess, D. E., & McAvoy, P. (2014). *The political classroom: Evidence and ethics in democratic education*. New York: Routledge.

Hess, R. D., & Torney, J. V. (1967). *The development of political attitudes in children*. New Brunswick, NJ: Aldine Transaction.

Hessel, S. (2011). *Time for outrage: Indignez-vous!* (M. Duvert, Trans.). New York: Hachette.

Hooghe, M., & Stiers, D. (2020). Political discussion begins at home: Household dynamics following the enfranchisement of adolescent children. *Applied Developmental Science*, Advance online publication.

Hope, E. C., & Spencer, M. B. (2017). Civic engagement as an adaptive coping response to conditions of inequality: An application of phenomenological variant of ecological systems theory (PVEST). In N. J. Cabrera & B. Leyendecker (Eds.), *Handbook on positive development of minority children and youth* (pp. 421–435).Cham: Springer.

Hufer, A., Kornadt, A. E., Kandler, C., & Riemann, R. (2019). Genetic and environmental variation in political orientation in adolescence and early adulthood: A nuclear twin family analysis. *Journal of Personality and Social Psychology*, *118*(4), 762–776.

Human Rights Watch. (2019, August 14). Hong Kong: Police should exercise restraint. Retrieved from https://www.hrw.org/news/2019/08/14/hong-kong-police-should-exercise-restraint#.

Hyman, J. B. (2002). Exploring social capital and civic engagement to create a framework for community building. *Applied Developmental Science*, *6*(4), 196–202.

Jagers, R. J., Lozada, F. T., Rivas-Drake, D., & Guillaume, C. (2017). Classroom and school predictors of civic engagement among black and Latino middle school youth. *Child Development*, *88*(4), 1125–1138.

Jemal, A. (2018). Transformative consciousness of health inequities: Oppression is a virus and critical consciousness is the antidote. *Journal of Human Rights and Social Work*, *3*(4), 202–215.

Jenkins, H., Shresthova, S., Gamber-Thompson, L., Kligler-Vilenchik, N., & Zimmerman, A. (2018). *By any media necessary: The new youth activism* (Vol. 3). New York: NYU Press.

Kagitçibasi, C. (1997). Individualism and collectivism. In J. W. Berry, M. H. Segall, & C. Kagitçibasi (Eds.), *Handbook of cross-cultural psychology: Social behavior and applications* (Vol. 3, pp. 1–49). Boston, MA: Allyn & Bacon.

Kahne, J., & Middaugh, E. (2008). *Democracy for some: The civic opportunity gap in high school* (Working Paper 59). CIRCLE, College Park, MD.

Kassimir, R. (2006). Youth activism: International and transnational. In L. R. Sherrod, C. Flanagan, R. Kassimer, & A. Syvertsen (Eds.), *Youth activism: An international encyclopedia*. (Vol. 1, pp. 20–28). Westport, CT: Greenwood Press.

Kassimir, R., & Flanagan, C. (2010). Youth civic engagement in the developing world: Challenges and opportunities. In L. R. Sherrod, J. Torney-Purta, & C. A. Flanagan (Eds.), *Handbook of research on civic engagement in youth* (pp. 91–113). Hoboken, NJ: Wiley.

Keyes, C. L. (2007). Promoting and protecting mental health as flourishing: A complementary strategy for improving national mental health. *American Psychologist*, *62*(2), 95–108.

Kim, J., & Pai, M. (2010). Volunteering and trajectories of depression. *Journal of Aging and Health*, *22*(1), 84–105.

Kim, Y., & Stattin, H. (2019). Parent–youth discussions about politics from age 13 to 28. *Journal of Applied Developmental Psychology*, *62*, 249–259.

Klofstad, C. A. (2009). Civic talk and civic participation: The moderating effect of individual predispositions. *American Politics Research*, *37*, 856–878.

Kracke, B., Noack, P., Hofer, M., & Klein-Allermann, E. (1993). Die rechte Gesinnung: Familiale Bedingungen autoritärer Orientierungen ost- und westdeutscher Jugendlicher [The rightist attitude: Family related conditions of authoritarian orientations among young people from East and West Germany]. *Zeitschrift für Pädagogik, 39*(6), 971–988.

Kuhn, R. (2012). On the role of human development in the Arab Spring. *Population and Development Review, 38*(4), 649–683.

Lauglo, J., & Øia, T. (2006). *Education and civic engagement among Norwegian youths (NOVA Report 14/06)*. Oslo: Norwegian Social Research.

Lee, N. J., Shah, D. V., & McLeod, J. M. (2013). Processes of political socialization: A communication mediation approach to youth civic engagement. *Communication Research, 40*(5), 669–697.

Lerner, R. M., Alberts, A. E., Jelicic, H., & Smith, L. M. (2006). Young people are resources to be developed: Promoting positive youth development through adult–youth relations and community assets. In E. G. Clary & J. E. Rhodes (Eds.), *Mobilizing adults for positive youth development: Strategies for closing the gap between beliefs and behaviors* (pp. 19–39). New York: Springer.

Lerner, R. M., Dowling, E. M., & Anderson, P. M. (2003). Positive youth development: Thriving as the basis of personhood and civil society. *Applied Developmental Science, 7*(3), 172–180.

Lerner, R. M., Wang, J., Champine, R. B., Warren, D. J., & Erickson, K. (2014). Development of civic engagement: Theoretical and methodological issues. *International Journal of Developmental Science, 8*(3–4), 69–79.

Levine, P., & Higgins-D'Alessandro, A. (2010). Youth civic engagement: Normative issues. In L. R. Sherrod, J. Torney-Purta, & C. A. Flanagan (Eds.), *Handbook of research on civic engagement in youth* (pp. 115–138). Hoboken, NJ: Wiley.

Levinsen, K., & Yndigegn, C. (2015). Political discussions with family and friends: Exploring the impact of political distance. *The Sociological Review, 63*, 72–91.

Levinson, M. (2012). *No citizen left behind* (Vol. 13). Cambridge, MA: Harvard University Press.

Mahatmya, D., & Lohman, B. J. (2012). Predictors and pathways to civic involvement in emerging adulthood: Neighborhood, family, and school influences. *Journal of Youth and Adolescence, 41*(9), 1168–1183.

Mannheim, K. (1952). The problem of generations. In P. Kecskemeti (Ed.), *Essays on the sociology of knowledge by Karl Mannheim*. New York: Routledge.

Markus, H. R., & Kitayama, S. (1991). Culture and the self: Implications for cognition, emotion, and motivation. *Psychological Review, 98*(2), 224–253.

Marta, E., Pozzi, M., & Marzana, D. (2010). Volunteers and ex-volunteers: Paths to civic engagement through volunteerism. *Psykhe, 19*(2), 5–17.

Martínez, M. L., Peñaloza, P., & Valenzuela, C. (2012). Civic commitment in young activists: Emergent processes in the development of personal and collective identity. *Journal of Adolescence, 35*(3), 474–484.

Marzana, D., Marta, E., & Pozzi, M. (2012). Social action in young adults: Voluntary and political engagement. *Journal of Adolescence, 35*(3), 497–507.

Mavros, T. (2012, March 8). Catastrophe spawns social transformation among Japanese youth. CNN. Retrieved August 2, 2012, from http://www.cnn.com/2012/03/08/world/asia/vice-tokyo-rising/index.html.

McAdam, D. (1986). Recruitment to high-risk activism: The case of freedom summer. *American Journal of Sociology, 92*(1), 64–90.

McAdam, D. (1988). *Freedom summer*. New York: Oxford University Press.

McBride, A. M., Sherraden, M. S., & Pritzker, S. (2006). Civic engagement among low-income and low-wealth families: In their words. *Family Relations, 55*(2), 152–162.

McDevitt, M., & Chaffee, S. (2000). Closing gaps in political communication and knowledge: Effects of a school intervention. *Communication Research, 27*(3), 259–292.

McIntosh, H., Hart, D., & Youniss, J. (2007). The influence of political discussion on youth civic development: Which parent qualities matter? *PS: Political Science & Politics, 40*, 495–499.

Metz, E., & Youniss, J. (2005). Longitudinal gains in civic development through school-based required service. *Political Psychology, 26*(3), 413–437.

Metzger, A., Alvis, L. M., Oosterhoff, B., Babskie, E., Syvertsen, A., & Wray-Lake, L. (2018). The intersection of emotional and sociocognitive competencies with civic engagement in middle childhood and adolescence. *Journal of Youth and Adolescence, 47*(8), 1663–1683.

Metzger, A., & Smetana, J. G. (2010). Social cognitive development and adolescent civic engagement. In L. R. Sherrod, J. Torney-Purta, & C. A. Flanagan (Eds.), *Handbook of research on civic engagement in youth* (pp. 221–248). Hoboken, NJ: Wiley.

Miklikowska, M. (2016). Like parent, like child? Development of prejudice and tolerance towards immigrants. *British Journal of Psychology, 107*(1), 95–116.

Mitra, D. L., & Serriere, S. C. (2012). Student voice in elementary school reform: Examining youth development in fifth graders. *American Educational Research Journal, 49*(4), 743–774.

Mounk, Y. (2018). *The people vs. democracy: Why our freedom is in danger and how to save it.* Cambridge, MA: Harvard University Press.

Mueller, M. K., Phelps, E., Bowers, E. P., Agans, J. P., Urban, J. B., & Lerner, R. M. (2011). Youth development program participation and intentional self-regulation skills: Contextual and Individual bases of pathways to positive youth development. *Journal of Adolescence, 34*, 1115–1125.

Musick, M. A., & Wilson, J. (2003). Volunteering and depression: The role of psychological and social resources in different age groups. *Social Science & Medicine, 56*(2), 259–269.

Neundorf, A., Niemi, R. G., & Smets, K. (2016). The compensation effect of civic education on political engagement: How civics classes make up for missing parental socialization. *Political Behavior, 38*(4), 921–949.

Nogueira, F., & Moreira, A. (2011). Civic education – Portuguese students' perceptions. *Procedia – Social and Behavioral Sciences, 15*, 1771–1776.

Ojeda, C., & Hatemi, P. K. (2015). Accounting for the child in the transmission of party identification. *American Sociological Review, 80*(6), 1150–1174.

Oosterhoff, B., & Metzger, A. (2016). Mother–adolescent civic messages: Associations with adolescent civic behavior and civic judgments. *Journal of Applied Developmental Psychology, 43*, 62–70.

Oosterhoff, B., Wray-Lake, L., Palmer, C. A., & Kaplow, J. B. (2020). Historical trends in concerns about social issues across four decades among US adolescents. *Journal of Research on Adolescence, 30*(S2), 485–498.

Pathak-Shelat, M., & Bhatia, K. V. (2019). Young people as global citizens: Negotiation of youth civic participation in adult-managed online spaces. *Journal of Youth Studies, 22*(1), 87–107.

Patterson, M. M., Bigler, R. S., Pahlke, E., Brown, C. S., Hayes, A. R., Ramirez, M. C., & Nelson, A. (2019). Toward a developmental science of politics. *Monographs of the Society for Research in Child Development, 84*(3), 7–185.

Pavlova, M. K., Silbereisen, R. K., Ranta, M., & Salmela-Aro, K. (2016). Warm and supportive parenting can discourage offspring's civic engagement in the transition to adulthood. *Journal of Youth and Adolescence, 45*(11), 2197–2217.

Peñafiel, R., & Doran, M. C. (2018). New modes of youth political action and democracy in the Americas: From the Chilean spring to the maple spring in Quebec. In S. Pickard & J. Bessant (Eds.), *Young people re-generating politics in times of crises* (pp. 349–373). Cham: Palgrave Macmillan.

Perez, W., Espinoza, R., Ramos, K., Coronado, H., & Cortes, R. (2010). Civic engagement patterns of undocumented Mexican students. *Journal of Hispanic Higher Education, 9*(3), 245–265.

Petersen, A. C., Koller, S. H., Motti-Stefanidi, F., & Verma, S. (Eds.). (2016). *Positive youth development in global contexts of social and economic change.* New York: Taylor & Francis.

Phillips, D., & Gershoff, E. T. (2006). Youth activism responses to terrorism. In L. Sherrod, C. Flanagan, R. Kassimir, & A. K. Syvertsen (Eds.), *Youth activism: An international encyclopedia* (pp. 635–639). Westport, CT: Greenwood.

Piliavin, J. A., & Siegl, E. (2015). Health and well-being consequences of formal volunteering. In D. A. Schroeder & W. G. Graziano (Eds.), *The Oxford handbook of prosocial behavior* (pp. 494–523). New York: Oxford University Press.

Putnam, R. (2000). *Bowling alone: The collapse and revival of American community*. New York: Simon & Schuster.

Quaranta, M., & Dotti Sani, G. M. (2016). The relationship between the civic engagement of parents and children. *Nonprofit and Voluntary Sector Quarterly*, *45*(6), 1091–1112.

Quintelier, E. (2013). Engaging adolescents in politics. *Youth & Society*, *47*(1), 51–69.

Rossi, A. S. (Ed.). (2001). *Caring and doing for others: Social responsibility in the domains of family, work, and community*. Chicago: University of Chicago Press.

Rousseau, J. J. (1987). On the social contract. In D. A. Cress (Eds.), *Jean-Jacques Rousseau: The basic political writings*. Indianapolis, IN: Hackett. (Original work published 1762)

Sanchez-Jankowski, M. (2002). Minority youth and civic engagement: The impact of group relations. *Applied Developmental Science*, *6*(4), 237–245.

Santos, C. E., & VanDaalen, R. A. (2018). Associations among psychological distress, high-risk activism, and conflict between ethnic-racial and sexual minority identities in lesbian, gay, bisexual racial/ethnic minority adults. *Journal of Counselling Psychology*, *65*(2), 194–203.

Scarr, S., & McCartney, K. (1983). How people make their own environments: A theory of genotype greater than environment effects. *Child Development*, *54*, 424–435.

Schlozman, K. L., Verba, S., & Brady, H. E. (2012). *The unheavenly chorus: Unequal political voice and the broken promise of American democracy*. Princeton, NJ: Princeton University Press.

Schmid, C. (2012). The value "social responsibility" as a motivating factor for adolescents' readiness to participate in different types of political actions, and its socialization in parent and peer contexts. *Journal of Adolescence*, *35*(3), 533–547.

Schreier, H. M., Schonert-Reichl, K. A., & Chen, E. (2013). Effect of volunteering on risk factors for cardiovascular disease in adolescents: A randomized controlled trial. *JAMA Pediatrics*, *167*(4), 327–332.

Schulz, W., Ainley, J., Fraillon, J., Kerr, D., & Losito, B. (2010). *ICCS 2009 international report: Civic knowledge, attitudes and engagement among lower secondary school students in thirty-eight countries*. Amsterdam: International Association for the Evaluation of Educational Achievement.

Schulz, W., Ainley, J., Fraillon, J., Losito, B., Agrusti, G., & Friedman, T. (2018). Explaining variation in students' civic knowledge and expected civic engagement. In *Becoming citizens in a changing world: IEA international civic and citizenship education study 2016 international report* (pp. 177–198). Cham: Springer.

Schwadel, P., & Garneau, C. R. (2014). An age–period–cohort analysis of political tolerance in the United States. *The Sociological Quarterly*, *55*(2), 421–452.

Sears, D. O., & Valentino, N. A. (1997). Politics matters: Political events as catalysts for preadult socialization. *American Political Science Review*, *91*, 45–65.

Šerek, J., Lacinová, L., & Macek, P. (2012). Does family experience influence political beliefs? Relation between interparental conflict perceptions and political efficacy in late adolescence. *Journal of Adolescence*, *35*(3), 577–586.

Šerek, J., & Machackova, H. (2017). Role of school climate and personality in the development of Czech adolescents' political self-efficacy. *Applied Developmental Science*, *23*(3), 203–213.

Šerek, J., & Umemura, T. (2015). Changes in late adolescents' voting intentions during the election campaign: Disentangling the effects of political communication with parents, peers and media. *European Journal of Communication*, *30*(3), 285–300.

Sherrod, L. R., & Lauckhardt, J. (2009). The development of citizenship. In R. M. Lerner & L. Steinberg (Eds.), *Handbook of adolescent psychology. Vol. 2: Contextual influences on adolescent development* (3rd ed., pp. 372–408). Hoboken, NJ: Wiley.

Sherrod, L. R., Torney-Purta, J., & Flanagan, C. (2010). Research on the development of citizenship: A field comes of age. In L. R. Sherrod, J. Torney-Purta, & C. A. Flanagan (Eds.), *Handbook of research on civic engagement in youth* (pp. 23–42). Hoboken, NJ: Wiley.

Sibley, C. G., & Duckitt, J. (2013). The dual process model of ideology and prejudice: A longitudinal test during a global recession. *The Journal of Social Psychology, 153*(4), 448–466.

Singh, S. (2012). India's proposal for government control of internet to be discussed in Geneva. *The Hindu*. Retrieved August 2, 2012, from http://www.thehindu.com/news/national/article3423018.ece.

Stattin, H., Hussein, O., Özdemir, M., & Russo, S. (2017). Why do some adolescents encounter everyday events that increase their civic interest whereas others do not? *Developmental Psychology, 53*(2), 306–318.

Stürmer, S., & Simon, B. (2004). The role of collective identification in social movement participation: A panel study in the context of the German gay movement. *Personality and Social Psychology Bulletin, 30*, 263–277.

Teorell, J., Torcal, M., & Montero, J. R. (2007). Political participation: Mapping the terrain. In J. van Deth, J. R. Montero, & A. Westholm (Eds.), *Citizenship and involvement in European democracies: A comparative analysis* (pp. 334–357). London: Routledge.

Ter Bogt, T. F. M., Meeus, W. H. J., Raaijmakers, Q. A. W., & Vollebergh, W. A. M. (2001). Youth centrism and the formation of political orientations in adolescence and young adulthood. *Journal of Cross-Cultural Psychology, 32*(2), 229–240.

Theiss-Morse, E., & Hibbing, J. R. (2005). Citizenship and civic engagement. *Annual Review of Political Science, 8*, 227–249.

Torney-Purta, J. (2002). The school's role in developing civic engagement: A study of adolescents in twenty-eight countries. *Applied Developmental Science, 6*(4), 203–212.

Torney-Purta, J., Lehmann, R., Oswald, H., & Schulz, W. (2001). *Citizenship and education in twenty-eight countries: Civic knowledge and engagement at age fourteen*. Amsterdam: International Association for the Evaluation of Educational Achievement.

Torney-Purta, J., Richardson, W. K., & Barber, C. (2005). Teachers' educational experience and confidence in relation to students' civic knowledge across countries. *International Journal of Citizenship and Teacher Education, 1*(1), 32–57.

Torney-Purta, J., Wilkenfeld, B., & Barber, C. (2008). How adolescents in 27 countries understand, support, and practice human rights. *Journal of Social Issues, 64*(4), 857–880.

Triandis, H. C. (1995). *Individualism and collectivism*. San Francisco, CA: Westview Press.

Uslaner, E. M. (2002). *The moral foundations of trust*. Cambridge: Cambridge University Press.

Van Goethem, A. A., Van Hoof, A., Van Aken, M. A., Raaijmakers, Q. A., Boom, J., & De Castro, B. O. (2012). The role of adolescents' morality and identity in volunteering: Age and gender differences in a process model. *Journal of Adolescence, 35*(3), 509–520.

Van Zalk, M. H., Kerr, M., Van Zalk, N., & Stattin, H. (2013). Xenophobia and tolerance toward immigrants in adolescence: Cross-influence processes within friendship. *Journal of Abnormal Child Psychology, 41*, 627–639.

Verba, S., & Nie, N. H. (1972). *Participation in America: Political democracy and social equality*. New York: Harper & Row.

Verba, S., Schlozman, K. L., & Brady, H. E. (1995). *Voice and equality: Civic voluntarism in American politics*. Cambridge, MA: Harvard University Press.

Villegas-Reimers, E. (1994). *Civic education in the school systems of Latin America and the Caribbean (Working Papers No. 3)*. Economic and Human Resources Division, Bureau of Latin America and the Caribbean, US Agency for International Development. Washington, DC: Academy for Educational Development.

Vogt, M., Bormann, N. C., & Cederman, L. E. (2016). Democracy, ethnic exclusion, and civil conflict. In D. Backer, R. Bhavnani, & P. Huth (Eds.), *Peace and Conflict* (pp. 57–66). New York: Routledge.

Wahlström, M., Sommer, M., Kocyba, P., De Vydt, M., De Moor, J., Davies, S., . . . Buzogany, A. (2019). Protest for a future: Composition, mobilization and motives of the participants in Fridays for future climate protests on 15 March, 2019 in 13 European cities. Retrieved from http://eprints.keele.ac.uk/6571.

Walzer, M. (1989). Citizenship. In T. Ball, J. Farrand, & R. Hanson (Eds.), *Political innovation and conceptual change* (pp. 211–219). Cambridge: Cambridge University Press.

Watts, R. J., Diemer, M. A., & Voight, A. M. (2011). Critical consciousness: Current status and future directions. *New Directions for Child and Adolescent Development, 201*(134), 43–57.

Watts, R. J., & Guessous, O. (2006). Sociopolitical development: The missing link in research and policy on adolescents. In S. Ginwright, P. Noguera, & J. Cammarota (Eds.), *Beyond resistance: Youth activism and community change* (pp. 59–80). New York: Routledge.

Weinstein, N., & Ryan, R. M. (2010). When helping helps: Autonomous motivation for prosocial behavior and its influence on well-being for the helper and recipient. *Journal of Personality and Social Psychology, 98*(2), 222–244.

Westheimer, J., & Kahne, J. (2004). What kind of citizen? The politics of educating for democracy. *American Educational Research Journal, 41,* 237–269.

White, E. S., & Mistry, R. S. (2019). Teachers' civic socialization practices and children's civic engagement. *Applied Developmental Science, 23*(2), 183–202.

Wray-Lake, L. (2019). How do young people become politically engaged? *Child Development Perspectives, 13*(2), 127–132.

Wray-Lake, L., & Abrams, L. S. (2020). Pathways to civic engagement among urban youth of color. *SRCD Monographs, 85*(2), 7–154.

Wray-Lake, L., DeHaan, C., Shubert, J., & Ryan, R. (2019). Examining links from civic engagement to daily well-being from a self-determination theory perspective. *Journal of Positive Psychology, 14,* 166–177.

Wray-Lake, L., & Flanagan, C. A. (2012). Parenting practices and the development of adolescents' social trust. *Journal of Adolescence, 35*(3), 549–560.

Wray-Lake, L., Maggs, J. L., Johnston, L., Bachman, J., O'Malley, P., & Schulenberg, J. (2012). Associations between community attachments and adolescent substance use in nationally representative samples. *Journal of Adolescent Health, 51,* 325–331.

Wray-Lake, L., Metzger, A., & Syvertsen, A. K. (2017). Testing multidimensional models of youth civic engagement: Model comparisons, measurement invariance, and age differences. *Applied Developmental Science, 21*(4), 266–284.

Wray-Lake, L., & Shubert, J. (2019). Understanding stability and change in civic engagement across adolescence: A typology approach. *Developmental Psychology, 55*(10), 2169–2180.

Wray-Lake, L., & Sloper, M. A. (2016). Investigating general and specific links from adolescents' perceptions of ecological assets to their civic actions. *Applied Developmental Science, 20*(4), 250–266.

Wray-Lake, L., Wilf, S., & Oosterhoff, B. (2020). Reconsidering the voting age in Los Angeles and California. In D. J. B. Mitchell (Ed.), *California Policy Options 2020.* Los Angeles, CA: UCLA School of Public Affairs.

Wrench, J., Rea, A., & Ouali, N. (Eds.). (2016). *Migrants, ethnic minorities and the labour market: Integration and exclusion in Europe.* London: Palgrave Macmillan.

Xenos, M. A., Vromen, A., & Loader, B. D. (2014). The great equalizer? Patterns of social media use and youth political engagement in three advanced democracies. In B. D. Loader, A. Vromen, & M. Xenos (Eds.), *The networked young citizen* (pp. 33–54). New York: Routledge.

Youniss, J., Bales, S., Christmas-Best, V., Diversi, M., McLaughlin, M., & Silbereisen, R. (2002). Youth civic engagement in the twenty-first century. *Journal of Research on Adolescence, 12*(1), 121–148.

Zaff, J., Boyd, M., Li, Y., Lerner, J. V., & Lerner, R. M. (2010). Active and engaged citizenship: Multigroup and longitudinal factorial analysis of an integrated construct of civic engagement. *Journal of Youth and Adolescence, 39*(7), 736–750.

Zeldin, S., Camino, L., & Mook, C. (2005). The adoption of innovation in youth organizations: Creating the conditions for youth–adult partnerships. *Journal of Community Psychology, 33*(1), 121–135.

## 11

# The Ups and Downs of Love: What Makes Love Go Well, or Badly?

Robert J. Sternberg

I started studying love when I was in a failing relationship. I wished it had been my only failed relationship, but it wasn't. I started to wonder why the relationship was failing and what I would need to do to make that relationship, or any other, succeed? I realized then that I had reached the point where I questioned whether I had what it took to make any relationship work. I grew up in a household with parents whose relationship had failed and maybe, I thought, I was doomed to repeat my parents' experience. But then, maybe not. So what could I do to set things right again, in that relationship or perhaps in some other future one?

Now many years have passed and I have studied loving relationships – on and off – for most of my career. This research fits directly into the framework of positive psychology, because, potentially, there are few if any experiences more positive in life than love. And thus love is yet another aspect of human strengths and modes of flourishing (Lopez, Pedrotti, & Snyder, 2018). My research has taught me a lot both about what works and what doesn't work. My goal in this chapter is to share with you what I have learned. So, here is what I have learned!

## Love is Not a Single Thing: Analyze What Is Going Right or Wrong

In my first empirical foray into studying love, Susan Grajek and I (Sternberg & Grajek, 1984) studied whether love is best understood as a single entity, a few overlapping entities, or a large number of distinct entities that may feel like one thing but that are really multiple. We had our participants fill out the Rubin love

*Positive Psychology: An International Perspective*, First Edition.
Edited by Aleksandra Kostić and Derek Chadee.

(and liking) scales (Rubin, 1970) and then sought to determine what exactly underlay scores on the scales.

The results were clearly in favor of the last hypothesis: Love comprises multiple entities that may feel like one thing but that are in fact many things, such as trust, caring, compassion, communication, understanding, and so on. The number of elements is quite large. The implication of this work was that if you are unhappy in love, to improve your relationship, you have to find out exactly which things are going wrong. If you don't, not only is your current relationship likely to fail, but so is your next and the one after that. It may be that there is something you do (or that is being done to you) that not only is harming your current relationship, but that also will harm future relationships. To succeed in love, therefore, you need to *feel holistically*, for sure, but to *think analytically* – to ask yourself what is going right and what is going wrong.

## The Role of Ideals

In a subsequent study (Sternberg & Barnes, 1985), Michael Barnes and I asked the question of whether analyzing what works well and what does not work as well in a relationship might be partially a matter of looking, first, at your actual love relationship, but also, second, at your ideal love relationship. It seemed to us that part of the "love equation" was figuring out the difference between your actual relationship and your ideal relationship – in other words, how close is what you have to what you want? In this study, we had individuals rate not only how they felt about their partner and how, ideally, they would like to feel, but also how they thought their partner felt and how they ideally wanted their partner to feel.

What we discovered was, first, and most basically and predictably, that the amount you love your partner predicts your happiness and satisfaction in a loving relationship. No surprise there. Much more interesting was the fact that ideals played a much more important role in the success of a relationship than we ever had expected. The really good predictors of happiness were those related to the difference between what you ideally wanted in a relationship and what you felt you were getting in that relationship. The single best predictor of your satisfaction was the difference between what you felt you were getting from your partner and what you actually wanted from your partner. In other words, the single best predictor was not about how much you loved your partner, but rather about how you thought your partner felt versus what you wanted your partner to feel. Also important was the difference between the way you felt toward your partner and the way you would have liked to feel in your "ideal" relationship.

I keep emphasizing terms like "how you think your partner feels about you" rather than "how your partner feels about you" for a very simple reason. In this study, we also had the partners of our participants rate how they felt about the relationship and how they thought the participants felt about it. So, we had both the subjects' impressions and their partners' impressions. It turned out that how one's partner actually felt and how one thought the partner felt were only rather modestly correlated – about 0.3 on a 0–1 scale. What this result means is that people are not very good judges of how their partners feel. Moreover, when we, the experimenters, predicted satisfaction in relationships, how the partner actually felt about the participant mattered not at all after entering into the prediction equation how the participant thought the partner felt. Put another way, all that matters for one's satisfaction is how one thinks one's partner feels, not how one's partner actually reports feeling.

We live in a sort of bubble. We do not know and have no way of knowing how our partners actually feel. We have available to us only our perceptions of our partner's feelings, and those perceptions are not, on average, particularly accurate. If you want to improve your relationship, do everything you can to ensure the accuracy of your perceptions. Talk to your partner; watch how your partner acts; watch what your partner does for you and what you do for your partner. Don't jump to conclusions. A relationship can be destroyed by our inaccurate perceptions of our partner's feelings. In particular, the love may be there, but we just don't see it. Or worse, the love may not be there, even though we think we see it.

Arthur Aron (Aron & Aron, 1986; Aron & Tomlinson, 2019) has proposed that love involves an expansion of the self. We fall in love with people who help expand our horizons in some way that makes us feel more fulfilled and self-actualized. Our findings support this idea. We are happiest when we are with someone who helps bring us closer to our ideal self. But there is a flip side as well: We need to be chary of people who expand ourselves in ways that do not represent our ideal. When I was in the failing relationship to which I referred at the beginning of the article, I had definitely expanded in the relationship, but not in a way that was bringing me closer to my ideal; rather, I was expanding in a way that brought me toward a self I really didn't like. Many of us end up becoming people other than those we ideally want to be in relationships. So, a question we need to ask ourselves in a relationship is whether we are moving and expanding toward a self that is closer to our ideal, or rather, a self that is further away from our ideal self.

## Triangulating Love

Eventually, in my research, I came back to the question of trying to figure out what the multiple components of love are (Sternberg, 1986, 1987, 1991, 2019). I started, as I usually do when I construct a new theory, by looking at my own past experiences. Three experiences stood out as especially relevant.

When I was young, before I even started school, there was a girl who lived nearby named Mary (not her real name). She and I were the best of friends. We could talk about anything. We trusted and confided in each other. We were close and the best of friends. What I had with Mary was *intimacy*. Mary moved away soon thereafter.

Years later, when I was 16, there was a girl in my biology class named Julia (also not her real name). I took one look at Julia and fell madly in love with her. I didn't even know her. I spent much of my year staring at her, pining away for her, feeling like I just could not go on without Julia. Too bad, New Year's Eve, she met a guy she actually liked and fell for him. That made it even worse. I couldn't stand being without her. What I experienced for Julia was *passion*.

And then there was, shortly thereafter, Susan (again, not a real name). Susan and I got into a relationship that worked well enough at first; but eventually whatever flame there might once have been, died. We ended up in a relationship where all I eventually felt was commitment. Whatever intimacy and passion we once had was gone for good, at least for me.

Each of the three components of love has a set of actions associated with it. For example, intimacy might be manifested in action through sharing one's possessions and time, expressing empathy for another, communicating honestly with another, and so on. Passion might be manifested through gazing, touching, making love, and so on. Commitment might be manifested through sexual fidelity, engagement, marriage, and so on. Of course, the actions that express a particular component of love can differ somewhat from one person to another, from one relationship to another, or from one situation to another.

Such was the beginning of my triangular theory of love (Sternberg, 1986, 1988a, 1988b, 1998a). The basic idea is that a full love relationship involves intimacy, passion, and commitment. Intimacy entails feelings of closeness, connectedness, trust, communication, respect, and so forth (see also Hendrick & Hendrick, 2019; Mikulincer & Shaver, 2019). Passion involves feelings of not being able to live without the loved one, of intense need, of longing, of overwhelming desire (see also Feybesse & Hatfield, 2019). Commitment involves feelings that one is in a relationship for good – that this is it! Different kinds of love emerge from different combinations of these components (see Table 11.1). Although love clearly has part of its basis in biology (Cacioppo, 2019; Fisher, 2004) and evolutionary mechanisms (Buss, 2019), the environment profoundly affects how we choose to define love as it applies in our own individual life.

**Table 11.1**    Taxonomy of kinds of triangles of love (based on Sternberg, 1986).

| Type of love | Intimacy | Passion | Commitment |
| --- | --- | --- | --- |
| Nonlove | No | No | No |
| Friendship | Yes | No | No |
| Infatuated love | No | Yes | No |
| Empty love | No | No | Yes |
| Romantic love | Yes | Yes | No |
| Companionate love | Yes | No | Yes |
| Fatuous love | No | Yes | Yes |
| Consummate love | Yes | Yes | Yes |

So what leads to success in romantic relationships? We have at least some answers (Sternberg, 1997, 2013a, 2013b).

First, you need to know you and your partner's triangles of love. If you don't know the triangles, you can't figure out what you have, what your partner has, and whether they match. The full Sternberg Triangular Love Scale is in Sternberg (1988a), although an abbreviated and slightly modified version is shown in Box 11.1.

Second, you need to ask whether your "triangle of love" is just large enough. Is there enough intimacy, passion, and commitment to form and sustain a loving relationship?

Third, you need to ask whether your triangle of love is a good match to your partner's. In some ways, this question of match is even more important than the question of size of your triangle. If, for example, commitment is important to you but not to your partner, you are in trouble. Or if you find intimacy challenging, but your partner wants more and more of it, the relationship also is likely to degenerate. You both need to want the same things out of a relationship.

Fourth, you need to ask whether the triangle you have is close enough to your ideal triangle to make the relationship work. That is, you may have a large triangle, and you may have one that matches that of your partner, but is it the triangle you want? How close is it to what you ideally would like to have?

---

**Box 11.1**   Examples of kinds of items from the triangular love scale (based on Sternberg 1997, 1998a)

*Intimacy*
1. Can you count on your partner in times of need?
2. Is your partner emotionally supportive of you?
3. Do you communicate well with your partner?

*Passion*
1. Does your partner excite you?
2. Do you find yourself thinking about your partner frequently during the day?
3. Is your relationship with your partner romantic?

*Commitment*
1. Do you know you care about your partner?
2. Are you committed to maintaining your relationship with your partner?
3. Do you have confidence in the stability of your relationship with your partner?

*Note*: On the actual scale, items are rated on a Likert scale rather than being presented in yes/no format.

Fifth, you need to ask whether your and your partner's "action triangles" match the triangles representing your feelings. Sometimes, one finds oneself with a partner, say, who feels love for one but just cannot show it. So the love may be there, but hidden behind a relatively cold and reserved exterior. Can you deal with the way your partner shows – or fails to show – their love?

Sixth, is the triangle you have sustainable? We found that love triangles change over time. For example, intimacy can go up and it can go down. Is your intimacy sustainable? Passion usually (not always) declines over time. Is there enough there in your relationship to sustain the relationship if passion were to decline? Is your commitment genuine – is it based on what you know about your partner, or what you wish were true about your partner? You need to ask whether the triangle of love you have is sustainable over time.

Your answers to these questions will give you a sense of your levels of intimacy, passion, and commitment in your relationship with your partner.

A question kept coming up as I thought about love. So, I had some sense of what the components of love are. But how do these components come to be? Why do some people, say, emphasize intimacy, others passion, and still others nothing at all?

## Love as a Story

As I thought about what makes love relationships succeed or fail, I found myself thinking about love stories – not only those in books or movies, but also, those in my own life and those in the lives of others I had observed. As a result of these reflections, I generated what I came to call a theory of love as a story (Sternberg, 1994, 1995, 1996, 1998b; Sternberg, Hojjat, & Barnes, 2001). The idea is that from the time we are very young, we start to formulate stories about love.

Love triangles emanate, in part, from stories about love. Almost all of us encounter large numbers of diverse stories about love that suggest to us different ideas about how love can be manifested and understood. Some of the stories that we observe may be purposely intended to serve as love stories; other stories may have become love stories without anyone intending them to become stories of love. Either way, our lives present many and varied opportunities – through our own experience, as well as through literature, media such as television and movies, and so on – to observe multiple stories regarding what love can be. As a consequence of our exposure to such diverse love stories, we develop our own personal stories of what love is, can be, or should be.

The interaction of our personality traits and personal dispositions with the environment – which we, in part, create – leads to our creating stories about love. We then seek to fulfill these stories in our own lives. During the course of our lifetime, we will meet a variety of potential partners. Each of these potential partners will fit these idealized stories in greater or lesser degree.

## Kinds of stories

The number of possible love stories is endless. But certain genres of stories keep emerging, again and again, in our research. Analyses we have done of literature, film, and people's oral descriptions of relationships keep leading to the same basic set of stories. Keep in mind that the love stories we have analyzed all were from individuals living in the United States. Thus, our list of stories almost certainly shows some amount of cultural bias.

The various stories partially overlap with each other. That is, people who prefer certain stories are likely also to prefer others. Stories my colleagues and I have found to be particularly prevalent in people's folk theories of love are displayed in Box 11.2 (see also Fehr, 2019, for more detail on folk or implicit theories of love). This list is non-exhaustive. The list is based on reviews of love stories underlying narratives in literature, on previous research in psychology by myself and others, and on analyses of informally gathered case studies of people's narratives about their love experiences.

---

**Box 11.2**    Taxonomy of some love stories (based on Sternberg, 1998b)

1. *Addiction*. Strong anxious attachment; clinging behavior; anxiety at thought of losing partner.
2. *Art*. Love of partner for physical attractiveness; importance to person of partner's always looking good.
3. *Business*. Relationships as business propositions; money is power; partners in close relationships as business partners.
4. *Collection*. Partner viewed as "fitting in" to some overall scheme; partner viewed in a detached way.
5. *Cookbook*. Doing things a certain way (recipe), results is relationship being more likely to work out; departure from recipe for success leads to increased likelihood of failure.
6. *Fantasy*. Often expects to be saved by a knight in shining armor or to marry a princess and live happily ever after.
7. *Game*. Love as a game or sport.
8. *Gardening*. Relationships need to be continually nurtured and tended to.
9. *Government*. (a) *Autocratic:* One partner dominates or even controls other. (b) *Democratic:* Two partners equally share power.
10. *History*. Events of relationship form an indelible record; keep a lot of records – mental or physical.
11. *Horror*. Relationships become interesting when you terrorize or are terrorized by your partner.
12. *House and Home*. Relationships have their core in the home, through its development and maintenance.

13. *Humor.* Love is strange and funny.
14. *Mystery.* Love is a mystery and you shouldn't let too much of yourself be known.
15. *Police.* You've got to keep close tabs on your partner to make sure they toe the line, or you need to be under surveillance to make sure you behave.
16. *Pornography.* Live is dirty, and to love is to degrade or be degraded.
17. *Recovery.* Survivor mentality; view that after past trauma, person can get through practically anything.
18. *Religion.* Either views love as a religion, or love as a set of feelings and activities dictated by religion.
19. *Sacrifice.* To love is to give of oneself or for someone to give of themself to you.
20. *Science.* Love can be understood, analyzed, and dissected, just like any other natural phenomenon.
21. *Science Fiction.* Feeling that partner is like an alien – incomprehensible and very strange.
22. *Sewing.* Love is whatever you make it.
23. *Theater.* Love is scripted, with predictable acts, scenes, and lines.
24. *Travel.* Love is a journey.
25. *War.* Love is a series of battles in a devastating but continuing war.
26. *Student-teacher.* Love is a relationship between a student and a teacher.

## Aspects of stories

Several aspects of the stories of love are common across the various stories.

First, the current taxonomy listing 26 kinds of love stories displays a wide range of folk theories of what love can be and, for individuals, is. Some of the conceptions are more common (e.g., love as a garden, love as a path to be traveled) than are other conceptions (e.g., love as a horror story, love as pornographic).

Second, each story has a typical mode of thought and a typical mode of how thought is translated into behavior. For example, an individual who views love as a business will think of a relationship as a series of transactions between two business partners in a personal relationship; the relationship is highly transactional, as are businesses. In contrast, an individual who views love as a fairy tale will be looking at how a prince and a princess can live happily ever after, serving each other communally rather than transactionally (Clark, Hirsch, & Monin, 2019).

Third, one's particular love story produces one's depictions of what it means to have a loving relationship. Typically, we are not even aware of the stories we have or that they may be quite idiosyncratic. Instead, we often will look at our conceptions of love as common depictions of what love is or should be. In other words, we assume others mostly share our views. As a result, we view partners or potential partners who fail to measure up according to our stories as being inadequate. Sometimes, it is not a lover who is viewed as falling short. We may view ourselves as failing to make the grade if we cannot fulfill our own love story. Thus, if an individual views love as a fairy tale but can't form a fairy-tale relationship, perhaps even after several attempts, the individual may view themself as incompetent in love.

Fourth, love stories each contain within them complementary roles. The roles can be either symmetrical or asymmetrical. We seek a partner who matches, at least approximately, our hierarchy of stories or who at least has stories that are sufficiently compatible with our own that we can make things work. But in asymmetrical stories, we look for someone who is somewhat different – for example, someone with an autocratic-government story may seek someone to boss around or who will boss them around.

Fifth, stories are adaptive in greater or lesser degree to a given cultural milieu. One culture may view a fairy-tale story as highly desirable and useful, whereas another culture may view it as totally unrealistic (see Beall & Sternberg, 1995).

Sixth, particular stories seem simply to have greater chances for success than do other stories. Some stories, for instance, may run themselves out quickly. For example, an art story generally has a short shelf life, in that people's appearances change over time, regrettably, often for the worse. The art story thus lacks durability over the long term.

Seventh, stories interact with other events in our lives. The stories we bring to relationships may lead us to behave in particular ways; but they also bring about particular behavior from others. Our own personal development and our various interactions with other people also may shape and change the stories we have and thus carry into our relationships. Our stories are so enmeshed with the rest of our lives that it would be impossible definitively to determine what is cause and what is effect.

We have used a Likert-type scale to measure love stories. Such a scale presenting items representing various stories allows people to show their levels of preference for multiple stories. Examples of love-story items are displayed in Box 11.3.

We have found that stories differ widely in popularity (Sternberg et al., 2001). The most popular stories are travel, gardening, democratic government, and history (in that order). Least popular stories are horror, collectors, autocratic government, and game (in that order). We found significant sex differences favoring men for art, pornography, sacrifice, and science fiction. There was a significant difference favoring women for travel.

Whereas all of the three components of the triangular theory of love (Sternberg, 1986) – intimacy, passion, and commitment – positively predicted satisfaction, those stories that showed significant correlations with satisfaction all negatively predicted the satisfaction ratings. The stories with significant negative correlations were business, collector, game, governor, governed, horror (both terrorist and victim), humor (comedian), mystery (mystery figure), police (officer), recovery (helper), science fiction, and theater (both actor and audience). It seems, therefore, that stories that are maladaptive can produce dissatisfaction in relationships; but adaptive stories do not necessarily produce satisfaction.

**Box 11.3**    Love Stories Scale: Sample items (based on Sternberg 1998b)

1. Addiction
   If my partner were to leave me, my life would be completely empty.
2. Art
   Physical attractiveness is quite honestly the most essential characteristic that I look for in a partner.
3. Business
   I believe close relationships are partnerships, just like most business relationships.
4. Collection
   I like dating different partners simultaneously; each partner should fit a particular need.
5. Cookbook
   I believe that to have a good relationship you need to follow all the necessary steps one by one.
6. Fantasy
   I think people owe it to themselves to wait for the partner they have always dreamed about.
7. Game
   I view my relationships as games; the uncertainty of winning or losing is part of the excitement of the game.
8. Garden
   I believe a good relationship is attainable only if you are willing to spend the time and energy to care for it, just as you need to care for a garden.
9. Government
   *Autocratic (governor)*
   I think it is important to let my partner know from the outset that I will be in charge.
   *Autocratic (governed)*
   I think it is actually more efficient if only one person takes control of the important decisions in a relationship, and I don't mind if that person is not me.
   *Democratic*
   I believe, contrary to what many people believe, that the issues of love and power can be resolved, provided partners are willing to share both love and power.
10. History
    I often think about all the moments that I have shared with my partner and how much this common history means to me.
11. Horror
    *Terrorizer*
    I actually find it exciting when I feel my partner is somewhat frightened of me.
    *Victim*
    I tend to end up with people who sometimes frighten me.
12. House and home
    When I do things for our home, I feel like I am doing things for my close relationship.

13. Humor

*Audience*

I think taking a relationship too seriously can spoil it; that's why I like partners who have a sense of humor.

*Comedian*

I admit that I sometimes try to use humor to avoid facing a problem in my relationship.

14. Mystery

*Sleuth*

I like it when my partner is a bit hard to figure out.

*Mystery figure*

I believe it is good to keep your partner guessing about yourself in a relationship.

15. Police

*Officer*

I believe it is foolish to let your guard down and to trust your partner completely.

*Suspect*

My partner gets very upset if I don't let them know exactly where I have been.

16. Pornography

*Object*

I confess that it is very important to me to be able to gratify all my partner's sexual desires and whims, even if other people might view them as debasing me.

*Subject*

I can never be happy with a partner who is not very adventurous, in a pornographic sort of a way, in their sex life.

17. Recovery

*Codependent*

I often end up with people who face a specific problem in their past or present life, and I find myself helping them get their life back in order.

*Recoverer*

I believe that a relationship can save me from a life that is crumbling around me.

18. Religion

*Religion in relationship*

My devotion to my partner can only be seen in the larger context of my devotion to God.

*Relationship as a religion*

I seem to seek salvation in relationships, much as other people do in religion.

19. Sacrifice

I often enjoy making sacrifices for the sake of my partner.

20. Science

I believe understanding a love relationship is like understanding any other natural phenomenon; you need to uncover its governing rules.

21.  Science-fiction
     I often find myself attracted to individuals who have unusual and strange characteristics, almost what you would expect of someone from another planet.
22.  Sewing and knitting
     I believe involvement in a close relationship is like sewing a dress or a shirt; it is in your own hands to make it fit just right.
23.  Theater
     *Actor*
     I think of my relationship as acting in a play, except that I create my own unique surprise ending.

     *Fan*
     I like partners who have a sense of drama about themselves, like actors in a play.
24.  Travel
     I believe that beginning a relationship is like starting a new journey that promises to be both exciting and challenging.
25.  War
     I think arguing is healthy for a close relationship.

We further tested similarity with respect to love stories, as well as other aspects of love. In general, the results were consistent with the notion that having more similar stories (as well as triangular profiles of love) is related to higher levels of satisfaction in close relationships. We found a strong correlation (0.65) between the story profiles of the two members of couples involved in close relationships. Moreover, the degree of discrepancy, or difference in couples' profiles of love stories was also negatively correlated with participants' ratings of relationship satisfaction (−0.45), as was predicted by the theory of love as a story.

So, where does all this leave us with respect to stories that will lead to success in an intimate relationship?

First, you need to know your stories and your partner's. The full love-story scales can be found in Sternberg (1998b). Very few of us have even a clue as to what our hierarchy of stories looks like. In our early research, we just asked people to tell us their love stories. We got virtually no useful data. In order to know whether your stories correspond to your partner's, you need to know where you both stand with respect to which stories you like more, and which stories you like less.

Second, you need to ascertain whether your profile of stories is a good match to your partner's. In intimate relationships, we usually look first at physical attractiveness, then at whether values and basic beliefs (political, religious, social, etc.) match. But eventually, usually much later, stories begin increasingly to matter. Sometimes, we may find a partner to be physically attractive and to have matching values, and yet something is not right. That something often is the partner's preferred stories. If one person has a fairy-tale story and the other a business story, it will be hard to make the relationship work, no matter how well matched the partners are in other respects.

Third, you need to ascertain whether you have one of the stories mentioned above that are negatively correlated with relationship success. If you have a horror story, it is hard to make a relationship work, even if your partner has exactly the same preferred story. If one person terrorizes the other, then the future of the relationship is bleak. Why would anyone willingly seek to be a villain or a victim in a loving relationship? Good question, and yet it does happen. For example, sometimes a person may have a need for abasement, and at the same time have observed relationships in which a terrorizer attacks a victim. The horror story then may be internalized. Of course, such a person may not view themselves as having a horror story. In such an instance, what is likely to happen is that the individual repeatedly gets into bad relationships, and attributes the bad relationships to bad luck, or meeting the wrong people, or falling for the wrong people, or whatever. But until the horror story changes or is pushed down lower in the hierarchy, it will be hard for someone with a horror story to make their relationships work in a way that is satisfactory to both partners.

Fourth, you want to ask whether the story you have with your partner is high enough in your hierarchy of stories to sustain the relationship over time. Say, for example, that you have a travel story and so does your partner, but it is not at or even near the top of your hierarchy. In this case, the relationship may initially succeed. But what will be more challenging will be to maintain it over the long term. Why? Because the relationship always will be susceptible to external threats. If you later meet someone with a top story in your hierarchy higher than that of the person with whom you have a current relationship, the current relationship will come under threat. The threat will come from the current relationship being displaced by the partner for whom the partner with the new story represents one higher in your hierarchy. Thus, going for a second or third choice in a relationship exposes one to the threat that the relationship won't last if someone else comes along who is viewed as more desirable. This issue brings us to the last set of considerations, those pertaining to jealousy.

## The Role of Jealousy

More recently, I have become interested in how jealousy and envy can sustain or, more likely, destroy relationships. In work with Navjot Kaur and Elisabeth Mistur (Sternberg, Kaur, & Mistur, 2019), I have looked at how jealousy and envy function in relationships. Jealousy occurs when you fear that you are losing your partner to an external threat (usually another person) and envy occurs when you seek to have a relationship with someone currently involved with someone else.

We expected there to be two kinds of variables that would affect levels of jealousy and envy. The first kind of variable would be *personal* – it would involve the jealous or envious individual's feelings about the actual or hoped-for partner and, more generally, relationship. The second kind of variable would be *situational* – things not directly under the jealous or envious individual's control, such as the level of threat posed by some third party. In two studies, we examined whether these two kinds of factors would indeed make the difference in levels of jealousy and envy. Here, I will discuss only the jealousy studies.

In the first study, we presented a series of scenarios about two people in a close relationship, say, Chad and Victoria. A third party, Anthony, was acting in ways that might be perceived by Chad as threatening his relationship with Victoria. Then we asked a series of questions: How much does Chad want to have an intimate relationship with Victoria? How much does Chad deserve Victoria? How fair is Victoria's treatment of Chad? How much does Victoria care about Chad? How much does Chad care about Victoria? How realistic was Chad and Victoria's relationship before Anthony entered the picture? How much does Chad need Victoria, either practically or emotionally? How much does Chad trust Victoria? How big of a threat is Anthony to Chad and Victoria's relationship? How jealous is Chad of Anthony? How jealous would you be if you were in Chad's situation? (You might or might not react the same way Chad did.) How likely is the relationship between Chad and Victoria to work out, given all the circumstances?

We were interested in the internal variables (e.g., How much does Chad care about Victoria) and a particular external variable (How much of a threat is Anthony to the relationship between Chad and Victoria?). To what extent would they predict feelings of jealousy? Our findings were simple. When participants rated hypothetical others in scenarios, both internal variables and the external variable (threat from a third party) affected their ratings of jealousy. But when they instead rated themselves in a current or recent relationship, only the external variable – threat – mattered. In other words, for people's own relationships, the participants discounted the internal variables.

What do these findings imply for our own relationships?

First, if you feel jealousy, you likely will view the jealousy only in terms of the external threat you perceive from some third party. But ask yourself: How important is this relationship to me? How much do I care for my partner, or need my partner, or want my partner? Because the threat may have originated from your not being all that invested in the relationship, with the result that your partner sought someone else. If you are not all so invested in the relationship, consider using the current circumstance as an opportunity to move on.

Second, if you feel jealousy and indeed are invested in the relationship, can you think of anything you may have done to contribute to the current situation? Is there anything you can change in your own behavior to reduce the current threat or future ones?

Third, ask yourself whether your feelings of jealousy even are justified. People with certain kinds of stories, such as a police story or an art story, are likely to be more susceptible to jealousy than people with other kinds of stories, such as a travel story or a history story. Ask yourself whether your feelings of jealousy are justified, and if not, how you can overcome those feelings?

Fourth, if you are convinced your feelings of jealousy are justified, is the relationship worth saving? Or is it so far gone that you may want to use these feelings as an opportunity to let go?

Fifth, if you want to save the relationship, how can you work with your partner – and to solve the problem, you will need to work with your partner – to remedy the situation and prevent it from happening again? Your feelings of jealousy may actually be highly adaptive, and lead you and your partner in the long run to having a better relationship.

## Conclusion

Research on love can point the way to improving your love relationships. In this chapter, I have discussed some particular research. First, I discussed research showing that love consists of many elements, not just a single one. Second, I discussed the role of ideals in romantic relationships. Third, I showed how love can be understood in terms of a "triangular" theory of love. Fourth, I expanded upon the role of "love stories" in the success or failure of relationships. Finally, I talked about how jealousy can harm relationships or actually, in the long run, help them.

In my experience, the greatest mistake people regularly make in close relationships is not monitoring them – not keep track of how they are going at a given time and in a given place. Often, people encode a relationship in a certain way when the relationship starts, and then are reluctant to let go of that encoding. But our research has shown that relationships change, often radically, over time. Our triangles change, our stories may change, we may become jealous, and so on. We all need constantly to be monitoring our relationships to ensure that they are the relationships we want. And if they are not what we want, we need to communicate with our partner. A lot of relationships die when things start to be secret. If we don't continually monitor our relationships, they still will change, but the change will be unobserved by us. In the long run, that usually leads to nowhere good. If you have a valuable possession, you may monitor it to make sure that all is well with it. Look at your intimate relationship as your most valuable, or at least as one of your most valuable possessions. Monitor it, make it the best you can, and if you can't bring it to where you want, figure out where you want to go from there.

## References

Aron, A., & Aron, E. (1986). *Love and the expansion of self: Understanding attraction and satisfaction*. New York: Hemisphere.

Aron, A., & Tomlinson, J. M. (2019). Love as expansion of the self. In R. J. Sternberg & K. Sternberg (Eds.), *The new psychology of love* (2nd ed., pp. 1–24). New York: Cambridge University Press.

Beall, A. E., & Sternberg, R. J. (1995). The social construction of love. *Journal of Social and Personal Relationships, 12*(3), 417–438.

Buss, D. M. (2019). The evolution of love in humans. In R. J. Sternberg & K. Sternberg (Eds.), *The new psychology of love* (2nd ed., pp. 42–63). New York: Cambridge University Press.

Cacioppo, S. (2019). Neuroimaging of love in the twenty-first century. In R. J. Sternberg & K. Sternberg (Eds.), *The new psychology of love* (2nd ed., pp. 64–83). New York: Cambridge University Press.

Clark, M. S., Hirsch, J. L., & Monin, J. K. (2019). Love conceptualized as mutual communal responsiveness. In R. J. Sternberg & K. Sternberg (Eds.), *The new psychology of love* (2nd ed., pp. 84–116). New York: Cambridge University Press.

Fehr, B. (2019). Everyday conceptions of love. In R. J. Sternberg & K. Sternberg (Eds.), *The new psychology of love* (2nd ed., pp. 154–182). New York: Cambridge University Press.

Feybesse, C., & Hatfield, E. (2019). Passionate love. In R. J. Sternberg & K. Sternberg (Eds.), *The new psychology of love* (2nd ed., pp. 183–207). New York: Cambridge University Press.

Fisher, H. (2004). *Why we love*. New York: Holt.

Hendrick, C., & Hendrick, S. S. (2019). Styles of romantic love. In R. J. Sternberg & K. Sternberg (Eds.), *The new psychology of love* (2nd ed., pp. 223–239). New York: Cambridge University Press.

Lopez, S. J., Pedrotti, J. T., & Snyder, C. R. (2018). *Positive psychology: The scientific and practical explorations of human strengths* (4th ed.). Thousand Oaks, CA: Sage.

Mikulincer, M., & Shaver, P. R. (2019). A behavioral systems approach to romantic love relationships: Attachment, caregiving, and sex. In R. J. Sternberg & K. Sternberg (Eds.), *The new psychology of love* (2nd ed., pp. 259–279). New York: Cambridge University Press.

Rubin, Z. (1970). Measurement of romantic love. *Journal of Personality and Social Psychology, 16,* 265–273.

Sternberg, R. J. (1986). A triangular theory of love. *Psychological Review, 93,* 119–135.

Sternberg, R. J. (1987). Explorations of love. In D. Perlman & W. Jones (Eds.), *Advances in personal relationships* (Vol. 1, pp. 171–196). Greenwich, CT: JAI Press.

Sternberg, R. J. (1988a). *The triangle of love.* New York: Basic.

Sternberg, R. J. (1988b). Triangulating love. In R. J. Sternberg & M. Barnes (Eds.), *The psychology of love* (pp. 119–138). New Haven, CT: Yale University Press.

Sternberg, R. J. (1991). *Love the way you want it.* New York: Bantam.

Sternberg, R. J. (1994). Love is a story. *The General Psychologist, 30,* 1–11.

Sternberg, R. J. (1995). Love as a story. *Journal of Social and Personal Relationships, 12,* 541–546.

Sternberg, R. J. (1996). Love stories. *Personal Relationships, 3,* 59–79.

Sternberg, R. J. (1997). Construct validation of a triangular love scale. *European Journal of Social Psychology, 27*(3), 313–335.

Sternberg, R. J. (1998a). *Cupid's arrow: The course of love through time.* New York: Cambridge University Press.

Sternberg, R. J. (1998b). *Love is a story.* New York: Oxford University Press.

Sternberg, R. J. (2013a). Measuring love. *The Psychologist, 26*(2), 101.

Sternberg, R. J. (2013b). Searching for love. *The Psychologist, 26*(2), 98–101.

Sternberg, R. J. (2019). When love goes awry (Part 1): Applications of the duplex theory of love and its development to relationships gone bad. In R. J. Sternberg & K. Sternberg (Eds.), *The new psychology of love* (2nd ed., pp. 280–299). New York: Cambridge University Press.

Sternberg, R. J., & Barnes, M. (1985). Real and ideal others in romantic relationships: Is four a crowd? *Journal of Personality and Social Psychology, 49,* 1586–1608.

Sternberg, R. J., & Grajek, S. (1984). The nature of love. *Journal of Personality and Social Psychology, 47,* 312–329.

Sternberg, R. J., Hojjat, M., & Barnes, M. L. (2001). Empirical aspects of a theory of love as a story. *European Journal of Personality, 15,* 199–218.

Sternberg, R. J., Kaur, N., & Mistur, E. J. (2019). When love goes awry (Part 2): Application of an augmented triangular theory of love to personal and situational factors in jealousy and envy. In R. J. Sternberg & K. Sternberg (Eds.), *The new psychology of love* (2nd ed., pp. 300–330). New York: Cambridge University Press.

# 12

# Flow: A Component of the Good Life

## Mihaly Csikszentmihalyi

When I started studying psychology in college, I realized that this discipline had probed broadly and deeply the chasms and valleys of human behavior; but told us very little about the peaks and vistas that made life meaningful and exciting. Therefore, during my years as a student, I tried to figure out what was missing from the perspective that science had developed about being human and to see whether it was possible to provide the missing link.

My first start in this direction was to study the psychology of art and creativity – two activities that are important to our species but seem to have little or no impact in the lives of other living beings. My doctoral dissertation explored how young artists approached their work, and what they had to do to persevere in it, despite the innumerable obstacles that the choice implied. One result that I found particularly interesting was that the motivation to persevere seemed to result more from the experience the young artist derived from doing the work itself, and not from any external reward they may obtain later from selling it. In other words, the *intrinsic* rewards of doing art appeared to take precedence over the eventual *extrinsic* rewards that the artists might expect from the marketplace. I came to give the name of "flow" to this experience that seemed to be the *intrinsic* reward the artists were experiencing and seeking.

After a career in teaching college and developing this research interests, it seemed important to find out whether other activities provided similar rewards to what art did, and why. During the following decades, I presented the results of my work and that of colleagues on this topic in many articles and several books (e.g., Csikszentmihalyi, 1975/2000, 1991). Reflecting on the significance of "flow" in the

*Positive Psychology: An International Perspective*, First Edition.
Edited by Aleksandra Kostić and Derek Chadee.
© 2021 John Wiley & Sons Ltd. Published 2021 by John Wiley & Sons Ltd.

context of larger questions about the good life is something that, at 85 years of age, seemed apropos.

## Flow and Measuring Experience

Rather that beginning with a description of flow, I want to explain the key methodological innovation that serves as its foundation, the experience sampling method (ESM), and how it serves as the foundation of the flow concept. The ESM grew from a conviction that questionnaires and tests were too distant from ordinary life experience, and that people tended to answer them by drawing on what they learned in school, rather than on their actual experiences. That is, testing in schools was a good indication of what the culture thought was important to know, but this had little to do with what the students felt or thought for themselves. Today, psychologists recognize the crucial distinction between our experience and what we remember about that experience some time afterward. The ESM tries to assess experience as soon as is possible after it occurs.

In the early 1970s, "pagers" were generally associated with physicians. Rectangular boxes that would emit a loud beeping sound when the doctor got a call (we tended to call them "beepers"), and display a phone number that the doctor needed to call back. So we thought of using pagers to signal subjects at random times and ask them to immediately fill out a questionnaire reporting their activities and state at that moment, seeking to minimize the gap between actual experience and self-reports. We tried to measure what people did at the moment, and ask why they did it, in a way that avoided the conscious self-presentation so common in interview situations. Pagers allowed us to take a random cross-section of experience, and ask people to respond immediately, using scales that allowed a quick response.

The questionnaire itself sought to describe the participant's experience along a number of axes. Originally, respondents reported their emotional and physical states during the past 48 hours (e.g., hungry, relaxed, headache), then their mood along a variety of scales (e.g., hostile to friendly, excited to bored), and finally they answered questions to pin down any ways in which their general psychological state differed from that of an average day (Csikszentmihalyi & Larson, 1987). By correlating what they were doing with their experiential state, or different dimensions of experience with one another, we created a window into people's inner lives that allowed us to see how that inner experience correlated to their outer lives, for instance, to things like how students did in school.

Patients in analysis process their lived experiences by creating a narrative that reflects their view of their most important experiences, and which have already been processed according to their understanding of what made them happy or sad. While modern psychologists do not need to be convinced of the value of experimental approaches, it is hard to overstate the degree to which, at that time, scholarly discussions of enjoyment relied on conventional understandings of emotional needs and mediated accounts of experience. While the ESM could not completely break free from such constraints, it was a significant advance in terms of describing ordinary human experience. By following the correlations, we found that these self-reports of experience drastically undercut conventional ideas about enjoyment. One example is the way that people turned to television after experiencing low moods, and yet reported very low levels of concentration and enjoyment while watching television (Kubey and Csikszentmihalyi, 1990). The pattern that emerged that had the most significance for me personally involved the way that the boredom and anxiety scales correlated negatively with enjoyment. That correlation was the empirical basis for the concept of flow.

## Flow in Leisure and Work

In addition to the pager study, we conducted interviews, and the qualitative responses from people who cited enjoyment as their motivation for certain activities – such as chess players, rock climbers, and dancers – helped us formulate our description of the conditions for entering the flow state. In 1991, I used the example of a tennis player to illustrate how flow occurs in a narrow band of experience that avoids both anxiety and boredom. The tennis player is anxious when their skills do not rise to the level of the challenges, and bored when the challenges do not rise to the level of their skills. It is when those skills match the challenges that the tennis player describes the positive affective states that are characteristic of the flow experience (Csikszentmihalyi, 1991, pp. 72–77). The example has the advantage of illustrating how, because the player's skills increase as they play, flow is not fixed but dynamic – that is, the game that produced this experience as a novice would be boring to a professional.

As the tennis player's skills increase, their ability to adjust in such a way as to continue to find the flow state is what we started to call *complexity*. Defining complexity as "the self-regulative capacity to move toward optimal experiences by negotiating a better fit or synchrony of self with environment" (Csikszentmihalyi & Rathunde, 2014, pp. 31–32), we sought to identify what, in both leisure and work, allowed people to change in a consistent way that kept them from becoming bored by or anxious about what they were doing.

The characteristics that began to emerge as part of a complex personality included the ability to seek out challenges that stretch existing skills and a reliance on feedback to understand the progress being made. In addition, interactions lead to clear proximal goals, which in turn shape motivation in a way that responds to what just happened and to what happens next. This dynamic intentional structure we called "emergent motivation" (Csikszentmihalyi, 1985). Importantly, we found that flow was not just an aspect of leisure activities but also an aspect of the experience of surgeons and artists when they feel their work went well. This aspect of the flow experience, I believe, is the reason that disparate experiences like child care, religious observance, and gardening may be experienced as drudgery in some cases, but, when other variables allow it, can also be a source of flow.

Entering into the state of flow, respondents described it as one of intense concentration in which they tended to lose self-consciousness. Some of the other key features of this state include having a sense of being in control of their actions, the sensation that time is distorting, and a sense that the experience was its own reward (Nakamura & Csikszentmihalyi, 2020). The qualitative aspects of these interviews allowed us to expand the description of the flow state in ways that complemented the raw data of experiential sampling, and to develop a more robust description of the subjective experience of the flow state than the one that the sampling method had led us to discover.

These findings also suggested that many aspects of human behavior were more easily understood by assuming that in addition to the conventional *extrinsic* rewards such as physical comfort, safety, property, food, or sexual stimulation which are built into our central nervous system and are necessary for survival, we also learn to pursue goals that are *intrinsic* to the individual selves that we have become – what we learned to prize through our experiences of living. We usually seek food because our body tells us it is time to eat, whereas we might pick up a racket because we have learned that playing tennis was a good way to pass the time. Satisfying such intrinsic goals may not add to our chances of survival, but it makes the process of living more enjoyable and rewarding. Of course, this process, while it feels good at the moment, might cause problems in the long run. The pleasure we get from food or from sex has been indispensable for the survival of our species, but if it takes up too much of our conscious energy, it becomes a threat to further development. So this brings up the question of how people may live and avoid the pitfalls of solely responding to extrinsic rewards. The next section of this chapter includes my recent reflections on that question.

## Flow in the Good Life

The question of the role of flow in the "good life" is, of course, dependent on the much-contested issue of how to define the good life. This is something that philosophers and psychologists – the former group more explicitly – are still debating. Positive psychology, roughly speaking, may be traced all the way back to Aristotle's writing in the fourth century BC. What Aristotle said about *eudaimonia* – a good or prosperous life – contains a valuable critique that we are still in the process of rediscovering. He wrote in *Book I* of the *Ethics* that while everyone identifies a good life with being happy, only the wise person realizes that *eudaimonia* is not simply a matter of pleasure, wealth, and honor (Aristotle, 1980, para. 1095a). The founder of the Lyceum believed that unless a person reflects, not only might they mistake *eudaimonia* for extrinsic goals like those, but also implied that the pursuit of such extrinsic goals may never prove satisfying – the particular extrinsic goals a person seeks will change depending on what they have and what they lack. Aristotle approached the problem by contrasting what he saw as the good life with the conventional view of it taught by society or culture. These insights started making sense to me when I was quite young.

Growing up as a refugee in Rome in the late 1940s, I attended the classical *gymnasium* called Torquato Tasso, where I first read Aristotle. It was not until the 1950s, though, that I attended a lecture that confirmed for me that psychology also had answers to these questions, and that psychologists were doing the work that I wanted to do. At the time, I was already interested in psychology, but did not know much about it. On a rare trip to Switzerland, I saw a notice about a lecture on UFOs in a newspaper that sounded entertaining and had the added attraction that it was free. The lecture was by the Swiss psychiatrist Carl Jung, and he published a version of it under the title "On Flying Saucers" (Jung, 1954/1976). Attending Jung's lecture motivated me to seek out the advice of the Italian psychologist Agostino Gemelli, and I started reading Italian translations of Jung's work.

There is no question that if it was not for Jung, I would not have ended up in psychology. This is perhaps of little interest to many people, since these days the field has changed so much, and the ideas of earlier generations seem less important. When I was younger, however, the works of Freud and Jung were still widely taken as gospel in psychology. Of the two, Jung appealed much more to me. I felt that, for Jung, the dynamics of human psychology could not be reduced to libidinal satisfaction, and he had a broader view of human interests and motivations. Of course, he also believed in an unconscious that was part of our inheritance as a species. While I do not think that was really something that bears on my work, I imagine that one could translate his view into a more modern idiom, so that this collective unconscious is actually the set of automatic responses that have proven useful to survival in the past, even if now these are less important or are actually misleading. This collective heritage, and the similar solutions that cultures develop to the issues that it raises, perhaps accounts for Jung's perception that all humans share a set of basic instincts and archetypes.

At the time, however, it was in the United States that departments of psychology were doing the most interesting work, in part because in Europe the discipline was somewhat discredited after the war. Having immigrated to the United States in 1956 from Italy, I completed my PhD under Jacob Getzels at the University of Chicago. My training was in empirically based approaches to psychology, in the use of interviews, questionnaires, and statistical methods, all of which culminated in the development of the ESM already described above.

The goal was to follow the data to understand human experience, something that both drew from and differed from the work of pioneers like William James and Abraham Maslow. Both the former's "healthy-mindedness" and the latter's "self-actualization" sought to push the boundaries of psychology beyond the study of types of illness, and they were models for the study of creativity and enjoyment.

However, these positive states were defined in opposition to neurosis or fixation, and were often seen as curative ones. "Peak experience" (Maslow, 1964), in particular, was an important attempt to describe one kind of phenomenon we ended up trying to isolate and explain. For Maslow, of course, peak experience was teleological, a kind of euphoria especially available to self-actualized individuals. Our studies, by contrast, tried to naturalistically map the continuum of ordinary daily experience, and look for quantitative correlations that could lead to qualitative conclusions about the psychological states that our participants reported.

While coding the responses was arduous in an era when IBM punch cards were the best way to crunch large amounts of data, the resulting descriptions of the things people did, and how they were feeling as they were doing them, formed an unprecedented database of daily human experience. Since then, similar databases have been developed across the world, and the information has been mined by myriads of studies. The description of the flow state that came out of this data was also a key foundation of the field of positive psychology, which in the span of four decades has grown far beyond the expectations of its founders.

While the potential of these methodologies geared around measuring human experience is to better understand both human beings' positive and negative states, the promise of positive psychology is in its connection to the question of the good life. Much of psychology is still built around adjusting people to fulfill extrinsic goals, or how to help people advance within society. Positive psychology is sometimes misconstrued in this way, as a tool to keep people functioning in society. For this reason, some assume that the goals of positive psychology are to boost the amount of relaxation one derives from one's leisure time or to teach people how to "whistle while they work." The mistake in this assumption is that such goals are still a type of personal adjustment to maximize measurements external to the individual, rather than a focus on intrinsic motivation and experience in the context of that individual's life. That is, the focus must not be on a single solution in a particular domain, but on a way of approaching solutions in any domain that fits one's own skills and goals. In the previous section, I described how concepts like complexity and emergent motivation have emerged in recent decades from research into the flow state, and such concepts give us a vocabulary to talk about individual well-being that is an alternative to concepts concerned with external norms like "cure" or "adjustment."

Maintaining such a focus is key to what I originally described as the "autotelic" personality, one that shifts from extrinsic motivations to intrinsic ones. In 1975, I defined an autotelic activity as one that "required formal and extensive energy output . . . yet provided few if any conventional rewards" (Csikszentmihalyi, 1975/2000, p. 10). The skills required of the autotelic personality are the ones that allow one to embrace the complexity of life in a way that attunes one to the nature of one's own motivations, and seek out autotelic activities. Absorption in an activity and high levels of concentration have been shown to be correlated with positive feelings related to the mastery of complex situations (Baumann & Scheffer, 2010). This is not a recipe for Aristotle's "pleasure, wealth, and honor," as much as a way of living that becomes available once one releases oneself from the goal of passively pursuing them.

Individuals exists within a set of institutions that provide the context for our lives, and a focus on personal intrinsic motivation does not mean we can ignore this context. Families, schools, and workplaces are key proximal institutions that impact well-being. Just as important are the effects on individual psychology of economic and social inequality. Even as we work to understand the nature of individual well-being better, we cannot ignore the connections between it and human well-being on a macro level. Disentangling the reliance on eudaimonic well-being from hedonistic well-being and the active pursuit of flow from the passive pursuit of extrinsic goals like wealth create the preconditions for rethinking society in a way that promises a better future. Research on psychosocial connections, asking questions about the values that can sustain efforts to transform patterns in everyday experience to focus attention on institutional change, is an important task that psychology is only now beginning to take up (Inghilleri, Riva, & Riva, 2014). This attention to values and worldview is a direction in which positive psychology needs to continue to go.

Another way of saying this is that psychologists cannot afford to leave the issue of defining the good life solely to the philosophers. We do not elevate "value" over "fact" when we ask questions about how the way people structure their inner lives supports, and is supported by, particular values and forms of social organization. We may even go a step further and say that, as social scientists, the way we formulate questions and select the topics to which we pay attention reflects and reinforces particular views of how the individual fits within society, and what a good life entails. Indeed, I began this chapter with a description of the way we tried to unlock everyday human experience through the ESM in part to underline the importance of psychological method to the kind of intervention that a researcher ultimately can make. The perspectives that our datasets provide are unavailable to philosophers, and are one reason that the most robust answers to questions about the good life will emerge from conversations that include psychologists and philosophers (and a variety of other fields as well).

Throughout my career, I've tried to focus on the good life by looking at a set of questions that complemented those that many psychologists have asked, but a set that is also fundamentally different from theirs. It strikes me that most goals necessary for survival are already programmed in our genome. We do not have to learn to enjoy food when we are hungry, or to enjoy sleep when we are tired. We do not have to learn how to respond to loving parents, or friendly peers. These responses have helped us survive, and those individuals who lacked them were less able to survive, grow to maturity, and leave offspring; then the remaining patterns have become part of what we now call "human nature," the process Charles Darwin first described, and has called *evolution*. Human societies have existed for thousands of years without knowing about evolution, and many of them have disappeared from the face of the Earth, and even from history, because they inadvertently ignored the conditions that make the survival of human beings possible – from the Inca and the Maya in the New World, to the great empires of Africa, Europe, and Asia in the east. This history resembles a series of brightening and then dimming lights in an otherwise dark, empty, and uninhabited space. The question that we need to answer is whether there is anything humankind can do to avoid continuing this dismal pattern?

In the past, our ancestors have often believed that the pursuit of power and wealth would get them on the path to happiness. Now at the end of the twentieth century of our era, this goal looks elusive, and has not done our planet any favors. In particular, the unreflective pursuit of extrinsic goals like economic prosperity can cloud our judgment about how to respond to existential threats like pandemics or environmental threats like climate change. Of course, our ancestors have also provided alternative meaningful goals, like that of placing our hope in an afterlife – but for many the wait for a better existence after death seems a difficult and uncertain proposition. The great world religions have contributed much to the evolution of our species, but are probably not the last words. Those are still to be found, and may not be found for a few more thousand years. But we are here now, and we should start the journey.

# References

Aristotle. (1980). *The Nicomachean ethics* (D. Ross & L. Brown, Transe.). Oxford: Oxford University Press.

Baumann, N., & Scheffer, D. (2010). Seeing and mastering difficulty: The role of affective change in achievement flow. *Cognition and Emotion, 24,* 1304–1328.

Csikszentmihalyi, M. (1985). Emergent motivation and the evolution of the self. In D. A. Kleiber & M. L. Maehr (Eds.), *Advances in motivation and achievement* (Vol. 4, pp. 93–119). Greenwich, CT: JAI Press.

Csikszentmihalyi, M. (1991). *Flow: The psychology of optimal experience.* New York: Harper Perennial.

Csikszentmihalyi, M. (2000). *Beyond boredom and anxiety.* San Francisco, CA: Wiley. (Original work published 1975).

Csikszentmihalyi, M., & Larson, R. (1987). Validity and reliability of the experience sampling method. *Journal of Nervous and Mental Disease, 175,* 526–536.

Csikszentmihalyi, M., & Rathunde, K. (2014). The development of the person: An experiential perspective on the ontogenesis of psychological complexity. In *Applications of flow in human development and education: The collected works of Mihaly Csikszentmihalyi.* Claremont, CA: Springer.

Inghilleri, P., Riva, G., & Riva, E. (Ed.). (2014). *Enabling positive change: Flow and complexity in daily life.* Berlin: De Gruyter Open.

Jung, C G. (1976). On flying saucers. In G. Adler & R. F. C. Hull (Eds.), *Collected works of C. G. Jung. Vol. 18: The symbolic life: Miscellaneous writings* (pp. 626–633). Princeton, NJ: Princeton University Press. (Original work published 1954).

Kubey, R. W., & Csikszentmihalyi, M. (1990). *Television and the quality of life: How viewing shapes everyday experience.* Hillsdale, NJ: Lawrence Erlbaum.

Maslow, A. H. (1964). *Religions, values, and peak experiences.* London: Penguin Books.

Nakamura, J., & Csikszentmihalyi, M. (2020). The experience of flow: Theory and research. In C. R. Snyder, S. J. Lopez, L. M. Edwards, & S. C. Marques (Eds.), *The Oxford handbook of positive psychology* (3rd ed.). New York: Oxford University Press.

# 13

# Global Perspectives on Positive Psychological Science

## Stewart I. Donaldson, Saeideh Heshmati, and Scott I. Donaldson

In the late 1990s, Mihayi Csikszentmihalyi and Martin Seligman made the astute observation that the study of psychology would benefit from being rebalanced. Much of the focus of psychological research at that point had been on psychological pathology and how to help people heal and strive for "normal" functioning in everyday life. What they envisioned for the next couple of decades of psychological research was much more research on positive subjective experiences, positive psychological traits, and positive institutions (Seligman & Csikszentmihalyi, 2000). They put out a call to the next generation of psychological scientists to expand their focus to topics that would contribute to a new framework for a science of positive psychology. Positive psychological science would aim to shed light on how to build the factors that allow individuals, organizations, communities, and societies to flourish, and prevent the pathologies that arise when life is barren and meaningless (Seligman & Csikszentmihalyi, 2000).

## Call for More Positive Psychological Science

Two decades later it is clear that the call for more positive psychological science put forward at the 1998 American Psychological Association and in the January 2000 special issue of the *American Psychologist* on happiness, excellence, and optimal human functioning has been answered (Donaldson, Cabrera, & Gaffaney, under review; Donaldson, Dollwet, & Rao, 2015; Donaldson, Heshmati, Lee, & Donaldson, 2020). This new research activity was further fueled by generous prizes to honor stellar research and achievement, and a wealth of research funding from major philanthropic foundations and from a range of government funders, including the

*Positive Psychology: An International Perspective*, First Edition.
Edited by Aleksandra Kostić and Derek Chadee.
© 2021 John Wiley & Sons Ltd. Published 2021 by John Wiley & Sons Ltd.

202

National Institutes of Health (Donaldson, 2020a). Many faculties across the world now teach positive psychology courses and seek students to work with them on topics within positive psychological science (Positive Psychology Center, 2020; https://ppc.sas.upenn.edu/educational-programs/faculty-universities).

Under the leadership of Professors Martin Seligman and James Pawleski, a highly visible professional master's program in applied positive psychology (MAPP) at the University of Pennsylvania is thriving, and has spawned numerous other MAPP programs across the world (see https://www.sas.upenn.edu/lps/graduate/mapp). The first doctoral and research focused master's programs focused on positive psychological science were established over a decade ago at Claremont Graduate University under the leadership of Professors Mihaly Csikszentmihalyi, Stewart Donaldson, and Jeanne Nakamura. The *Journal of Positive Psychology* was established in 2006, and the International Positive Psychology Association (IPPA), formed in 1998, is now home to approximately 3,000 professionals worldwide who are interested in positive psychology.

Rusk and Waters (2013) estimated the size, reach, impact, and breath of positive psychology. Casting a very wide net, they found that over 18,000 documents in 700 PsycINFO® journals covering the fields of psychology, psychiatry, neuroscience, management, business, public health, and sport science had discussed a wide range of positive psychology topics. While the findings of these analyses using semantic and bibliographic methods confirmed that the positive psychology literature had been growing rapidly, it was still unclear how much of that literature was based on the scientific study of positive psychology theories and principles.

In an effort to take stock and understand how much of this activity met the call for more positive psychological science published in peer-reviewed journals, Donaldson et al. (2015) specifically examined the positive psychological science that has accumulated, and published their results in a highly cited paper in the *Journal of Positive Psychology* titled "Happiness, Excellence, and Optimal Human Functioning Revisited: Examining the Peer-reviewed Literature linked to Positive Psychology." This systematic review found and analyzed 1,336 peer-reviewed articles linked to positive psychology, with more than 750 of these articles demonstrating empirical tests of positive psychology theories, principles, and interventions. The content of this new body of science revealed that a large number of the empirical studies ($n$ = 339) investigated well-being or one of its subcomponents as the outcome variable. These studies investigated constructs such as gratitude, mindfulness/meditation, strengths, coaching, hope, or spirituality, as key predictors of well-being. Empirical findings on the antecedents and consequences of well-being, as well as findings from studies on performance, growth, and the effectiveness of 161 positive psychological interventions were discussed. This systematic review provided clear evidence that the call had been answered, and found that positive psychological scientists had been actively seeking to provide a better understanding of well-being, excellence, and optimal human functioning. The authors concluded that by 2015 positive psychological science was a growing and vibrant subarea within the broader discipline of psychology committed to using rigorous scientific methods.

## Globalization of Positive Psychological Science

Despite its popularity and widespread interest, positive psychology has sometimes been criticized for being an elite North American phenomenon (see Bacigalupe, 2001; Pedrotti & Edwards, 2017; Rao & Donaldson, 2015; Warren, Donaldson, Lee, & Donaldson, 2019). After all, it was founded in the United States, and first announced broadly in a presidential address at the American Psychological Association and later as a special issue of the *American Psychologist*. In fact, the first four International Positive Psychology Association (IPPA) world congresses of positive psychology were held in the United States, and the fifth was also held in North America in Montreal, Canada. Just a few months ago, for the first time, the sixth IPPA World Congress of Positive Psychology was held overseas in Melbourne Australia (July 2019). However, a growing list of national and regional positive psychology professional associations has emerged, and associated positive psychology research conferences are now going on all across the globe (see Table 13.1). Furthermore, a recent systematic review of the international landscape of positive psychological science revealed there is now a large and growing global presence, perspective, and visibility. No longer can it be claimed that positive psychological science is just a United States and/or Western phenomenon.

Kim, Doiron, Warren, and Donaldson (2018) identified and analyzed 863 peer-reviewed positive psychology articles in an effort to map the current international landscape of positive psychological science. They found published research in positive psychology across five continents and 63 countries. The number of articles published outside of the United States encompassed 52% of the articles in their dataset, including those from five continents, namely, Europe ($k = 209$), Asia ($k = 114$), the Americas ($k = 52$), Oceania ($k = 46$), and Africa ($k = 25$). The remaining 7% ($k = 67$) was comprised of multinational articles. Although these numbers are smaller than the articles produced in the United States, the percentage of research taking place outside of the United States appears to be increasing every year (see Figure 13.1). Examination of the dataset revealed that empirical research was produced in 62 countries other than the United States, and the top locations were the United Kingdom ($k = 78$), Canada ($k = 57$), and Australia ($k = 55$). China ($k = 31$) was ranked fifth and was the top country in Asia, and South Africa ($k = 25$) was ranked seventh and was the top country in Africa (see Table 13.2).

This first systematic review of the global landscape of positive psychological science clearly shows its growing influence across the world. This detailed analysis of the prevalence, characteristics, and influence of empirical research in positive

**Table 13.1**    Illustrative sample of associations and degree programs by continent.

| Area | Associations | Courses and Degrees |
|---|---|---|
| Europe | • European Network of Positive Psychology<br>• German-Speaking Association of Positive Psychology (German speaking areas)<br>• German Society for Positive Psychology Research<br>• French and Francophone Positive Psychology Association (Francophone areas)<br>• Czech Positive Psychology Center<br>• Hellenic Association of Positive Psychology<br>• Italian Society of Positive Psychology<br>• Polish Positive Psychology Association<br>• Portuguese Association for Studies and Intervention in Positive Psychology<br>• Spanish Society for Positive Psychology (SEPP)<br>• Swiss Positive Psychology Association<br>• Turkish Positive Psychology Association | • Oslo Summer School (Norway)<br>• Aarhus University (Denmark)<br>• Universiteit Twente; Maastricht University (The Netherlands)<br>• Universidade de Lisboa (Portugal)<br>• IE University (Spain)<br>• University of East London; City University of London; University of Glasgow; Middlesex University London; Anglia Ruskin University; Buckinghamshire New University (UK) |
| Asia | • Asian Center for Applied Positive Psychology<br>• Global Chinese Positive Psychology Association<br>• National Positive Psychology Association, India<br>• Japan Positive Psychology Association<br>• Informal groups in South Korea | • Lebanese American University (Lebanon)<br>• The Chinese University of Hong Kong; Hong Kong Shue Yan University (Hong Kong)<br>• Jerusalem University (Israel)<br>• School of Positive Psychology (Singapore) |
| Americas | • Associação de Psicologia Positiva da América Latina (Latin America)<br>• Western Positive Psychology Association<br>• Canadian Positive Psychology Association<br>• Informal groups in Mexico and Brazil | • Instituto Chileno de Psicologia Positiva (Chile)<br>• Universidad Iberoamericana (Mexico)<br>• TecMillenio University (Mexico)<br>• Claremont Graduate University; University of Pennsylvania; University of Utah; Harvard University; Stanford University; University of California Los Angeles [UCLA] Extension; University of Michigan; Case Western Reserve University; University of Missouri (US) |
| Oceania | • New Zealand Association of Positive Psychology | • University of Sydney; University of Melbourne: RMIT University; TAFE South Australia |
| Africa | | • North-West University (South Africa) |

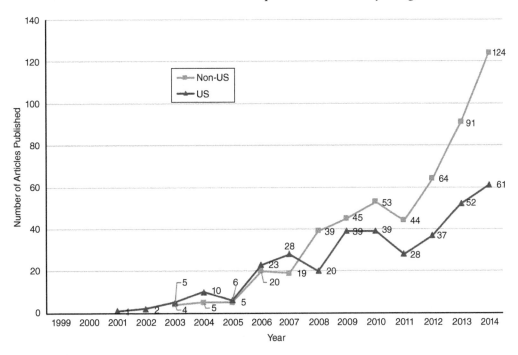

**Figure 13.1** The number of articles published outside the United States versus in the United States by year.

**Table 13.2** Number of publications by country.

| Country | Region | Number of publications |
|---------|--------|------------------------|
| United Kingdom | Northern Europe | 78 |
| Canada | Northern America | 57 |
| Australia | Oceania | 55 |
| Germany | Western Europe | 36 |
| China | East Asia | 31 |
| Spain | Southern Europe | 25 |
| Israel | Middle East/North Africa | 25 |
| South Africa | Southern Africa | 25 |
| Netherlands | Northern Europe | 23 |
| Switzerland | Western Europe | 20 |
| Italy | Southern Europe | 16 |
| India | South Asia | 14 |
| Sweden | Northern Europe | 13 |
| Japan, Taiwan | East Asia | 11 |
| Norway | Northern Europe | 11 |
| Belgium | Western Europe | 9 |
| Hong Kong | East Asia | 8 |
| South Korea | East Asia | 8 |

*(Continued)*

**Table 13.2**    (Continued)

| Country | Region | Number of publications |
| --- | --- | --- |
| Turkey | Eastern Europe | 77 |
| Iran | Middle East/North Africa | 7 |
| New Zealand | Oceania | 6 |
| Singapore | Southeast Asia | 6 |
| Russia | Eastern Europe | 5 |
| Denmark | Northern Europe | 5 |
| Brazil | South and Central America | 5 |
| Romania | Eastern Europe | 4 |
| Ireland | Northern Europe | 4 |
| Austria | Western Europe | 4 |
| Croatia | Eastern Europe | 3 |
| Finland | Northern Europe | 3 |
| France | Western Europe | 3 |
| Poland | Eastern Europe | 2 |
| Argentina | South and Central America | 2 |
| Indonesia, Malaysia | Southeast Asia | 2 |
| Portugal, Greece | Southern Europe | 2 |
| Cameroon, Nigeria | Central and Western Africa | 1 |
| Kenya, Malawi, Tanzania, Uganda, Zimbabwe | East Africa | 1 |
| Hungary, Kosovo, Serbia | Eastern Europe | 1 |
| Kuwait, Afghanistan, Algeria, Jordan, Egypt | Middle East/North Africa | 1 |
| Northern Ireland | Northern Europe | 1 |
| El Salvador, Nicaragua, Bolivia | South and Central America | 1 |
| Lesotho | Southern Africa | 1 |
| Pakistan | South Asia | 1 |
| Thailand | Southeast Asia | 1 |
| Malta | Southern Europe | |

psychology reveals that it is time to acknowledge the global nature of our science. It was also very interesting to learn about the variety and frequency of topics being studied across continents and regions (see Table 13.2). Kim et al. (2018) noted that the global perspective, influence, and popularity of positive psychological science has grown to such a large extent that in addition to contributions in mainstream psychology journals, new journals dedicated to indigenous positive psychology scholarship are being developed (e.g., the Middle East and North Africa: *Middle East Journal of Positive Psychology*; India: *Indian Journal of Positive Psychology*). A more culturally responsive field of positive psychological science that is committed to the advancement of flourishing and well-being in the global context is now clearly on the horizon.

## Scientific Foundation of Positive Psychological Science

Perhaps the harshest critiques of positive psychology have been wagered against its scientific foundation. Despite the rapid growth in research and scholarship, the perceptions of positive psychology as unscientific self-help and popular press psychology have persisted over time. This inspired a team of scientists to systematically review how constructs in positive psychological science have been operationalized, measured, validated, cited, and used to build the science (Ackerman, Warren, & Donaldson, 2018).

Based on an archive of 972 empirical articles linked to positive psychology, this review found that 762 articles used at least one measurement scale; whereas 312 measures were created or adapted. The most fundamental positive psychological science constructs and the scales used to measure them seem to be well-established. Findings also revealed a wide range of scales being used to measure a variety of constructs, including scales on both life-enhancing and life-depleting constructs.

There is now evidence from this review that shows the recent development of a range of constructs and measures, and prolific growth in their application (e.g., via adaptations of scales in new contexts). Interestingly, the most frequently measured and studied topics in positive psychological science were not found to be those of stereotypical happiness and positivity, but rather, topics such as meaning, purpose, character strengths, values, positive relationships, social support, gratitude, spirituality, self-esteem, and self-efficacy. While it was found that some reliability analyses and validations are occurring within the field, the creation of new measures far outpaced the validation of existing measures. It was also found that 78% of the studies used self-report measures, which opens up some positive psychological science to the threats of monomethod and self-report bias (see Donaldson, 2020a; Donaldson et al., 2020; Donaldson & Grant-Vallone, 2002). Overall, the scientific foundation of positive psychological science was found to be much stronger than some critics have suggested, but more validation studies, cross-pollination, and synthesis across studies would be desirable for building an even more scientifically robust area of inquiry.

## Workings of Positive Psychology Interventions

Fortunately, there is now enough research on interventions based on positive psychological science that we can begin to understand their potential. For example, a number of meta-analyses have been conducted to examine the effects of various types of positive psychology interventions (e.g., Bolier et al., 2013; Donaldson, Cabrera, & Gaffaney, under review; Donaldson, Lee, & Donaldson, 2019a; Hendriks, Schotanus-Dijkstra, Hassankhan, De Jong, & Bohlmeijer, 2019; Schueller, Kashdan, & Parks, 2014; Sin & Lyubomirsky, 2009). Two recent meta-analyses published in 2019 provide us with a synthesis of findings from the most rigorous interventions studies to date. These recent meta-analyses based on thousands of participants reveal some of the conditions under which these interventions appear to be most effective.

First, Hendriks et al. (2019) meta-analyzed 50 randomized controlled trials (RCTs) including 6,141 participants to examine the efficacy of multicomponent positive psychological science interventions (MPPIs). After controlling for study quality and other important covariates, they concluded that MPPIs studies had an overall small effect on subjective well-being and depression, and a small to moderate effect on psychological well-being. In addition, they suggest MPPIs had an overall small to moderate effect on anxiety and a moderate effect on stress. However, even though this may be the largest meta-analysis of rigorous experiments to determine the effectiveness of MMPIs to date, they caution us that definite conclusions about the effects of MPPIs on these outcomes cannot me made.

Donaldson et al. (2019a) recently published a meta-analysis of the most rigorous positive psychological science intervention studies conducted in the workplace. The best 22 studies were included in the meta-analysis containing 52 independent samples. The total number of participants in this meta-analysis was 6027 ($n$(treat) = 2187; $n$(control) = 3840), representing 10 nations (e.g., Australia, China, Netherlands, Sweden, United States, etc.). It was found that the workplace interventions had a small to moderate positive effects across both desirable and undesirable work outcomes (e.g., job stress), including well-being, engagement, leader member exchange, organization-based self-esteem, workplace trust, forgiveness, prosocial behavior, leadership, and calling. Donaldson, Lee, and Donaldson (2019b) followed up this meta-analysis with a more in-depth analysis of why and under what conditions PPI's are the most effective. This work shed more light on implementation issues and on the effectiveness of PPIs at work based on some of the most popular theory-driven approaches such as PsyCap, job crafting, strengths, gratitude, and employee well-being (PERMA) interventions.

Taken together, these recent meta-analyses based on numerous empirical tests and thousands of participants illustrate the conditions under which positive psychological interventions can improve well-being and optimal human functioning. There has now been enough sound evidence accumulated over the past two decades to conclude that interventions based on positive psychology theory and science can make measurable differences in everyday life, health and well-being, work, education, and societies across the globe (see Donaldson, Csikszentmihalyi, & Nakamura, 2020).

## New Directions in Positive Psychological Science

Three new volumes, focused on what we have learned from positive psychological science over the past two decades, suggest a range of new topics that seem ripe for future research and exploration. *Scientific Advances in Positive Psychology* presents a wide range of new directions for positive psychological science (see Warren & Donaldson, 2017). One possible new direction emphasized that will be elaborated on below involves developing a better understanding of the cultural context in positive psychological science and more exploration of issues related to diversity, equity, and inclusion. *Toward a Positive Psychology of Relationships: New Directions in Theory and Research* and *Positive Psychological Science: Improving Everyday Life, Work, Education, and Societies Across the Globe* also suggest a wide range of new research opportunities as well as underscore the importance of relationships in terms of our well-being and optimal functioning (see Donaldson et al., 2020; Warren & Donaldson, 2018). We will also elaborate on possible new directions for studies on positive relationships.

One new direction that has been emerging is the development of more science taking a global perspective on diversity, equity, and inclusion issues (DEI). Rao and Donaldson (2015) found that although women are overrepresented as participants in positive psychology research, they are underrepresented as first authors, and discussions of issues relevant to women and gender are relatively scarce. Further, empirical research studies conducted across the world are based largely on White samples, and there is little research focused on race and ethnicity or individuals at the intersections of gender, race, and ethnicity. Both Rao and Donaldson (2015) and Pedrotti and Edwards (2017) have provided recommendations on how to focus positive psychological science more on gender, race and ethnicity, social class, disability, sexual orientation, and cross-cultural issues to help build a more culturally responsive field.

Warren et al. (2019) provided a very recent example of how taking a positive psychology perspective on a major DEI issue may reinvigorate an area of research that is in decline. They underscored that gender inequality is a widespread organizational challenge, however, research on gender in the workplace suffers from stagnation in the mainstream. They proposed that a positive work and organizations perspective has the capacity to augment problem-focused gender research with new approaches to boosting gender equity. Four themes that emerged from their systematic review that could stimulate more gender research from a positive perspective were performance, social integration, well-being, and justice/moral matters. They highlighted pathways to organizational flourishing through positive diversity, equity, and inclusion behaviors and practices (see Figure 13.2).

A related issue involves encouraging more globally oriented positive psychological research to focus on better understanding positive relationships within and across cultures. One of the most robust findings across many peer-reviewed scientific studies is that the quality of our social relationships most often emerges as the strongest predictor of our well-being (Diener & Biswas-Diener, 2011) and a central component in the network of well-being (Heshmati, Oravecz, Brick, & Roeser, 2020). This global evidence base makes it clear that the quality of our relationships with significant others, family, friends, coworkers, and work supervisors, among others, "matter" in terms of our well-being over time and on a daily basis (see Dutton, Morgan Roberts, & Bednar, 2020; Heshmati et al., 2019; Oravecz, Warren & Donaldson, 2018). The evidence is so strong that Martin

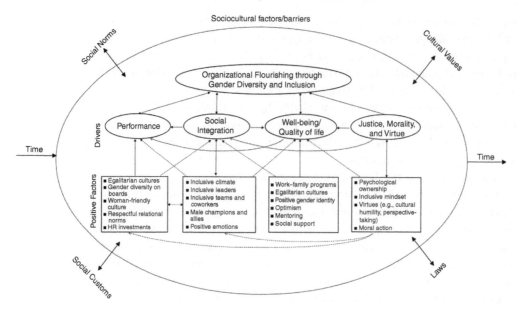

**Figure 13.2**    Proposed positive factors, drivers, and sociocultural factors and their interrelationships underlying organizational flourishing through gender DEI.

Seligman extended his theory of well-being, PERMA, to explicitly include the quality of our relationships as one of the five most important aspects of human flourishing (Seligman, 2011).

Warren and Donaldson (2018) engaged leading experts from around the world to contribute their latest positive psychological science theory and research to a volume, *Toward a Positive Psychology of Relationships: New Directions in Theory and Research*. The authors in this volume attempted to uncover a wide range of ways that positive psychological science has and could advance our understanding of well-being, flourishing, and optimal functioning across the globe. One of the topics that emerged focused on inspiring more research on positive relationships in the context of diversity, culture, and collective well-being (Harrell, 2018).

Another exciting new direction that could be explored is the importance of positivity resonance or love across our relationships (Fredrickson, 2013, 2016). That is, one of the most important ingredients for a positive relationship that has emerged across the positive psychological science literature is positivity resonance (West & Fredrickson, 2020; Heshmati et al., 2019). That is, positivity resonance and a wide variety of forms of love appear essential for developing and maintaining high quality relationships or connections with other people. Heshmati and Donaldson (2020) have provided a new framework intended to inspire more positive psychological science focused on understanding the mechanisms leading to well-being from positive relationships and love.

# Conclusion

This chapter has focused on the peer-reviewed science that has resulted from the call for more scientific studies that shed light on how to build the factors that allow individuals, organizations, communities, and societies to flourish (Seligman & Csikszentmihalyi, 2000). One purpose of this new science is to provide knowledge that can help prevent the pathologies that arise when life is barren and meaningless. It is important to point out that positive psychological science is a rather small sample of the vast literature linked to positive psychology. As Rusk and Waters (2013) have documented, there is also a plethora of books, chapters, popular press articles, commentaries, and so on, that discuss positive psychology ideas, perspectives, and issues. Many of the critics of positive psychology have focused their critiques on this vast literature that has not passed the scrutiny of scientific peer review (Donaldson, 2020b).

We have identified and summarized some of the most credible and actionable evidence now available on positive psychology topics and interventions (Donaldson, Christie, & Mark, 2008). Most evidence hierarchies suggest systematic reviews and meta-analyses often provide us with the most rigorous and actionable knowledge about a topic. We are fortunate that the relatively new field of positive psychological science is now at the place in its development that there is enough sound research to learn new insights from systematic reviews and meta-analyses. It is our hope that the global perspective on positive psychological science that we have presented in this chapter will inspire much more, sound peer-reviewed research and facilitate the design and evaluation of many more evidence-based positive psychology interventions across the world.

# References

Ackerman, C., Warren, M. A., & Donaldson, S. I. (2018). Scaling the heights of positive psychology: A systematic review of measurement scales. *International Journal of Wellbeing, 8*(2), 1–21.

Bacigalupe, G. (2001). Is positive psychology only White psychology? *American Psychologist, 56,* 82–83.

Bolier, L., Haverman, M., Westerhof, G., Riper, H., Smit, F., & Bohlmeijer, E. (2013). Positive psychology interventions: A meta-analysis of randomized controlled studies. *BMC Public Health, 13,* Article 119.

Diener, E., & Biswas-Diener, R. (2011). *Happiness: Unlocking the mysteries of psychological wealth.* New York: Wiley.

Donaldson, S. I. (2020a). Theory-driven positive psychological science: A global perspective. In S. I. Donaldson, M. Csikszentmihalyi, & J. Nakamura (Eds.), *Positive psychological science: Improving everyday life, well-being, work, education, and societies across the globe* (2nd ed., pp. 1–10). New York: Routledge Academic.

Donaldson, S. I. (2020b). Using positive psychological science to design and evaluate interventions. In S. I. Donaldson, M. Csikszentmihalyi, & J. Nakamura (Eds.), *Positive psychological science: Improving everyday life, well-being, work, education, and societies across the globe* (2nd ed., pp. 246–255). New York: Routledge Academic.

Donaldson, S. I., Cabrera, V., & Gaffaney, J. (under review). Following the positive psychology intervention science to generate well-being in a global pandemic. Manuscript submitted for publication.

Donaldson, S. I., Christie, C. A., & Mark, M. M. (2008). *What counts as credible evidence in applied research and evaluation practice?* Newbury Park, CA: Sage Publications.

Donaldson, S. I., Csikszentmihalyi, M., & Nakamura, J. (2020). *Positive psychological science: Improving everyday life, well-being, work, education, and societies across the globe* (2nd ed.). New York: Routledge Academic.

Donaldson, S. I., Dollwet, M., & Rao, M. (2015). Happiness, excellence, and optimal human functioning revisited: Examining the peer-reviewed literature linked to positive psychology. *Journal of Positive Psychology, 10*(3), 185–195.

Donaldson, S. I., & Grant-Vallone, E. J. (2002). Understanding self-report bias in organizational behavior research. *Journal of Business and Psychology, 17*(2), 245–262.

Donaldson, S. I., Heshmati, S., Lee, J. Y., & Donaldson, S. I. (2020). Examining building blocks of well-being beyond PERMA and self-report bias. *The Journal of Positive Psychology*, https://doi.org/10.1080/17439760.2020.1818813.

Donaldson, S. I., Lee, J. Y., & Donaldson, S. I. (2019a). Evaluating positive psychology interventions at work: A systematic review and meta-analysis. *International Journal of Applied Positive Psychology, 4*, 113–134.

Donaldson, S. I., Lee, J. Y, & Donaldson, S. I. (2019b). The effectiveness of positive psychology interventions in the workplace: A theory-driven evaluation perspective. In S. Rothman, L. E. van Zyl, & I. Rothman (Eds.), *Theoretical approaches to multi-cultural positive psychology interventions* (pp. 115–160). New York: Springer.

Dutton, J. E., Morgan Roberts, L., & Bednar, J. (2020). Prosocial practices, positive identity, and flourishing at work. In S. I. Donaldson, M. Csikszentmihalyi, & J. Nakamura (Eds.), *Positive psychological science: Improving everyday life, well-being, work, education, and societies across the globe* (2nd ed., pp. 128–144). New York: Routledge Academic.

Fredrickson, B. L. (2013). *Love 2.0: How our supreme emotion affects everything we feel, think, do, and become.* New York: Hudson Street Press.

Fredrickson, B. L. (2016). Love: Positivity resonance as a fresh, evidence-based perspective on an age-old topic. In L. F. Barrett, M. Lewis, & J. M. Haviland-Jones (Eds.), *Handbook of emotions* (4th ed., pp. 847–858). New York: Guilford Press.

Harrell, S. P. (2018). "Being human together": Positive relationships in the context of diversity, culture, and collective well-being. In M. A. Warren & S. I. Donaldson (Eds.), *Toward a positive psychology of relationships: New directions in theory and research* (pp. 247–284). Santa Barbara, CA: Praeger/ABC-CLIO.

Hendriks, T., Schotanus-Dijkstra, M., Hassankhan A., De Jong, J., & Bohlmeijer, E. (2019). The efficacy of multi-component positive psychological interventions: A systematic review and meta-analysis of randomized controlled trials. *Journal of Happiness Studies, 21*(1), 357–390.

Heshmati, S., & Donaldson, S. I. (2020). The science of positive relationships and love. In S. I. Donaldson, M. Csikszentmihalyi, & J. Nakamura (Eds.), *Positive psychological science: Improving everyday life, well-being, work, education, and societies across the globe* (2nd ed., pp. 52–63). New York: Routledge Academic.

Heshmati, S., Oravecz, Z., Brick, T. R., & Roeser, R. W. (2020). Assessing psychological well-being in early adulthood: Empirical evidence for the structure of daily well-being via network analysis. *Applied Developmental Science.* Advance online publication.

Heshmati, S., Oravecz, Z., Pressman, S., Batchelder, W. H., Muth, C., & Vandekerckhove, J. (2019). What does it mean to feel loved: Cultural consensus and individual differences in felt love. *Journal of Social and Personal Relationships, 36*(1), 214–243.

Kim, H., Doiron, K., Warren, M. A., & Donaldson, S. I. (2018). The international landscape of positive psychology research: A systematic review. *International Journal of WellBeing, 8*(1), 50–70.

Pedrotti, J. T., & Edwards, L. M. (2017). Cultural context in positive psychology: History, research, and opportunities for growth. In M. A. Warren & S. I. Donaldson (Eds.), *Scientific advances in positive psychology* (pp. 257–288). Santa Barbara, CA: Praeger/ABC-CLIO.

Positive Psychology Center. (2020). Faculty at universities. Retrieved from https://ppc.sas.upenn.edu/educational-programs/faculty-universities.

Rao, M., & Donaldson, S. I. (2015). Expanding opportunities for diverse populations in positive psychology: An examination of gender, race, and ethnicity. *Canadian Psychology/Psychologie canadienne, 56*(3), 271–282. (Special issue on positive psychology).

Rusk, R. D., & Waters, L. E. (2013). Tracing the size, reach, impact, and breadth of positive psychology. *The Journal of Positive Psychology, 8*, 207–221.

Schueller, S. M., Kashdan, T. B., & Parks, A. C. (2014). Synthesizing positive psychological interventions: Suggestions for conducting and interpreting meta-analyses. *International Journal of Wellbeing, 4*(1), 91–98.

Seligman, M. E. P. (2011). *Flourish: A visionary new understanding of happiness and well-being*. New York: Free Press.

Seligman, M. E. P., & Csikszentmihalyi, M. (2000). Positive psychology: An introduction. *American Psychologist, 55,* 5–14.

Sin, N., & Lyubomirsky, S. (2009). Enhancing well-being and alleviating depressive symptoms with positive psychology interventions: A practice-friendly meta-analysis. *Journal of Clinical Psychology, 65*(5), 467–487.

Warren, M. A., & Donaldson, S. I. (2017). *Scientific advances in positive psychology*. Westport, CT: Praeger.

Warren, M. A., & Donaldson, S. I. (2018). *Toward a positive psychology of relationships: New directions in theory and research*. Westport, CT: Praeger.

Warren, M. A., Donaldson, S. I., Lee, J. Y., & Donaldson, S. I. (2019). Reinvigorating research on gender in the workplace using a positive work and organizations perspective. *International Management Reviews, 21*(4), 498–518.

West, T. N., & Fredrickson, B. L. (2020). Cultivating positive emotions to enhance human flourishing. In S. I. Donaldson, M. Csikszentmihalyi, & J. Nakamura (Eds.), *Positive psychological science: Improving everyday life, well-being, work, education, and societies across the globe* (2nd ed., pp. 38–51). New York: Routledge Academic.

# 14

# Self-Efficacy, Collective Efficacy and Positive Psychology

Shari Young Kuchenbecker

Humanity seems to be at a crossroads. Many authoritarian leaders have emerged internationally (Kakkar & Sivanathan, 2017a, 2017b). The current president of Russia – thought by some to be the most powerful and wealthiest individual alive – revels in his personal influence and is maneuvering to remain in power for life (Khurshudyan, 2020). The 2017–2021 president of the United States made pronouncements daily that exposed his own poor mental health and, more importantly, the shaky foundation of America's democracy. Everywhere, scientists warn that climate change is within a decade of fundamentally changing all human relations (United Nations Intergovernmental Panel on Climate Change, 2018), and while some corrective measures have begun, the US withdrawal from the Climate Accord in 2019 ceding leadership to China raised concerns that others soon would withdraw. Those worries appear unfounded, but the pandemic may stall many societies' efforts taking the needed corrective measures (Climate Action Tracker, 2020). Some scholars see the global corona virus pandemic as a symptom of the catastrophic connection between humanity and nature (Lewis, 2020).

Now, more than ever, we need the insights that come from the field of positive psychology. When traditional texts dwell on psychopathology and substance abuse, they often underestimate people's capacity to overcome less-than-optimal life circumstances. But, as positive psychologists note, there are astounding numbers of people worldwide who face challenging inequities and continue to report high levels of happiness (Helliwell, Layard, & Sachs, 2019). Subjective well-being is not independent of political, health, or socioeconomic context; nor are these single factors absolute determinants of life satisfaction which also reflects culture, values, and supportive social relationships (Diener, Oishi, & Tay, 2018).

*Positive Psychology: An International Perspective*, First Edition.
Edited by Aleksandra Kostić and Derek Chadee.

One of the leading researchers contributing to the foundations of positive psychology is Albert Bandura. Working over the decades on models of human development (Bandura, 1976, 1986, 2006a, 2008, 2011a), Bandura is now best known for his social cognitive theory (SCT). SCT explains that all people strive to influence the events affecting their lives (Bandura, 1997). It is fundamental to human nature to work for desired futures and to avoid unwanted outcomes. Although the specific expressions of human agency are shaped by cultures, ethnicities, and families, human agency is at the core of human life.

At the heart of agency is self-efficacy – the belief that one can take actions that will produce desired effects. According to Bandura (2008), without self-efficacy, there is little incentive to act or to face difficulties. Hope and optimism are our lay terms expressing agency.

The aim of this chapter is to expand on Bandura's insights by reminding readers that *self*-efficacy is, fundamentally, only a beginning. Unlike some other scholars who see agency as entirely distinct from community, Bandura demonstrates that agency is inherently interpersonal and dynamically intertwined in the social relationships in which it is embedded and from whence it arises. The last section of this chapter and the last chapter of his book, *Self-Efficacy: The Exercise of Control* (Bandura, 1997) looks at how people can take collective actions that are prosocial, proactive, and pro-global. Collective agency is greatly needed, perhaps now more than ever.

## Bandura's Theories

Albert Bandura, a Canadian-born American psychologist, began his academic career exploring observable human behaviors and replicable phenomena. His first two books dealt with social learning and adolescent aggression (Bandura & Walters, 1959, 1963). Both featured a theme of reciprocal determinism, the idea that actions are created dynamically through interactions between people.

Bandura early recognized that what people know and what people do are separable. Fighting against the then-dominant mechanistic stimulus and response (S-R) theories of learning, Bandura made a couple of very important observations. First, he noted that people do not always express the behaviors that they know how to do. Second, he noted that people can learn through social observation.

In the early 1960s Bandura's research concentrated on vicarious learning (Bandura, Ross, & Ross, 1961, 1963a, 1963b, 1963c). At the time, the influential view in developmental psychology emphasized instrumental learning such that individuals increased responses for which they were rewarded. Bandura, Ross and Ross – in collaboration with their inflatable partner, Bobo – debunked the notion that the only way to acquire behaviors was through direct personal experience. Role models helped individuals learn both general and specific behaviors, whether or not the behaviors were displayed immediately after acquisition.

Consistently over the decades, Bandura has noted that motivation plays a big part in behavior (Bandura, 2016). People's attitudes and context matter. People who think they can succeed behave differently than people who believe they cannot.

What makes people feel they can succeed? The first contributing factor is social learning – role models – seeing how others act and what then occurs. Second, people's self-efficacy (optimism) is influenced by their own past mastery experiences. Those who have experienced past success in similar tasks usually are most optimistic about new successes and are more willing to try. Third, encouragement and persuasion from others matter. When individuals are supported by others to engage in behaviors, told that they have what it takes to succeed, they are more likely to strive harder than when others seek to discourage or disparage them. Fourth and last, contributing to people's motivation is their physiological state at the time when the behavior might be performed. This includes current health (illness), age, condition (injury), and even weariness. A flu or sore muscles will dampen enthusiasm, self-efficacy beliefs, and action. Notably, as researchers and clinicians have noted, each one of these four factors can be a point of intervention for increasing a desired behavior, thus increasing self-efficacy beliefs and an individual's willingness to take action.

Substantial research supports many aspects of Bandura's theories. Research shows that people can overcome fear of snakes via observational learning and desensitization (Bandura, Blanchard, & Ritter, 1969); can unlearn phobias (Bandura, Jeffery, & Gajdos, 1975); and can manage depression (Holahan & Holahan, 1987). Self-efficacy beliefs even influence career choices (Betz & Hackett, 1986).

Bandura's ability to fashion useful theories has earned him unparalleled respect and recognition. Bandura leads the eminent psychologists' list in total citations and is the author of psychology's most-cited article (Diener, Oishi, & Park, 2014). Enter the term "self-efficacy" and 2,190,000 Google Scholar results appear. Search for Bobo Doll, and you will find over 6,320 Google Scholar references. Bandura is the most-cited psychologist. His name appears on every list of psychology's greatest contributors along with Freud, Piaget, and Skinner (American Psychological Association, 2002). In 2016, President Obama awarded Bandura the US National Medal of Science.

## Self and the Collective

Bandura's work always has been intertwined with recognition that people are social creatures. What is now known as SCT had its origin in Bandura's social learning theory – a clear indication that Bandura always has valued the social component of our behaviors. Bandura points out that behavior results from our attention, retention, reproduction, and motivation (Bandura, 2011b), thus emphasizing his respect for individuals attending to others. Similarly, his focus on indirect learning and on encouragement from others as builders of a sense of efficacy shows that Bandura consistently supports that people need other people to succeed. The assumption that people can and must join with others for success is the central principal in the concept of "collective efficacy."

Given the enormous popularity of Bandura's work, it may not be surprising that his highly nuanced ideas sometimes can become distorted. The term "self-efficacy" invites a misunderstanding, especially as it has been contrasted with the term "collective efficacy." In some instances, practitioners and researchers assume that self-efficacy means that an individual believes they can accomplish something on their own, an illusion, for example, more common among men than women in STEM careers (Zeldin, Britner, & Pajares, 2008).

The central purpose of this chapter is to remind scholars of the interpersonal nature of self-efficacy. I propose that at the core of self-efficacy is the ability to connect to others. Through connection, the dependent infant survives. By caring for an infant, building trust, empathy, and social responsibility in children, the social contract continues despite the destructive pull of egotism and aggression. It will be through connection that we as a species might survive despite the vast challenges that face us today.

## Surviving Impossible Odds of Infancy

Let's put things into perspective by asking: How likely is it that a baby could survive a week or even a single day on its own? Not very likely.

Yet the vast majority of completely dependent babies survive beyond infancy. Deemed "helpless" by some, babies arrive equipped with reflexes and instincts that support survival. The instincts are deeply intertwined in both infant and parent(s), dynamically interacting to assure survival of the species (Feldman, 2015, 2016).

Nature equips the newborn with five senses (smell, taste, touch, hearing, sight) and a host of reflexes. When the bladder is full, the infant urinates. When solid waste needs to exit, the baby defecates. Hold an infant vertically with feet touching a flat surface and they'll make walking movements (walking/stepping reflex). Place your finger across the palm of newborns, and their fingers will curl around yours, clinging (palmar grasp). Soon after the first breath, touch the side of a newborn's mouth and you'll elicit turning toward the touch and feeling around with his or her tiny mouth (rooting). If their mouth is lucky enough in the rooting reflex to encounter a nipple, they start automatically to suck.

Babies cry. They cry when they feel uncomfortable, are hungry, or otherwise need help. Infants' cries communicate their needs.

Caregivers respond. A crying baby constitutes an attention-demanding stimulus with most caregivers' heartrates, blood pressure, and motor potentiation rising (Parsons, Young, Parsons, Stein, & Kringelbach, 2011). A smiling and cooing baby gives reinforcement. Most people like babies, but not everyone and like all of nature's gifts, there may be a bell-like curve. This much almost everyone understands. And from this simple observation, we know that babies survive because a happy baby constitutes a very positive stimulus for most adults – and a baby's smile is tremendously rewarding.

Yet the extraordinary degree of the symbiosis is only now being understood by researchers. Studies shows that infant cries are tuned to an easily heard frequency. What is even more astonishing, the cries of an infant activate areas of the brain involved in oxytocin production and generally in empathic responsiveness (Parsons, Young, Murray, Stein, & Kringelbach, 2010; Riem et al., 2011).

Like other humans, babies are agentic; but to an extraordinary degree, their efficaciousness works through the capabilities of other humans. In fact, Bandura noted that agency can be by self-actions, by proxy – getting others to do your desired action(s), or by collective agency, working together (Bandura, 1997).

Across the early months and years of life, the developing infant's job is to communicate what they need, thereby their agency is by proxy. Crying is babies' universal language and nicely enough, within a few weeks of birth, the attentive caregiver can differentiate between their baby's hungry cry and "I am wet, cold, and uncomfortable, change me!" cry.

Caregivers know that they feel emotions when they are around babies. Caregivers infer that babies feel emotions too, thus, when the baby gurgles and giggles, adults assume the child feels happiness. Mirrored smiling often ensues and the relationship becomes reciprocal (Feldman, Gordon, Influs, Gutbir, & Ebstein, 2013). Dynamically, caregiver and infant learn from each other via sustaining instincts (Young et al., 2016). They reinforce, withhold reward, and sometimes even punish and withhold punishment from each other but the core of reciprocal social interaction is more than simple reinforcement.

Indeed, the agentic model of early development is dynamic. The infant, and later the child, plays a proactive role in adapting to the environment (Bandura, 1997; Bandura, Pastorelli, Barbaranelli, & Caprara, 1999). Certain types of child-rearing, furthermore, enhance the child's sense of being capable, encouraging them to be curious and proactive. Children who are lucky enough to receive contingent caregiving, where the adult's behavior responds and shapes to that child's needs, tend to be more connected to others (Feldman, Weller, Zagoory-Sharon, & Levine, 2007), develop a deeper sense of trust (Maslow, 1943, 1971), and are more capable of handling stress (Schanberg & Field, 1988) than others.

Consistent with the idea that babies feel emotions, early studies demonstrated that babies need more than just food. Harry Harlow's (Harlow, 1958, 1962; Harlow, Dodsworth, & Harlow, 1965; Harlow & Suomi, 1971) famous laboratory recordings of rhesus monkeys convinced the scientific community that infant mammals require more than mere sustenance. The same message was evident in infant development, care, and orphanage studies conducted in the first half of the twentieth century (Bowlby, 1952, 1958; Skeels & Dye, 1939; Spitz, 1946) where, lacking adequate holding and touch, social withdrawal ensues. Delayed development, infant wasting (marasmus), and even infant death in these conditions inspired laws mandating minimum 3 : 1 infant/caregiver ratios in most settings. With touch and cuddling, infants develop more rapidly, premature and sick infants heal and could go home sooner than those left untouched in the sanitary, but isolated incubator (Field et al., 1986).

Babies need care. Most babies, and certainly most neuro-typical babies, orient toward the human face and particularly eyes (Baron-Cohen, 1994a, 1994b; Farroni et al., 2005). Imitating simple behaviors like tongue thrust, infants begin their mirroring adult facial behaviors early (Meltzoff & Moore, 1977).

Smiles beget smiles. In fact, many two- to three-month-old babies respond reciprocally to simple changes in the human face. A smiling caregiver's face is welcome versus the caregiver's still face which will elicit longer looking, attempts to engage (movement and vocalizations) but failing, crying often ensues. Recognizing their own caregiver's unique face by five to six months is when stranger anxiety may set in.

Dynamic face-to-face interplay between infant and caregiver becomes an important part of social development. For the infant, contingent reciprocated smiling contributes to a sense of efficacy and social competence. Studies support that emotional expressiveness in later life has deep roots in infancy and early childhood (Meltzoff, 1990a, 1990b; Meltzoff & Decety, 2003) with skills developing through years of practice (Nozadi, Spinrad, Johnson, & Eisenberg, 2018).

## Hope and Caring for Others

### Building efficacy in kids

Just as in infancy, so in childhood caregivers can build a sense of efficacy in the young ones. Hess and Shipman (1965) set the stage showing that almost all parents mean to help their children; but despite good intentions, may undermine their child's own capable development. Watching mother–child pairs interact on several tasks including drawing a figure with an Etch-a-Sketch, they found a supportive mother would verbally instruct her child how to move the dials, praising successful efforts, and suggesting (but not doing) helpful actions. The less-skilled mother was more likely to be hasty, use negative words, and belittle her child's independent efforts. She typically would reach in, move the dials herself, overlooking that she had just undermined her child's own developing capabilities. Regrettably, the drawn figure may look good, but her child's self-efficacy was diminished and learning was colored by negative emotion.

As children mature beyond the first months and years of life, their caregivers are ideally less and less involved in meeting basic needs of the child and more and more involved in teaching the child how to meet his or her own needs. By early childhood, little people might not prepare their own food, but they are increasingly capable of conveying it from plate to mouth and, early on, can pack their own snacks and lunches. Indeed, caregiver and child agree the efficacy of children managing their own bodily functions. "I can do it by myself," the capable child insists. And increasingly, children manage social interactions, regulating their emotional responses in ways that others find palatable. With supportive guiding positive feedback, thus efficacy and quality development proceeds.

## Caring in kids

Watch children at any age, and you will notice that some children seem more socially adept than others. While this may vary from day to day, particularly among the very young, as children mature, their social behaviors become more consistent across situations and time.

The difference among children relates not just to social competence in general, but specifically to differences in the ability to plan and perform prosocial behaviors. Prosocial behaviors are defined as voluntary actions intended to benefit another person (or group) performed without pressure to do so (Eisenberg & Mussen, 1989; Mussen & Eisenberg-Berg, 1977). On the surface, doing anything for someone else may look prosocial, but may be self-serving as, for example, when someone makes a big display of generosity simply to win approval.

White (1973) documented the importance of social skills in his longitudinal study of children from birth through six years old. Distinguishing that social skills contributed instrumentally to building linguistic abilities, intellectual competence, dual attention, and executive planning, White noted that there were seven important aspects of social competence. These include the abilities to:

- get and maintain attention of adults in socially acceptable ways;
- use adults as resources;
- express both affection and hostility to adults and to peers;
- lead and follow peers;
- compete with peers;
- show pride in oneself and accomplishments; and
- become involved in adult role model imitation play.

While White and his team showed that these social skills can be learned at later ages, competencies tend to emerge early, build on themselves, becoming increasingly stable over time, thus supporting the value of early learning and intervention.

Notably, not all developing children are able to build caring connections. Boys and adolescent males are particularly at risk for having limited or poor social skills (Zimbardo & Coulombe, 2016; Zimbardo & Duncan, 2012). Over or misuse of modern technologies must bear some of the responsibility. Playing video games alone in their bedrooms means the boys are not hanging out with other kids, they are not interacting with others, and they are not learning the social skills they need to become contributive members of society (Carducci, Riggio, Zimbardo, & Kuchenbecker, 2015).

If social influences can, in essence, teach children to be isolated, educational influences can also teach connections. Psychologists early on looked at social skills to create school and parental curricula to help guide children's social behavior. One of the first was Lois Murphy and her work on children's sympathy and prosocial behavior in the 1930s (Murphy, 1937). Eisenberg and Mussen (1989) conducted germinal work on prosocial behavior. Other early researchers contributed by looking at gender roles and development (Maccoby & Jacklin, 1974; Sears, Maccoby, & Levin, 1957), helping behavior (Staub, 1971), altruism (Hoffman, 1975), empathy (Feshbach & Feshbach, 1982; Feshbach & Kuchenbecker, 1974; Feshbach & Roe, 1968; Kuchenbecker, 1976, 1977), social learning (Bandura, 1976), and others.

Many researchers are now looking into social and emotional learning (SEL) and a social emotional curriculum for early and elementary schools. The splendid CASEL program at the University of Chicago, Illinois (Graczyk et al., 2000), reveals that this field is richly promising. People can, indeed, learn to forge good connections with others.

One particular variable of interest in the field is emotional regulation (ER). In the mid-1990s, emotional regulation emerged as a distinct research area differentiated from the previous developmental, clinical, and research domains (Campos, Campos, & Barrett, 1989; Gross & Munoz, 1995; Izard, 1990; Thompson, 1994), and interest has grown exponentially since then (Gross, 2015; McRae & Gross, 2020). ER acknowledges both positive and negative feelings as potentially independently active at the same time, even supporting the dynamic interplay of positive emotions which may serve to buffer the harmful effects of negative emotions. Early ER work underscored the superiority of personal and social cognitive reframing compared to emotion suppression (Gross & John, 2003). Recent research with adolescents supports intervention strategies using initial affective control as a building block in exercising cognitive reappraisal/reframing strategies (Schweizer, Gotlib, & Blakemore, 2020), thereby increasing self-efficacy.

Socially competent people do more than regulate their own emotions. They respond appropriately to the emotions of others. Appropriate responses can occur, obviously, only if people actually attend to and correctly decode the emotions of others. Very young children across cultures are given the greatest latitude of emotional expression with increasingly constrained guidelines as to what is considered "appropriate" expressiveness for children of increasing ages in public and/or specific situations.

To respond appropriately to the emotions of others you must observe and be able to recognize what those emotions are (Ekman, 1992; Keltner & Lerner, 2010; Keltner, Sauter, Tracy, & Cowen, 2019.) The human body gives clues to emotion and one of the best ways to know the emotions of others is to read their faces (Ekman, 1993, 2011; Ekman & Friesen, 1975, 1976; Ekman et al., 1987; Ekman, Levenson, & Friesen, 1983). Ekman and his colleagues identify several negative and positive emotional facial expressions, distinguishing anger, fear, sadness, disgust, contempt, surprise, and happiness cues displayed in subtle macro-expressions (1–4 seconds) and briefer micro-expressions (1/15–1/25th second).

Recent research describes how attending to facial expressions can facilitate responding to other's emotions and can support interpersonal connections, thus opening a promising avenue for future research (Lwi, Haase, Shiota, Newton, & Levenson, 2019). Notably, the universality of human facial movements to convey accurate emotional experiences remains controversial (Barrett, Adolphs, Marsella, Martinez, & Pollak, 2019), but others' facial expressions nonetheless potentially provide some clues to others' social emotional processes.

## Connection between Caring and Competence

Caprara, Barbaranelli, Pastorelli, Bandura, and Zimbardo (2000) looked at children's academic achievement in middle school. Academic success in 8th grade was best predicted by prosocial behavior in third grade, not raw academic achievement in third grade. Here, prosocialness was determined by self-ratings of helpfulness, sharing, kindness, and cooperativeness (Caprara & Pastorelli, 1993), peer nominations of children who cooperated, shared, consoled, and helped others, as well as teacher ratings of prosocial behavior using the same scale that the children used to assess themselves. In fact, when controlling for prosocial behavior as a latent variable, early academic achievement did not contribute anything to the middle-school academic success. Social skills matter most.

Additional research shows similar connections between caring and success. More specifically, we've found that positive social skills were instrumental in advancing athletic development (Kuchenbecker 2000; Kuchenbecker et al. 1999). We asked 658 coaches for different sports and age groups to name three characteristics of a young athlete who was "a real winner." Positive psychological characteristics made up 2.9 out of 3 qualities coaches cited, not physical attributes. Only one in ten coaches even mentioned physical skills. Next, when coaches were asked to pick five qualities from a list of 120 characteristics, half physical and half psychological, the five top choices were:

| | |
|---|---|
| Loves to play | 43% |
| Positive attitude | 33% |
| Coachable | 30% |
| Self-motivated | 27% |
| Team player | 26% |

Natural physical ability was mentioned by only 10% of the coaches and physically giftedness by only 6%.

Notably, youth, middle-school, and collegiate coaches all rated "Loves to Play" highest, but coaches working with high school aged athletes gave top billing to "Coachable" (46%), followed by "Positive Attitude" (39%). Apparently, their experiences with high schoolers particularly taught them that physical gifts were of little value if the young athlete could not listen and take direction.

Across the life span, social skills and friendships also yield additional health and longevity benefits (Holt-Lunstad, 2017, 2018a, 2018b; Holt-Lunstad, Ditzen, & Light, 2019; Holt-Lunstad, Smith, & Layton, 2010). Having solid friendships adds both to the quality of life, and it also increases life span. In their meta-analysis including 148 studies, people with stronger social relationships enjoyed a 50% increased chance of survival and this effect held across mortality age, sex, initial health status, cause of death, and follow-up. Interestingly, the effect sizes were greatest when assessing complex social integration measures and most modest for binary factors like living alone as opposed to living with others. On average, supportive relationships translated to 6.5 years of extended life, a difference equivalent halting a known health-damaging behavior like smoking.

Summarizing, from infancy through early childhood (White, 1973), from grade school to high school (Caprara et al., 2000), across developmental athletic trajectories (Kuchenbecker, 2000; Kuchenbecker et al., 1999) and adding years to life (Holt-Lunstad et al., 2010), social competency, positive social skills, and social relationships contribute to life success. Most parents, caregivers, and educators understand this. From the dependent crying infant to becoming an independent contributing adult, the developing child needs a language to communicate their emotions and needs (beyond crying) and social emotional and behavioral guidance to become successful contributing adults. This hidden parenting/caregiving curriculum must build needed self-efficacy in the context of an individual growing within a family, community, culture, and global collective.

Urie Bronfenbrenner, cofounder of the US Head Start program, proposed the ecological systems theory of human development including individual, microsystem, mesosystem, exosystem, and macrosystem across time (chronosystem) (Bronfenbrenner, 1979, 1994, 1999). With the family and community's central developmental role, a child's positive trajectory was enmeshed in early and later social ecological experiences.

Positive developmental psychology is a field sharing deep foundations and advances with life-span research clarifying positive parenting (Kyriazos & Stalikas, 2018) and coming from Jeanne Nakamura and Claremont Graduate University's positive psychology labs revealing mentor's cultivation of virtue within a systems perspective (Nakamura & Condren, 2018), the family of positive emotions (Graham, Thomson, Nakamura, Brandt, & Siegel, 2019), flow's life-span developmental trajectory (Tse, Nakamura, & Csikszentmihalyi, 2020), and more.

## Positive Psychology and Efficacy Beyond Self

Positive psychology is sometimes misunderstood as a movement that eschews recognition of the negative aspects of life. Positive psychology is occasionally cast as a viewpoint that unflinchingly adheres to a positive evaluation and smiling emojis. In this view, positive psychologists all would be saying: "if you don't have something nice to say, don't say anything at all."

I believe a more accurate view understands positive psychology as a branch of psychology that seeks to promote human flourishing. Acknowledging problems openly – especially with the goal to then solve the problems – is one way to promote flourishing. Positive psychology does not deny that challenges exist. Research supports using a positive lens to see and frame problems and thereby guide the work toward solutions.

Consistent with this characterization of positive psychology is Langer's (2005) guidance toward mindfulness in the process of all judgement and evaluation. Mindfulness, according to Langer, is a flexible state of mind with an openness to novelty. Situated in the present, mindfulness appreciates situation and perspective. The mindful person is willing to accept uncertainty and also willing to embrace imperfections. "By becoming less judgmental, we are likely to come to value other people and ourselves. All told, it would seem that being mindful would lead us to be optimistic, obviating the necessity for learning how to be positive" (p. 228).

In almost every study that my students and I conducted between 2007 and 2013, a strong positive correlation between well-being and empathy emerged. Whether we were studying time perspective, helping behavior, cyberspace positivity, role modeling, preschool teachers, Prop 8 voting behavior, the making of optimistic attributions, or framing personal challenges, we found the two constructs to be related. In the United States and elsewhere, self-reported empathy was consistently, significantly, and positively related to well-being.

The first two components of empathy are cognitive – comprehending the situation and understanding the other person's feelings. The third component and by far the most dynamic is sharing matched feelings (Feshbach & Kuchenbecker, 1974; Feshbach & Roe, 1968). Indeed, neuroscience research supports empathy's dual cognitive and affective contributions (Decety, 2011; Decety & Meltzoff, 2011; Hein & Singer, 2008) and most standard empathy measures, such as the interpersonal reactivity index (IRI; Davis, 1983), feature dual components – perspective taking and empathic concern.

While beyond the scope of this chapter, the association between empathy and well-being draws upon acceptance, mindfulness, and positive affect, which, as seen in other studies, expand resources and open social relationships (Fredrickson, Cohn, Coffey, Pek, & Finkel, 2008).

There are people who insist on one right way to live – a way they will argue is wholly positive. In our research, we found that a judgmental style was associated with limited empathy for others who are not like them (Jablonski & Kuchenbecker, 2008; Kuchenbecker, Cosme, Brown, & Pepino, 2009). And people with diminished empathy open the gateway to judging and visiting harm on others and can do so without any sense of guilt or self-sanction.

This is one of many insights offered by Bandura in his important monograph and later in his book on moral disengagement (1999, 2016). In the book, *Moral Disengagement*, Bandura admonishes: "to function humanely, societies must establish social systems that uphold compassion and curb cruelty ... whether carried out individually, organizationally or institutionally, it should be made difficult for people to delete humanity from their actions" (Bandura, 2016, p. 446).

Published in 2016, *Moral Disengagement* identifies eight common mechanisms whereby individuals and groups of people do harm to others, seemingly oblivious or ignoring the injuries they are inflicting. Bandura includes examples of moral disengagement in action from the tobacco, coal/oil, corporate, entertainment, gun industries, and more.

Moral agency is founded in a humanitarian ethic hallmarked by its dualistic foundation featuring proactive as well as inhibitive functions (Rorty, 1993). Moral engagement involves active self-monitoring committed to doing no harm and ideally helping others. Moral disengagement works by stripping away moral self-sanctions, allowing people to live in peace with themselves despite violating their own moral standards.

The eight mechanisms of moral disengagement are: (a) moral justification, (b) palliative favorable comparisons, (c) euphemistic language, (d) displacement of responsibility, (e) diffusion of responsibilities, (f) minimizing, ignoring, or denying harmful effects, (g) attribution of blame, and (h) dehumanization (Bandura, 2016; personal communication, March 30, 2020, "Widespread practices in all walks of life in which people violate their moral standards"). Bandura's book richly describes each, with across industry examples, but I will offer only a few.

First, in moral justification, people sanctify harmful actions by investing them with worthy social or moral purposes. For example, the US president claimed in late March 2020 that opening up the middle of America for business and trade was necessary in light of the certain catastrophic economic damage, despite medical experts' advice to the contrary. Never mind the lives that would be lost, the rationalization capitalizes on jobs, money, and economic loss.

Second, using palliative comparisons paint harmful conduct as benign or even altruistic through advantageous comparison, thus the harm one inflicts is minor compared with the harm others perpetuate. To exemplify, some industries demand removing all restrictions on US factory and auto emissions claiming the US emissions levels are better than China's. They say the United States cannot allow China to dominate the United States economically by cutting the US emissions any more than they already have.

The third mechanism allows harmful actions to be cloaked in euphemistic or innocuous language that removes the humanity. In the entertainment industry, for example, physical violence is labeled "action and adventure." In drone warfare, killing actions are cast in sports language with drone strikes called "touchdowns" and suspected terrorists who are on a list called "baseball card" (Bandura, 2017).

Fourth and fifth, in displacement of responsibility and diffusion of responsibilities people absolve themselves of personal accountability for harmful conduct by blaming someone else (e.g., their boss, wife, coworker) or spreading the accountability around so widely that no single person is to blame. For example, diesel cars give off more emissions and are banned in some European cities, but many countries have no bans, nor have any bans been made in US cities. The US auto industry argues that if people are still buying diesel vehicles and large SUVs with low miles per gallon, it is the will of the people, thus they are only conforming to what the people want. The gun industry continues to make guns with escalating lethal power, claiming it is only serving public demand.

Sixth, perpetuators of harm can minimize, ignore, deny, or misconstrue the consequences of their actions and thereby falsely keep their high self-regard intact. For example, many people claim to be "environmentally conscious," but will not use the correct bins for recycling, saying to themselves, "Really, my one straw, my one aluminum can, my one plastic bag won't make any difference."

The seventh moral disengagement mechanism is attributing blame to the victim. Here, the injured person or people are blamed for bringing the harm on themselves, thus the smoker with lung cancer is at fault. The more they smoked, the worse the harm, thus the lawyers reasoned, the tobacco industry was not to blame.

Last, dehumanization is done by removing the humanity from another person, distancing even attributing animalistic qualities to them. Belittling and name-calling are common. For example, silicosis in an occupational lung disease caused by inhaling silica dust, seen among workers in stonework, cement manufacturing, glassmaking, mining, road construction and more; the defense teams for those industries labeled the lawyers who brought lawsuits against them as "ambulance chasers," "racketeering lawyers," and the doctors were "quacks" (Hirth, 1936, in Bandura, 2016, p. 265).

Examples abound. Some current politicians are quick to label their opponents with demeaning nicknames. Such immature name calling serves to expose the name caller's moral disengagement and likely increases the schism between groups of swayable people. Regrettably, media is all too quick to perpetuate this role model of moral disengagement and the needed critical thinking practices of many people are sorely under-practiced.

Moral disengagement mechanisms often are combined as people seek to excuse themselves and their behavior. Moreover, moral disengagement occurs daily across all walks of life, across all countries, in social, political, financial, entertainment, educational, environmental, military, and all industries (Bandura, 2016, 2018).

In fact, the flip side of moral disengagement is moral engagement. Collective efficacy succeeds *because* each person *can* make a difference by working together. For the environment, we each can contribute to saving the planet by voting mindfully for measures/politicians supporting a global climate change vision committed to taking needed actions; by using our one recyclable straw, bag, and water bottle every day, taking one small action at a time individually, contributing – together! Such is the foundation of collective efficacy.

## Recognizing Challenges and Working for the Good

Acknowledging our many social problems, including overpopulation, disease spread, prejudice and discrimination, Bandura turned his attention to understanding the foundations to achieve widespread social change (Bandura, 2002). He partnered with

Miguel Sabido, creative producer of Televisia. The Population Communications International (PCI), Population Media Center (PCM), and researchers have been leaders in picking up this campaign and offer instrumental role models for tackling global problems positively (Poindexter, 2004; Ryerson, 1999). For example, honoring cultures, Sabido (1981) and their researchers enlist local leaders to identify their greatest community concerns and obstacles. They then create serial dramas, fashioning realistic characters and engaging plotlines with the target behavioral changes needed as the story curriculum to instigate social change (Papa et al., 2000). Notably, their story construction reflects both social cognitive theory, role models, change, and the values of human dignity, equitable opportunities in social practices, and shared human aspirations approved by the United Nations.

Reviewing the programs, Bandura (2008, 2011a) describes the very successful serial drama programs addressing national literacy in Mexico, family planning in Mexico and China, girls' and women's equality in China, India, and Africa, and HIV/AIDS transmission reduction in Tanzania, Kenya, and Ethiopia. Engaging characters (role models – positive, negative, and transitioning) and intersecting plotlines in Sudan, for example, addressed family planning education for daughters, injustices of forced marriage, early childbearing risks, preventing HIV infection and Muslim clerics denouncing female genital mutilation resulting in reduced incidences of all compared to match control communities without the programs.

Bandura underscores the profound real-world outcomes that these televised and radio programs achieve, showing such results as family planning contraceptive use increasing three-to-five-fold and some areas showing 58% increases compared to control communities (Westoff & Rodriguez, 1995). These research findings and many more support community action serial drama program efficacy and the capability of accomplishing social changes needed through educational programming based on social cognitive theory (Bandura, 2006b; McKusick, Coates, Morin, Pollack, & Hoff, 1990; Rogers et al., 1999; Singhal, Cody, Rogers, & Sabido, 2004; Singhal & Rogers, 1999; Vaughan, Rogers, Singhal, & Swalehe, 2000).

Most recently, Bandura has turned to the climate crisis. In a review published in the *American Psychologist*, he argues that the greatest challenge facing humanity in early 2020 is preserving a habitable planet (Bandura, personal communication 2020). Ecological support systems loss threatens our future led by factors including deforestation, desertification, topsoil erosion, decreased fertile farm land, floods, extreme weather, and massive loss of biodiversity, all precipitously related to global warming (Bandura, 2016). We have less than two decades left to take the needed actions to halt downward spiraling planet changes (Plumer, 2019).

The mass youth protests across the United States calling for sensible gun reform highlighted the power of the youth to take action (March, 2018). Bandura recognized the youths' perspective that the adult generations has had decades of failing stewardship for our planet earth marked by inertia and irresponsibility.

Bandura identified youth leadership as a key and agentically promoted the plan for a solution (Bandura, 2018, 2019, personal communication 2020). The plan includes the three psychosocial components working in concert. First, he brought the theoretical model to the fore, that is, the social cognitive theory. Second, he presented the translational and implementation conversion of theory into an innovative program (content, strategy, mode); and third, he presented the social diffusion method using diverse social media. To do this, Bandura joined with Lynne Cherry and *Young Voices for the Planet* (YVP) in celebrating the power of youth and their potential to right our decades of irresponsibility. The YVP video series – which can be accessed on their website (www.youngvoicesfortheplanet. com) – features brief videos of children sharing their community action stories demonstrating (role modeling) their power to achieve climate change initiatives around the world (Bandura & Cherry, 2020).

In so doing, Bandura's life's work presents a roadmap for our positive psychology community. Circling back to Bandura, in Ross and Ross's early studies, individuals *and* communities learn by observing role models. The serial dramas Bandura and Sabido created addressing identified community problems offer one set of examples. The YVP video series offers another. Phil Zimbardo's Heroic Imagination Project (HIP), offering training programs around the world on seven social psychology problems offers yet one more (Zimbardo, 2020). What social actions do you think are needed in your community? Listen to youth. Support youth endeavors.

Second, past mastery experiences contribute to efficacy. Both individuals and community share a boost from past successes. Recalling that efficacy is task/action specific, be willing to search out multiple role models for guided action and enlist youth and experienced people when possible. Persevere in the face of challenges!

Third, behavior and efficacy can be increased through encouragement. Cheering each other along helps, plus many countries' governments offer grants and subsidies for initiatives that they believe are important. So do private philanthropic organizations. Many are building programs using these funds. What more might we do to utilize and share these resources as a community?

Finally, for individuals, the physiological state at the time influences willingness to take action. As a community, we must look at our global well-being in relation to depleted natural resources, threatened biodiversity, unclean water, climate change, and the short-sighted decisions of many governments. We, as a positive psychology community all committed to human flourishing, have strength working together. Our strength is in our community and our collective efficacy. We must attend to the environment; "that's the only thing worth attending to because otherwise, we're going to pass on an unlivable environment" (A. Bandura, personal communication, December 17, 2020).

Self-efficacy and collective efficacy cannot be disambiguated. Unless people feel hope, they will not act. But without action – taken by individuals in concert with others around the globe – the future will indeed become hopeless. If you want change, you have to do it collectively. "Considering the pressing worldwide problems that loom ahead, people can ill afford to trade efficacious endeavors for public apathy or mutual immobilization. The times call for social initiatives that build people's sense of collective efficacy to influence the conditions that shape their lives and those of future generations" (Bandura, 1997, p. 525.)

Now is the moment to act, efficaciously, beyond the self – together – collectively.

## References

American Psychological Association. (2002). *Eminent psychologists of the 20th century.* Washington, DC: Author. Retrieved from https://www.apa.org/monitor/julaug02/eminent.

Bandura, A. (1976). *Social learning theory.* Englewood Cliffs, NJ: Prentice-Hall.

Bandura, A. (1986). *Social foundations of thought and action: A social cognitive theory.* Englewood Cliffs, NJ: Prentice-Hall.

Bandura, A. (1997). *Self-efficacy: The exercise of control.* New York: W. H. Freeman.

Bandura, A. (1999). Moral disengagement in the perpetration of inhumanities. *Personality and Social Psychology Review, 3,* 193–209. (Special issue on evil and violence.)

Bandura, A. (2002). Environmental sustainability by sociocognitive deceleration of population growth. In P. Schmuck & W. Schultz (Eds.), *The psychology of sustainable development* (pp. 209–238). Dordrecht, Netherlands: Kluwer.

Bandura, A. (2006a). Toward a psychology of human agency. *Perspectives on Psychological Science, 1,* 164–180.

Bandura, A. (2006b). Going global with social cognitive theory: From prospect to paydirt. In S. I. Donaldson, D. E. Berger, & K. Pezdek (Eds.), *Applied psychology: New frontiers and rewarding careers* (pp. 53–79). Mahwah, NJ: Lawrence Erlbaum.

Bandura, A. (2008). An agentic perspective on positive psychology. In S. J. Lopez (Ed.), *Positive psychology: Exploring the best in people* (Vol. 1, pp. 167–196). New York: Praeger.

Bandura, A. (2011a). A social cognitive perspective on positive psychology. *Revista de Psicologia Social, 26*(1), 7–20.

Bandura, A. (2011b). But what about that gigantic elephant in the room? In R. Arkin (Ed.), *Most underappreciated: 50 prominent social psychologists describe their most unloved work* (pp. 51–59). Oxford: Oxford University Press.

Bandura, A. (2016). *Moral disengagement: How people do harm and live with themselves.* New York: Worth.

Bandura, A. (2017). Disengaging morality from robotic war. *The Psychologist, 38–45.*

Bandura, A. (2018). Toward a psychology of human agency: Pathways and reflections. *Perspectives on Psychological Science, 13,* 130–136.

Bandura, A. (2019). Applying theory for human betterment. *Perspectives on Psychological Science, 14,* 12–15.

Bandura, A., Blanchard, E. B., & Ritter, B. (1969). Relative efficacy of desensitization and modeling approaches for inducing behavioral, affective, and attitudinal changes. *Journal of Personality and Social Psychology, 13*(3), 173–199.

Bandura, A., & Cherry, L. (2020). Enlisting the power of youth for climate change. *American Psychologist, 75*(7), 945–951.

Bandura, A., Jeffery, R. W., & Gajdos, E. (1975). Generalizing change through participant modeling with self-directed mastery. *Behaviour Research and Therapy, 13,* 141–152.

Bandura, A., Pastorelli, C., Barbaranelli, C., & Caprara, G. V. (1999). Self-efficacy pathways to childhood depression. *Journal of Personality and Social Psychology, 76,* 258–269.

Bandura, A., Ross, D. M., & Ross, S. A. (1961). Transmission of aggression through imitation of aggressive models. *Journal of Abnormal and Social Psychology, 63*(3), 575–582.

Bandura, A., Ross, D. M., & Ross, S. A. (1963a). Imitation of film-mediated aggressive models. *Journal of Abnormal and Social Psychology, 66,* 3–11.

Bandura, A., Ross, D. M., & Ross, S. A. (1963b). A comparative test of the status envy, social power, and secondary reinforcement theories of identificatory learning. *Journal of Abnormal and Social Psychology, 67*(6), 527–534.

Bandura, A., Ross, D. M., & Ross, S. A. (1963c). Vicarious reinforcement and imitative learning. *Journal of Abnormal and Social Psychology, 67,* 601–607.

Bandura, A., & Walters, R. H. (1959). *Adolescent aggression: A study of the influence of child-training practices and family interrelationships.* New York: Ronald Press.

Bandura, A., & Walters, R. H. (1963). *Social learning and personality development.* New York: Holt, Rinehart & Winston.

Baron-Cohen, S. (1994a). How to build a baby that can read minds: Cognitive mechanisms in mindreading. *Cahiers de Psychologie Cognitive/Current Psychology of Cognition, 13,* 513–552.

Baron-Cohen, S. (1994b). The mindreading system: New directions for research. *Cahiers de Psychologie Cognitive/Current Psychology of Cognition, 13,* 724–750.

Barrett, L. F., Adolphs, R., Marsella, S., Martinez, A. M., & Pollak, S. D. (2019). Emotional expressions reconsidered: Challenges to inferring emotion from human facial movements. *Psychological Science in the Public Interest, 20*(1), 1–68.

Betz, N. E., & Hackett, G. (1986). Applications of self-efficacy theory to understanding career choice behavior. *Journal of Social and Clinical Psychology, 4,* 279–289.

Bowlby, J. (1952). *Maternal care and mental health (World Health Organization monograph series, 20).* Geneva, Switzerland: World Health Organization. Retrieved from http://apps.who.int/iris/handle/10665/40724.

Bowlby, J. (1958). The nature of the child's tie to his mother. *The International Journal of Psychoanalysis, 39,* 350–373.

Bronfenbrenner, U. (1979). *The ecology of human development.* Cambridge, MA: Harvard University Press.

Bronfenbrenner, U. (1994). Ecological models of human development. In T. Husen & T. N. Postletwaite (Eds.), *International encyclopedia of education* (2nd ed., Vol. 3, pp. 1643–1647). Oxford: Elsevier.

Bronfenbrenner, U. (1999). Environments in developmental perspective: Theoretical and operational models. In S. L. Friedman & T. D. Wachs (Eds.), *Measuring environment across the life span: Emerging methods and concepts* (1st ed., pp. 3–28). Washington DC: American Psychological Association.

Campos, J. J., Campos, R. G., & Barrett, K. C. (1989). Emergent themes in the study of emotional development and emotion regulation. *Developmental Psychology, 25*(3), 394–402.

Caprara, G. V., Barbaranelli, C., Pastorelli, C., Bandura, A., & Zimbardo, P. G. (2000). Prosocial foundations of children's academic achievement. *Psychological Science, 11*(4), 302–306.

Caprara, G., & Pastorelli, C. (1993). Early emotional instability, prosocial behaviour, and aggression: Some methodological aspects. *European Journal of Personality, 7,* 19–36.

Carducci, B., Riggio, R., Zimbardo, P., & Kuchenbecker, S. Y. (2015). *The demise of guys.* Invited symposium presented at the 14th European Congress of Psychology. Milan, Italy.

Climate Action Tracker. (2020). Effect of the US withdrawal from the Paris Agreement. Retrieved March 27, 2020, from https://climateactiontracker.org/press/effect-of-the-us-withdrawal-from-the-paris-agreement.

Davis, M. H. (1983). Measuring individual differences in empathy: Evidence for a multidimensional approach. *Journal of Personality and Social Psychology, 44*(1), 113–126.

Decety, J. (2011). Dissecting the neural mechanisms mediating empathy. *Emotion Review, 3*(1), 92–108.

Decety, J., & Meltzoff, A. N. (2011). Empathy, imitation and the social brain. In A. Coplan & P. Goldie (Eds.), *Empathy: Philosophical and psychological perspectives* (pp. 58–81). Oxford: Oxford University Press.

Diener, E., Oishi, S., & Park, J. Y. (2014). An incomplete list of eminent psychologists of the modern era. *Archives of Scientific Psychology, 2,* 20–32.

Diener, E., Oishi, S., & Tay, L. (2018). Advances in subjective well-being research. *Nature Human Behaviour, 2,* 253–260.

Eisenberg, N., & Mussen, P. H. (1989). *The roots of prosocial behavior in children.* New York: Cambridge University Press.

Ekman, P. (1992). Facial expressions of emotion: New findings, new questions. *Psychological Science, 3*(1), 34–38.

Ekman, P. (1993). Facial expression and emotion. *American Psychologist, 48*(4), 384–392.

Ekman, P. (2011). The face suite (earlier version of METT and SETT training). Purchased and used with permission from P. Ekman. Retrieved from http://www.paulekman.com/product-category/research-products.

Ekman, P., & Friesen, W. V. (1975). *Unmasking the face.* Englewood Cliffs, NJ: Prentice Hall.

Ekman, P., & Friesen, W. V. (1976). Measuring facial movement. *Environmental Psychology and Nonverbal Behavior, 1*(1), 56–75.

Ekman, P., Friesen, W. V., O'Sullivan, M., Chan, A., Diacoyanni-Tarlatzis, I., Heider, K., . . . Tzavaras, A. (1987). Universals and cultural differences in the judgments of facial expressions of emotion. *Journal of Personality and Social Psychology, 53*(4), 712–717.

Ekman, P., Levenson, R. W., & Friesen, W. V. (1983). Autonomic nervous system activity distinguishes among emotions. *Science, 221*(4616), 1208–1210.

Farroni, T., Johnson, M. H., Menon, E., Zulian, L., Faraguna, D., & Csibra, G. (2005). Newborns' preference for face-relevant stimuli: Effects of contrast polarity. *Proceedings of the National Academy of Sciences, 102*(47), 17245–17250.

Feldman, R. (2015). The adaptive human parental brain: Implications for children's social development. *Trends in Neurosciences, 38*(6), 387–399.

Feldman, R. (2016). The neurobiology of mammalian parenting and the biosocial context of human caregiving. *Hormones and Behavior, 77,* 3–17.

Feldman, R., Gordon, I., Influs, M., Gutbir, T., & Ebstein, R. P. (2013). Parental oxytocin and early caregiving jointly shape children's oxytocin response and social reciprocity. *Neuropsychopharmacology, 38*(7), 1154–1162.

Feldman, R., Weller, A., Zagoory-Sharon, O., & Levine, I. (2007). Evidence for neuroendocrinological foundations of human affiliation: Plasma oxytocin levels across pregnancy and the postpartum period predict mother–infant bonding. *Psychological Science, 18*(11), 965–970.

Feshbach, N., & Feshbach, S. (1982). Empathy training and the regulation of aggression: Potentialities and limitations. *Academic Psychological Bulletin, 4,* 399–413.

Feshbach, N. D., & Kuchenbecker, S. Y. (1974). *A three-component model of empathy (ERIC Number: ED 101-242).* Paper presented as part of an invited symposium on The Concept of Empathy: Bond between Cognition and Social Behavior at the annual meeting of American Psychological Association, New Orleans, Louisiana.

Feshbach, N. D., & Roe, K. (1968). Empathy in six- and seven-year-olds. *Child Development, 39*(1), 133–145.

Field, T. M., Schanberg, S. M., Scafidi, F., Bauer, C. R., Vega-Lahr, N., Garcia, R., . . . Kuhn, C. M. (1986). Tactile/kinesthetic stimulation effects on preterm neonates. *Pediatrics, 77*(5), 654–658.

Fredrickson, B. L., Cohn, M. A., Coffey, K. A., Pek, J., & Finkel, S. M. (2008). Open hearts build lives: Positive emotions, induced through loving-kindness meditation, build consequential personal resources. *Journal of Personality and Social Psychology, 95*(5), 1045–1062.

Graczyk, P., Matjasko, J., Weissberg, R., Greenberg, M., Elias, M., & Zins, J. (2000). The role of the collaborative to advance social and emotional learning (CASEL) in supporting the implementation of quality school-based prevention programs. *Journal of Educational and Psychological Consultation, 11*(1), 3–6.

Graham, L. E., Thomson, A. L., Nakamura, J., Brandt, I. A., & Siegel, J. T. (2019). Finding a family: A categorization of enjoyable emotions. *The Journal of Positive Psychology, 14*(2), 206–229.

Gross, J. J. (2015). Emotion regulation: Current status and future prospects. *Psychological Inquiry, 26*(1), 1–26.

Gross, J. J., & John, O. P. (2003). Individual differences in two emotion regulation processes: Implications for affect, relationships, and well-being. *Journal of Personality and Social Psychology, 85,* 348–362.

Gross, J. J., & Muñoz, R. F. (1995). Emotion regulation and mental health. *Clinical Psychology: Science and Practice, 2,* 151–164.

Harlow, H. F. (1958). The nature of love. *American Psychologist, 13*(12), 673–685.

Harlow, H. F. (1962). Development of affection in primates. In E. L. Bliss (Ed.), *Roots of behavior* (pp. 157–166). New York: Harper.

Harlow, H. F., Dodsworth, R. O., & Harlow, M. K. (1965). Total social isolation in monkeys. *Proceedings of the National Academy of Sciences, 54*(1), 90–97.

Harlow, H. F., & Suomi, S. J. (1971). Social recovery by isolation-reared monkeys. *Proceedings of the National Academy of Sciences, 68*(7), 1534–1538.

Hein, G., & Singer, T. (2008). I feel how you feel but not always: The empathic brain and its modulation. *Current Opinions in Neurobiology, 18*(2), 153–158.

Helliwell, J. F., Layard, R., & Sachs, J. D. (Eds.). (2019). *World happiness report – 2019.* New York: Sustainable Development Solutions Network.

Hess, R. D., & Shipman, V. C. (1965). Early experience and the socialization of cognitive modes in children. *Child Development, 36*(4), 869–886.

Hoffman, M. (1975). Altruistic behavior and the parent–child relationship. *Journal of Personality and Social Psychology, 31,* 937–943.

Holahan, C. K., & Holahan, C. J. (1987). Self-efficacy, social support, and depression in aging: A longitudinal analysis. *Journal of Gerontology, 42,* 65–68.

Holt-Lunstad, J. (2017). The potential public health relevance of social isolation and loneliness: Prevalence, epidemiology, and risk factors. *Public Policy & Aging Report, 27*(4), 127–130.

Holt-Lunstad, J. (2018a). Why social relationships are important for physical health: A systems approach to understanding and modifying risk and protection. *Annual Review of Psychology, 69,* 437–458.

Holt-Lunstad, J. (2018b). Relationships and physical health. In A. L. Vangelisti & D. Perlman (Eds.), *The Cambridge handbook of personal relationships* (pp. 449–463). Cambridge: Cambridge University Press.

Holt-Lunstad, J., Ditzen, B., & Light, K. C. (2019). Oxytocin, social relationships, and health: An introduction to the special issue. *International Journal of Psychophysiology, 136,* 1–4.

Holt-Lunstad, J., Smith, T. B., & Layton, J. B. (2010). Social relationships and mortality risk: A meta-analytic review. *PLoS Medicine, 7,* Article e1000316.

Izard, C. E. (1990). Facial expressions and the regulation of emotions. *Journal of Personality and Social Psychology, 58,* 487–498.

Jablonski, J., & Kuchenbecker, S. (2008). Empathy and/or personal experience related to decreased sexual orientation discrimination. *Poster presented at the 88th annual meeting of Western Psychological Association (WPA),* Irvine, California.

Kakkar, H., & Sivanathan, N. (2017a). When the appeal of a dominant leader is greater than a prestige leader. *PANAS, 114*(26), 6734–6739.

Kakkar, H., & Sivanathan, N. (2017b, August 11). Why we prefer dominant leaders in uncertain times. *Harvard Business Review.* Retrieved March 27, 2020, from https://hbr.org/2017/08/why-we-prefer-dominant-leaders-in-uncertain-times.

Keltner, D., & Lerner, J. S. (2010). Emotion. In S. T. Fiske, D. T. Gilbert, & G. Lindzey (Eds.), *Handbook of social psychology* (5th ed., Vol. 1, pp. 317–352.) Hoboken, NJ: Wiley.

Keltner, D., Sauter, D., Tracy, J., & Cowen, A. (2019). Emotional expression: Advances in basic emotion theory. *Journal of Nonverbal Behavior, 43*(2), 133–160.

Khurshudyan, I. (2020, November 11). Putin once told Russians he did not want to be the "eternal president." Now it appears he does. Washington Post. Retrieved March 26, 2020, from https://www.washingtonpost.com/world/europe/putin-once-told-russians-he-didnt-want-to-be-the-eternal-president-now-it-appears-he-does/2020/03/11/5391b5f0-638e-11ea-8a8e-5c5336b32760_story.html.

Kuchenbecker, S. Y. (1976). *A developmental investigation of children's behavioral, cognitive, and affective responses to empathically stimulating situations (Doctoral dissertation).* University of California, Los Angeles.

Kuchenbecker, S. Y. (1977). *A personality trait of empathy in children? Paper presented in a symposium with Daryl Bem and Andrea Allen at the annual meeting of the American Psychological Association*, San Francisco, CA.

Kuchenbecker, S. Y. (2000). *Raising winners: A parent's guide to helping kids succeed on and off the playing field*. New York: Crown Random House.

Kuchenbecker, S. Y., Cosme, D., Brown, B., & Pepino, C. (2009). *Empathy, open-mindedness, well-being: Prop 8 voting behavior, and political party affiliation*. Presented at the presidential theme poster session: Emotional Ups and Downs at the 21st Annual Convention of American Psychological Society (APS), San Francisco, CA.

Kuchenbecker, S. Y., Rigg, C., Weglarz, C., Alvarez, E., Fleming, K., Ribera, S., . . . French, M. (1999). *Who's a winner? Coaches' views of winning young athletes*. Poster presented at the annual meeting of American Psychological Association, Boston, MA.

Kyriazos, T. A., & Stalikas, A. (2018). Positive parenting or positive psychology parenting? Towards a conceptual framework of positive psychology parenting. *Psychology, 9*, 1761–1788.

Langer, E. (2005). Well-being: Mindfulness versus positive evaluation. In C. R. Snyder & S. J. Lopez (Eds.), *Handbook of positive psychology* (pp. 214–230). New York: Oxford University Press.

Lewis, G. (2020). Reducing global catastrophic biological risks. 80,000 Hours. Retrieved March 28, 2020, from https://80000hours.org/problem-profiles/global-catastrophic-biological-risks.

Lwi, S. J., Haase, C. M., Shiota, M. N., Newton, S. L., & Levenson, R. W. (2019). Responding to the emotions of others: Age differences in facial expressions and age-specific associations with relational connectedness. *Emotion, 19*(8), 1437–1449.

Maccoby, E. E., & Jacklin, C. N. (1974). *The psychology of sex differences*. Stanford, CA: Stanford University Press.

Maslow, A. H. (1943). A theory of human motivation. *Psychological Review, 50*(4), 370–396.

Maslow, A. H. (1971). *The farther reaches of human nature*. New York: Viking Press.

McKusick, L., Coates, T. J., Morin, S. F., Pollack, L., & Hoff, C. (1990). Longitudinal predictors of reductions in unprotected anal intercourse among gay men in San Francisco: The AIDS behavioral research project. *American Journal of Public Health, 80*, 978–983.

McRae, K., & Gross, J. J. (2020). Emotion regulation. *Emotion, 20*(1), 1–9.

Meltzoff, A. N. (1990a). Towards a developmental cognitive science: The implications of cross-modal matching and imitation for the development of representation and memory in infancy. *Annals of the New York Academy of Sciences, 608*, 1–37.

Meltzoff, A. N. (1990b). Foundations for developing a concept of self: The role of imitation in relating self to other, and the value of social mirroring, social modeling, and self-practice in infancy. In D. Cicchetti & M. Beeghly (Eds.), *The self in transition: Infancy to childhood (The John D. and Catherine T. MacArthur foundation series on mental health and development, pp. 139–164)*. Chicago, IL: University of Chicago Press.

Meltzoff, A. N., & Decety, J. (2003). What imitation tells us about social cognition: A rapprochement between developmental psychology and cognitive neuroscience. *Philosophical Transactions B, 358*, 491–500.

Meltzoff, A. N., & Moore, M. K. (1977). Imitation of facial and gestures by manual human neonates. *Science, 198*(4312), 75–78.

Murphy, L. (1937). *Social behavior and child personality: An exploratory study on some roots of sympathy*. New York: Columbia University Press.

Mussen, P., & Eisenberg-Berg, N. (1977). *Roots of caring, sharing, and helping: The development of prosocial behavior in children*. San Francisco, CA: Freeman.

Nakamura, J., & Condren, M. (2018). A systems perspective on the role mentors play in the cultivation of virtue. *Journal of Moral Education, 47*(3), 316–332.

Nozadi, S. S., Spinrad, T. L., Johnson, S. P., & Eisenberg, N. (2018). Relations of emotion-related temperamental characteristics to attentional biases and social functioning. *Emotion, 18*(4), 481–492.

Papa, M. J., Singhal, A., Law, S., Pant, S., Sood, S., Rogers, E. M., & Shefner-Rogers, C. L. (2000). Entertainment-education and social change: an analysis of parasocial interaction, social learning, collective efficacy, and paradoxical communication. *Journal of Communication, 5,* 31–55.

Parsons, C. E., Young, K. S., Murray, L., Stein, A., & Kringelbach, M. L. (2010). The functional neuroanatomy of evolving parent–infant relationship. *Progress in Neurobiology, 91*(3), 220–241.

Parsons, C. E., Young, K. S., Parsons, E., Stein, A., & Kringelbach, M. L. (2011). Listening to infant distress vocalizations enhances effortful motor performance. *Acta Paediatrica, 101*(4), e189–e191.

Plumer, B. (2019, May 6). Humans are speeding extinction and altering the natural world at an "unprecedented" pace. *The New York Times.* Retrieved from https://www.nytimes.com/2019/05/06/climate/biodiversity-extinction-united-nations.html.

Poindexter, D. O. (2004). A history of entertainment-education, 1958–2000: The origins of entertainment-education. In A. Singhal, M. J. Cody, E. M. Rogers, & M. Sabido (Eds.), *Entertainment-education and social change: History, research, and practice* (pp. 21–32). Mahwah, NJ: Lawrence Erlbaum.

Riem, M. M., Bakermans-Kranenburg, M. J., Pieper, S., Tops, M., Boksem, M. A., Vermeiren, R. R., . . . Rombouts, S. A. (2011). Oxytocin modulates amygdala, insula, and inferior frontal gyrus responses to infant crying: A randomized controlled trial. *Biological Psychiatry, 70*(3), 291–297.

Rogers, E. M., Vaughan, P. W., Swalehe, R. M. A., Rao, N. I., Svenkerud, P., & Sood, S. (1999). Effects of an entertainment-education radio soap opera on family planning behavior in Tanzania. *Studies in Family Planning, 30,* 193–211.

Rorty, A. O. (1993). What it takes to be good. In G. Noam & T. E. Wren (Eds.), *The moral self* (pp. 28–55). Cambridge, MA: MIT Press.

Ryerson, W. N. (1999). Population Media Center. Retrieved from https://www.populationmedia.org.

Sabido, M. (1981). *Towards the social use of soap opera.* Mexico City: Institute for Communication Research.

Schanberg, S., & Field, T. (1988). Maternal deprivation and supplemental stimulation. In T. Field, P.

McCabe, & N. Schneiderman (Eds.), *Stress and coping across development* (pp. 112–119). Hillsdale, NJ: Lawrence Erlbaum.

Schweizer, S., Gotlib, I., & Blakemore, S.-J. (2020). The role of affective control in emotion regulation during adolescence. *Emotion, 20*(1), 80–86.

Sears, R. R., Maccoby, E. E., & Levin, H. (1957). *Patterns of child rearing.* Evanston, IL: Row, Peterson.

Singhal, A., Cody, M. J., Rogers, E. M., & Sabido, M. (Eds.). (2004). *Entertainment-education and social change: History, research, and practice.* Mahwah, NJ: Lawrence Erlbaum.

Singhal, A., & Rogers, E. M. (1999). *Entertainment-education: A communication strategy for social change.* Mahwah, NJ: Lawrence Erlbaum.

Sivanathan, N., & Kakkar, H. (2017). Explaining the global rise of "dominance" leadership. *Scientific American.*

Skeels, H. M., & Dye, H. A. (1939). A study of the effects of differential stimulation on mentally retarded children. *Proceedings of the American Association on Mental Deficiency, 44,* 114–136.

Spitz, R. A., & Wolf, K. M. (1946). Anaclitic depression: An inquiry into the genesis of psychiatric conditions in early childhood. *The Psychoanalytic Study of the Child, 2,* 313–342.

Staub, E. (1971). Helping a person in distress: The influence of implicit and explicit "rules" of conduct on children and adults. *Journal of Personality and Social Psychology, 17,* 137–145.

Strack, F., Martin, L. L., & Stepper, S. (1988). Inhibiting and facilitating conditions of the human smile: A nonobtrusive test of the facial feedback hypothesis. *Journal of Personality and Social Psychology, 54,* 768–777.

Thompson, R. A. (1994). Emotion regulation: A theme in search of definition. *Monographs of the Society for Research in Child Development, 59,* 25–52.

Tse, D. W., Nakamura, J., & Csikszentmihalyi, M. (2020). Beyond challenge-seeking and skill-building: Toward the lifespan developmental perspective on flow theory. *The Journal of Positive Psychology, 15*(2), 171–182.

United Nations Intergovernmental Panel on Climate Change. (2018). *UN climate change: Annual Report – 2018.* Bonn, Germany: UNFCC.

Vaughan, P. W., Rogers, E. M., Singhal, A., & Swalehe, R. M. A. (2000). Entertainment-education and HIV/AIDS prevention: A field experiment in Tanzania. *Journal of Health Communication, 5,* 81–100.

Westoff, C. F., & Rodriguez, G. (1995). The mass media and family planning in Kenya. *International Family Planning Perspectives, 21,* 26–36.

White, B. L. (1973). *Experience and environment: Major influences on the development of the young child* (Vol. 1). Englewood Cliffs, NJ: Prentice Hall.

Young, K. S., Parsons, C. S., Jegindoe Elmholdt, E.-M., Woolrich, E. W., Van Hartevelt, T. J., Stevner, A. B. A., . . . Kringelbach, M. L. (2016). Evidence for a caregiving instinct: Rapid differentiation of infant from adult vocalizations using magnetoencephalography. *Cerebral Cortex, 1309–1321.*

Zeldin, A. L., Britner, S. L., & Pajares, F. (2008). A comparative study of the self-efficacy beliefs of successful men and women in mathematics, science, and technology careers. *Journal of Research in Science Teaching, 45*(9), 1036–1058.

Zimbardo, P. (2020). The heroic imagination project: Train everyday heroes. Retrieved March 30, 2020, from https://heroicimaginationproject. squarespace.com.

Zimbardo, P., & Coulombe, N. (2016). *Man, interrupted: Why young men are struggling and what we can do about it.* Newburyport, MA: Red Wheel.

Zimbardo, P., & Duncan, N. (2012). *The demise of guys: Why boys are struggling and what we can do about it.* Amazon Kindle: https://www.amazon. com/Demise-Guys-Boys-Struggling-About-ebook/dp/B00850HTHO.

## 15

# Creating and Disseminating Positive Psychology Interventions: Going Viral to Staying Vital

Everett L. Worthington, Jr.

The purpose of this book is to bring together researchers on positive psychology to discuss current themes and research. In this chapter, I briefly review the history of development of the REACH Forgiveness intervention and summarize the intervention research on it. My intention is to use it as a case study to inform interventionists of ways they might create and promote positive psychology interventions. However, instead of reviewing a lot of research as the focal point, I will provide suggestions for developing interventions in general (based on some of my experiences) and then disseminating one's intervention as widely as possible – after it has been scientifically established as an evidence-based practice in positive psychology. This will involve dissemination through scientific publications and presentations, books, public speaking, web presence, local presence, and using principles of marketing. My intent is to marry scientifically respectable positive clinical psychology interventions with efforts to make those interventions available to the widest group of people. I confess that my title is a bit misleading. I actually have never made a positive psychology intervention actually go viral, if we literally mean getting over a half million hits on YouTube. But, I have created several well-used interventions within positive psychology, and those have been sustainable.

While I don't want to come across as a crotchety old obscure uncle handing out who-asked-for-*that* advice, I do want to provide ideas that are both helpful and practical for you if you wish to create a positive psychology intervention that is widely disseminated. The target audiences of this book are undergraduates, graduate students, academicians, and basic and clinical researchers who study positive psychology. So, if you are early in your career, perhaps this chapter can set

*Positive Psychology: An International Perspective*, First Edition.
Edited by Aleksandra Kostić and Derek Chadee.
© 2021 John Wiley & Sons Ltd. Published 2021 by John Wiley & Sons Ltd.

you to creating interventions that are based on basic science, intervention science, and translational science (i.e., using basic research within evidence-based interventions). Then, perhaps you'll be inspired to study the efficacy of your intervention to establish it as an evidence-based positive psychological intervention. If you are midcareer or later, you might have already invested in developing and scientifically establishing an intervention. If so, great! I have spent the last year and a half reading and thinking about how to disseminate such interventions, so I hope you'll find this helpful as well – though you might want to skip some of the more basic aspects of creating and testing your intervention.

## Creating Your Intervention

### REACH forgiveness: My focal intervention

After describing the forming of the REACH Forgiveness intervention based on my clinical practice, I describe its systematic elaboration. Over time and experience, I added components and conducted outcome studies to test the efficacy of results – including testing some individual components of the method. Finally, the REACH Forgiveness approach was fully developed (though it continues to be refined). Studies from other laboratories have provided independent outcome evaluations. A meta-analysis of 22 efficacy studies published through 2013 signified a general clinical scientific acceptability of the method (see Wade, Hoyt, Kidwell, & Worthington, 2014), so attention was turned to effectiveness (within various communities) and dissemination (McHugh & Barlow, 2012).

What is REACH Forgiveness? It is a brief positive psychological intervention that has been used by itself and within other interventions, in psychoeducation and psychotherapy formats, to help people forgive bothersome hurts and help people become generally more forgiving people. That is, it is concerned with building and exercising character strengths. The five steps to REACH emotional forgiveness are as follows:

R = Recall the hurt
E = Empathize (sympathize, feel compassion for, love) the transgressor
A = give an Altruistic gift of forgiveness
C = Commit to the emotional forgiveness one experienced
H = Hold on to forgiveness when doubts arise

The REACH Forgiveness intervention by itself is primarily available in two formats – as a psychoeducational group intervention and as a do-it-yourself workbook. Neither groups nor workbooks is targeted at a specific type of interpersonal transgression. Rather anyone can use them. The REACH Forgiveness intervention is also embedded within three other interventions. First, the hope-focused approach (HFA) to couple enrichment and therapy (Ripley & Worthington, 2014;

Worthington, 2005) has two components (see Worthington et al., 2015). Handling Our Problems Effectively (HOPE) teaches skills at communication and conflict resolution. Forgiveness and Reconciliation through Experiencing Empathy (FREE) coaches couples in forgiveness (which incorporates REACH Forgiveness within it) and reconciliation. Second, the six steps to forgiving yourself intervention (Worthington, 2013), which uses a dual process model of responsible self-forgiveness (Griffin et al., 2015), uses the REACH Forgiveness acrostic applied to self-forgiveness. Third, community-based forgiveness awareness-raising campaigns, which have been tested within Christian communities but which could apply to any community, also employ the REACH Forgiveness (Griffin et al., 2019).

## Where Do Ideas for Interventions Come From?

Sometimes clinicians who have not developed interventions are intimidated by the prospect. They might prefer to stick with evidence-based practices already long-established or they want to develop their own intervention but think that a long process of basic research must be carried out to have an adequate empirical base for the intervention. Either way, they wonder where ideas to create interventions might originate.

### Practice

*Clients.* Many interventions I have developed came from my initial work with clients. For years, I had a small part-time (three cases) private practice in couple therapy. From those struggles trying to help specific couples deal with their relationship problems, I developed the beginning of the hope-focused couple approach for couple therapy and couple enrichment (Worthington, 2005). Dealing with clients and group members who were applying my suggestions required me to react to issues introduced by the couples or group members.

*Idealized theorizing.* When I develop an intervention, I try to think up hard questions and objections. That keeps me from too many unproductive rabbit trails once I take the intervention into the field. But when I try any fledgling intervention out with a troubled couple or a group, they often raise questions and problems that I have not anticipated.

### Teaching

*Teaching courses.* A teacher meets with a class face-to-face for about 45 hours each semester. I must say that those interactions have led to the creation and refinement of many positive psychology interventions. I have taught large lectures in Introductory Psychology, Positive Psychology (for undergraduates), Personal Adjustment, and Personality. I had to explain positive psychology to undergraduates, and that was great practice for communicating with clients, psychoeducational groups, public audiences, and people who use my interventions.

The Positive Psychology course was particularly helpful. I developed hope-focused approach (Worthington, 1989) and the REACH Forgiveness intervention (Worthington & DiBlasio, 1990) and had done multiple studies of each when positive psychology got underway. As positive psychology gained momentum, however, I put together a course for undergraduates as a senior finishing course, which I taught for 8 years. I billed positive psychology as "the positive half" of psychology. My lectures paralleled Introductory Psychology, but I found studies and theories of "positive psychology" before it was positive psychology. That course gave me a broad background in understanding character strengths and subjective well-being.

Moving from the general to the specific, I also taught a graduate seminar in "Forgiveness: Theory, Research, and Application" and an undergraduate "Spotlight on Research" course for seniors on "Forgiveness." Both courses helped me organize the material in my area of emphasis but beyond my own narrow research on forgiveness. Recently I taught an adult education commercial course on "The Science of Forgiveness and Reconciliation," which is marketed as a commercial course by Now You Know Media (Worthington, 2018). The point here is that teaching deepened my knowledge base of positive psychology and forced me to articulate clearly the ideas within positive psychology.

The graduate-level Psychological Assessment and Psychometrics course also helped with intervention. By teaching that course, I better learned how to create measures of positive psychology. By developing a measure we must understand its definition and composition. This adds to our understanding of positive psychological constructs and makes it easier to communicate to lay people within interventions – and in teaching and public talks.

## Graduate students, undergraduate students, and collaborators

I have had the privilege of advising and teaching many outstanding, award-winning, psychologists who have studied positive psychology in either basic or clinical science or both. Each of these has far surpassed what I can do. My mentoring strategy was to try to aim them and get out of their way and hold onto their coattails. With each of my graduate students, I have learned far more than I have taught. One thing with which I am most pleased in my career is that I have made these lifelong friends and still often collaborate with most. In more recent years, as I neared retirement, my laboratory at VCU collapsed as graduate students got their doctoral degrees. I established many international collaborations with highly talented professionals. Through these multinational, intercultural interactions I have also learned how I often needed to adjust interventions for culture.

## Reflection on life events

Life intrudes on our professional activities. After developing the REACH Forgiveness and the hope-focused approach, including doing many studies, writing conceptual articles, and even writing books about forgiveness and hope, my mother was murdered in January 1996. I had to practice what I was teaching others – maintain hope and forgive. My brother had discovered my mother's body, and he could never erase the images from his mind. Ten years later (May 2005), he committed suicide. I had already created some interventions to promote self-forgiveness, but dealing with the realities of my personal failures to help my brother when he needed it, I was able to deepen my understanding of self-condemnation and different ways of dealing with it, such as self-compassion, self-acceptance, and self-forgiveness. Even more recently, I have watched my wife Kirby's struggles with multiple physical degenerative problems and pain. I marvel at her strength, faith, and hope. Those observations have led to working on a new measure of hope – persistence in the face of what seems like intractable troubles with little perceived likelihood of achieving a positive outcome – at least on this side of life (Bury, Wenzel, & Woodyatt, 2016).

Life also provides a variety of wise models for us. These come often from family. My mother-in-law, Rena Canipe, was the basis for my scientific and intervention programs in humility. After years of observing my humble mother-in-law, I realized that other-reports of humility might be more trusted than one's self-report (Worthington, 2006). So, we developed other-report measures of relational humility (Davis, Worthington, & Hook, 2010; Davis et al. 2011), and we soon developed an intervention to promote humility (Lavelock et al., 2014, 2017).

Life challenges are difficult teachers. I must keep reminding myself that my experiences are not necessarily like the people's experiences who might seek an intervention. Yet, we can learn from personal reflection on struggles and from those who handle struggles well.

## Other reading

Ideas often come about because we intentionally attend to unrelated subject matter. For me, I gave up listening to country music in 2006, and thus I gave up all hope of finding out the resolution to life's mysteries of where a person's truck, dog, gun, and long-lost love ever come together. But – coping with these disappointments, I started listening in my car, on CD, to The Great Courses on history, art, music, philosophy, science, the humanities, and even a couple on psychology. I also read eclectically. Thinking about disparate topics spurs creativity. As scholars we forever run our experiences through a filter of our own research and practice. Life is a fertile ground for innovation in research, theory, and clinical intervention.

## Reading and doing basic science

I get many ideas for intervention from reading about and doing basic science on forgiveness, humility, relationships, and religion and spirituality. Now I am always seeking to do studies that overlap my three areas of research and practice. Can I study forgiveness in religious couples or humility in spiritually oriented families? When I read ideas in the basic science literature, I want to take the ideas into the laboratory and test them. Here are some examples.

*Injustice gap.* I developed the idea of the injustice gap (Davis et al., 2016; Worthington, 2003) when reading literature and doing studies on apology and restitution, restorative justice, organizational psychology, and forgiveness in couples. I saw common threads. When people were offended, they create an implicit accounting – the more injustice they dwelt on (i.e., the larger the injustice gap), the harder it was to deal with the injustice.

*Handling injustice.* Furthermore, people seemed to have multiple ways of handling injustice – by revenge, seeking or observing justice, turning the matter over to God, forbearing, accepting and moving on, and forgiving to name a few (Wade & Worthington, 2003). Different people employed different combinations of strategies. If an offender could reduce the size off the injustice gap using any of those strategies and could convince the offended partner that the offender would try not to repeat the offense, that reduced the size of the injustice gap and made it easier for the hurt person to forbear, accept, or forgive the offense.

*Interventions are time-dependent.* Another time when research informed intervention was thinking about the implications of the Wade et al. (2014) meta-analysis of all existing forgiveness interventions. Regardless of whose intervention we examined, seriously trying to forgive an offender brought about 0.1 standard deviations (SDs) per hour of forgiveness and increased hope similarly. Interventions also reduced anxiety and depression. That might be the most important finding (to date) in forgiveness intervention research. Forgiveness within an intervention is all about time!

The implications are practical. A clinician will not usually have 10 hours to work with a client on forgiveness. Insurance companies will not compensate for forgiveness therapy. Chances are that a clinician will have about two hours to work on forgiveness within a course of treatment. Partners in a group practice could constitute enough participants for a six-hour Saturday morning psychoeducational REACH Forgiveness group about once a month. Such a group would yield 0.6 SDs of forgiveness, 0.6 SDs of hope, and 0.3 SDs of improvement in depression and anxiety – at group rates for the patients. Or the patient could even be directed to go online at www.EvWorthington-forgiveness.com and download a six-hour do-it-yourself (DIY) workbook without cost, getting about the same benefits. Then, two hours of psychotherapy could be efficiently used to deal with forgiveness difficulties.

Interventions are not "natural"

An intervention's content is often drawn from basic science, but don't mistake the intervention for a natural process. There have been many interventions developed to promote forgiveness, for example. Yet, the processes that clinicians lead clients through are not like what happens in the natural not-psychotherapy-aided situation. McCullough, Luna, Berry, Tabak, and Bono (2010) assessed people who had been hurt or offended to seek to determine what happened with forgiveness as a natural process. They had students who had been hurt or offended come to the laboratory within the first few hours (and no longer than 24 hours) and be assessed for avoidant, revenge, and benevolent motives. McCullough et al. arrived at a wonderfully elegant curve representing the results – a power curve. The unforgiveness (sum of avoidant and revenge motives) was high at first, but within three or four days had fallen to about 10 to 15% of the initial value and after the unforgiveness declined sufficiently, the person began to have a sense of benevolent motives toward the offender.

But science is about averages, and individuals are different – as clinicians, clinical scientists, and basic scientists know. McCullough et al. (2010) showed graphs for individual participants. Most decreased in forgiveness quickly. However, others seemed not to change in unforgiving motivations at all, and some exploded into chronic or increasing rage or bitterness. Those are the people more often seen in psychotherapy – although having high unforgiveness is certainly no sure predictive criterion for seeking psychotherapy. Psychotherapy is expensive and time consuming. Many people just do not want to seek psychotherapy due to culture, stigma, family background, or simple time availability. Yet, those are the very people for whom an intervention might help.

An intervention does not tell us anything about what usually happens when people seek to forgive. How individuals respond is individual and variable (see McCullough et al., 2010). An intervention is an ordered set of *engineered* experiences. The interventionist walks a person through guided experiences, and at least 85% of the patients will eventually forgive.

## Turn Your Idea into an Actual Intervention

There is no substitute for using an intervention with people who are seeking help

As we move from an idea to a systematic method that can help many patients or participants, it is important to have tried using it with as many people as possible. I like to test interventions out in university classes (as applied exercises or home-work exercises), in workshops, with patients, with formal or informal groups, or with focus groups. In all of those I can get feedback about what does and does not work with the people I am seeking to help.

When I have worked out many of the bugs, I do an efficacy trial – usually comparing it to a waiting list, who also get the intervention after a suitable waiting time. The design is (using Stanley and Campbell's nomenclature with O as an observation point, and X as treatment):

$$O_D O_1 \quad X \quad O_2 \qquad O_3 \quad (IT)$$

$$O_D O_1 \qquad O_2 \quad X \quad O_3 \quad (WC)$$

In this particular design, I test all people the same week for demographics and person variables, $O_D$, and also give my measures I will use to track whether the intervention worked $O_1$. The immediate treatment (IT) condition gets the treatment (X), while the wait-list condition (WC) gets nothing. All participants are assessed again ($O_2$). Comparing the two conditions in change from $O_1$ to $O_2$ helps me see whether the treatment helps people improve relative to waiting. After that, the WC condition gets the treatment (X) and all are assessed at $O_3$, which helps me see whether the treatment will replicate. The IT condition gets nothing between $O_2$ and $O_3$. This helps me see whether the treatment gains are maintained over time.

Typically, I try to get such studies published in peer-reviewed journals to provide initial scientific validation. However, in the climate of clinical psychological science today, submitting a one-study article might not be enough. I usually try to include a second study replicating the first and often examining some personal characteristic in a treatment by personal attribute design is needed to assure reviewers that the effect is replicable.

If you are in clinical practice or don't have access to people in which to conduct a randomized controlled study, you can do an $N = 1$ study. This is not a case report. It reports outcomes of several individual cases. In each, the client is assessed multiple times. Perhaps, after five to ten individual clients, I might even have a sense of whether the intervention will work.

The most basic answer, then, to the question of how an idea is transformed into an intervention that you have confidence in is: gradually. The process is often trial and error and, though usually I can get some things right from the outset, I inevitably get things wrong. Let me illustrate this by using my REACH Forgiveness intervention.

## The initial development of REACH forgiveness: A case study

Throughout the 1980s, I was a full-time academician. Besides training and supervising counselors-in-training, I directed the MidLife Counseling Service, which was a department-based community clinic. I occasionally saw couples as a co-therapist with a student. I also saw about three couples a week in a part-time solo practice. From these experiences, I developed the hope-focused approach (HFA), which included promoting forgiveness and reconciliation. In 1990, Worthington and DiBlasio (1990) published a brief intervention that emphasized making a decision to forgive, which McCullough and Worthington (1995) tested in a one-hour intervention study. We compared it to telling groups self-benefit information – that it was good for their own mental and physical health to forgive. Ironically, the self-benefit condition out-performed the decision-based forgiveness intervention. For self-benefit, the pre- to postintervention change was about 0.2 SDs; for decision-based forgiving, the change was about 0.1 SDs.

McCullough, Worthington, and Rachal (1997) expanded the theory of forgiveness. We saw it as a decision to forgive plus empathy-stimulated altruism, giving an undeserved gift of forgiveness to an offender and thus experiencing some emotional transformation based on the altruism. Using an eight-hour version of a proto-REACH Forgiveness (mostly REA), we compared it to an eight-hour elaboration of the self-benefit intervention (again about 0.2 SDs of lasting change). For REA, the mean effect size for forgiveness measures was about 1.2 SDs at both postintervention and follow-up. Sandage added a necessary sense of humility to the treatment. We called this the empathy-humility-forgiveness model and tested it as a six-hour psychoeducational group against a six-hour self-benefit control group (Sandage & Worthington, 2010). The effect size for the treatment was about 0.6 SDs at both postintervention and follow-up; like the two previous studies, the lasting change of the self-benefit group was 0.2 SDs. In 1998, in a conceptual article, I added the necessity of committing to the forgiveness one experiences to enhance maintenance (Worthington, 1998a). Also, realizing that explicit attention to maintenance was needed, I added that as a fifth stage. That completed the five steps of REACH Forgiveness, but I called it a "pyramid model" (Worthington, 1998b) instead of "REACH Forgiveness."

As we reflect on the development of this clinical model, we note several things. First, it was a practical, clinically based model. Second, it grew organically. Third, with each addition, we put it to a limited test and used the feedback (clinical and research) to correct course. Fourth, we stayed alert to unanticipated findings, which resulted in at least three major modifications to the intervention. (a) When we found that helping people make a decision to forgive had a small but positive effect, we incorporated it in the model and shifted our emphasis from decision (McCullough & Worthington, 1995) to emotional forgiveness (McCullough et al., 1997). (b) When we found that our self-benefit control condition consistently produced 0.2 SDs of forgiveness, we incorporated it in the model. (c) When we found that maintenance required giving explicit attention to holding onto the forgiveness one had experienced, we added two steps to the model to commit to the forgiveness experience to better maintain gains. Fifth, clinically, we noticed that we needed to define forgiveness at the beginning of each intervention (Wade, Worthington, & Meyer, 2005). When we did not, people tended to verbally disagree about what forgiveness actually meant – often confusing it with reconciliation. Those disagreements derailed progress in REACH Forgiveness groups.

I have always admired people who could create an efficacious intervention instantly. Clinical geniuses like Milton H. Erickson, Jay Haley, or Salvadore Minuchin could pull this off. I could not. Progress comes by making clinical mistakes and getting feedback from my clinical supervisors, collaborators, clients, and basic and clinical science research studies.

## Systematic Efficacy Trials for REACH Forgiveness

With the intervention developed, we and other scientists conducted randomized controlled efficacy trials, which established the efficacy of REACH Forgiveness. By 2005, Wade et al. (2005) meta-analyzed over 44 studies involving 63 empirical tests from all interventions regardless of originator – some were actually control conditions like out self-benefit control – and we looked for evidence of commonality along the lines of the steps in the REACH Forgiveness method. The time spent in each intervention was correlated with outcome measures. Besides R, E, A, C, and H, we found two other steps: definition (D) and overcoming unforgiveness (OU; i.e., acceptance, forbearing, distraction, etc.). Correlations were as follows: D = 0.37; R = 0.43; E = 0.51; A = 0.32; C = 0.52; H = 0.29; and OU = 0.44.

By 2000, I had developed a life mission – to do all I can to promote forgiveness in every *willing* heart, home, and homeland. In 1998, I co-directed a John Templeton Foundation request for proposals for research on forgiveness. Over 100 proposals were submitted. About US$3 million was used to fund about 20. We formed a 501c(3) corporation, A Campaign for Forgiveness Research, and, as executive director, I helped with money to support others' research in forgiveness (about $6.4 million in seven years). That put me in frequent media contact, speaking about the science of forgiveness in general. Also, despite an active travel and speaking schedule, my scientific efforts at dissemination of the REACH Forgiveness intervention were passive. I published journal articles and books and expected that clinicians who were interested would find and use them and that clinicians would find and use REACH Forgiveness.

The meta-analysis of interventions by Wade et al. (2014) yielded several conclusions. First, REACH Forgiveness and Enright's process model of forgiveness were investigated equally often in randomized controlled trials (RCTs), and all other interventions combined were equal to the number of studies on each of those (about 22). Second, regardless of whose intervention was tested, the Cohen's *d* (number of effect sizes change in forgiveness relative to the control group) was about 0.1 per hour of intervention. Third, when anxiety, depression, and hope were assessed, changes in forgiveness were mirrored by lower anxiety and depression and increased hope, and the effect size was about 0.05 per hour of treatment. Thus, a 10-hour psychoeducational group to promote forgiveness would typically produce 1.0 SDs of improvement in forgiveness, 0.5 SDs lowering of anxiety and depression, and 1.0 SDs of increase in hope. (For perspective, 26 weeks of hourly cognitive-behavior therapy for anxiety or for depression will yield an effect size of about 1.2.) Fourth, while efficacy for most interventions had been established, the needs were for effectiveness and dissemination research. Almost no work had systematically examined moving interventions from the laboratory to the practitioner's office or to the wider community – which is effectiveness. The growth of forgiveness studies was continuing, but clearly something additional was needed to promote the findings more widely (McHugh & Barlow, 2012), which is dissemination.

## Disseminating Your Intervention

### Scientific publication and presentations

For most of us, dissemination of clinical science boils down to publishing empirical research on its efficacy. Perhaps, if we do a big study or a grant-funded study and our university public relations group puts out a press release, then we can have our 15 minutes of fame (in my case, more like a six-second sound bite) as we tout the findings. Besides articles, most of us use presentations at scientific conferences as a way to organize an early version of an article and getting the students a line on the CV. Another way to gain visibility for our interventions is to write chapters.

### Dissemination through books

Similarly, I have written almost 40 books. Those have included edited heavy tomes, books for practitioners, basic conceptual and theoretical books, and trade books for lay people. Each type makes dissemination inroads into an audience. Books have also been a great way for me to unify by thinking about basic research findings, theory, application, and dissemination. The common knowledge is that a book's prestige is inversely proportional to the number of copies sold. (If that were the case, I'd have a lot of prestige, because both of the people who have bought one of my books enjoyed it.) But besides disseminating to nonarticle-reading audiences, I find that book writing has been one of the most helpful things I do in honing interventions. I must systematically integrate basic and applied research, theory, and clinical and personal experience. And I must articulate the ideas coherently and simply.

### Dissemination through public speaking

I give workshops at professional organizations and universities, and I am invited often to speak or give workshops at professional counseling practices, which often organize continuing education training experiences for their own practitioners and those in the surrounding area. Presentations to practicing professionals are useful because they raise practical issues that lead to modifications in interventions so that they will actually be used in practice.

## Dissemination through local presence

If we wish to disseminate our intervention locally, we need to be present. That means local television, radio, podcasts, and word of mouth. We must cultivate the local network and keep email lists if we intend to get our intervention known within the local professional network, and especially if we expect to be known within a referral catchment area.

## Dissemination through web presence

These days, dissemination can usually mean putting our interventions on a webpage. Psychologists do not always do a good job at web presence. But perhaps this is just "projection" of my own web-naiveté to others. My first effort created websites that were centered on me. They marketed my intervention in an information-heavy format that provided the details of the intervention and the studies supporting it. But most people who go to the internet these days are attuned to the four-minute YouTube information video (seven minutes tops). When people are surfing, looking for interventions, often the effort they put toward understanding our website is what shows up on the Google page, and if they do click on our link, we have only a few seconds to hook them. How can we be better at this?

## Dissemination through application of marketing principles

By 2014, the efficacy of REACH Forgiveness had been well established, but I did not seem to be making as much headway in widely promoting REACH Forgiveness as I would have liked. I felt like practitioners were using it in practice, researchers were using it in RCTs, lay people were using it in their daily life, and people in non-USA countries and cultures were using it. REACH Forgiveness was becoming a "brand name" for use in psychoeducational groups, and both secular and Christian-accommodated versions had been shown to be efficacious. But clearly, it could be more widely disseminated.

Recently, I have thought about what makes things go viral and stay vital, reflecting the new wave of marketing on building perennial winners instead of short-term winners (see Ryan Holiday's [2017], *Perennial Seller*). Moving from establishing efficacy to dissemination necessitated that I change my focus from thinking primarily about translational research (i.e., from basic research on forgiveness to applying it) to reading about and applying marketing research. That sent me on a 2-year pilgrimage through marketing literature (see Table 15.1). In the following two sections, I trace a brief history of marketing ideas that positive psychologists can use to disseminate their psychological intervention.

**Table 15.1**    Marketing resources for the positive psychology interventionist.

| Author/s | Year | Main points |
| --- | --- | --- |
| Berger | 2013 | Getting ideas to become contagious. |
| Coker | 2016 | How to take internet advertising viral. |
| Gladwell | 2000 | What tips one idea to something that is qualitatively different from what it was previously. |
| Goldberg, Mazursky, and Solomon | 1999 | The fundamental templates of quality advertisements (article). |
| Heath and Heath | 2007 | Using cognitive psychology to show why some ideas survive (i.e., stick) and others die. |
| Heath and Heath | 2010 | Using cognitive psychology to show how to change things when change is hard. |
| Heath and Heath | 2013 | Using cognitive psychology to show how to make better choices in life and work. |
| Holiday | 2014 | A primer on the future of PR, marketing, and advertising. It's all going to be about a list of people who will instantly buy your idea. (Draws on Rogers's diffusion of information.) |
| Holiday | 2017 | The art of making and marketing work that lasts. Go for quality, not for fads. Find the right audience and match perfectly to that. |
| Miller | 2017 | Clarify your message so customers will listen. People want a story, and they are the central character. You are providing something to help them achieve their dreams. Don't sell your product. Get them to see that they can use your product to achieve what they want to accomplish. |
| Moore | 2014 | Getting ideas to go viral (i.e., cross the chasm). |
| Reis and Trout | 1986 | Marketing warfare. |
| Reis and Trout | 1993 | The 22 immutable laws of marketing as of 1993 – today, not so immutable. |
| Rogers | 2003 | Diffusion occurs because some jump on new ideas quickly; others require nudging; others require being sold; others will never come. Get the sure things and nudge and sell. |
| Sinek | 2009 | Begin with the deep purpose you want to accomplish, not the characteristics of your product. |

*Note*: Consult references section for the full reference.

## Going Viral

### The 22 (perhaps not so) immutable laws of marketing

In 1993, Reis and Trout wrote a classic book, *The 22 Immutable Laws of Marketing: Violate Them at Your Own Risk*. In the intervening 25 years, we have discovered that many of these are not so immutable. The *law of leadership* advises people to create a category in which you can be first. Reis and Trout say it is better to be first than to be better than the competitors. The *law of the category* says that, if you can't be first, create a new category you can be first in. The *law of focus* says that the most important and powerful concept in marketing is owning a word – in my case, that would be "forgiveness." In branding, one cannot stand for something if one chases after everything, so settle on one word and seek to own it. The *law of exclusivity* states that two companies cannot own the same word in a prospect's mind. The *law of the mind* says that it is better to be first in the mind than in the market-place. Thus, seek to have a simple, easy-to-remember name. The *law of perception* claims that marketing is not a battle of products, but of perceptions. In summary, success requires focus.

*Initial applications of the laws.* When I began to study forgiveness (our first empirical study was McCullough & Worthington, 1995), Enright's process model was already being tested (Hebl & Enright, 1993). Before our second study (McCullough et al., 1997), Enright had published two studies in the *Journal of Consulting and Clinical Psychology* (Coyle & Enright, 1997; Freedman & Enright, 1996) that were targeted at forgiving clinically relevant problems – incest and partners who had had an abortion. Since then, Enright's forgiveness therapy has become the unquestioned leader in long treatment of severe psychological forgiveness-related problems (see Enright & Fitzgibbons, 2015). REACH Forgiveness was not first in the forgiveness therapy market (i.e., the law of the market). My focus was psychoeducation, not psychotherapy (see the law of the category). Psychoeducation is widely available to all, not just to people with severe unforgiveness issues. Also, not everyone had the resources or wanted to invest in weekly long-term forgiveness therapy. So, I occupied a category that did not compete with forgiveness therapy (see the law of exclusivity). In addition, I was primarily a couple therapist, not individual psychotherapist, so I also continued to develop the HFA, and include forgiveness with couples. Again, instead of competing with forgiveness therapy, I sought to find a complementary category. Reis and Trout's *law of the ladder* argues that your strategy depends on which rung on the ladder you occupy. The *law of the opposite* says that to be in second place, do not try to be "better" than the leader. Try to be different.

*Settling into established operation.* After a time, markets settle. Companies usually have half the market share of the company above and twice the market share of the company below. Reis and Trout argue that every market eventually becomes two teams (the *law of duality*), which might not be an immutable law. Note the market for cars, fast food, and so on. In forgiveness, by Wade et al.'s (2014) meta-analysis, there were only two main interventions.

*Resist ambitious expansion.* Successful companies want to expand. Whether that is a good idea depends on how they seek expansion. Instead of chasing fads, look for trends and position yourself on the leading edge of a long-term trend. A classic mistake is extending one's line of products into new arenas. The *law of perspective* says, after initial success, line extension usually undermines one part of the line. The *law of line extension* says, resist the overwhelming pressure to extend the brand – it is better to stay strong somewhere than to be weak everywhere. The *law of sacrifice* says, one must give up something to get something. A generalist is weak. A wider net does not catch more customers; it allows more to simply fall between the cords. I have maintained focus on REACH Forgiveness – in psychoeducational groups and workbooks – and not extended my line. Finally, the *law of unpredictability* says, we cannot predict the future. Therefore, stay humble. Companies change. Extrapolation of current trends is a good general guess about the future, but all markets change. Growth curves bend over. The *law of success* says, success often leads to arrogance, which leads to failure. And the *law of failure* says, expect failures, accept them, and learn from them. The most important lessons I learned from Reis and Trout are to focus and to stay humble.

## Start with why

Why start with WHY (Sinek, 2009)? Something *viral* resonates on such a visceral level that we share it with those we know and love. Something *vital* has a *why* that keeps inspiring us. Two stone masons were lifting heavy rocks from a quarry. A man asked each, "What are you doing?" One said, "Finding the best pieces of rock I can." The other said, "Building a cathedral." If people know the why of what they are doing, they will be inspired and stay inspired.

I must communicate my WHY. So I do not introduce my REACH Forgiveness method by saying, "I have a great simple program to help you forgive: REACH Forgiveness." Nor do I introduce it by saying, "REACH Forgiveness is evidence-based, easy to use, easy to remember, free, available on my website in several versions (i.e., group, DIY, Christian and secular, couple, culturally adapted)." Rather, I try to appeal to deep motivations by saying, "REACH Forgiveness is tangible manifestation of what I believe – that we can all be more virtuous – people of high character strength who can live more intimately with the Sacred, other people, and other nations." After the why, I introduce the *how* and the *what*.

*Why forgive?* Be more forgiving to be free of corrosive bitterness and to live in a way that elevates others and pleases what you call Sacred. *What?* Forgiveness can help you achieve your personal goals by improving your physical health, mental health, relationships, and spiritual life. *How?* REACH Forgiveness can help you forgive through a psychoeducational group or do-it-yourself (DIY) manual. *Because?* It is evidence-based, easy to use, easy to remember, free, available on my website, has several versions (i.e., group, DIY, Christian and secular, couple, culturally adapted).

## Crossing the chasm – the law of diffusion

Rogers (2003) and Moore (2014) have suggested that ideas diffuse across a population described roughly by a normal distribution. About 2.5% of the population are innovators, who will be attracted to many new ideas without seeking to attract them. Innovators pursue new ideas and products aggressively, are intrigued by fundamental advances, and define themselves largely by being first. About 13.5% are early adopters. Early adopters appreciate new ideas, quick to recognize advantages, and willing to put up with inconveniences to use the advantages. They rely on intuition and trust their gut. They will be attracted to *good* new ideas, and many will jump on board quickly after being exposed to the idea. About 34% are the early majority, and they must be sold before they will adopt the idea. The early majority are swept up in the trend. They generally won't try a new idea or product until it has been tried and proven by others. About 34% are the late majority, and they will adopt new ideas only when the ideas are markedly better than alternatives. They join in only after everything is running smoothly. About 16% are laggards, who might never adopt the idea or, if they do, it is only because nothing else is available. According to the law of diffusion, success requires penetrating at least 15 to 18% of the market – that is, one must attract some of the people who must be persuaded to change and attract most of the innovators and early adopters. That point is the tipping point. Sinek (2009) suggests that about 10% of people might come aboard on any new idea. That involves innovators (about 2.5%) plus early-early adopters (about 7.5%). But for a *viral* movement, one must also win the harder-to-convince last 6% of the early adopters and some of the early majority. To attract as many early adopters as possible, focus on the *why*.

To make your intervention go forward, you must inspire people to talk about it, include it in the context of their lifestyle, and (especially) share it with others. The key is not flashy websites or email campaigns but to get people to *talk about* the intervention. People must be engaged so that the intervention taps into their me-centered values. Then get people talking to spread their own *me-centered values* (and coincidentally, your intervention). Good dissemination will do so by spreading the intervention. But, how do we do this?

## Create a clear message

Miller (2017) provided valuable advice on clarifying our message. He begins his book, "Customers don't generally care about your story; they care about their own. Your customer should be the hero of the story, not your brand" (p. ix). "Pretty websites don't sell things. Words sell things. And if we haven't clarified our message, customers won't listen" (p. 4). Miller identifies two fatal mistakes:

(a) failing to focus on the things that will help users survive and thrive, and (b) making potential users work too hard to understand what you are offering. Thus, the narrative coming out of a company and existing within the company *must* be clear.

Miller uses the metaphor of creating a story to get your message out. The elements of a story are predictable. A character has a problem, meets a guide, who gives the character a plan that calls the character to action. The result will either avoid a painful failure or end in success (or both). Miller then offers principles to construct a clear story.

Principle 1:    The customer is the hero, not your brand.

Principle 2:    Companies try to sell solutions to *external* problems. Users buy solutions to *internal* problems. For example, an external problem is, "Why am I letting this offender (external) get me down?" But an internal problem is, "Do I have what it takes to forgive?" "Can I deal with my unforgiving emotions and motivations?" "Can I be a person who can act in ways leading to better health, mental health, relationships, and spirituality?"

Principal 3:    Users of your intervention are not looking for another hero (i.e., your intervention). They are the hero. They are looking for a guide.

Principle 4:    Users trust a guide who has a plan.

Principle 5:    Users won't act unless they are challenged to act.

Principle 6:    Everyone is trying to avoid a tragic ending.

Principle 7:    Never assume people understand *how* your brand can change their lives. Tell them.

After I read Miller's book, I redesigned my website. Prior to Miller's book, my REACH Forgiveness website cast both me and REACH Forgiveness as heroes in a buddy story. But my purpose was to give away resources to help people forgive. So, after Miller's book, my banner heading became this: "LET ME HELP YOU REACH PEACE IN YOUR PERSONAL LIFE, RELATIONSHIPS, AND GROUPS." Then, next were active links to get resources, labeled "No-cost resources": DIY workbooks, Run groups, Help couples, Transform groups you identify with, secular and explicitly Christian, books that can further equip you, and Contact Ev (i.e., giving my contact information).

## Creating a tipping point

Gladwell (2000) suggested that the best way to spread the word is to think of it as an epidemic. By understanding how epidemics happen, we get ideas about how to disseminate interventions. Usually, epidemics begin with concentrated "infection." That is, only one or two people are initially infected. This is called the *law of the few*. Thus, infections are spread in the margins by many one-on-one contacts by "carriers." Three kinds of people are needed to spread an infection, or to disseminate an intervention. *Connectors* have contacts with many people. Usually, the connector is not a member of one's inner circle because a good connector belongs to many diverse networks of people. Often people within our own network are just going to spread the word within our network. We need to connect with other networks. *Mavens* have two essential characteristics: (a) They figure out that your practice or your research is great. (b) Then they tell others about it without some agenda other than the need to share with others. They have knowledge, social skills, and inspirational and storytelling abilities. *Salespeople* are also needed. Some people have to be persuaded, so sales people are necessary to "cross the chasm." Recall that about 18% of the people must adopt our intervention to make it go viral, and that requires persuading people in the early majority to adopt the intervention. A good sales person has personally winsome qualities, of course, like energy, enthusiasm, charm, and optimism. But effective sales people are not just positive people. Their defining characteristic is that they have more and better answers to people's objections. Thus, to spread an intervention we need to arm sales people with answers to common objections.

## Stay Vital

### The Heaths's *made to stick*

Gladwell (2000) addressed the staying power of a new idea. His main points were that our practice or research needs to be easily findable and then accessible. We must remove practical barriers to people finding and using it. For example, on my website (www.EvWorthington-forgiveness.com), my resources are free and easy to download.

In designing an intervention, we want to convey it in a way that "sticks." Chip Heath and Dan Heath (2007) furthered Gladwell's initial reflections on how to make ideas "sticky." First, what makes messages and ideas *not* stick? One thing is the "curse of knowledge." When we understand a concept well, we can think that others understand it too. Not explaining things clearly can make our intervention slippery, not sticky.

Second, what makes an intervention sticky? The Heaths identify six qualities of ideas that make an impact and also have staying power. They use an acrostic, SUCCESs. That is, sticky ideas or interventions (i.e., interventions that remain vital) are those that are *s*imple, *u*nexpected, *c*oncrete, *c*redible, *e*motional, and *s*tory-based.

*Simple* means that we have found the core of our intervention and can clearly communicate it. For example, what is the *core* of the science of forgiveness? The science of forgiveness tells us to decide to forgive and free yourself emotionally, empathize with the one who hurt you, and give an altruistic (often self-sacrificing) gift of forgiveness. A slogan that captures the core might be, "Forgiving is for giving."

*Unexpected* approaches get attention by surprise and hold attention by appealing to people's interest. Surprise makes us pay attention and think. It prompts us to hunt for underlying causes, to imagine other possibilities, to figure out how to avoid unpleasant surprises in the future. But, after the surprise, we must return the listener to a relatively comfortable place. Completely discordant information will usually be rejected. For forgiveness, I surprise listeners by presenting some unusual ways of thinking about forgiving. Here are three examples. First, an injustice creates an injustice gap (Davis et al., 2016). Forgiveness is not the only way to reduce this gap. People can also see justice done, turn the matter over to the sacred, forbear, accept and move on, and other ways. Second, I describe two different types of forgiveness – not two halves of one experience – and people might experience either or both (Exline, Worthington, Hill, & McCullough, 2003). *Decisional forgiveness* is a decision about how one intends to behave toward an offender (i.e., without revenge and by valuing the person). *Emotional forgiveness* is an emotional replacement of negative with positive other-oriented emotions. Most people believe that forgiving is an act of will and therefore, if we will hard enough, we can force forgiveness. I treat a decision to forgive as controllable, but not emotional forgiveness. Third, McCullough and his colleagues (2010) found that over 90% of hurts heal within three days. A few hurts last weeks, months, or years. Just knowing one should forgive won't work for those. For those, people need something more than knowing what one "should" do and then willing oneself to do it.

*Concrete* concepts help people understand and remember. The Velcro theory of memory suggests that, like Velcro, for an event to be remembered it needs to have many "hooks" that can catch the loops of one or more mental associations. Goldberg, Mazursky, and Solomon (1999) examined memorable television advertisements. They identified six fundamental templates that described most of the adverts. (a) Pictorial analogies are easy to remember. Most people who saw the public service announcement of a Native American rowing through garbage and landing on garbage-covered beach can remember that mental picture. (b) Pictorial analogies with extreme circumstances are memorable. In one Nike advert, a man on the roof of a 20-story building looks down and see firemen with a large Nike shoe to catch the man. Voice: "Something soft between you and the pavement." (c) Extreme situations can dramatize properties (i.e., false teeth adhesive holds weight). (d) Competition has been often evoked (i.e., Coke vs. Pepsi taste test; Burger King vs. McDonalds; Hertz vs. Avis). (e) Interactive experiments challenge the watcher to test for themselves (i.e., use Right Guard under left arm and your brand under right arm). (f) Alteration (i.e., suggesting a leap in time that shows long-term benefit of investing).

To apply this to forgiveness make appeals concrete. For example, I might say, "If you complete a two-hour REACH Forgiveness workbook, you can forgive about

0.4 SD of a hard-to-forgive event you've been struggling with." Although that is a concrete statement, numbers are abstract. They wash over people without penetrating the skin. Here is an alternative. "Have you been struggling for months to forgive a hard-to-forgive event? In the time it would take to watch a video movie, you can get rid of two-thirds of any unforgiveness, resentment, bitterness, anger, and pay-back motivation that is troubling you. After that, it is just mopping up."

*Credibility* of the source is important. Sources of credibility can be authorities, experts, celebrities, or even anti-authorities (i.e., a woman who had smoked since her early teens but at age 31, with lung cancer, spoke out against smoking and died shortly after). Recently, research has shown that honesty and trustworthiness affect people more positively than mere high status.

*Emotional* appeals are not manipulative tear-jerkers. They engage emotions by making people care or they appeal to identity. With Christian churches, I encourage people by saying, Christians are forgiving people. We need to live into our identity. Also, an emotional appeal can rely on facts. One might ask, "Why hold a grudge that makes you angry, bitter, depressed, physically unwell, or conflicted in relationships?" Another emotion-engaging metaphor is this: "Forgiveness is useful for its own ends. It helps you be healthier, more psychologically free from depression, anxiety, anger, and stress, more fulfilled, have better family, work, and friendship networks. But forgiveness is also virtue-building 'weight training.' Forgiveness is hard. You have to strive to do it well. By learning to be patient in negative responding, to be other-oriented and humble, to be self-controlled and disciplined, to be compassionate for those who have harmed or offended you and do not deserve your compassion and love, and to practice forgiveness when it is difficult – by doing those – you also build strength of character."

*Stories* get people to act. Stories as simulations (they tell people how to act). Stories stick. For example, in the media was a story of Chris Carrier (https://www. sun-sentinel.com/news/fl-xpm-1996-09-15-9609140223-story.html), a man I met on *The Lisa Show* years earlier. Chris was abducted as a ten-year-old, stabbed repeatedly, shot through the temple with the exit wound taking his eye. Yet Chris survived. Years later, he had the opportunity to confront the man who wounded him – David McAllister – on the man's death-bed. Instead of condemn, though, Carrier ended up caring for McAllister during the last two weeks of McAllister's life. There are many lessons to learn from Carrier's story, but among those are the following. (a) It really matters on what one dwells over time. Carrier did not dwell on his wounds or his loss, but as a Christian, he dwelt on forgiveness and loving-kindness of Jesus, which led Chris to be a Christian and youth minister. (b) A police officer advised a just confrontation, which was within Carrier's rights. But instead, Carrier was moved by McAllister's suffering. Through empathy, Carrier was able to give an altruistic gift of forgiveness, then he made public his commitment by actively caring for McAllister and that helped Carrier hold onto his forgiveness. Sharing stories that are powerful – and there are many of those publicly available – inspire and move people.

## Use an easy-to-disseminate format

When professionals hear "easy-to-disseminate," they usually think "internet." For developed nations, that is a key to dissemination. English fluency is likely. While an intervention developed in the United States, like REACH Forgiveness is rooted in USA culture, we have sought to make it easily adaptable to other cultures. Culture-specific examples can be replaced with culturally tailored examples. But there are downsides to relying on the internet for dissemination. Throughout the world, not everyone has access to the internet. Rural villages might not have energy to power computers. Many cannot afford computers. Even with internet access, internet has disadvantages. People must find your website. That is not a trivial problem. Even if people find it through Google or a referral, a six- to seven-hour intervention, like we studied in Nation, Wertheim, and Worthington (2018), is not likely to be completed without monitoring, reminders, and so on. People often approach the internet seeking a four-minute YouTube solution, an 18-minute TED talk, or a 45-minute podcast to solve all problems. A seven-hour intervention can be daunting. People start it with good intentions, but when they leave to fix dinner two hours later, it is out of sight and out of mind. Nation et al. had 74% attrition.

We became convinced that the future of interventions needed to provide ways that people could access interventions online by downloading workbooks in Word documents but work with them on their own (Kazdin & Rabbitt, 2013; Walton, 2014). We have published three randomized controlled trials on REACH Forgiveness workbooks, all about seven hours long. Two have assessed changes in trait forgivingness with mean effect sizes of 0.59 (Lavelock et al., 2017) and 0.70 (Greer, Worthington, Lin, Lavelock, & Griffin, 2014). On state measures of decisional forgiveness, emotional forgiveness, and motivation to forgive, the effect sizes have been between 0.74 and 1.56 for Harper et al. (2014) and Greer et al. (2014). These gains are about twice what we saw in psychoeducational group interventions.

Attrition was about 10–15%, but the participants were college students getting credit for participation. If workbooks were available from the internet but even shorter, we suspect that attrition would not be a problem. (a) The mentality of people working on a Word document or a hard copy of the Word document is different than the same content presented as an internet intervention. (b) A writing-based intervention can in itself have therapeutic effects even beyond what a personal or group-based intervention has (see Pennebaker, 2004). (c) A shorter intervention to forgive, like a two-hour hard copy workbook intervention, which is repeatable when additional harms are experienced, might be one of the best interventions. It is like a dose of penicillin. No single dose changes the user's life forever. But it is available for use again and again, every time a person needs infection treatment. *That* changes people's lives. Penicillin costs money. REACH Forgiveness workbooks do not. Penicillin must be obtained through a physician. REACH Forgiveness workbooks are Word documents. They are available via internet but only one person in a remote village needs internet access to download or print, making it widely available in the remotest areas. These workbooks will be readily available.

# Conclusion

Throughout this chapter, I have sought to use a practical case study of how I have developed, efficacy tested, and sought to disseminate the REACH Forgiveness intervention. The practical lessons I hope the reader will take away are these. Designing interventions that are helpful to many people is a marriage of basic and applied research, practice, life, and intentional efforts to spread the word so that the maximum number of people can be helped. This dissemination will likely not just spontaneously happen regardless of how much clinical genius one has. The development, efficacy testing, and dissemination of any positive psychology intervention is a product of one's own efforts, but also crucially depends on one's colleagues, collaborators, clients, and students. The people to whom we present our ideas will be needed to sharpen our thoughts and products, and it takes a certain amount of humility to stay open to the feedback and keep honing the product until it truly is helpful. In addition, we need to expand our horizons beyond typical academic publication outlets, and I recommended attending to marketing literature for ideas.

# References

Berger, J. (2013). *Contagious: How to build word of mouth in the digital age*. New York: Simon & Schuster.

Bury, S. M., Wenzel, M., & Woodyatt, L. (2016). Giving hope a sporting chance: Hope and distinct from optimism when events are possible but not probable. *Motivation and Emotion*, *40*, 588–601.

Coker, B. (2016). *Going viral: The 9 secrets of irresistible marketing*. Harlow: FT Press (Pearson).

Coyle, C. T., & Enright, R. D. (1997). Forgiveness intervention with post-abortion men. *Journal of Consulting and Clinical Psychology*, *65*, 1042–1045.

Davis, D. E., Hook, J. N., Worthington, E. L., Jr., Van Tongeren, D. R., Gartner, A. L., Jennings, D. J., & Emmons, R. A. (2011). Humility as personality judgment: Conceptualization and development of the relational humility scale (RHS). *Journal of Personality Assessment*, *93*, 225–234.

Davis, D. E., Worthington, E. L., Jr., & Hook, J. N. (2010). Humility: Review of measurement strategies and conceptualization as personality judgment. *The Journal of Positive Psychology*, *5*(4), 243–252.

Davis, D. E., Yang, X., DeBlaere, C., McElroy, S. E., Van Tongeren, D. R., Hook, J. N., & Worthington, E. L., Jr. (2016). The injustice gap. *Psychology of Religion and Spirituality*, *8*(3), 175–184.

Enright, R. D., & Fitzgibbons, R. P. (2015). *Forgiveness therapy: An empirical guide for resolving anger and restoring hope*. Washington, DC: American Psychological Association.

Exline, J. J., Worthington, E. L., Jr., Hill, P. C., & McCullough, M. E. (2003). Forgiveness and justice: A research agenda for social and personality psychology. *Personality and Social Psychology Review*, *7*, 337–348.

Freedman, S. R., & Enright, R. D. (1996). Forgiveness as an intervention with incest survivors. *Journal of Consulting and Clinical Psychology*, *64*, 983–992.

Gladwell, M. (2000). *The tipping point: How little things can make a big difference*. Boston, MA: Little, Brown.

Goldberg, J., Mazursky, D., & Solomon, S. (1999). The fundamental templates of quality ads. *Marketing Science*, *18*, 333–351.

Greer, C. L., Worthington, E. L., Jr., Lin, Y., Lavelock, C. R., & Griffin, B. J. (2014). Efficacy of a self-directed forgiveness workbook for Christian victims of within-congregation offenders. *Spirituality in Clinical Practice*, *1*(3), 218–230.

Griffin, B. J., Toussaint, L. L., Zoelzer, M., Worthington, E. L., Jr., Coleman, J., Lavelock, C. R., ... Rye, M. (2019). Evaluating the effectiveness of a community-based forgiveness campaign. *The Journal of Positive Psychology, 14*(3), 354–361.

Griffin, B. J., Worthington, E. L., Jr., Lavelock, C. R., Greer, C. L., Lin, Y., Davis, D. E., & Hook, J. N. (2015). Efficacy of a self-forgiveness workbook: A randomized controlled trial with interpersonal offenders. *Journal of Counselling Psychology, 62*(2), 124–136.

Harper, Q., Worthington, E. L., Jr., Griffin, B. J., Lavelock, C. R., Hook, J. N., Vrana, S. R., & Greer, C. L. (2014). Efficacy of a workbook to promote forgiveness: A randomized controlled trial with university students. *Journal of Clinical Psychology, 70*(12), 1158–1169.

Heath, C., & Heath, D. (2007). *Made to stick: Why some ideas survive and others die.* New York: Random House.

Heath, C., & Heath, D. (2010). *Switch: How to change things when change is hard.* New York: Broadway Books.

Heath, C., & Heath, D. (2013). *Decisive: How to make better choices in life and work.* New York: Crown Business.

Hebl, J., & Enright, R. D. (1993). Forgiveness as a psychotherapeutic goal with elderly females. *Psychotherapy, 30,* 658–667.

Holiday, R. (2014). *Growth hacker marketing: A primer on the future of PR, marketing, and advertising, revised and expanded.* New York: Penguin Books.

Holiday, R. (2017). *Perennial seller: The art of making and marketing work that lasts.* New York: Penguin Books.

Kazdin, A. E., & Rabbitt, S. M. (2013). Novel models for delivering mental health services and reducing the burdens of mental illness. *Clinical Psychological Science, 1*(2), 170–191.

Lavelock, C. R., Worthington, E. L., Jr., Davis, D. E., Griffin, B. J., Reid, C., Hook, J. N., & Van Tongren, D. R. (2014). The quiet virtue speaks: An intervention to promote humility. *Journal of Psychology and Theology, 42*(1), 99–110.

Lavelock, C. R., Worthington, E. L., Jr., Elnasseh, A., Griffin, B. J., Garthe, R. C., Davis, D. E., & Hook, J. N. (2017). Still waters run deep: Humility as a master virtue. *Journal of Psychology and Theology, 45*(4), 286–303.

McCullough, M. E., Luna, L. R., Berry, J. W., Tabak, B. A., & Bono, G. (2010). On the form and function of forgiving: Modeling the time-forgiveness relationship and testing the valuable relationships hypothesis. *Emotion, 10,* 358–376.

McCullough, M. E., & Worthington, E. L., Jr. (1995). Promoting forgiveness: A comparison of two psychoeducational group interventions with a waiting-list control. *Counseling and Values, 40,* 55–68.

McCullough, M. E., Worthington, E. L., Jr., & Rachal, K. C. (1997). Interpersonal forgiving in close relationships. *Journal of Personality and Social Psychology, 73,* 321–336.

McHugh, R. K., & Barlow, D. H. (Eds.). (2012). *Dissemination and implementation of evidence-based psychological interventions.* Oxford: Oxford University Press.

Miller, D. (2017). *Building a storybrand: Clarify your message so customers will listen.* New York: HarperCollins.

Moore, G. A. (2014). *Crossing the chasm* (3rd ed.). New York: HarperCollins.

Nation, J., Wertheim, E., & Worthington, E. L., Jr. (2018). Evaluation of an online self-help version of the *REACH forgiveness* program: Outcomes and predictors of persistence in a community sample. *Journal of Clinical Psychology, 74*(6), 819–838.

Pennebaker, J. W. (2004). *Writing to heal: A guided journal for recovering from trauma and emotional upheaval.* Oakland, CA: New Harbinger.

Reis, A., & Trout, J. (1986). *Marketing warfare.* New York: McGraw-Hill.

Reis, A., & Trout, J. (1993). *The 22 immutable laws of marketing: Violate them at your own risk.* New York: Harper.

Ripley, J. S., & Worthington, E. L., Jr. (2014). *Couple therapy: A new hope-focused approach.* Downers Grove, IL: InterVarsity Press.

Rogers, E. M. (2003). *Diffusion of innovations* (5th ed.). New York: Free Press.

Sandage, S. J., & Worthington, E. L., Jr. (2010). Comparison of two group interventions to promote forgiveness: Empathy as a mediator of change. *Journal of Mental Health Counselling, 32*(1), 35–57.

Sinek, S. (2009). *Start with why: How great leaders inspire everyone to take action.* New York: Penguin Books.

Wade, N. G., Hoyt, W. T., Kidwell, J. E. M., & Worthington, E. L., Jr. (2014). Efficacy of psychotherapeutic interventions to promote forgiveness: A meta-analysis. *Journal of Consulting and Clinical Psychology, 82*(1), 154–170.

Wade, N. G., & Worthington, E. L., Jr. (2003). Overcoming interpersonal offenses: Is forgiveness the only way to deal with unforgiveness? *Journal of Counseling and Development, 81,* 343–353.

Wade, N. G., Worthington, E. L., Jr., & Meyer, J. (2005). But do they really work? Meta-analysis of group interventions to promote forgiveness. In E. L. Worthington Jr. (Ed.), *Handbook of forgiveness* (pp. 423–440). New York: Brunner-Routledge.

Walton, G. M. (2014). The new science of wise psychological interventions. *Current Directions in Psychological Science, 23*(1), 73–82.

Worthington, E. L., Jr. (1989). *Marriage counseling: A Christian approach to counseling couples.* Downers Grove, IL: InterVarsity Press.

Worthington, E. L., Jr. (1998a). An empathy-humility-commitment model of forgiveness applied within family dyads. *Journal of Family Therapy, 20,* 59–76.

Worthington, E. L., Jr. (1998b). The pyramid model of forgiveness: Some interdisciplinary speculations about unforgiveness and the promotion of forgiveness. In E. L. Worthington Jr. (Ed.), *Dimensions of forgiveness: Psychological research and theological perspectives* (pp. 107–137). Philadelphia, PA: Templeton Foundation Press.

Worthington, E. L., Jr. (2003). *Forgiving and reconciling: Bridges to wholeness and hope.* Downers Grove, IL: InterVarsity Press.

Worthington, E. L., Jr. (2005). *Hope-focused marriage counselling: A guide to brief therapy* (rev. ed.). Downers Grove, IL: InterVarsity Press.

Worthington, E. L., Jr. (2013). *Moving forward: Six steps to forgiving yourself and breaking free from the past.* Colorado Springs, CO: WaterBrook/Multnomah.

Worthington, E. L., Jr. (2018). *The science of forgiveness and reconciliation (15-lecture video course).* Silver Spring, MD: Now You Know Media.

Worthington, E. L., Jr., Berry, J. W., Hook, J. N., Davis, D. E., Scherer, M., Griffin, B. J., . . . Campana, K. L. (2015). Forgiveness-reconciliation and communication-conflict-resolution interventions versus rested controls in early married couples. *Journal of Counseling Psychology, 62*(1), 14–27.

Worthington, E. L., Jr., & DiBlasio, F. A. (1990). Promoting mutual forgiveness within the fractured relationship. *Psychotherapy, 27,* 219–223.

# 16

# From Serbia with Positive Orientation: The Serbian Studies

Vesna Petrović, Dragan Žuljević, and Gian Vittorio Caprara

## Introduction

One issue that has in recent years increasingly come under the focus of researchers is the differences in a human's individual psychological strengths and their role in promoting optimal adjustment across different domains of functioning and in moderating vulnerability to adversities and illness.

In psychological literature, it is well known that self-esteem (Baumeister, 1993; Greenberg et al., 1992; Kernis, 2003), life satisfaction (Diener, Emmons, Larsen, & Griffin, 1985), and dispositional optimism (Kernis, 2003) have been repeatedly associated with well-being and successful adaptation. Life satisfaction refers to a person's general evaluation of various activities and relationships that make someone's life worth living (Diener, 1984). Self-esteem denotes an individual's general self-regard and level of self-acceptance (Harter, 1999). Optimism refers to one's perspective on future personal and social events in which one sees an abundance of good things and a scarcity of bad things (Carver & Scheier, 2002). Whereas several studies have shown a relatively high level of intercorrelation among the judgments that people hold about themselves, their life, and their future (Diener & Diener, 1995; Lucas, Diener, & Suh, 1996), Caprara and his colleagues found that these judgments can be traced to a common latent component (Caprara et al., 2009). This component was originally named positive thinking and then positive orientation, positivity, or, in short, POS (Caprara et al., 2009; Caprara & Steca, 2005; Caprara, Steca, Alessandri, Abela, & McWhinnie, 2010).

*Positive Psychology: An International Perspective*, First Edition.
Edited by Aleksandra Kostić and Derek Chadee.

In a relatively short time, a significant amount of research has attested to the positive impact of positive orientation on an individuals' health, adjustment, and achievements (Caprara & Alessandri, 2014; Caprara, Alessandri, & Caprara, 2019).

The aim of this chapter is to present the major findings of five studies conducted in Serbia that corroborate the validity of the positivity scale and that further document the impact of positive orientation on psychosocial functioning.

## Positivity

A large number of studies that have included thousands of participants across a diverse range of cultures have led to positive orientation being posited as the common latent factor underlying self-esteem, life satisfaction, and dispositional optimism (Caprara, Alessandri, Eisenberg, et al., 2012; Caprara, Alessandri, Trommsdorff, et al., 2012). Results from twin studies have led to the estimate that heritability accounts for about 50% of the variance of this latent dimension (Fagnani, Medda, Stazi, Caprara, & Alessandri, 2014). This may account for the relative stability of POS over the course of development.

Several findings attest to the positive impact of positive orientation across diverse domains of functioning, including health, work performance, psychological well-being, and social adjustment, while little residual variance has been shown to be due to self-esteem, life satisfaction, and optimism once their common component was taken into account (Alessandri, Caprara, & De Pascalis, 2015; Alessandri, Caprara, & Tisak, 2012; Alessandri, Vecchione, et al., 2012).

Caprara and colleagues have argued that POS is a stable evaluative disposition that enables humans to cope well with life in the face of adversities, failures, and loss (Caprara et al., 2009), and whose major expressions are self-esteem, life satisfaction, and optimism.

The positivity scale that has been used by many related studies includes eight items selected to provide a direct measure of positive orientation (Caprara, Alessandri, Eisenberg, et al., 2012; Caprara, Alessandri, Trommsdorff, et al., 2012). Excellent psychometric properties attesting to its unidimensionality have been confirmed across various cultural contexts, including in Brazil, Canada, China, Germany, Israel, Italy, Japan, the Netherlands, Poland, Serbia, Spain, Turkey, the UK, and the USA (Borsa, Damásio, Souza, Koller, & Caprara, 2015; Çıkrıkçı, Çiftçi, & Gençdoğan, 2015; Heikamp et al., 2014; Łaguna, Oleś, & Filipiuk, 2011; Tian, Zhang, & Huebner, 2018).

In presenting the five Serbian studies on positivity, we shall start with the study which is in accordance with the process of discovering the positivity that Caprara and colleagues experienced (Caprara et al., 2009; Caprara, Steca, et al., 2010), starting with the research on the structure of positivity and developing the concept. Thus, the first study presented in this chapter is the replication of the original study done in Italy and subsequently corroborated in other countries, tracing self-esteem, optimism, and life satisfaction to a common latent construct.

## Study 1: Positivity Underlying the Constructs of Self-Esteem, Life Satisfaction, and Optimism

The aim of this study was to link the standard measures of self-esteem, life satisfaction, and dispositional optimism to the common factor of positivity, attesting to a similar factorial structure as demonstrated in Japan, Germany, and Italy (Caprara, Alessandri, Trommsdorff, et al., 2012).

### Participants

A total of 1,332 Serbian adults (51.1% females; M age = 41.86, SD = 14.17, age range 19–79) participated in the study. Table 16.1 presents a detailed description of the study sample.

### Instruments

The Serbian translation of the revised life orientation test (LOT-R; Scheier, Carver, & Bridges, 1994) was used to assess dispositional optimism. The LOT-R consists of 10 items (4 filler items), rated across a five-point Likert-type scale, ranging from 1 (strongly disagree) to 5 (strongly agree). Three items are positively worded

**Table 16.1**   Study 1 sample description.

| Variable | | Percentage |
| --- | --- | --- |
| Age | 19–29 | 26.3% |
| | 30–39 | 20.9% |
| | 40–49 | 18.4% |
| | 50–59 | 23.2% |
| | > 60 | 11.2% |
| Gender | Male | 48.9% |
| | Female | 51.1% |
| Marital status | Single | 21.9% |
| | Married | 49.5% |
| | In a relationship | 13.5% |
| | Divorced | 9.3% |
| | Widowed | 5.8% |
| Education | No or elementary school | 3.8% |
| | High school | 51.7% |
| | Student | 15.8% |
| | University degree | 28.7% |
| Employment | Unemployed | 22.9% |
| | Temporarily employed | 15.3% |
| | Permanently employed | 50.2% |
| | Retired | 11.6% |

(e.g., "Overall, I expect more good things to happen to me than bad") and three are negatively worded (e.g., "If something can go wrong for me, it will"). The reliability and validity of the LOT-R have proven sufficient (Jovanović & Gavrilov-Jerković, 2013), as was also the case in this research ($\alpha = 0.74$).

The Serbian translation of the Rosenberg self-esteem scale (RSES; Rosenberg, 1965) was used to assess self-esteem. The RSES consists of 10 items (e.g., "I feel that I have a number of good qualities"), followed by a 5-point Likert scale ranging from 1 (strongly disagree) to 5 (strongly agree). The scale translated into Serbian has shown good internal consistency (Jovanović & Žuljević, 2013), as was also demonstrated in this research ($\alpha = 0.88$).

The Serbian translation of the satisfaction with life scale (SWLS; Diener et al., 1985) was used to assess life satisfaction. The responses to each of the five items (e.g., "If I could live my life over, I would change almost nothing") range from 1 (strongly disagree), to 7 (strongly agree). This translation of the scale has been widely used and has shown good psychometric properties (Jovanović, 2016; Vasić, Šarčević, & Trogrlić, 2011). In this research, the scale demonstrated a high internal consistency ($\alpha = 0.88$).

## Results

The latent model establishing positivity as a common factor underlying the standard measures of self-esteem, life satisfaction, and dispositional optimism was tested by confirmatory factor analysis (CFA) within EQS 6.1 for Windows (Bentler, 2006). Keeping in mind that the Mardia coefficient of multivariate kurtosis ($g = 134.22$) was significantly higher than the criterion (Bentler, 2006), the robust method of estimation was used (Satorra & Bentler, 1994). For the fit estimation, the following criteria were used: the Satorra–Bentler chi square (SB$\chi^2$), the SB$\chi^2$ ratio (SB$\chi^2/df$), the root mean square error of approximation (RMSEA; Steiger, 2016), the standardized root mean square residual (SRMR), the comparative fit index (CFI; Bentler, 1989), and the Bentler-Bonett normed fit index (NFI; Bentler & Bonett, 1980). Good fit indices are considered to be: SB$\chi^2/df < 3$, RMSEA and SRMR $< 0.05$, CFI and NFI $> 0.95$ (Hu & Bentler, 1998, 1999; Kline, 2005; Schumacker & Lomax, 1996).

Data analyses revealed a very good fit of the hypothesized model: SB$\chi^2(df) =$ 493.94 (170); SB$\chi^2/df = 2.90$; RMSEA (90% CI) $= 0.044$ (0.040–0.049); SRMR $=$ 0.057; CFI $= 0.94$; NFI $= 0.92$. Although the SB$\chi^2$ was large and significant, the ratio to degrees of freedom satisfied the criterion (under 3), followed by the alternative fit indexes, which satisfied the more restrictive cut-off criteria. As we can see in Figure 16.1, item loadings were high and significant (all above 0.40), except for three items of self-esteem and one in optimism. Moreover, the loadings of the three first-order factors on positive orientation were large and significant, all 0.70 and higher. This was particularly the case for self-esteem – its variance was almost completely taken over by the second-order positive orientation factor.

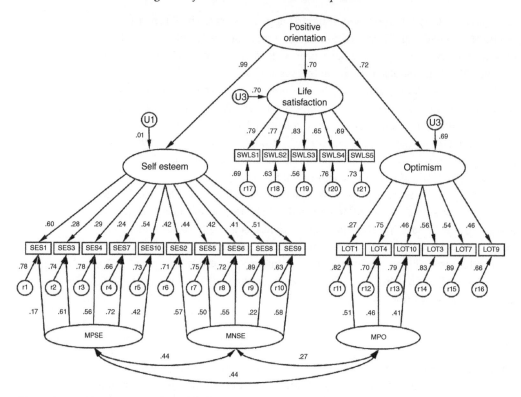

**Figure 16.1**   The measurement model of positive orientation with standardized parameter estimates.

*Note*: All paths are significant on the *p* < 0.01 level. *r1–r21* = Unique items and error variance; U = Factor unique variance; MPS = Method factor associated with positively worded items from the RSES; MNS = Method factor associated with negatively worded items from the RSES; MPO = Method factor associated with positively worded items from the LOT-R.

## Discussion of Study 1

The latent model establishing positivity as a common factor underlying the self-esteem, life satisfaction, and dispositional optimism was tested by confirmatory factor analysis. Data analysis revealed a very good fit of the hypothesized model.

Many previous studies have attested to the reliability of directly assessing positive orientation by using the common measures of self-esteem, life satisfaction, and optimism. Confirmative factor analysis models in which self-esteem, life satisfaction, and optimism were modeled as indicators of a common latent positive orientation factor have attested to a good match between the conceptual model and the observed data across various linguistic and cultural contexts, such as in Canada, China, Italy, Japan, Poland, and Turkey (Caprara, Alessandri, Trommsdorff, et al., 2012; Çıkrıkçı & Gençdoğan, 2016; Oleś et al., 2013; Tian et al., 2018). Models carried out in Serbia have now also reported excellent results in this regard.

## Study 2: Positivity Scale – Psychometric Properties of Serbian Translation

The aim of this study was to investigate the descriptives of the positivity scale translated into the Serbian language, and also to evaluate the latent structure of the scale by testing the general hypothesized model, as well as its invariance across gender and age. The descriptive analyses for these items and the total scale were performed in the program IBM SPSS 22, while the general structural model and its age and gender invariance were tested in EQS 6.1.

### Participants

A total of 2,791 Serbian adults (52.7% females; M age = 34.45, SD = 13.15, age range 18–80) participated in this study. Table 16.2 presents a detailed description of the study sample. For this study, as for all of the subsequent studies presented in this chapter, the participants were recruited via convenience, and the snowball sampling method (Goodman, 1961) was performed by undergraduate students at the Faculty of Law and Business Studies in Novi Sad, Serbia. Participation was voluntary and anonymous and respondents were not compensated for their participation.

**Table 16.2**  Study 2 sample description.

| Variable | | Percentage |
| --- | --- | --- |
| Age | 18–29 | 46.9% |
| | 30–39 | 20.5% |
| | 40–49 | 15.7% |
| | 50–59 | 11.6% |
| | > 60 | 5.3% |
| Gender | Male | 47.3% |
| | Female | 52.7% |
| Marital status | Single | 42.5% |
| | Married | 29.4% |
| | In a relationship | 13.9% |
| | Divorced | 11.3% |
| | Widowed | 2.9% |
| Education | No or elementary school | 2.2% |
| | High school | 47.9% |
| | Student | 16.2% |
| | University degree | 33.7% |
| Employment | Unemployed | 35.6% |
| | Temporarily employed | 17.1% |
| | Permanently employed | 41.8% |
| | Retired | 5.5% |

### Instrument

The positivity scale (PS; Caprara, Alessandri, Eisenberg, et al., 2012) is an 8-item self-report questionnaire aimed at assessing positive orientation, or, in short, positivity. The respondents provide their responses by using a 5-point scale ranging from 1 (strongly disagree) to 5 (strongly agree) for each of the items. All of the items are positively worded, except one (*At times, the future seems unclear to me*), which needs recoding into reverse values. The total score (ranging from 8 to 40) indicates the level of one's general positive orientation toward oneself (e.g., *On the whole, I am satisfied with myself*), other people (e.g., *Others are generally here for me when I need them*), and the future (e.g., *I have great faith in the future*). The instrument was translated into Serbian by the back-translation procedure with the consent of the author and under his supervision.

### Results

The positivity scale demonstrated good internal consistency, both in the total sample and in the male and female subsamples. The female subsample discretely overperformed against the male subsample in mean score distribution (Table 16.3; $t(2,786) = 1.98$; $p = 0.05$; $d = 0.08$), but at a marginal level of statistical significance. Also, in all samples tested, there was a minor deviation from the normal distribution of total scores.

In the Table 16.4 the descriptives for each of the PS items are presented. All of the items demonstrate good interitem correlation, except for item 4 (*At times, the future seems unclear to me*), which contributes to the total item variance, with only 3% indicating a specificity of the Serbian translation as compared to the original (Caprara, Alessandri, Eisenberg, et al., 2012).

The latent structure of the positivity scale was tested by CFA using EQS 6.1 for Windows (Bentler, 2006). Keeping in mind that the Mardia coefficient of multivariate kurtosis ($g = 39.21$) was significantly higher than the criterion (Bentler, 2006), the robust method of estimation was used (Satorra & Bentler, 1994). The cut-off criteria for fit indices, implicating a good model fit to the covariance matrix, were the same (Hu & Bentler, 1998, 1999; Kline, 2005; Schumacker & Lomax, 1996), as mentioned above in Study 1.

**Table 16.3**  Descriptives of the positivity scale score distribution.

|  | M | SD | α | MIC | Sk | Ku | Z |
|---|---|---|---|---|---|---|---|
| Female | 30.49 | 4.87 | 0.81 | 0.36 (0.05–0.62) | −0.68 | 0.68 | 3.09** |
| Male | 30.10 | 5.23 | 0.82 | 0.39 (0.05–0.67) | −0.67 | 0.66 | 2.91** |
| Total sample | 30.29 | 5.04 | 0.81 | 0.37 (0.05–0.65) | −0.68 | 0.69 | 4.26** |

*Note*: M = Mean score; SD = Standard deviation; α = Cronbach alpha; MIC = Mean interitem correlation; Sk = Skewness; Ku = Kurtosis; Z = Kolmogorov-Smirnov test of distribution normality; **$p < 0.01$.

**Table 16.4** Item descriptives.

| Item | M | SD | Sk | Ku | rit | $r^2$ | α |
|------|---|----|----|----|----|----|----|
| 1. Snažno verujem u budućnost [I have great faith in the future] | 3.91 | 1.00 | −0.87 | 0.47 | 0.60 | 0.44 | 0.79 |
| 2. Drugi su generalno tu za mene kada su mi potrebni [Others are generally here for me when I need them] | 3.71 | 1.03 | −0.76 | 0.10 | 0.38 | 0.19 | 0.82 |
| 3. Zadovoljan/na sam svojim životom [I am satisfied with my life] | 3.86 | 0.91 | −0.83 | 0.71 | 0.66 | 0.49 | 0.77 |
| 4. Povremeno, budućnost mi izgleda nejasno (R) [At times, the future seems unclear to me] | 2.78 | 1.06 | 0.32 | −0.46 | 0.16 | 0.03 | 0.85 |
| 5. Generalno se osećam siguran/na a u sebe [I generally feel confident in myself] | 3.90 | 0.92 | −0.85 | 0.66 | 0.63 | 0.46 | 0.78 |
| 6. Očekujem budućnost sa nadom i entuzijazmom [I look forward to the future with hope and enthusiasm] | 3.94 | 0.93 | −0.83 | 0.60 | 0.65 | 0.49 | 0.79 |
| 7. Osećam da ima mnogo stvari na koje treba da budem ponosan [I feel I have many things to be proud of] | 4.12 | 0.89 | −1.06 | 1.09 | 0.61 | 0.44 | 0.78 |
| 8. U celini, zadovoljan/na sam sobom [On the whole, I am satisfied with myself] | 4.08 | 0.88 | −1.08 | 1.37 | 0.71 | 0.60 | 0.77 |

*Note*: M = Mean score; SD = Standard deviation; Sk = Skewness; Ku = Kurtosis; *rit* = Corrected mean interitem correlation; $r^2$ = Squared multiple correlation; α = Cronbach alpha; R = Negatively worded item.

**Table 16.5** Fit indices for tested models.

| Model | Sample | SBχ² | df | SBχ²/df | RMSEA (90% CI) | SRMR | CFI | NFI |
|-------|--------|------|----|---------|----------------|------|-----|-----|
| 1 | Total (N = 2,791) | 163.43 | 20 | 8.17 | 0.051 (0.044–0.058) | 0.031 | 0.96 | 0.96 |
| 2 | Total (N = 2,791) | 69.16 | 19 | 3.64 | 0.031 (0.023–0.039) | 0.021 | 0.99 | 0.98 |
| | Male (N = 1,321) | 65.12 | 19 | 3.42 | 0.030 (0.020–0.037) | 0.020 | 0.99 | 0.98 |
| | Female (N = 1,470) | 73.12 | 19 | 3.84 | 0.032 (0.025–0.041) | 0.023 | 0.98 | 0.98 |

*Note*: 1 = The original model; 2 = The original model with correlated residuals of items 1 and 6; SBχ² = Satorra–Bentler corrected χ²; RMSEA = Root mean square error of approximation; SRMR = Standardized root mean square residual; CFI = Comparative fit index; NFI = Normed fit index.

Two models were tested. The first one hypothesized a one factor model and resulted in fair fit indices, but also suggested some unexplained variance by both general and residual indices (SBχ²/*df* and RMSEA; Table 16.5). The second model was based on sequential fit diagnostic evaluation using the Lagrange multiplier test, which indicated that the points of ill fit pertained to the error covariances of Items 1 and 6 (Table 16.6). This exact issue was also reported for the original scale (Caprara, Alessandri, Eisenberg, et al., 2012). This model resulted in excellent fit indices and statistically significant factor loadings, both for the total sample (Figure 16.2) and for the subsamples divided by gender variable (Table 16.5).

Testing the gender invariance of the model by multigroup analysis with factor loadings unconstrained to be equal across the genders demonstrated an excellent

**Table 16.6**　Multivariate Lagrange multiplier test results.

| Step | Item residual pairs | | Cumulative increment | | Univariate increment | |
|---|---|---|---|---|---|---|
| | | | $\Delta\chi^2$ | df | $\Delta\chi^2$ | df |
| 1 | PS6 | PS1 | 144.89 | 1 | 144.89** | 20 |
| 2 | PS7 | PS3 | 175.94 | 2 | 31.05 | 19 |
| 3 | PS3 | PS2 | 193.23 | 3 | 17.29 | 18 |
| 4 | PS2 | PS1 | 213.99 | 4 | 20.76 | 17 |
| 5 | PS8 | PS6 | 225.72 | 5 | 11.73 | 16 |
| 6 | PS6 | PS4 | 233.14 | 6 | 7.42 | 15 |
| 7 | PS6 | PS3 | 238.28 | 7 | 5.11 | 14 |

*Note:* $\Delta\chi^2$ = Univariate incremental change of absolute mode fit; **$p < 0.01$.

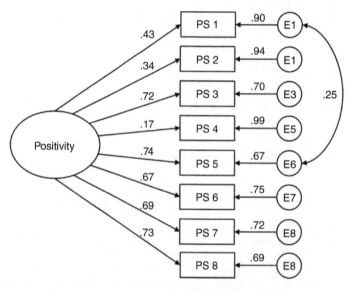

**Figure 16.2**　The latent structure model of the positivity scale.

fit to the data (Table 16.7), as did the following models with additional constraints imposed, thus suggesting model invariance across genders.

## Discussion of Study 2

The results in this study obtained from a large Serbian sample strongly support the good psychometric properties and unidimensionality of the positivity scale, as well as its invariance across the factors of both gender and age. At the same time, these findings accord absolutely with the data on the properties of the scale when applied in different cultural contexts (Borsa et al., 2015; Çıkrıkçı et al., 2015;

**Table 16.7**   Fit indices for models in multigroup analyses.

| Model | Constrains | SBχ² | df | SBχ²/df | RMSEA (90% CI) | SRMR | CFI | NFI |
|---|---|---|---|---|---|---|---|---|
| 1 | None | 163.43 | 38 | 3.63 | 0.033 (0.024–0.040) | 0.028 | 0.96 | 0.96 |
| 2 | Measurement weights | 149.41 | 45 | 3.32 | 0.031 (0.020–0.038) | 0.031 | 0.99 | 0.98 |
| 3 | Structural covariance | 140.76 | 46 | 3.06 | 0.030 (0.019–0.036) | 0.034 | 0.98 | 0.98 |
| 4 | Measurement residuals | 171.05 | 55 | 3.11 | 0.030 (0.021–0.039) | 0.037 | 0.98 | 0.98 |

*Note*: SBχ² = Satorra–Bentler corrected χ²; RMSEA = Root mean square error of approximation; SRMR = Standardized root mean square residual; CFI = Comparative fit index; NFI = Normed fit index.

Heikamp et al., 2014; Łaguna et al., 2011; Tian et al., 2018), regarding good internal consistency, the latent structure of the positivity scale, and the gender invariance of the model, with an excellent fit to the data.

Thus, these psychometric findings documenting the validity of the positivity scale in Serbia adds one further example to a convincing, growing body of evidence of positivity as a basic disposition across cultures that enables humans to view life and to approach the world with a positive outlook.

## Study 3: Composite Positivity Measure Versus the Positivity Scale: Comparing the Potential to Predict Depression and Self-Efficacy

The first aim of this study was to trace the relations of positivity to demographical variables on a new, different sample. The second aim was to compare the measure of positivity operationalized via the first-order constructs of self-esteem, life satisfaction, and dispositional optimism while controlling the positivity. The third goal of the study was to compare the independent measure of positivity to the composite second-order common factor score of positive orientation in predicting levels of depression and general self-efficacy.

### Participants

The same sample was used as in Study 1. A total of 1332 Serbian adults (51.1% females; M age = 41.86, SD = 14.17, age range 19–79) participated in the study. Table 16.1 presents a detailed description of the study sample.

### Instruments

Along with the Serbian translation of the positivity scale described above in Study 2 (PS; Caprara, Alessandri, Eisenberg, et al., 2012), additional tools were used in Study 3.

The Serbian translation of the general self-efficacy scale (GSES; Schwarzer & Jerusalem, 1995) was also employed. The GSES is a 10-item self-report measure aimed at assessing one's general sense of self-efficacy (e.g., "If I am in trouble, I can usually think of a solution"). Respondents rate each item using a 4-point Likert-type scale (0 = not at all true to 3 = exactly true). The GSES has been found to possess excellent psychometric properties and a one-dimensional structure in previous research (Scholz, Gutiérrez-Doña, Sud, & Schwarzer, 2002). Excellent internal consistency was also supported by this research ($\alpha = 0.90$).

The Serbian translation of the Center for Epidemiologic Studies depression scale (CES–D; Radloff, 1977) was used to assess participants' level of depressive symptoms. The scale consists of 20 items (e.g., *I was bothered by things that usually don't bother me*), measuring symptoms that characterize depression, such as despondency, hopelessness, sleep disturbance, crying bouts, loss of appetite and interest in pleasurable activities, loss of initiative, and self-deprecation. The items were rated on the basis of frequency of occurrence during the previous week using a 4-point Likert-type scale from 1 (*rarely or none of the time*) to 4 (*most or all of the time*). In this research, the scale demonstrated a high internal consistency ($\alpha = 0.89$).

## Results

In this study's sample, positivity was shown to negatively correlated with age ($r = -0.14$; $p < 0.01$), suggesting that younger adults demonstrate higher levels of positivity. In contrast to the results presented in Study 1, the male and the female subsamples did not demonstrate a significant difference in positivity ($t$ (1,330) = 0.39; $p = 0.69$; $d = 0.01$). There were no differences shown in positivity regarding current employment status (F = 1.51; $p = 0.21$), nor regarding marital status (F = 1.37; $p = 0.25$). On the other hand, participants with no schooling or who had completed either elementary or high school demonstrated lower positivity than students or participants with a university degree (F = 10.10; $p < 0.01$). This subsample of students demonstrated the highest level of positivity in comparison to all other subsample groups. The results of the least significant difference (LSD) test post hoc comparison is presented in Table 16.8.

After successfully replicating the model of positive orientation as a general construct incorporating self-esteem, life satisfaction, and dispositional optimism in Study 1, a decision was made to perform a series of hierarchical regression analyses in order to compare the predictive power of three alternatives of positive orientation operationalization. First, after controlling for the age and gender effect in every equation, the unique predictive power of first-order positivity constructs while controlling the incremental predictive power of positivity scale scores were evaluated. Second, the general composite score of positive orientation to the score of the 8-item positivity scale (Caprara, Alessandri, Eisenberg, et al., 2012) were compared according to their levels of predicting depression and self-efficacy. In all

**Table 16.8**   The mean differences between subsamples divided by education.

|  | High school | Student | University degree |
|---|---|---|---|
| No or elementary school | −0.35 | 2.29** | 0.98* |
| High school | 1.00 | 3.23** | 1.32** |
| Student |  | 1.00 | −1.91** |

*Note:* **$p < 0.01$; *$p < 0.05$.

**Table 16.9**   Hierarchical regression analyses predicting depression and self-efficacy by positivity measured by the positivity scale and components of positive orientation.

|  | Depression | | | | Self-efficacy | | | |
|---|---|---|---|---|---|---|---|---|
|  | $R^2$ | $\Delta R^2$ | F change | $\beta$ | $R^2$ | $\Delta R^2$ | F change | $\beta$ |
| *Step 1 – Age and gender* |  |  |  |  |  |  |  |  |
|  | 0.01 | 0.01 | 6.11** |  | 0.01 | 0.01 | 4.19* |  |
| Age |  |  |  | 0.06* |  |  |  | 0.04 |
| Gender |  |  |  | 0.08** |  |  |  | −0.07** |
| *Step 2 – Age, gender, and components of positive orientation* |  |  |  |  |  |  |  |  |
|  | 0.26 | 0.25 | 459.29** |  | 0.33 | 0.32 | 641.96** |  |
| Age |  |  |  | −0.01 |  |  |  | 0.04 |
| Gender |  |  |  | −0.07** |  |  |  | −0.06* |
| PS positivity |  |  |  | −0.51** |  |  |  | 0.58** |
| *Step3 – Age, gender, components of positivity, and Positivity Scale score* |  |  |  |  |  |  |  |  |
|  | 0.33 | 0.07 | 44.90** |  | 0.37 | 0.04 | 30.70** |  |
| Age |  |  |  | −0.02 |  |  |  | 0.05* |
| Gender |  |  |  | −0.05* |  |  |  | −0.05* |
| PS positivity |  |  |  | −0.25** |  |  |  | 0.37** |
| Optimism |  |  |  | −0.28** |  |  |  | 0.20** |
| Self-esteem |  |  |  | −0.09** |  |  |  | 0.10** |
| Life satisfaction |  |  |  | −0.07* |  |  |  | 0.06* |

*Note:* **$p < 0.01$; *$p < 0.05$.

tested models, the indices of multicollinearity were high above the cut-off of 0.20 for tolerance and under 5 for the variance inflation factor (O'Brien, 2007), suggesting no multicollinearity among predictors.

Table 16.9 presents the results of the hierarchical regression analyses which evaluated the unique predictive power of the positive orientation components while controlling for the positivity measured by the positivity scale. Positivity itself explained 25% of depression and 32% of self-efficacy, while adding all of the three components of positive orientation explained 7% and 4% of the criterion variables. These findings also support the construct of positivity as a superordinate to self-esteem, life satisfaction, and dispositional optimism.

**Table 16.10**    Hierarchical regression analyses predicting depression and self-efficacy via two methods of measuring positivity.

| | Depression | | | | Self-efficacy | | | |
|---|---|---|---|---|---|---|---|---|
| | $R^2$ | $\Delta R^2$ | F change | β | $R^2$ | $\Delta R^2$ | F change | β |
| *Model 1 – Age and gender* | | | | | | | | |
| Step 1 | 0.01 | 0.01 | 6.11** | | 0.01 | 0.01 | 4.19* | |
| Age | | | | 0.06* | | | | 0.04 |
| Gender | | | | 0.08** | | | | −0.07** |
| *Model 2 – Age, gender, and composite positivity score* | | | | | | | | |
| Step 2 | 0.25 | 0.24 | 434.36** | | 0.28 | 0.27 | 494.13** | |
| Age | | | | 0.02 | | | | 0.00 |
| Gender | | | | 0.04 | | | | −0.04 |
| Comp. positivity | | | | −0.49** | | | | 0.52** |
| *Model 3 – Age, gender, and Positivity Scale score* | | | | | | | | |
| Step 2 | 0.26 | 0.25 | 459.29** | | 0.33 | 0.32 | 641.96** | |
| Age | | | | −0.01 | | | | 0.04 |
| Gender | | | | −0.07** | | | | −0.06* |
| PS positivity | | | | −0.51** | | | | 0.58** |

*Note:* **$p < 0.01$; *$p < 0.05$.

As can be seen in Table 16.10, a minor significant effect of age and gender were detected, possibly due to the large sample, which can increase the statistical power of detecting irrelevant parameters as significant (Cohen, 1988). Also, the positivity scale score slightly overperformed in the composite measure of positive orientation in both predicting depression and self-esteem, indicating that the construct of positive orientation is a broader and more general construct than a simple sum of the subordinate constructs of dispositional optimism, life satisfaction, and self-esteem.

## Discussion of Study 3

*Positivity and demographical variables.* Regarding the relation between positivity and the demographical variables, the results obtained in this study suggest that younger adults and more educated individuals possess a higher level of positivity. The importance of an individual's education and its influence on the level of positivity, clearly demonstrated in this study, could serve as evidence for the argument that environmental factors such as these account significantly for the level of individual positivity. Based on this result, education and knowledge could serve as possible tools of intervention for enriching or enhancing positivity.

An interesting result obtained in this study was the relation between age and positivity. Younger people showed a higher level of positivity, with students indicated as possessing the highest of all. This brings up the question of why? What happens after a student's period of study in Serbia? Are there biological factors or factors of environmental influence that could account for difference between young students and their older counterparts? Environmental influence would not, as was demonstrated in other studies in various cultural context, support such findings. If it is somehow the influence of learning and good expectations regarding one's future that stimulate positivity, then a natural consideration would be the promotion of lifelong learning and simply believing in a beautiful future. Before any such course might be suggested, however, this exceptional finding needs to be more precisely explored, even in Serbia itself. Indeed, these findings from Serbia are not in accordance with the data from previous studies (Caprara, Caprara, & Steca, 2003; Caprara & Steca, 2005, 2006) in which men reported higher levels of positive orientation and no significant differences due to age were found.

The extent to which gender differences reflect socialization processes and adaptation strategies in the various life contexts remains unclear. In previous studies (Caprara et al., 2003) a tendency toward declining positivity had been noticed in very old age, though Diener and Diener (1996) reported that happiness and life satisfaction remain relatively stable across ages.

Perhaps an even more interesting result indicated by an analysis of the demographical variables is that current unemployment status, marital status, and gender differences do not appear to be related to positivity. Although the findings of this study indicating no gender differences were not supported by the results of Study 1 in this chapter, they do raise questions about the certainty of any such findings. These results also offer some support for ideas about an indirect argument that positivity is influenced by heredity, as some studies have reported (Fagnani et al., 2014), and that biological underpinning is related to positivity in human functioning (Alessandri et al., 2015). Likewise, the pervasiveness of positivity on an individual's functioning in different cultural contexts could also bolster the argument for positivity's biological underpinnings.

*Predictive power of positivity for depression and self-efficacy.* Following findings in Study 3 of this chapter, a series of hierarchical regression analyses were employed, showing the predictive power of positivity in predicting levels of depression and self-efficacy, compared with the predictive power of its components; life satisfaction, self-esteem, and optimism. Positivity itself explained 25% of depression and 32% of self-efficacy, while all three components of positive orientation explained 7% and 4% of the criterion variables. These findings additionally, yet clearly and precisely, support the construct of positivity as a superordinate to self-esteem, life satisfaction, and dispositional optimism. These results strongly corroborated that the construct of positive orientation is a broader and more general construct than a simple sum of the subordinate constructs of life satisfaction, self-esteem, and dispositional optimism.

Likewise, the results also documented the relation between positivity and depression and positivity and self-efficacy. These findings are inspirational and important, as they opened up an important and interesting questions and possible conclusions.

Regarding the relation between positivity and self-efficacy, it is useful to look at the research and results of Oleś and colleagues (2013). This study considered the question of whether general self-efficacy could be traced together with self-esteem, life satisfaction, and optimism to a common latent dimension, namely, POS or positivity. The findings corroborated the previous findings tracing self-esteem, life satisfaction, and optimism to positivity while leaving general self-efficacy as a separate but correlated factor (Caprara, Alessandri, & Barbaranelli, 2010). They explored the model's fit by adding general self-efficacy to the triad of self-esteem, life satisfaction, and optimism and concluded that by adding general self-efficacy, the model's fit decreased. Although we did not explore the relation between positivity and general self-efficacy in this way, as we were interested in the power of positivity to predict depression and self-efficacy, findings of Oleś et al. (2013) were in close accordance with our research. As it is clear from the results in Study 3 in this chapter, when we added all three components of positive orientation, they explained only 7% and 4% of the criterion variables. In comparison to the predictive power of positivity in predicting levels of depression and self-efficacy, it could be seen as a significant decreasing effect.

Oleś et al. (2013) emphasized that the results they obtained add support to the opinion that individuals who score high on positivity feel a stronger confidence in their potentialities and strengths, yet these two sets of beliefs are distinct.

What are the important and interesting questions that open up when contrasting Oleś et al. (2013) with research and findings on the Serbian sample? Some of them are: what interventions we could choose or create to support positivity, what style of bringing up children we can recommend, what schooling we could support, what we could offer to adults in promoting positivity, and many other similar questions. When we add to this discussion similar question regarding the results obtained about the relation of positivity and depression, we are on a way to support and promote positive mental health and to make an important contribution to mental health in general.

The significance of these findings for mental health in general and positive mental health in particular is quite important. It is well known that depression is increasing in Serbia, in Europe, and across the world. If we could predict depression by positivity and significantly prevent it, then we would have a powerful tool for designing approaches for enhancing positive mental health in people. Also, self-efficacy is a very promising concept, generally important and particularly so given the human world's contemporary rhythms. The authors of this chapter believe that it would be very useful to gain more insight into how positivity operates so that accomplished knowledge could be more efficiently utilized. Łaguna (2019) offered a valuable contribution to this aim, explaining how positive orientation may relate to activity engagement and stimulate persistence in action.

## Study 4: Positivity and Personality Traits

The aim of this study was twofold: first, to test the relations between positivity and personality traits, tracing its potential determinants, and exploring the variance of positivity explained by personality traits; second, to examine the predictive power of personality traits in relation to depression and self-efficacy, focusing on the unique increment of positivity in these relations and suggesting its potential mediating role in relations between personality and subjective well-being.

### Participants

A total of 1,010 Serbian adults (50.4% females; M age = 41.86, SD = 14.17, age range 19–79) participated in the study. Table 16.11 presents a detailed description of the study sample.

### Instruments

In this study, the Serbian translation of the positivity scale described above in Study 1 was employed (PS; Caprara, Alessandri, Eisenberg, et al., 2012), as were

**Table 16.11**    Study 4 sample description.

| Variable | | Percentage |
|---|---|---|
| Age | 19–29 | 59.3% |
| | 30–39 | 20.3% |
| | 40–49 | 14.5% |
| | 50–59 | 5.2% |
| | > 60 | 0.7% |
| Gender | Male | 49.6% |
| | Female | 50.4% |
| Marital status | Single | 47.0% |
| | Married | 29.5% |
| | In a relationship | 14.3% |
| | Divorced | 8% |
| | Widowed | 1.2% |
| Education | No or elementary school | 1.6% |
| | High school | 48.2% |
| | Student | 21.5% |
| | University degree | 28.7% |
| Employment | Unemployed | 43% |
| | Temporarily employed | 17.9% |
| | Permanently employed | 37.9% |
| | Retired | 1.2% |

the Serbian translation of the GSES (Schwarzer & Jerusalem, 1995) and the Serbian translation of the CES–D (Radloff, 1977), both described above in Study 3.

Also, the personality traits were measured through a Serbian translation of the short versions of the Big Five questionnaire (BFQ; Caprara, Barbaranelli, & Borgogni, 1993). The BFQ contains 60 items that form five domain scales: energy/extraversion, agreeableness, conscientiousness, emotional stability, and openness, each incorporating 12 items. The responses to each item are indicated on a 5-point Likert scale ranging from 1 (very false for me), to 5 (very true for me). The Cronbach's alpha coefficients in this research ranged from 0.70 (energy/extraversion) to 0.81 (emotional stability).

## Results

As can be seen in Table 16.12 describing total sample and male and female subsamples separately, positivity demonstrated highly significant correlations with self-efficacy and depression in a negative manner. It was also seen to correlate moderately with personality traits such as energy/extraversion and emotional stability, and to a low but still significant level with agreeableness.

To test the potential mediating effect of positivity in the relation between personality traits and depression and general self-efficacy, yet having in mind that mediation can be said to occur when (a) the independent variable (IV) significantly affects the mediator, (b) the IV significantly affects the dependent variable (DV) in the absence of the mediator, (c) the mediator has a significant unique effect on the DV, and (d) the effect of the IV on the DV shrinks upon the addition of the mediator to the model (Baron & Kenny, 1986), all of these conditions were tested.

After controlling for age and gender effect, positivity was shown to be significantly predicted by energy/extraversion, emotional stability, and conscientiousness (Table 16.13).

These three personality traits also directly and significantly predicted self-efficacy and, reversely, the level of depression (Table 16.14), while agreeableness and openness failed to predict either positivity or the criteria of depression and self-efficacy.

After entering positivity in the equation of personality traits predicting the level of depression, it significantly overtook the predictive variance of all three traits, lowering their regression coefficient to a level still significant (Table 16.14). The partial mediation role of positivity in predicting depression by personality traits was confirmed by Sobel tests for energy/extraversion ($z = -6.50$; $p < 0.01$), conscientiousness ($z = -4.09$; $p < 0.01$), and emotional stability ($z = -7.74$; $p < 0.01$).

Conversely, the level of general self-efficacy was shown to be predicted by three personality traits – energy/extraversion, conscientiousness, and emotional stability. After entering positivity in Step 3 of the equation, the standardized regression coefficient lowered for the energy/extraversion trait, indicating the partial mediation role of positivity, which was confirmed by a Sobel test ($z = 7.93$; $p < 0.01$), as

**Table 16.12** Descriptive statistics and correlations between variables in Study 4.

| | M | SD | r Positivity | r Depression | r General self-efficacy |
|---|---|---|---|---|---|
| **Total sample (N = 1,332)** | | | | | |
| Positivity | 3.65 | 0.62 | — | — | — |
| Depression | 0.69 | 0.48 | −0.50** | — | — |
| General self-efficacy | 3.22 | 0.51 | 0.55** | −0.46** | — |
| Energy/extraversion | 3.30 | 0.44 | 0.37** | −0.28** | 0.37** |
| Conscientiousness | 3.38 | 0.56 | 0.28** | −0.30** | 0.38** |
| Agreeableness | 3.11 | 0.45 | 0.19** | −0.15** | 0.10* |
| Emotional stability | 3.12 | 0.67 | 0.37** | −0.42** | 0.26** |
| Openness | 3.21 | 0.57 | 0.23** | −0.20** | 0.28** |
| **Male subsample (N = 501)** | | | | | |
| Positivity | 3.66 | 0.61 | — | — | — |
| Depression | 0.66 | 0.46 | −0.46** | — | — |
| General self-efficacy | 3.25 | 0.51 | 0.53** | −0.43** | — |
| Energy/extraversion | 3.32 | 0.43 | 0.36** | −0.24** | 0.34** |
| Conscientiousness | 3.34 | 0.55 | 0.33** | −0.30** | 0.42** |
| Agreeableness | 3.11 | 0.45 | 0.14** | −0.12** | 0.05 |
| Emotional stability | 3.12 | 0.67 | 0.37** | −0.38** | 0.27** |
| Openness | 3.25 | 0.59 | 0.21** | −0.19** | 0.28** |
| **Female subsample (N = 509)** | | | | | |
| Positivity | 3.65 | 0.62 | — | — | — |
| Depression | 0.73 | 0.51 | −0.53** | — | — |
| General self-efficacy | 3.18 | 0.52 | 0.56** | −0.46** | — |
| Energy/extraversion | 3.27 | 0.45 | 0.37** | −0.32** | 0.39** |
| Conscientiousness | 3.41 | 0.57 | 0.25** | −0.32** | 0.35** |
| Agreeableness | 3.11 | 0.46 | 0.23** | −0.19** | 0.16** |
| Emotional stability | 3.04 | 0.67 | 0.36** | −0.46** | 0.25** |
| Openness | 3.17 | 0.57 | 0.25** | −0.20** | 0.27** |

*Note*: **$p < 0.01$; *$p < 0.05$.

**Table 16.13** Hierarchical regression analyses of personality traits predicting positivity.

| | $R^2$ | $\Delta R^2$ | F change | $\beta$ | Tol | VIF |
|---|---|---|---|---|---|---|
| Step 1: Gender and age | 0.02 | 0.02 | 9.6** | | | |
| Age | | | | −0.02 | 1.00 | 1.01 |
| Gender | | | | −0.14** | 1.00 | 1.01 |
| Step 2: | 0.26 | 0.24 | 63.55** | | | |
| Age | | | | 0.02 | 0.97 | 1.03 |
| Gender | | | | −0.08* | 0.97 | 1.04 |
| Energy/Extraversion | | | | 0.24** | 0.78 | 1.28 |
| Conscientiousness | | | | 0.13** | 0.80 | 1.25 |
| Agreeableness | | | | 0.02 | 0.88 | 1.14 |
| Emotional stability | | | | 0.29** | 0.91 | 1.10 |
| Openness | | | | 0.02 | 0.77 | 1.30 |

*Note*: Tol = tolerance; VIF = variance inflation factor; **$p < 0.01$; *$p < 0.05$.

**Table 16.14**    Hierarchical regression analyses of personality traits and positivity predicting depression and general self-efficacy.

|  | $R^2$ | $\Delta R^2$ | F change | β | Tol | VIF |
|---|---|---|---|---|---|---|
| *Model 1: Depression* | | | | | | |
| Step 1: Gender and age | 0.01 | 0.01 | 5.03** | | | |
| Age | | | | 0.08* | 1.00 | 1.00 |
| Gender | | | | 0.07* | 1.00 | 1.00 |
| Step 2: | 0.26 | 0.25 | 67.06** | | | |
| Age | | | | 0.04 | 0.99 | 1.01 |
| Gender | | | | 0.02 | 0.99 | 1.01 |
| Energy/Extraversion | | | | −0.15** | 0.78 | 1.28 |
| Conscientiousness | | | | −0.19** | 0.80 | 1.25 |
| Agreeableness | | | | −0.01 | 0.87 | 1.00 |
| Emotional stability | | | | −0.36** | 0.91 | 1.11 |
| Openness | | | | 0.01 | 0.77 | 1.30 |
| Step 3: | 0.35 | 0.09 | 132.75** | | | |
| Age | | | | 0.05 | 0.97 | 1.03 |
| Gender | | | | 0.01 | 0.96 | 1.05 |
| Energy/Extraversion | | | | −0.07* | 0.74 | 1.36 |
| Conscientiousness | | | | −0.15** | 0.78 | 1.27 |
| Agreeableness | | | | 0.01 | 0.87 | 1.14 |
| Emotional stability | | | | −0.26** | 0.82 | 1.22 |
| Openness | | | | 0.01 | 0.77 | 1.30 |
| Positivity | | | | −0.34** | 0.75 | 1.34 |
| *Model 2: General self-efficacy* | | | | | | |
| Step 1: Gender and age | 0.01 | 0.01 | 2.66 | | | |
| Age | | | | −0.04 | 1.00 | 1.00 |
| Gender | | | | −0.03 | 1.00 | 1.00 |
| Step 2: | 0.25 | 0.24 | 65.10** | | | |
| Age | | | | −0.04 | 0.97 | 1.03 |
| Gender | | | | −0.03 | 0.96 | 1.04 |
| Energy/Extraversion | | | | 0.25** | 0.78 | 1.28 |
| Conscientiousness | | | | 0.25** | 0.80 | 1.25 |
| Agreeableness | | | | −0.06 | 0.88 | 1.14 |
| Emotional stability | | | | 0.17** | 0.91 | 1.10 |
| Openness | | | | 0.08 | 0.77 | 1.30 |
| Step 3: | 0.39 | 0.14 | 223.54** | | | |
| Age | | | | −0.05 | 0.97 | 1.03 |
| Gender | | | | 0.06 | 0.96 | 1.04 |
| Energy/Extraversion | | | | 0.14** | 0.73 | 1.36 |
| Conscientiousness | | | | 0.19** | 0.78 | 1.28 |
| Agreeableness | | | | −0.07 | 0.87 | 1.14 |
| Emotional stability | | | | 0.05 | 0.82 | 1.22 |
| Openness | | | | 0.07 | 0.77 | 1.30 |
| Positivity | | | | 0.43** | 0.75 | 1.34 |

*Note*: Tol = tolerance; VIF = variance inflation factor; **$p < 0.01$; *$p < 0.05$.

was also the case for conscientiousness ($z = 6.25$; $p < 0.01$). In the case of emotional stability, the standardized regression coefficient in Step 3 lowered insignificantly, suggesting a potential full mediation by positivity, which was confirmed by a Sobel test ($z = 7.82$; $p < 0.01$).

## Discussion of Study 4

It is important to note that Caprara and his colleagues (2018) have emphasized that positive orientation differs from other basic dispositions like those that are commonly investigated under the five-factor model (Digman, 1990; John & Srivastava, 1999). Whereas the so-called Big Five are related to behavioral dispositions, positive orientation represents a basic attitude that is present and is important in facing major challenges of human life, such as illness, aging, and death. Additionally, Caprara and his colleagues (2019) have asserted that more than any of the Big Five, positive orientation rests on human beings' unique capacities to reflect upon their experience and to make sense of their life.

The results of Study 4 in this chapter support the main findings of other research (Caprara, Alessandri, Eisenberg, et al., 2012; Lauriola & Iani, 2015; Miciuk, Jankowski, Laskowska, & Oleś, 2016) which have explored the relation between positivity and personality traits inside the Big Five model. For the sample drawn from Serbia, positivity correlated moderately with energy/extraversion and emotional stability and low with agreeableness and it was shown to be significantly predicted by energy/extraversion, emotional stability, and conscientiousness. Such findings could be useful in developing and planning interventions for improving positivity. Although much more needs to be done to understand better how, and by what mechanisms, positivity is operating as an element in human's experiencing and acting in this world, these findings could serve as a springboard, as well as a directional tool, for planning psychological programs which promote expressive techniques and positive reflections about oneself, one's life, and one's future, including positive appraisals of events which could further nourish positive feelings.

The findings also support the importance of positivity for mental health, as emotional stability is a variable that contributes significantly to overall stability and health. Likewise, the findings suggest that energy as a human resource and the expression (energy/extraversion) of inner psychological states and processes could serve as some sort of base for overall well-being. Lauriola and Iani (2015) explored the positive mediational role of positive orientation in the relation between the Big Five and happiness. These authors reported initial evidence that positive orientation might be a mediator of the relation between both extraversion and neuroticism and subjective happiness.

In this study the predictive power of personality traits in regard to depression and self- efficacy was also examined, with special focus put on the contribution of positivity. The partial mediation role of positivity in predicting depression by personality traits was confirmed for energy/extraversion, conscientiousness, and emotional stability. From the obtained data, the significant mediating role of positivity in predicting depression by personality traits was also apparent. This would seem to suggest then that positivity has a special mediating role in predicting depression, which is beyond the contribution of personality traits included in the Big Five traits.

The level of general self-efficacy was also shown to be predicted by energy/extraversion, conscientiousness, and emotional stability. After entering positivity in this prediction, its partial mediation role regarding energy/extraversion and conscientiousness and full mediation in the case of emotional stability was observed. From this, it could be said that positivity has a very important mediating role in predicting self-efficacy, even rendering the prediction power of self-efficacy by emotional stability insignificant. These findings then raise the questions: Is positivity broader in scope than emotional stability and in what sense? Or, can one's self-efficacy stem directly from, or account for, a positive view about oneself, life, and future? Yet, without controlling or entering positivity in the prediction, the trait of emotional stability was shown to predict self-efficacy. It seems that this could support the argument that positivity is a wider concept than are the personality traits inside the Big Five model of personality, at least when we are exploring emotional stability. Comparing the contributions of positivity and emotional stability in predicting self-efficacy, it becomes clear that positivity is not only a more broadly applicable trait than those dispositions inside the Big Five model, at least certainly wider than emotional stability, but also, based on these and other results, that positivity could be viewed as functioning like a major or fundamental disposition responsible for positive mental health and well-being in general. But a question lingers: to what degree does emotional stability contribute to positive affectivity and positive mental health? Or does it not? Emotional stability could serve as testament that one is not mentally ill, but this does not necessarily mean that one is mentally healthy in the frame of positive mental health criteria. What is clear is that these questions and hypotheses arising from the results of this study need to be tested further.

## Study 5: Positivity, Early Family Traumatization, and Subjective Well-Being

The aim of this study was to investigate the potential mediating role of positivity in the relation between unresolved family traumatization and variables of subjective well-being. In order to do so, several mediation analyses were conducted by hierarchical regression using the IBM SPSS 22. In all of the models tested, age and gender effect were controlled by entering these factors in the first step of building the equation. In the second step of building the models the predictive power of unresolved family traumatization was evaluated, while in the third step the positivity variable was added. The analyses were conducted on standardized scores of all the variables.

## Participants

A total of 1,781 Serbian adults (54% females; M age = 30.16, SD = 10.31, age range 18–80) participated in the present study. Table 16.15 presents a detailed description of the study sample. Participation in the study was voluntary, anonymous, and respondents received no compensation for their participation. Participants were recruited via convenience, and the snowball sampling method (Goodman, 1961) was performed by undergraduate students at the Faculty of Law and Business Studies in Novi Sad, Serbia.

## Instruments

Along with the Serbian translation of the positivity scale described above in Study 1 (PS; Caprara, Alessandri, Eisenberg, et al., 2012) several other instruments were used.

The unresolved family traumatization scale (UPIPAV-NPT; Hanak, 2004) is a subscale of the questionnaire for assessment of adult and adolescent attachment

**Table 16.15**  Study 5 sample description.

| Variable | | Percentage |
| --- | --- | --- |
| Age | 19–29 | 59.3% |
| | 30–39 | 20.3% |
| | 40–49 | 14.5% |
| | 50–59 | 5.2% |
| | > 60 | 0.7% |
| Gender | Male | 46% |
| | Female | 54% |
| Marital status | Single | 47.0% |
| | Married | 29.5% |
| | In a relationship | 14.3% |
| | Divorced | 8% |
| | Widowed | 1.2% |
| Education | No or elementary school | 1.6% |
| | High school | 48.2% |
| | Student | 21.5% |
| | University degree | 28.7% |
| Employment | Unemployed | 43% |
| | Temporarily employed | 17.9% |
| | Permanently employed | 37.9% |
| | Retired | 1.2% |

(UPIPAV; Hanak, 2004). It was used to assess unresolved family traumatization, that is, the presence of painful feelings and negative attitudes toward a person's family during childhood and/or adolescence. The responses to each of the 11 UPIPAV-NPT items (e.g., *Because of bad experiences with my parents, I find it difficult to trust people*) range from 1 (strongly disagree) to 7 (strongly agree). The scale has demonstrated excellent psychometric properties (Hanak, 2004). In this research, the scale demonstrated a high internal consistency ($\alpha = 0.91$).

The Serbian version of the depression anxiety and stress scale (DASS-21; Lovibond & Lovibond, 1995) was used to assess negative affective states. The DASS-21 consists of 21 items and includes three subscales: depression (e.g., *I felt I wasn't worth much as a person*), anxiety (e.g., *I felt scared without any good reason*), and stress (e.g., *I tended to overreact to situations*). Responses are rated on a 4-point scale, from 0 (did not apply to me at all) to 3 (applied to me very much, or most of the time). The DASS-21 translation to Serbian has been widely used and has shown good psychometric properties both in adult and adolescent samples (Jovanović, Gavrilov-Jerković, Žuljević, & Brdarić, 2014; Jovanović, Žuljević, & Brdarić, 2011). For this particular study, only the DASS-21 total score was utilized ($\alpha = 0.93$).

The Serbian inventory of affect based on the positive and negative affect schedule-X (SIAB-PANAS; Novović & Mihić, 2008) is a Serbian translation and adaptation of the positive and negative affect schedule-X (PANAS-X; Watson & Clark, 1994). The scale has demonstrated excellent psychometric properties in previous studies (Novović, Mihić, Tovilović, & Jovanović, 2008). In this study, the short form of the scale was employed to measure positive affect (PA; $\alpha = 0.91$) and negative affect (NA; $\alpha = 0.92$), with 10 items each. Participants were asked to report how they feel in general, using a 5-point Likert scale ranging from 1 (never or almost never) to 5 (always or almost always).

## Results

In order to test the potential mediating effect of positivity within the predictive power of family traumatization on the variables of subjective well-being, and having in mind the conditions for mediation analysis (Baron & Kenny, 1986) mentioned above in Study 3, each of these conditions was tested sequentially. In Table 16.16, higher levels of unresolved family traumatization were shown to significantly predict lower levels of positivity, thus satisfying the first condition of mediation.

As presented in Steps 2 of all the models tested (Table 16.16), the unresolved family traumatization had a significant and unique effect on all of the well-being variables, predicting higher scores of general distress and negative affect, as well as lower scores of satisfaction with life and positive affect. In the opposite direction, these same findings were shown to be true for positivity. Also, the unique predictive power of family traumatization dropped after adding positivity in all of the

**Table 16.16**  Hierarchical regression analyses of unresolved family traumatization predicting positivity.

|  | $R^2$ | $\Delta R^2$ | F change | $\beta$ | Tol | VIF |
|---|---|---|---|---|---|---|
| Step 1: Gender and age | 0.01 | 0.01 | 2.04 |  |  |  |
| Age |  |  |  | 0.02 | 0.99 | 1.01 |
| Gender |  |  |  | 0.05 | 0.99 | 1.01 |
| Step 2: | 0.09 | 0.08 | 144.12** |  |  |  |
| Age |  |  |  | 0.02 | 0.99 | 1.01 |
| Gender |  |  |  | 0.05 | 0.99 | 1.01 |
| Family traumatization |  |  |  | −0.27** | 1.00 | 1.00 |

*Note*: Tol = tolerance; VIF = variance inflation factor; **$p < 0.01$; *$p < 0.05$.

models, suggesting a partial mediation effect in all of the models except for positive affect, where the mediation was full. The highly significant Sobel test statistic (Sobel, 1982) finally suggested that the mediational role of positivity in the relation between unresolved family traumatization and subjective well-being is unquestionable: $z = 9.34$, $p < 0.00$ for general depression; $z = 8.20$, $p < 0.00$ for general anxiety; $z = 8.12$, $p < 0.00$ for stress; $z = 9.73$ $p < 0.00$ for negative affect; and $z = -10.79$, $p < 0.00$ for positive affect (see Table 16.17).

## Discussion of Study 5

The results of Study 5 provide evidence that unresolved family traumatization has a significant unique effect on all of the well-being variables included in the research, as it predicted higher scores of general distress and negative affect, as well as lower scores of satisfaction with life and positive affect. The same can also be said for positivity, but in the opposite direction. It is worth noting that the unique predictive power of family traumatization lowered after taking into account the contribution of positivity on all included variables. Or, in other words, positivity demonstrated a partial mediation effect for all the variables included in the study with the exception for positive affect, where the mediation was full. Thus, the results suggest that the mediational role of positivity in the relation between unresolved family traumatization and subjective well-being is considerable and unquestionable.

This is a powerful data finding, as one could say that positivity is a protective factor against the psychological consequences of early family traumatization, especially in regard to variables of subjective well-being. Developmental psychological models (English, Wisener, & Bailey, 2018) have argued that early development and early traumatization have a considerable impact on the whole individual psychological functioning and in that sense are crucial for individual mental health. Positivity appears to serve as a partly protective factor for general depression, general anxiety, stress, and negative affect, while, particularly important, as

**Table 16.17**  Hierarchical regression analyses of unresolved family traumatization and positivity predicting subjective well-being.

|  | $R^2$ | $\Delta R^2$ | F change | $\beta$ | Tol | VIF |
|---|---|---|---|---|---|---|
| *Model 1: Depression* |  |  |  |  |  |  |
| Step 1: Gender and age | 0.01 | 0.01 | 0.78 |  |  |  |
| Age |  |  |  | 0.01 | 0.99 | 1.01 |
| Gender |  |  |  | 0.03 | 0.99 | 1.01 |
| Step 2: | 0.12 | 0.11 | 242.75** |  |  |  |
| Age |  |  |  | 0.01 | 0.99 | 1.01 |
| Gender |  |  |  | 0.02 | 0.99 | 1.01 |
| Family traumatization |  |  |  | 0.35** | 1.00 | 1.00 |
| Step 3: | 0.26 | 0.14 | 330.17** |  |  |  |
| Age |  |  |  | 0.01 | 0.99 | 1.00 |
| Gender |  |  |  | 0.04 | 0.99 | 1.00 |
| Family traumatization |  |  |  | 0.24** | 0.93 | 1.08 |
| Positivity |  |  |  | −0.39** | 0.92 | 1.09 |
| *Model 2: Anxiety* |  |  |  |  |  |  |
| Step 1: Gender and age | 0.01 | 0.01 | 9.19** |  |  |  |
| Age |  |  |  | −0.03 | 0.99 | 1.01 |
| Gender |  |  |  | 0.06* | 0.99 | 1.01 |
| Step 2: | 0.13 | 0.11 | 236.78** |  |  |  |
| Age |  |  |  | −0.03 | 0.99 | 1.01 |
| Gender |  |  |  | 0.05** | 0.99 | 1.01 |
| Family traumatization |  |  |  | 0.33** | 1.00 | 1.00 |
| Step 3: | 0.17 | 0.06 | 92.57** |  |  |  |
| Age |  |  |  | −0.03 | 0.99 | 1.00 |
| Gender |  |  |  | 0.06** | 0.99 | 1.00 |
| Family traumatization |  |  |  | 0.26** | 0.93 | 1.08 |
| Positivity |  |  |  | −0.24** | 0.92 | 1.08 |
| *Model 3: Stress* |  |  |  |  |  |  |
| Step 1: Gender and age | 0.01 | 0.01 | 3.41* |  |  |  |
| Age |  |  |  | −0.05* | 0.99 | 1.01 |
| Gender |  |  |  | 0.09** | 0.99 | 1.01 |
| Step 2: | 0.11 | 0.11 | 215.58** |  |  |  |
| Age |  |  |  | −0.06* | 0.99 | 1.01 |
| Gender |  |  |  | 0.08** | 0.99 | 1.01 |
| Family traumatization |  |  |  | 0.34** | 1.00 | 1.00 |
| Step 3: | 0.17 | 0.06 | 113.91** |  |  |  |
| Age |  |  |  | −0.05** | 0.99 | 1.00 |
| Gender |  |  |  | 0.09** | 0.99 | 1.00 |
| Family traumatization |  |  |  | 0.28** | 0.93 | 1.08 |
| Positivity |  |  |  | −0.22** | 0.92 | 1.08 |

**Table 16.17**  (Continued)

| | $R^2$ | $\Delta R^2$ | F change | $\beta$ | Tol | VIF |
|---|---|---|---|---|---|---|
| *Model 4: Negative affect* | | | | | | |
| Step 1: Gender and age | 0.01 | 0.01 | 11.33** | | | |
| Age | | | | −0.01 | 0.99 | 1.01 |
| Gender | | | | 0.11** | 0.99 | 1.01 |
| Step 2: | 0.09 | 0.08 | 160.75** | | | |
| Age | | | | −0.01 | 0.99 | 1.01 |
| Gender | | | | 0.11** | 0.99 | 1.01 |
| Family traumatization | | | | 0.29** | 1.00 | 1.00 |
| Step 3: | 0.21 | 0.12 | 259.71** | | | |
| Age | | | | −0.01 | 0.99 | 1.00 |
| Gender | | | | 0.13** | 0.99 | 1.00 |
| Family traumatization | | | | 0.19** | 0.93 | 1.08 |
| Positivity | | | | −0.35** | 0.92 | 1.09 |
| *Model 5: Negative affect* | | | | | | |
| Step 1: Gender and age | 0.01 | 0.01 | 3.26* | | | |
| Age | | | | 0.06* | 0.99 | 1.00 |
| Gender | | | | 0.01 | 0.99 | 1.00 |
| Step 2: | 0.02 | 0.02 | 41.98** | | | |
| Age | | | | 0.06* | 0.99 | 1.01 |
| Gender | | | | 0.02 | 0.99 | 1.01 |
| Family traumatization | | | | −0.15** | 1.00 | 1.00 |
| Step 3: | 0.29 | 0.26 | 660.49** | | | |
| Age | | | | 0.05* | 0.99 | 1.01 |
| Gender | | | | −0.01 | 0.99 | 1.01 |
| Family traumatization | | | | −0.01 | 0.93 | 1.08 |
| Positivity | | | | 0.54** | 0.92 | 1.08 |

*Note*: Tol = tolerance; VIF = variance inflation factor; **$p < 0.01$; *$p < 0.05$.

completely protective for positive affect. Thus, the data clearly demonstrated that the significance of positivity in the relation between unresolved family traumatization and subjective well-being is very important, while for positive affects it is crucial. This leads to the conclusion that the protective power of positivity in unresolved family traumatization should be more extensively applied as a possible practical application and in the promotion of overall mental health.

To gain greater insight into the obtained results regarding the relation between positivity and positive affectivity, the finding linking positive orientation to subjective happiness should be addressed. This finding comes from two studies that examined how the relations between positivity and positive affectivity operates or functions over time. Caprara, Eisenberg, and Alessandri (2016) have shown that positivity predicts positive affect over the course of development from adolescence to young adulthood, but the flow of influence does function inversely, from positive affect to positivity. The authors of another study (Alessandri, Zuffianò, Fabes, Vecchione, & Martin, 2014), using seven waves of daily evaluations of positive orientation across an entire week, reported a significant prediction of positive affect by positive orientation, but again, not inversely. The findings of both of these studies support one another, not only in attesting to the strong association between positive orientation and positive affect, but also in clearly recognizing the flow of influence from positive orientation to positive affect, and not the other way around. Indirectly, the finding from Study 4 of this chapter, utilizing a Serbian sample, added further confirmation with its findings, showing that positivity is fully predictive of positive affectivity. This deserves particular consideration, as there is a growing amount of research and literature reporting that positive affectivity is a major correlate and determinant of well-being, well adjustment, and health (Fredrickson & Losada, 2005; Lyubomirsky, King, & Diener, 2005).

## Toward Positivity

Five studies on positivity carried out on a Serbian sample mainly confirm the findings reported by a large number of the other investigations on positivity, administered to thousands of participants over the past 20 years and conducted across a large and varied array of countries, contexts, and cultures.

The studies (state years) on the Serbian sample attest to positivity being a common latent factor for self-esteem, life satisfaction, and dispositional optimism; that the measure of positivity obtained by an 8-item scale is an excellent representation of the conceptual model of positivity, as there is an excellent match between the conceptual model and the observed data; that the predictive power of positivity in predicting levels of depression and self-efficacy, compared with predictive power of its components, life satisfaction, self-esteem and optimism is much higher; that positivity has a special status inside personality, especially regarding the Big Five model; and that positivity should be regarded as a wider concept than basic dispositions inside a five-factor model. Finally, the last of the five studies done on the Serbian sample, exploring the relation between positivity and positive affectivity, suggest that positivity is a protective factor against the psychological consequences of early family traumatization, especially in regard to variables of subjective well-being. These five studies should serve as a worthy contribution toward a more accurate understanding of the theoretical concept of positivity, its measuring ability, and its relations to the other psychological concepts, personality, and subjective well-being, as well as of its potential applicability.

What has emerged as a "figure in front of a background," as a gestalt-oriented psychologist might say, is that positivity can predict depression at a high percentage, that positivity exceeds emotional stability in predicting a self-efficacy, that positivity decreases the consequences of early family traumatization and increases the likelihood and presence of positive affect. All these findings support the hypothesis that positivity may be a basic disposition correlated with positive mental health and in that sense is conductive to optimal adjustment across various domains of functioning, such as health, differing fields of achievement, job performance, and job satisfaction (Caprara et al., 2019). Following this logic, positivity also contributes significantly to subjective well-being (Caprara et al., 2016). The authors of this study emphasize that further studies must be done to test and refine this hypothesis so that a more thorough understanding of the fundamental psychological roots of positivity, its significance for human mental health, and its possible practical implementations may be gained.

Results gained from this study supplement those from previous studies regarding the relation between positive affect and positivity revealing that positivity significantly predicts positive affectivity across time rather than vice versa (Caprara et al., 2016) and similar findings (Alessandri et al., 2014) regarding the relation of positivity to positive affect supports the above hypothesis. Caprara et al. (2016) have also asserted that positivity has a fundamental role in creating the conditions to face, frame, and construe experience in ways that activate and promote positive affect. Basing their remarks on studies done regarding relations between positivity and different psychological variables, researchers (Caprara et al., 2016) have concluded that it is highly plausible that positivity contributes to an individual's mood by predisposing them to positive emotional experiences and by enhancing positive feelings. All these findings are especially noteworthy as positive affect has been associated with many health outcomes through its apparent effects on cognition and social relationships (Bolte, Goschkey, & Kuhl, 2003; Fredrickson & Branigan, 2005; Fredrickson & Joiner, 2002; Lyubomirsky et al., 2005; Rowe, Hirsh, & Anderson, 2007) as well as on various physiological functions, such as cardiovascular, endocrinal, and immunological processes (Pressman & Cohen, 2005).

Despite the strength of past findings, further research is still needed to clarify the path of influence between positivity and positive affectivity generally, across longitudinal studies, and over the course of development, as well as to clarify the influences of culture and life experiences on these constructs. Likewise, these findings have significant value in regard to mental health and overall health.

Certain results gained from Study 4 in this chapter merit further discussion. The protective function of positivity revealed in regard to consequences of early family traumatization and concepts like depression, anxiety, stress, and negative affect are truly significant. More precise further studies in these directions could prove significant in achieving a fuller understanding of how these relations might function over the full course of one's development and in different cultural contexts, as well as aid in clarifying the effects of additional life experience on these relations.

These five studies conducted in Serbia have attempted to confront the most fundamental and pressing questions regarding the theory, measuring, and practice of positivity, but they also have raised or further prompted, and perhaps even established a springboard for, questions demanding further research, most relevantly into the impact of positivity on different spheres of life and domains of functioning, such as physical health, family, job, coping, and other domains. Also, in the future, as Caprara et al. (2019) have stated, it would be useful to further clarify how and when different feelings about the self, life, and the future ultimately unite under a unique pervasive disposition. Viewing POS as a disposition opens a new field for research and practice in approaching the promotion of human potential and strengths. Recent research has indicated that positivity is stable, yet also flexible to change (Caprara, Steca, et al., 2010). Thus, research designed to test whether, and especially how, positivity operates as a beneficial function and whether and why a lack or excess of POS may carry negative consequences deserve further investigation. This kind of knowledge is crucial to designing interventions structured on practices that promote and sustain individuals' POS. Finally, a better understanding of the biological correlates of positivity and the ways that positivity may moderate stress, illness, and pain is likely to prove critical to promoting overall health and well-being.

# References

Alessandri, G., Caprara, G. V., & De Pascalis, V. (2015). Relations among EEG-alpha asymmetry and positivity personality trait. *Brain and Cognition*, 5(97), 10–21.

Alessandri, G., Caprara, G. V., & Tisak, J. (2012). A unified latent curve, latent state-trait analysis of the developmental trajectories and correlates of positive orientation. *Multivariate Behavioral Research*, 47, 341–368.

Alessandri, G., Vecchione, M., Tisak, J., Deiana, G., Caria, S., & Caprara, G. V. (2012). The utility of positive orientation in predicting job performance and organisational citizenship behaviors. *Applied Psychology: An International Review*, 61(4), 669–698.

Alessandri, G., Zuffianò, A., Fabes, R., Vecchione, M., & Martin, C. (2014). Linking positive affect and positive self-beliefs in daily life. *Journal of Happiness Studies*, 15, 1479–1493.

Baron, R. M., & Kenny, D. A. (1986). The moderator–mediator variable distinction in social psychological research: Conceptual, strategic, and statistical considerations. *Journal of Personality and Social Psychology*, 51, 1173–1182.

Baumeister, R. (Ed.). (1993). *Self-esteem: The puzzle of low self-regard*. New York: Plenum Press.

Bentler, P. M. (1989). *EQS: Structural equations program model*. Los Angeles, CA: BMDP Statistical Software.

Bentler, P. M. (2006). *EQS: Structural equations program manual*. Encino, CA: Multivariate Software.

Bentler, P. M., & Bonett, D. G. (1980). Significance tests and goodness of fit in the analysis of covariance structures. *Psychological Bulletin*, 88, 588–606.

Bolte, A., Goschkey, T., & Kuhl, J. (2003). Emotion and intuition: Effects of positive and negative mood on implicit judgments of semantic coherence. *Psychological Science*, 14, 416–421.

Borsa, J. C., Damásio, B. F., Souza, D. S. D., Koller, S. H., & Caprara, G. V. (2015). Psychometric properties of the positivity scale – Brazilian version. *Psicologia: Reflexão e Crítica*, 28, 61–67.

Caprara, G. V., & Alessandri, G. (2014). Optimal functioning. In S. Cooper & K. Ratele (Eds.), *Psychology serving humanity* (Vol. 2, pp. 202–214). Hove: Psychology Press.

Caprara, G. V., Alessandri, G., & Barbaranelli, C. (2010). Optimal functioning: Contribution of self-efficacy beliefs to positive orientation. *Psychotherapy and Psychosomatics*, 79(5), 328–330.

Caprara, G. V., Alessandri, G., & Caprara, M. (2019). Associations of positive orientation with health and psychosocial adaptation: A review of findings and perspectives. *Asian Journal of Social Psychology*, 22(2), 126–132.

Caprara, G. V., Alessandri, G., Eisenberg, N., Kupfer, A., Steca, P., Caprara, M. G., . . . Abela, J. (2012). The positivity scale. *Psychological Assessment, 24*(3), 701–712.

Caprara, G. V., Alessandri, G., Trommsdorff, G., Heikamp, T., Yamaguchi, S., & Suzuki, F. (2012). Positive orientation across three cultures. *Journal of Cross-Cultural Psychology, 43*, 77–83.

Caprara, G. V., Barbaranelli, C., & Borgogni, L. (1993). *BFQ: Big five questionnaire: Manuale*. Firenze, Italy: Organizzazioni Speciali.

Caprara, G. V., Caprara, M. G., & Steca, P. (2003). Personality correlates of adult development and aging. *European Psychologist, 8*, 131–147.

Caprara, G. V., Eisenberg, N., & Alessandri, G. (2016). Positivity: The dispositional basis of happiness. *Journal of Happiness Studies, 18*(2), 353–371.

Caprara, G. V., Fagnani, C., Alessandri, G., Steca, P., Gigantesco, A., Cavalli-Sforza, L., & Stazi, M. A. (2009). Human optimal functioning: The genetics of positive orientation towards self, life, and the future. *Behavior Genetics, 39*, 277–284.

Caprara, G. V., & Steca, P. (2005). Affective and social self-regulatory efficacy beliefs as determinants of positive thinking and happiness. *European Psychologist, 4*, 275–286.

Caprara, G. V., & Steca, P. (2006). The contribution of self-regulatory efficacy beliefs in managing affect and family relationships to positive thinking and hedonic balance. *Journal of Social and Clinical Psychology, 25*, 601–625.

Caprara, G. V., Steca, P., Alessandri, G., Abela, J. R., & McWhinnie, C. M. (2010). Positive orientation: Explorations on what is common to life satisfaction, self-esteem, and optimism. *Epidemiologia e psichiatria Sociale, 19*, 63–71.

Carver, C., & Scheier, M. (2002). Optimism. In C. R. Snyder & J. L. Lopez (Eds.), *Handbook of positive psychology* (pp. 231–243). New York. Oxford University Press.

Çıkrıkçı, Ö., Çiftçi, M., & Gençdoğan, G. (2015). Pozitiflik Ölçeği Türkçe Formu'nun psikometrik özellikleri [The psychometric properties of the Turkish form of the positivity scale]. *The Journal of Happiness and Well-Being, 3*(1), 57–76.

Çıkrıkçı, O., & Gençdoğan, B. (2016). Structuring the cognitive dimensions of well-being phenomenon:

Positive orientation model. *Journal of Graduate School of Social Sciences, 20*, 1435–1450.

Cohen, J. (1988). *Statistical power analysis for behavioral sciences* (2nd ed.). Mahwah, NJ: Lawrence Erlbaum.

Diener, E. (1984). Subjective well-being. *Psychological Bulletin, 95*, 542–575.

Diener, E., & Diener, C. (1996). Most people are happy. *Psychological Science, 7*, 181–185.

Diener, E., & Diener, M. (1995). Cross-cultural correlates of life satisfaction and self-esteem. *Journal of Personality and Social Psychology, 68*, 653–663.

Diener, E., Emmons, R. A., Larsen, R. J., & Griffin, S. (1985). The satisfaction with life scale. *Journal of Personality Assessment, 49*, 71–75.

Digman, J. M. (1990). Personality structure: Emergence of the five-factor model. *Annual Review of Psychology, 41*, 417–440.

English, L., Wisener, M., & Bailey, H. (2018). Childhood emotional maltreatment, anxiety, attachment and mindfulness: Associations with facial emotion recognition. *Child Abuse & Neglect, 80*, 146–160.

Fagnani, C., Medda, E., Stazi, M. A., Caprara, G. V., & Alessandri, G. (2014). Investigation of age and gender effects on positive orientation in Italian twins. *International Journal of Psychology, 6*, 453–461.

Fredrickson, B. L., & Branigan, C. A. (2005). Positive emotions broaden the scope of attention and thought–action repertoires. *Cognition and Emotion, 19*, 313–332.

Fredrickson, B. L., & Joiner, T. (2002). Positive emotions trigger upward spirals toward emotional wellbeing. *Psychological Science, 13*, 172–175.

Fredrickson, B. L., & Losada, M. F. (2005). Positive affect and the complex dynamics of human flourishing. *American Psychologist, 60*, 678–686.

Goodman, L. A. (1961). Snowball sampling. *Annals of Mathematical Statistics, 32*(1), 148–170.

Greenberg, J., Solomon, S., Pyszczynski, T., Rosenblatt, A., Burling, J., Lyon, D., . . . Pinel, E. (1992). Why do people need self-esteem? Converging evidence that self-esteem serves an anxiety-buffering function. *Journal of Personality and Social Psychology, 63*, 913–922.

Hanak, N. (2004). Konstruisanje novog instrumenta za procenu afektivnog vezivanja kod odraslih i adolescenata u Srbiji [Construction of the new instrument for assessment of adult and adolescent attachment]. *Psihologija, 37*(1), 123–142.

Harter, S. (1999). *The construction of the self: A developmental perspective.* New York: Guilford Press.

Heikamp, T., Alessandri, G., Łaguna, M., Petrović, V., Caprara, M. G., & Trommsdorff, G. (2014). Cross-cultural validation of the positivity scale in five European countries. *Personality and Individual Differences, 71*, 140–145.

Hu, L. T., & Bentler, P. M. (1998). Fit indices in covariance structure modeling: Sensitivity to underparameterized model misspecification. *Psychological Methods, 3*(4), 424–453.

Hu, L. T., & Bentler, P. M. (1999). Cutoff criteria for fit indexes in covariance structure analysis: Conventional criteria versus new alternatives. *Structural Equation Modeling, 6*(1), 1–55.

John, O. P., & Srivastava, S. (1999). The big five trait taxonomy: History, measurement, and theoretical perspectives. In L. A. Pervin & O. P. John (Eds.), *Handbook of personality: Theory and research* (2nd ed., pp. 102–138). New York: Guilford Press.

Jovanović, V. (2016). Trust and subjective well-being: The case of Serbia. *Personality and Individual Differences, 98*, 284–288.

Jovanović, V., & Gavrilov-Jerković, V. (2013). Dimensionality and validity of the Serbian version of the life orientation test – revised. *Journal of Happiness Studies, 14*(3), 771–782.

Jovanović, V., Gavrilov-Jerković, V., Žuljević, D., & Brdarić, D. (2014). Psihometrijska evaluacija Skale depresivnosti, anksioznosti i stresa–21 (DASS–21) na uzorku studenata u Srbiji [Psychometric properties of depression, anxiety and stress scale–21 (DASS–21) on a student sample in Serbia]. *Psihologija, 47*(1), 93–112.

Jovanović, V., & Žuljević, D. (2013). Psychometric evaluation of the Serbian version of the multidimensional students' satisfaction scale. *Social Indicators Research, 110*, 55–69.

Jovanović, V., Žuljević, D., & Brdarić, D. (2011). Skala depresivnosti, anksioznosti i stresa (DASS–21) – Struktura negativnog afekta kod adolescenata Srbiji [The depression, anxiety and stress

scale (DASS–21) – the structure of negative affect in Serbian adolescents]. *Engrami, 33*(2), 19–28.

Kernis, M. H. (2003). Toward a conceptualization of optimal self-esteem. *Psychological Inquiry, 14*, 1–26.

Kline, R. B. (2005). *Principles and practices of structural equation modeling* (2nd ed.). New York: Guilford Press.

Łaguna, M. (2019). Towards explaining the "how" of positive orientation: The beliefs-affect-engagement model. *Asian Journal of Social Psychology, 22*(2), 133–139.

Łaguna, M., Oleś, P. K., & Filipiuk, D. (2011). Orientacja pozytywna i jej pomiar: Polska adaptacja Skali Orientacji Pozytywnej [Positive orientation and its measure: Polish adaptation of the positivity scale]. *Studia Psychologiczne, 49*, 47–54.

Lauriola, M., & Iani, L. (2015). Does positivity mediate the relation of extraversion and neuroticism with subjective happiness? *PloS One, 10*, Article e0121991.

Lovibond, S. H., & Lovibond, P. F. (1995). *Manual for the depression anxiety stress scales* (2nd ed.). Sydney: Psychology Foundation.

Lucas, R. E., Diener, E., & Suh, E. (1996). Discriminant validity of well-being measures. *Journal of Personality and Social Psychology, 71*, 616–628.

Lyubomirsky, S., King, L., & Diener, E. (2005). The benefits of frequent positive affect: Does happiness lead to success? *Psychological Bulletin, 131*, 803–855.

Miciuk, L. R., Jankowski, T., Laskowska, A., & Oleś, P. (2016). Positive orientation and the five-factor model. *Polish Psychological Bulletin, 47*(1), 141–148.

Novović, Z., & Mihić, L. (2008). Srpski inventar afekata baziran na positive and negative affect schedule – X (SIAB-PANAS) [The Serbian inventory of affect based on the positive and negative affect schedule – X]. *Unpublished manuscript.* Novi Sad, Serbia: University of Novi Sad.

Novović, Z., Mihić, L., Tovilović, S., & Jovanović, V. (2008). Relations among positive and negative affect, dysphoria and anxiety. *Psihologija, 41*(4), 413–435.

O'Brien, R. M. (2007). A caution regarding rules of thumb for variance inflation factors. *Quality & Quantity, 41*(5), 673–690.

Oleś, P. K., Alessandri, G., Oleś, M., Bak, W., Jankowski, T., Łaguna, M., & Caprara, G. V. (2013). Positive orientation and generalized self-efficacy. *Studia Psychologica, 55*(1), 47–58.

Pressman, S. D., & Cohen, S. (2005). Does positive affect influence health? *Psychological Bulletin, 131,* 925–971.

Radloff, L. S. (1977). The CES–D Scale: A self-report depression scale for research in the general population. *Applied Psychological Measurement, 1,* 385–401.

Rosenberg, M. (1965). *Society and the adolescent self-image.* Princeton, NJ: Princeton University Press.

Rowe, G., Hirsh, J. B., & Anderson, A. K. (2007). Positive affect increases the breadth of attentional selection. *Proceedings of National Academy of Sciences, 104,* 383–388.

Satorra, A., & Bentler, P. M. (1994). Corrections to test statistics and standard errors in covariance structure analysis. In A. von Eye & C. C. Clogg (Eds.), *Latent variables analysis: Applications for developmental research* (pp. 399–419). Thousand Oaks, CA: Sage.

Scheier, M. F., Carver, C. S., & Bridges, M. W. (1994). Distinguishing optimism from neuroticism (and trait anxiety, self-mastery, and self-esteem): A reevaluation of the life orientation test. *Journal of Personality and Social Psychology, 67,* 1063–1078.

Scholz, U., Gutiérrez-Doña, B., Sud, S., & Schwarzer, R. (2002). Is general self-efficacy a universal construct? Psychometric findings from 25 countries. *European Journal of Psychological Assessment, 18,* 242–251.

Schumacker, R., & Lomax, R. (1996). *A beginner's guide to structural equation modeling.* Mahwah, NJ: Lawrence Erlbaum.

Schwarzer, R., & Jerusalem, M. (1995). Generalized self-efficacy scale. In J. Weinman, S. Wright, & M. Johnston (Eds.), *Measures in health psychology: A user's portfolio: Causal and control beliefs* (pp. 35–37). Windsor: NFER-Nelson.

Sobel, M. E. (1982). Asymptotic intervals for indirect effects in structural equations models. In S. Leinhart (Ed.), *Sociological methodology 1982* (pp. 290–312). San Francisco, CA: Jossey-Bass.

Steiger, J. H. (2016). Notes on the Steiger–Lind (1980) handout. *Structural Equation Modeling: A Multidisciplinary Journal, 23*(6), 777–781.

Tian, L., Zhang, D., & Huebner, E. S. (2018). Psychometric properties of the positivity scale among Chinese adults and early adolescents. *Frontiers in Psychology, 9,* Article 197.

Vasić, A., Šarčević, D., & Trogrlić, A. (2011). Zadovoljstvo životom u Srbiji [Satisfaction with life in Serbia]. *Primenjena Psihologija, 2,* 151–177.

Watson, D., & Clark, L. A. (1994). *The PANAS-X: Manual for the positive and negative affect schedule expanded form.* Iowa City: University of Iowa.

# Index